THE GOLDEN BOOK OF CHURCH PLAYS

The
GOLDEN BOOK OF CHURCH PLAYS

A Compilation of One-Act Plays and Pageants Selected and Adapted for Production by Teenagers and Adults for the Inspiration of Audiences and Participants.

by

LAWRENCE M. BRINGS, M.A.

Formerly professor of speech at Northwestern Lutheran Theological Seminary, Luther Theological Seminary, and the University of Minnesota.

Publishers

T. S. DENISON & COMPANY

Minneapolis

PRODUCTION RIGHTS

All the plays included in this book are available in separate pamphlet form at 50c a copy. Amateurs may produce any of these plays without payment of a royalty fee, provided that the required number of copies as specified in each instance are purchased.

The sole professional rights, motion picture, television and radio broadcasting rights are reserved. For professional rights, address the publishers of this book.

The attention of all producers of these plays is directed to the following:

This book is fully protected under the laws of the United States of America and in all countries included under the Universal Copyright Convention.

Violations of the Copyright Law are punishable by fine or imprisonment, or both.

The copying, or duplication of these plays or any part of them, by hand or by an process is an infringement of the copyright and will be vigorously prosecuted.

Other Books by Lawrence M. Brings

Prize Winning Orations for High School Contests

The Christmas Entertainment Book

Clever Introductions for Chairmen

The Modern Treasury of Christmas Plays

Humorous Introductions for Emcees

Choice Comedies for Junior High Schools

The Master Stunt Book

PREFACE

It has been my chief aim in compiling this collection of plays to meet the requirements of directors of religious education in churches and the affiliated type of organization who are interested in producing the type of play that will justify its presentation.

Selection has been made of plays that can be presented at a most significant season of the year — Easter. The other plays deal with moral, social and ethical themes that merit production by church groups. Many times spiritual truths can reach the hearts and minds of individuals through this medium and for this reason I have included only those plays that have a purpose for presentation.

The practical value of this collection is that it makes available to church producers a wide variety of selection under the covers of one volume. Practically all the plays have simple and easy stage settings; casts are usually small, but several plays have large groups of players. Both Biblical and modern settings are used. The playing time varies from thirty minutes to one hour.

Even though this compilation is aimed to serve church groups, the plays may be produced by almost any other type of amateur group. Several of these plays are suitable for drama contests and festivals.

I have directed many plays for church groups and it has been my observation that finding a suitable play for a specific situation was always a primary problem. I hope that this compilation will serve to alleviate the stress and strain of the last-minute search for an appropriate play. If it accomplishes this purpose, then my effort in assembling this material in one volume will not have been in vain.

—Lawrence M. Brings

CONTENTS

A CERTAIN MAN HAD TWO SONS

A DRAMA IN ONE ACT

By

ROBERT FINCH

PRODUCTION RIGHTS

11

A CERTAIN MAN HAD TWO SONS

CAST OF CHARACTERS

(For two women and three men)

KATE..........*The mother; a woman of late middle age*
JUDSON............*The father; a man of late middle age*
STEVE......................*The elder son, about 32*
EDDIE....................*The prodigal son, about 28*
LILY........................*The daughter, about 16*

THE TIME: *A morning in October.*

THE PLACE: *A farm, in the mid-west.*

THE SETTING: *The plain but comfortable living-room of the Manning farmhouse. There is a window in the Left wall, looking out over the fields. A doorway in the rear wall leads through a screen door and on to the low, wide front porch, the white, thin pillars of which can be seen through the door. Windows are on either side of the door. A swinging door in the Left wall leads to the kitchen. Downstage in the Left wall is a small, open entry, opening on to the stairs to the upper floor. At Right is a large, old-fashioned heating-stove, also a low bookcase with books. A dining-table is in the center of the room, with five chairs about it. Upstage of the kitchen door is an upright piano. A large, old-fashioned Morris chair up Right. The walls are papered in a cheerful, unobtrusive fashion; the windows have clean and cheery curtains. Several potted plants, mostly geraniums, stand in the windows. All in all, this is a very cheerful, comfortable room.*

At the Rise of the Curtain: *It is morning, and the sun streams cheerfully through the windows. At the table is* Steve, *dressed in overalls and workshirt, eating his breakfast.* Steve *is a man of perhaps 32, dark and a little bit dour in appearance, being too serious in his manner. A moment, then* Lily *enters.* Lily *is a dark-haired, pretty girl of fifteen or sixteen. She carries a plate of pancakes which she puts on the table.* Steve *silently hands her his coffee-cup, which she takes to the kitchen, returning immediately with the filled cup.* Lily *crosses to the window and looks out over the fields.*

Lily (*At the window.*) It's another wonderful, sunny day, Steve.

Steve. Clouds, boiling up in the northwest. See the big white thunderheads?

Lily. Oh, it won't rain. It's a day for *good* things to happen, not bad.

Steve. I hope you're right.

Lily. Oh!

Steve. What's up?

Lily. Oh, look! There's a great flock of geese. (*Breathlessly.*) So high . . . and flying so straight and sure . . . like arrows. They fly so fast . . . and they hardly move their wings at all.

Steve. They mean winter coming on, to me.

Lily. Oh, I know. But everything is so beautiful right now in October. It must be the finest month of all. It's *such* a beautiful day.

Steve. Well, we can use some more like it, if it's a good one. (Kate *appears in the doorway. She is a woman of late middle-age, but still strong and efficient-looking. Dressed in a house-dress, she looks clean and neat, but she*

13

is heated and red-faced from her work over the kitchen stove.)

KATE. You want any more eggs, Steve?

STEVE. Well now, I might, Mother.

KATE. Lily! (LILY *obediently jumps up to fetch the eggs. As she reaches the kitchen door, she looks upward, hearing a sound, a thump from the floor above.*)

LILY. Oh. I hear Father getting up! I'll fetch his pancakes, so they'll be ready for him when he comes down. (*She hurries into the kitchen.*)

KATE (*Quite soberly.*) How does it look, Steve, the harvest?

STEVE. All right, I guess, Mother. We ought to be finished by Saturday, if the weather holds.

KATE. Good. *Good.* That will please your father.

STEVE. But how can you win? We get a big harvest and the price drops. Sixty bushels o' barley to the acre, and it drops to eighty cents. The corn better'n it ever was and the price dropping lower every day. It's enough to sour a man.

KATE (*Philosophically.*) That's the way farming is. Always was and always will be, I guess.

STEVE. I guess. Well . . . (*Taking a last sup of coffee.*) I better be getting out to the field.

KATE. Eat your breakfast, son.

STEVE. I gotta get out there.

KATE. It's only a quarter to seven.

STEVE. The men are on the way already.

KATE. But you been up since daylight, getting the chores done.

STEVE. Only way to get 'em done is do 'em, Mother. I'm not like Eddie was. I want to *run* the farm, not sell it.

KATE. Don't talk against him this morning, Steve.

STEVE. I just can't help it. If we had the west forty, 'stead of Dad lettin' Ed sell it, we'd have forty acres of corn off it to sell. It just sets me afire to see a piece of the place in some other man's hands, with a fine crop on it.

KATE. Don't keep talking about it. It's been eight years since Eddie left.

STEVE. Eight years or eighty. I haven't forgotten.

KATE. Well, don't talk of it today.

STEVE. What's today I shouldn't talk?

KATE. It's his birthday. Ed's birthday.

STEVE (*Thoughtfully.*) That's so. I forgot. (*Stubbornly.*) Well, even so . . .

KATE. Hush, son. Please. (LILY *enters with cakes and eggs. Entering, she glances up the stairway and sees her father coming down.*)

LILY. Morning, Father. (JUDSON *is still unseen, but in his deep bass voice he greets her.*)

JUDSON. Morning, young one. (*He appears at the foot of the stairs.* JUDSON *is a man of late middle age, his hair almost white. But his cheeks are ruddy, and his shoulders broad and strong, his hands worn and knotted from labor. He is a big man, and it seems wrong that he should be walking, as he is, with the aid of a crutch, to support a heavily-bandaged foot. He gives* LILY *a kiss on the cheek as he passes her. He comes to* KATE *at the head of the table, gives her a hug and an affectionate whack on the back.*) Well, Kate, it looks good to me! (*Indicating the breakfast table. He greets* STEVE.) Steve.

STEVE. Morning, Dad. (JUDSON *laboriously tries to sit at the table;* KATE *attempts to help him.*)

JUDSON. Confound it, Kate, don't *help* me! You know anything makes me mad it's people helpin' me. Just 'cause a horse throwed me, it doesn't mean I got to be waited on hand and foot! (*Awkwardly he seats himself and is extremely uncomfortable, not being able to dispose of his bandaged foot. Loudly.*) All right! Get me the footstool, if you *must* help! (LILY *hurries to get the footstool and* JUDSON *makes himself fairly comfortable. He pitches right into his food, without ceremony.*) How's the corn in the upper field?

STEVE. She's ripening fast. It's good corn. Better'n last year.

JUDSON. Fine. Fine. The men doing all right? No trouble?

STEVE. No trouble.

15

JUDSON. You're doing a good job, Steve. (STEVE *says nothing, puts his napkin down.*) I sure wish I was out there, 'stead of settin' round the house doin' nothing.

STEVE. I better be gettin' out there myself. (*He rises.*) Yeah, the corn looks good in the upper field. But the best crop's in the west forty.

JUDSON (*Sternly.*) Never mind about that. (STEVE *shrugs.*) Keep those men on the move, now.

STEVE. I will. (*He goes out.* LILY *rises, takes* STEVE'S *dishes and starts toward the kitchen with them.*)

KATE. If you're through with your breakfast, you can start the cleaning, Lily.

LILY. Yes, Mother. (*She goes to the kitchen.*)

KATE (*Fanning herself with her napkin.*) It's getting hot already.

JUDSON. It's always hot at harvest time, Kate. Expect it.

KATE. I'm used to it. But I'm not crazy about it.

JUDSON. Hotter'n this twenty-eight years ago today, Kate. When Eddie came. And I walked up and down there on the veranda, with the sweat just a-pouring off me. And the sweat wasn't all from the heat, neither.

KATE (*She smiles affectionately at her husband.*) You worried about me—about us.

JUDSON. Certainly I worried. If we'd had twenty kids, I'd never stopped worrying, though, time like that.

KATE. I know. (*Suddenly she hears something beyond the open window, out in the fields.*) Listen!

JUDSON (*Lifts his head to listen.*) Hmph?

KATE. Hear it?

JUDSON. Cricket.

KATE. I never hear that sound without I think of Eddie. It's what I remember about it—the hot, dry day me lying upstairs there, me and Eddie—and that lazy, funny sewing-machine sound—the cricket. It always takes me back. (*There are tears in her eyes.*)

JUDSON (*Patting her arm.*) There, Kate. There.

KATE (*Somewhat self-consciously.*) Judson. There's

something in the kitchen I want to show you. (*She rises, goes to the kitchen door.*)

JUDSON. What is it?

KATE. You'll see. (*She goes in the kitchen, returns immediately with a big birthday cake, elaborately frosted. She holds it in front of* JUDSON *for his inspection.*)

JUDSON (*Reading.*) "Happy Birthday, Eddie." (*He is deeply touched.*) Ah, Kate, why do you hurt yourself like that?

KATE (*Sincerely.*) I'm not hurting myself. I *want* to remember. See, I'll put it here on the sideboard—and once in a while we'll see it, on his birthday. It'll be like he's here again, a boy once more, for just a moment.

JUDSON. We think about him too much. We ought not to keep his chair here at the table, after eight years. It hurts us both.

KATE. No. It's best to leave it where it is. (*Firmly.*) Some day he'll be coming back. It'll please him to see some things as they were. He'll be sitting in it again. I know it. (*Comfortingly,* JUDSON *takes her hand.*) All these years and never a letter for the last three. Why couldn't he write us? Just a post card. Anything. (JUDSON *shrugs, helplessly.*) I shouldn't talk about it, I guess. It's worse for you than for me. A woman cries— that helps somehow. (*She sits at the table, sadly, running the hem of her apron through her worn fingers.*)

JUDSON. I can't understand. A man works, drives himself all his life long, to make things good, for his family, to make everything right. And then his young ones doesn't want the things he has to give them—except to sell them, maybe.

KATE. We shouldn't have done it. It wasn't good for him. He was too young.

JUDSON. No. We did the best. He didn't like it here. He had to go. Better he should go with our blessing, with what money we could give him, than to run away from us, with nothing. The land we could get back, somehow. The thousand dollars we gave him to start his life with. Without money something might have happened to him.

17

(*A terrible thought.*)   Maybe something *has* happened.

KATE (*Firmly, but close to tears.*)   No—that isn't true. I would know.   But it's been such a long time.   I wonder what he looks like.   He must have changed.   (*Sorrowfully.*)   Maybe we wouldn't even know him if we saw him.

JUDSON.   *I* would.   (*Sadly.*)   But maybe he's forgotten us.

KATE.   I'd hate to think that.   But—yes—maybe he has —for a long time.   (*She jabs at her eyes with her apron.*) Well—I have to clear off this table and get back to the kitchen   (*She notices that* JUDSON *is staring fixedly out the window.   She puts an affectionate hand on his shoulder.*)   I guess we'd better not think about Eddie, like you say.   It just doesn't do any good.   (JUDSON *rouses himself, pats her hand affectionately.*)

JUDSON.   I know.   (*He pushes himself back from the table a little.*)   I'm going to sit here for a minute and take my time for my coffee.

KATE.   Shall I pour you some fresh?

JUDSON.   No.   This is fine.   (*He stretches and yawns, lazily.*)   It's nice here with the sun through the window.

KATE.   It's a fine day.   A fine day.   (*She picks up some of the dishes and goes to the kitchen.   Left alone,* JUDSON *settles himself more comfortably in his big chair, yawns again, his eyelids begin to droop.   He nods.* KATE *returns from the kitchen, gives him a glance, sees that he is sleepy, smiles affectionately on him, starts toward the kitchen.*)   Shall I bring you a pillow?

JUDSON (*An indignant, negative grunt.*)   Hmp-umgh. (*But* KATE *goes to the kitchen with the dishes, returns immediately, takes a pillow from the nearby rocking-chair, and places it behind* JUDSON'S *head.   He is nearly asleep but he appreciates the pillow and settles his head on it comfortably.* KATE *tiptoes out, closes the door quietly. Left alone,* JUDSON *blinks once or twice, yawns a little and then is sound asleep.   There is a pause.* JUDSON *stirs once, settles himself more comfortably.   Then there is a faint sound on the porch, outside the screen door; first a shadow appears, then the figure of a man.   He is a rough-*

*looking hobo, about 28, dressed in ragged overalls, shirt
and worn-out, dusty shoes, a battered old hat. His face is
heavily bearded with several days' stubble. He is dusty,
dirty and tired. He stands at the screen door a moment,
then taps lightly on the door.* JUDSON *stirs slightly.
Sleepily, not knowing what is going on.*) Hmpgh? (*The*
HOBO *knocks again.* JUDSON *only half-wakes, but dimly
realizes there is someone at the door.*) Hello.

HOBO. Howdy. (JUDSON *is rapidly dropping off to
sleep again, so the* HOBO *steps inside, quietly.*) I was
wondering if you need any harvest-hands.

JUDSON (*Still mostly asleep.*) Got a full crew now.
Only got two or three days left.

HOBO (*Disappointed.*) Oh-h. (*He starts to go, then
turns.*) I—maybe I could work for my board.

JUDSON (*Sleepy and confused, his eyes still shut.*)
Hmpgh? What did you say?

HOBO. I'd like to work for my meals if you'll let me.

JUDSON. Oh. (*This almost, but not quite registers.*)
That's fine if you want to. Go on out in the field. You
can eat with the men. If you want to help with the work,
you can.

HOBO. Thank you. Thanks a *million*. That's *swell*.
(*Quickly he opens the screen door, goes out, with just a
hurried, backward glance at* JUDSON. JUDSON *is left alone.
Now he is slowly waking up; he groans, yawns, stretches,
shifts in his chair, suddenly snaps wide-awake, with a
start.*)

JUDSON (*Bewildered, he looks about the room, sees no
one. He calls loudly.*) Kate! Kate! (KATE *appears in
the kitchen door.*)

KATE. What are you yelling about? What on earth's
the matter?

JUDSON. I— Kate— What happened to the man that
was in here a minute ago?

KATE. *Man?* What man?

JUDSON (*Indignantly.*) *What* man? Why, the man
that was in this room, not two minutes ago! He wanted
something. Something to eat—(*Vaguely.*)—or something.

KATE (*Laughing.*) Why, Judson, you've been dreaming, that's all.

JUDSON (*Uncertainly.*) Was I? Was that it?

KATE. Of course. Now go on back to sleep.

JUDSON (*Confused, scratching his head in mystification.*) Maybe—maybe I was. But there was something about his voice— (*Suddenly he shouts.*) Lily! (LILY, *frightened, appears in the kitchen door.*)

LILY. Yes, Father?

JUDSON (*Quiet, tense.*) Lily girl, there was a man here a minute ago. Least I think there was—(LILY *and* KATE *exchange a glance.*)—he cleared out 'fore I got a good look at him. Think he was going down in the field. I want you to go and see.

LILY (*Uncertainly.*) What did he look like?

JUDSON. Didn't ever see him real clear. Half asleep. Dark in here. I—uh—

LILY. Well, what sort of man was he?

JUDSON (*Scratching his head.*) Well—a hobo I guess. Sort of youngish-like. (*Impatiently.*) Go on out and look for a stranger on the place!

LILY. ' Yes, Father! (*She hurries to the door, looks back at her father, puzzled, then she is gone.*)

KATE (*She is wide-eyed with tension, almost afraid to ask* JUDSON *the question that is in her mind; quietly, in a strained voice.*) Jud! Jud! What are you all excited about? What is it?

JUDSON (*Afraid to hope, really.*) Now never mind, Kate. You just wait.

KATE. What did you send Lily for that man for?

JUDSON. Don't make me say it. I don't want to disappoint you. Nor me neither.

KATE. Do you—do you *really suppose*—?

JUDSON. Stop it! Stop, I tell you. Can't you leave a thing alone? I don't know till I see him. Till I talk with him again. (KATE *moves to the window, much agitated, and peers out.*) Go on away from that window! I tell you it's no good gettin' your hopes up so high. Not yet.

KATE (*Helplessly.*) Then why—why—?

JUDSON. Well, I was half asleep—didn't rightly see him at all. But there was something—something about his voice—I heard that voice somewheres before. If it'd been a stranger to me, it would've waked me right up.

KATE (*Close to tears.*) I—I don't know if I can stand it, if it isn't him—or if it *is,* either.

JUDSON. Now you hush. You can stand it if I can. Now you get over there and set at the table. Don't say a single word while I talk to him. (*Reluctantly she does so. They sit there tense and motionless, their eyes on the door. A step is heard on the veranda, and* LILY *appears, followed by the* HOBO. *She holds the door open and he reluctantly enters.*)

HOBO (*Feeling their intense gaze.*) The girl said you wanted to talk to me.

JUDSON (*After a searching look at the tramp.*) That's right. I do that. (*Kindly.*) Sit down, son.

HOBO. Thank you kindly. I'd just as leave stand. (*He waits.*)

JUDSON. Didn't rightly see you when you were here a minute ago.

HOBO. I didn't think you did. (*Wryly.*) Ain't much to see.

JUDSON. I've been thinking. We might be able to use another harvest hand, at that.

HOBO. I could use the work.

JUDSON. 'Course I'd like to know a bit about you first. Like to make a friend of a man when I hire him.

HOBO. Sure.

JUDSON (*Both he and* KATE *are watching the* HOBO *with the utmost intensity, hardly able to breathe from their eagerness to learn the truth.* KATE *twists her handkerchief, nervously, back and forth in her hands.*) Where did you come here from—if it ain't asking too much?

HOBO. Why no, that's all right. Came from up north.

JUDSON. Oh. (*Pause.*) You didn't come from Chicago?

HOBO. Nope. Stranger in Chicago myself. Came from North Dakota. Came down here for the harvest.

Figure on followin' the combines north again, up into Canada.

JUDSON. What part o' Dakota?

HOBO (*Vaguely.*) Oh—west part. West central, like. (*Quickly.*) If you got a job for me I'd best go out in the field and get at it.

JUDSON. The job can wait. You ever been in these parts before?

HOBO. No. Never been out of Dakota till lately. Real lately.

JUDSON. You never seen my face before? (*The* HOBO *stares at* JUDSON *a long moment, speaks very quietly.*)

HOBO. No.

JUDSON. You mind tellin' me your name?

HOBO. Name's Jack.

JUDSON. Jack what?

HOBO. Jack Brown.

JUDSON. Oh-h. (*He extends his hand.*) Glad to know you. My name's Manning. (*They shake hands.* JUDSON *exchanges a glance with* KATE, *in which their uncertainty is plain, their doubt of this man's identity.*) I—I guess you been wondering why I'm askin' you all these questions?

HOBO. You got a right to. Guess you want to know who you're hiring, most likely.

JUDSON. Yeah. That's right, I do. There's another reason, though. You see we used to have a boy. He'd be 'bout your age now. I—I thought maybe you might've seen him somewhere—run across him. I ask a lot o' people that travel around if they've seen my boy.

HOBO. How would I see him?

JUDSON. Oh, I don't know. You harvestin' men get around a lot.

HOBO. I don't think I did. What was his name?

JUDSON. Eddie. Eddie Manning.

HOBO. No-o—I don't recollect the name.

JUDSON. He was just a kid when he left here eight years ago. Sure have missed him. We were mighty fond of that boy. (*He sighs.*) But—well, he was kind of wild, I guess, you might call him that. This little place seemed pretty tame. He wanted to see the country, get out on his own. So—I sold part of the place, and I gave him his share of what he'd have comin'. He wrote us now and then for two or three years. Didn't seem to be able to get started somehow—he spent his money—pretty soon he stopped writin'. We sure have missed him. (*He stops, clears his throat awkwardly.*) That's his sister there— name's Lily. (LILY *gives a little awkward curtsey, and the* HOBO *gives a slight nod.*) He was a good youngster. Kind of wild, I guess. But he was good enough for us. Had a right good voice, too. Good voice for singin', that is. Of an evenin', sometimes we'd get him to sing, with his mother at the piano. (*Almost imperceptibly* JUDSON *indicates to* KATE *that she should go to the piano. She does so, sits there unobtrusively, silently.*) Favorite of our Eddie's was that old song, "Rock of Ages." You know that song?

HOBO (*After a pause.*) Yeah. I think so. I—I never cared much for it myself.

JUDSON. Our Eddie *liked* it. Crazy about it, he was. He thought it was a beautiful old tune. (KATE *very softly begins to play the song at the piano.*) Yuh. We were happy here then. One happy little family, and we'd set here and sing that old song together— (*The song is well begun now, and old* JUDSON *hesitatingly begins to sing, in a deep, tuneless rumble, with one sharp eye watching the* HOBO. *At first the* HOBO *does not respond in any way, but soon in spite of him the tears come, and soon he is silently weeping, the tears streaking his dusty face. old* JUDSON's *voice trembles as he sees this. Suddenly* JUDSON *shouts in triumph.*) Eddie! (*He grasps the boy's hand, and his own eyes are filled with tears.* KATE's *playing ends with a loud discord, and she rushes to the* HOBO, *she and* LILY *crowding around him, embracing him.* JUDSON *speaks in quiet, happy triumph.*) I *knew* it! I *knew* it was you, all the time!

KATE (*Crying.*) Eddie! You're home! (EDDIE *is laughing and crying all at once. He puts his arm around*

23

his mother, LILY *comes close and shyly nestles under his arm.*)

JUDSON. Why didn't you *tell* us it was you?

EDDIE. I didn't *want* you to know me. I'd failed. I disgraced myself. But I wanted to come home. I wanted to see you. I've changed so much. I thought I could come and see you, and you'd never recognize me.

KATE (*Sorrowfully.*) Oh, Eddie—look at your poor, ragged clothes. And you're so thin—so thin!

JUDSON. We'll fix that, now we have him home again.

KATE. Your old room's just like you left it. And there's clean clothes—Steve's—and your father's—hanging in the closet.

EDDIE. But look, Mother, I can't move back in the house like nothing happened.

JUDSON. And why not?

EDDIE. Why—because I *can't.* I took your money—let you sell your land for me. I never did a thing that was right. Everything was wrong. I—I'm not really a son to you.

JUDSON. Did I ask you what you've done? Did your mother ask? Do you think you're a fifteen-hundred-dollar son, or a two-thousand-dollar son, and no more?

KATE. You're *our* son.

EDDIE. No, I think it'd be better if I just work for you and live with the men. I haven't any right in the house.

KATE. Eddie! Hush, child.

JUDSON. You wouldn't do that to us. You wouldn't make us unhappy.

KATE. Upstairs with you! And clean up! You're a *terrible* sight!

JUDSON. Get up there with you! (EDDIE *laughs, turns to the stairs.*)

EDDIE. All right. (*At the stairway he turns.*) It's great to have you ordering me around the house again! (*He goes upstairs.*)

LILY. So that's Eddie! He's my brother!

JUDSON. He's home at last. (KATE *comes close to him; she speaks breathlessly.*)

KATE. I—I'm afraid I'll wake up. It must be a *dream.*

JUDSON. No, it's no dream. (*He sighs deeply.*) I thought I'd never last this long. I was afraid I couldn't. (*Suddenly he thinks of something, shouts.*) Kate! (KATE *looks at him in alarm.*) What are we waiting for? It's Eddie's birthday! He's home! Lily! Ring the dinner bell! Get the men in from work for a party! No work today! Eddie's home! (LILY *hurries out to do so.*) Kate! You get on the telephone! Get the neighbors over here! Get all our friends in to celebrate! (*Offstage the dinner gong begins to ring, a loud and triumphant clanging.* KATE *turns the crank of the old-fashioned phone, waits for the operator.* JUDSON, *greatly moved and close to tears, he speaks almost to himself.*) I just can't take it in! He's home! Eddie's home!

KATE (*At the phone.*) Hello! Operator! Lucy?— Get me the Brandons, Lucy, and hurry! I got a whole lot of calls to make! I— Lucy—Eddie's home! (*After a pause as she listens, she speaks quietly, sincerely.*) Thank you—*thank* you.

JUDSON (*Softly.*) Why, it's like he was dead, and now he's come to life again—like we'd lost him forever and ever, and found him all over again! (*He blows his nose, helplessly, dries his eyes.*)

KATE (*At the phone.*) Hello! Mrs. Brandon? This is Kate Manning— (*Breathlessly.*) Look! I want you should come over to our house, right away! You and all your family!—It's a party! A celebration!—It— (*With the utmost happiness in her voice.*) —Eddie's come back! He's home!—Yes! Hurry!—Thank you! Thank you! (*She hangs up, turns the crank once more to make another call, suddenly stops, as she realizes that the bell has suddenly stopped ringing, and there now is only silence. She turns to* JUDSON, *and though she speaks quietly she is plainly alarmed.*) Jud! Jud!

JUDSON (*Also plainly much concerned.*) The bell! It's stopped ringing! (LILY *comes hurrying in.*)

KATE. Child! Don't stop ringing the bell! Go back! Ring the bell!

LILY. It was Steve. He told me to stop.

KATE. Steve!

JUDSON. Steve told you to stop?

LILY. Yes, Father.

JUDSON (*After a puzzled glance at* KATE.) You go back and tell Steve that I want the bell to ring.

LILY. He's coming, Father. (STEVE *appears on the porch, enters. He looks even more glum and dour than before. He enters, stands before his father, ready for whatever may be said.*)

JUDSON. You stopped the bell?

STEVE. Yes. The men were quitting. They were coming in from the field.

JUDSON. I want they should stop their work.

STEVE. But they can't! The rain may come, anytime. They can't stop! (*He looks at his father defiantly, then speaks quietly.*) So he's come back?

JUDSON (*Happy at the thought of it.*) Yes! He's home.

STEVE. Well!

JUDSON (*In his own happiness he notices nothing wrong with* STEVE'S *attitude.*) He's upstairs now, in his old room.

STEVE. My room.

JUDSON. His room—yours—what does it matter? He's home—after eight years. He's home!

KATE. We're going to have a party for him, Steve. A celebration!

JUDSON. Sure we are! That's why we rang the bell. I want the men here to celebrate with us. And, Steve—the calf that you've been feeding—

STEVE. What about the calf?

JUDSON. There'll be a big crowd—maybe a hundred. We'll have to have plenty for them to eat. I—I want you should slaughter the calf.

STEVE: My calf! **Slaughter** *my* calf?

26

JUDSON. I paid for the mother that bore it. But it doesn't matter whose it is—it's ours.

STEVE. *I* paid for it. Like I pay for everything. With work. With sweat!

KATE (*Warningly.*) Son!

JUDSON. Steve! Steve! Aren't you glad to have your brother home?

STEVE (*Sullenly.*) *Glad?* Why should I be?

JUDSON. Because he's your brother!

STEVE. Sure. My brother. Good old Eddie. Upstairs right now, probably slipping on my best suit.

JUDSON. A suit! What is a suit?

STEVE. Nothing—to *you*. Now you've got your son back again. Not *this* son— (*Indicating himself.*) The other one. The one that means most to you both! (KATE *gasps at this outburst.*) He never liked it here. He hated it. All he could think of was getting to the city and seeing the bright lights, and the women!

KATE. Steve!

JUDSON. Stop it!

STEVE. You sold the best field we had to give him a stake! What did he do with it? *Nothing!* Now you'll probably sell the rest of the place to give him another stake to blow in, in the city! But *me*—does anyone ever do anything for me? Not much. Work like a dog, day in, day out. I've given everything I've got to this farm. Everything! Do I get a big party, a great big hoop-de-do thrown for me and my friends! I'll say I don't!

JUDSON (*Helplessly.*) Everything I have is yours. I don't begrudge you anything, Steve. But he's your brother. He's been gone for eight years. Why, he might have been dead for all we knew. And now he's alive— he's home. Here, with us!

STEVE. Sure he is. Because he's broke. Look, you explain it to me if you can. I run this place. I work sixteen hours a day to keep it going. For eight years I been doing it. What does he do? He *sells* his share, blows the money. He stayed away for eight years and didn't even write! Just comes home when there's no place else to go. And who gets the party? *He* does. I should kill my calf for him! He shouldn't have come back! (EDDIE *has come down the stairs and has heard this last speech. He is now shaved but is still dressed in his ragged clothes.*)

KATE (*Crying.*) Steve! You don't mean that! You couldn't!

JUDSON (*Heartbroken.*) There, there, Kate. Steve'll get over it. There, there.

EDDIE. Never mind, Mother.

JUDSON. Eddie!

EDDIE. Steve's right. It's what I've said to myself. Steve—I never meant to come right in the house like this, like nothing's happened, expect things to be like before. I gave up my rights when I left here eight years ago. It's no good, Pa, Mother. I don't belong here any more. If you'll just let me work in the fields, be a hired hand, for my eats—I'll stay a few days and move on. (*He moves to the door.*) I'll sleep in the bunkshack with the men. (*He goes out. When* EDDIE *is gone the others are momentarily stunned.* JUDSON *simply sits there, staring ahead of him, suddenly bangs his cane on the floor, in frustration.* KATE *turns away from the door in silence and defeat.* STEVE *is as amazed as they, but is inclined to bluster it out.*)

STEVE (*After watching his parents guiltily for a moment, he speaks defensively.*) Well—he should've known— He made his choice— He— (*His voice trails off into silence The parents say nothing.* STEVE *grows more and more uncomfortable.*) Gosh—he didn't need to pull out like *that*—mad, like. He didn't have to do that! (*The others say nothing.*) Why, I—I don't see why he couldn't stay in the *house*—with *us*—in his own room—while he's here, at least. *Golly*, after all, he— (*He blurts it out.*) he's one of the *family!* I— well— (*Suddenly he can stand it no longer.*) He can't *do* this to us! I'm goin' after him! (*He strides quickly out the door.* JUDSON *smiles in relief,* KATE *crosses to* JUDSON, *puts her hands on his shoulder; he pats her hand, happily.*)

JUDSON (*Quietly.*) Lily—

LILY. Yes, Father.

JUDSON. You can ring the bell now. (LILY *goes out, through the kitchen door. A moment, then* STEVE *and* EDDIE *are heard, laughing jovially, off Left, as they approach the house. They enter the room, both looking happy and much relieved.*)

STEVE. Well—I brought him back!

EDDIE. He sure did.

KATE (*Breathless with pleasure.*) That's wonderful— wonderful— (KATE *sits at the piano and begins to play the old hymn. The two brothers move to the piano, stand on either side of* KATE, *and they begin to sing,* JUDSON *joining in with his rumbling bass. After two or three bars, the triumphant pealing of the bell is heard, offstage.* STEVE *and* EDDIE *grin at each other,* STEVE *gives his brother an affectionate punch on the shoulder, as the curtain falls.*)

CURTAIN

THE ANSWER

A DRAMA IN ONE ACT

By

WILLARD S. SMITH

PRODUCTION RIGHTS

Copies of this play are available in single pamphlet form. The right to produce this play by one group of amateur players is authorized only by the purchase of four copies (one copy for each speaking part) at the current price of 50c each.

It is dishonest and illegal to copy parts.

THE ANSWER

CAST OF CHARACTERS

(For two women and three men)

BETTY..............*Eight-year-old daughter of the Elliots*
JENNIE...................................*Mrs. Elliot*
MARK ....*Mr. Elliot*
THE STRANGER
DR. MARTIN

———

The scene is the living room of the Elliots.

———

The time is a late winter afternoon with a blizzard raging.

THE ANSWER

The scene is the home of JENNIE *and* MARK ELLIOT.
*That they are not blessed with more than the average
amount of this world's goods is evidenced by the rather
plain furnishings of the room, and by the fact that what is
obviously the living room is also being used for a bedroom. For there is a bed up Left. Perhaps there is a good
reason for having the bed in the living room where the fire
in the stove, down Right, can make it more comfortable
for* BETTY, *the Elliots' eight-year-old daughter, who, sick
and feverish, tosses and turns restlessly in the bed. There
is a table in the center of the room with two or three chairs
around it, and a lamp on the table. Near the head of the
bed is a small stand with a lamp on it. The telephone, with
a chair handy, is down Left. There is a window up Center
against which a raging storm is swirling snow. The door
up Right leads directly out-of-doors.*

*The time is late afternoon and it is darkening fast. The
lamp by the bed is lit. It is not too bright and the shade
is adjusted so the light does not shine in* BETTY'S *eyes.*

*There is an atmosphere of anxiety in the room which the
audience feels at once, perhaps because of the attitude of*
MARK *who sits, plainly worried, by the table, perhaps
because of* JENNIE *just going toward the bed with a spoon
and a glass of fruit juice; certainly because of* BETTY'S *in-
coherent mumbling and tossing.*

JENNIE (*at the bedside*). Come, dear, just a spoonful.
It's orange juice that you like so much.

33

(BETTY *moves and mumbles and* JENNIE'S *efforts are of no avail. She puts the glass on the stand, then places her hand on* BETTY'S *forehead.*)

MARK. How is she?
JENNIE. If I only could get her to take a little of the juice it might help.
MARK (*lighting the lamp on the table*). Why couldn't this storm have held off until morning so Dr. Martin could get here?
JENNIE. He'll get here if he can.
MARK. Yes, if he can! And what if he can't? (MARK *goes listlessly to the window and looks out at the storm.*)

(JENNIE, *by the bed, keeps the bed-clothes smooth, strokes* BETTY'S *forehead and does the other little things a mother does naturally at the bedside of her sick child.*)

JENNIE. Why don't you try to get him again?
MARK. I tried ten minutes ago. The line's been out all afternoon.
JENNIE. But try, Mark! Try again!
MARK (*leaving the window and going to the phone*). O.K. But it won't do any good. Nothing will.
JENNIE. Mark! Don't!

(MARK *sits dejectedly in the chair by the phone and tries to get the operator—and plainly does not expect to. There is no response and he tries again.* BETTY *tosses and calls weakly, "Mommy!"*)

MARK (*after two or three attempts*). There's no chance of that line . . . (*He straightens up suddenly, new life in his voice.*) . . . Hello! Hello! Operator? (*Aside to* JENNIE.) It's the operator! I—— Hello, operator? Get me Dr. Martin at Hillsboro......Dr. Martin. M-A-R-T-I-N, Martin . . . and hurry! It's an emergency...... You bet I'll wait!

JENNIE. You got through!

MARK. Yeh, I got the operator. Now if I can get . . . Hello!

(*No response.* JENNIE *has come down to stand by* MARK'S *chair.*)

JENNIE. He'll come; I know he will!

MARK (*he reflects* JENNIE'S *hope*). Sure he will if . . . Hello! (*Pause.*) Hello! Dr. Martin? This is Mark Elliot up on the Tilson road. Yeh......No, Doc, she's worse . . . seems like she's burning up with fever......Yeh, we have but Jennie can't get her to take a thing......Can you get here, Doc? You......You've got to!......Yeh, I know and I hate to ask you but . . . but it's Betty! ......Thanks, Doc, (*with half a sob*) I knew you would! ......It sure is a bad one......O.K., Doc, we'll be looking for you......Hurry, won't you?......I know you will......So long, Doc. (*Hangs up.*)

JENNIE. He's coming?

MARK. Says he'll get here if he possibly can. (*Rises and goes to the window and looks out at the storm which seems to have grown worse.*)

JENNIE. Oh, God! Make a way for him through the storm!

MARK. I guess it will take our prayers all right, Jennie. The storm is getting worse.

JENNIE. Prayer always helps, dear. You've said so many times.

MARK. Sure it does. And I'm praying as hard as I know how that Doc will make it through this blizzard.

JENNIE. It would be a strange God who couldn't answer prayer because of a snowstorm, even one as bad as this.

MARK. But don't expect miracles, Jennie.

JENNIE. No, Mark. Just God answering our prayers.

BETTY. Mommy!

JENNIE (*going to the bed*). Yes, dear, Mommy's right here.

MARK. If we'd only known yesterday how sick she was getting. (*The phone rings.* JENNIE *and* MARK *look at each other a moment, then* MARK *hurries over to the phone.*) Hello! Hello! Yes, this is Mark Elliot...... Yeh, I can hear you but talk up good and loud......(*To* JENNIE.) It's the doctor's office......Where?......At Taft's Corner? I thought perhaps......The main road . . . to Shelby? That's ten miles longer!......Yes, I guess so, if they can keep it open.....Doctor who? Stanley?......Standish?......No, never met him......How'll he make it? Well, I hope so.....I say I hope so!...... No . . . she . . . Well, she's no better......What's that? ......Nelson's? O.K. Try from here......Thank you, Mrs. Martin. (*Hangs up.*)

JENNIE. Mrs. Martin?

MARK (*dejectedly*). Yeh. Drift's 'most five feet deep across Taft's Corner. Doc's already left. She says if we can get the Nelsons' at the crossroads Larry can head him off and send him around through Shelby on the main road. It's longer but the state plows will be on it so he may be able to get through.

JENNIE. And if Larry can't head him off?

MARK. He'll get stuck at Taft's Corner. Then he'll have to turn around and go all the way back to the crossroads.

JENNIE. And Betty needs him now!

MARK (*at the phone*). Operator! Operator!

JENNIE. Couldn't Mrs. Martin get the Nelsons' ?

MARK. No. She said . . . Operator? Hello, operator? I want to get the Nelsons, Larry Nelson, at the Shelby crossroads......O.K.

JENNIE. She said what?

MARK. She said the line was out from their side.

JENNIE. But ours is still open.

MARK. Thank God for that!

JENNIE. I do thank Him for that!

MARK. If only there was . . . Hello! Hello, Larry? This is Mark Elliot......Yeh, it sure is a bad one. Listen, Larry, we need your help......Betty is sick......I say

Betty is sick......Don't know but she is a pretty sick kid......Yeh, I got hold of Doc Martin awhile ago......I say I got Doc Martin......(*The storm has been increasing in fury. There is a sudden blast of wind, stronger than the others and the lights go out.*) Larry! Larry! Hello, Larry!......Operator! Operator!......The line has gone!

JENNIE. Oh, Mark!

MARK (*half sobbing*). Is *that* what you call an answer to prayer?

JENNIE. Mark! Don't!

BETTY. Mommy! It's dark!

JENNIE. Just for a minute, dear.

MARK (*lighting a match*). There are two candles in the drawer. . . . Why couldn't that phone have stayed in another minute, half a minute?

JENNIE (*bringing the candles, she lights one.* MARK *takes the other*) I don't know why the phone went out just when it did. And the lights. But I'm not going to let the light go out in my soul! (*It is not with desperation, but with faith that she speaks. The audience must sense this.*)

MARK. What light is there anywhere now?

(JENNIE *is holding the lighted candle which illumines her face as she stands facing the audience. It must be a natural pose, not a stilted tableau.*)

JENNIE. The light of faith! We have to keep that burning!

MARK. Faith, only faith, at a time like this? (*He lights the other candle from the one* JENNIE *holds.*)

JENNIE. Faith was meant for times like this. (*She goes to the stand by the bed and leaves the candle there.*)

(MARK *places the other one on the table. There are no candle-holders so they must be stuck to something with dripped wax.*)

MARK. I know, Jennie, I know. But . . . but Betty . . . she's so sick.

JENNIE. The doctor will get here. I know he will.

MARK. But when?

JENNIE. Who was the other doctor?

MARK. Standish. Dr. Standish over in Shelby. Mrs. Martin said she called the operator and asked her to get word to him. He lives right in town. He'll come if he can get through.

JENNIE. See? Two doctors on the way.

MARK. Yes, but will either of them get here in time?

(JENNIE *is at the bed.* BETTY *tosses and moans.*)

BETTY. Mommy!

MARK. How is she?

JENNIE. She's . . . just the same, I think.

MARK. Still hot?

JENNIE. Feels as if she is burning up, poor darling.

MARK. And all we can do is wait! Wait! Wait! (*He paces back and forth.*)

JENNIE. Wait—and pray.

MARK. Pray? With the wires down? The phone out? The road blocked?

JENNIE (*coming down, she takes the Bible and sits at the Left of the table*). Sit down, Mark. (*He sits Right of the table.*) Remember how the 91st psalm draws to a close with, " He shall call upon Me and I will answer him " ?

MARK. I remember all right, but I never thought I'd call on God for . . . for Betty . . .

(*Note:* BETTY *should not remain quiet for long at any time. But her restlessness should not distract the attention of the audience from* MARK *and* JENNIE.)

JENNIE (*reading*). " And they brought little children to Him that He should bless them, and His disciples rebuked those that brought them. But when Jesus saw it He was much displeased and said unto them, Suffer the little children to come unto Me, and forbid them not for of such is the kingdom of heaven. . . . Verily I say unto you, Whosoever shall not receive the kingdom of God as a little child shall no wise enter therein. . . . He that dwelleth in the secret place of the Most High shall abide under the shadow of the Almighty. I will say of the Lord, He is my refuge and my fortress: my God, in Him will I trust." We've got to trust in Him, Mark.

MARK. I know it, dear, I know it. But . . .

JENNIE (*reading*). "He shall call upon Me and I will answer him. I will be with him in trouble . . ."

MARK (*his head in his hands*). "He shall call upon Me and I will answer him . . ."

JENNIE. Oh, dear God, in our trouble we call upon Thee. Thy heart must have ached when Thy son suffered, so hear our prayer for our child. Make a way for the doctor through the storm. Look down on our Betty and make her well. I don't know how, oh God, I only know that we have done all that we can do, and the storm is worse, and our only help is in Thee. Oh, God . . . please, God! Make her better!

MARK. Please, God, make her better!

JENNIE. Amen.

MARK (*in a whisper*). Amen. (*Slight pause.*) And that's . . . that's all we can do.

JENNIE. Yes, dear, but that's everything.

MARK. I guess your faith is stronger than mine, Jennie. I'm . . . I'm afraid.

JENNIE. So am I. We've never had anyone sick like this before. And Betty is so awfully sick. But surely faith and prayer wouldn't be worth much if they didn't help when we need them most.

MARK. That's why I'm trying hard to believe our prayer will be answered.

JENNIE. It will be, Mark! It will be!

BETTY. Mommy!

JENNIE. Yes, dear; right here. (*She goes to the bed and* MARK *follows her.*)

MARK. Try the juice again.

JENNIE. I've tried and tried and she won't take a swallow. (*She takes the glass of juice.*)

MARK. Betty, take some for Daddy.

(BETTY *moans and tosses and refuses to take the spoonful of juice* JENNIE *offers.* MARK *and* JENNIE *are so intent on tending* BETTY *that they do not notice that the storm has died down a good deal. Nor do they notice the light that shines through the window as though someone were passing with a lantern. A moment later there is a knock at the door.* MARK *and* JENNIE *look at each other wondering if they have heard. The knock is repeated.*)

JENNIE. Mark! He made it! It's the doctor! Thank God!

MARK. Good old Doc! How on earth did he get here so soon?

JENNIE. Oh, Mark, our prayer has been answered! (MARK *opens the door. The* STRANGER *stands outside, snow-covered and dressed for the storm. He wears a beard.* MARK *and* JENNIE *are taken aback for a moment.*) Why, you're . . . you're not Dr. Martin!

STRANGER (*half-laughing*). I'm afraid not! But may I come in out of the storm?

MARK. Sure, sure, come in.

STRANGER. Dr. Martin couldn't make it for some time so I——

JENNIE. Oh, then you're Dr. Standish from Shelby. Mrs. Martin said she was going to try and reach you.

MARK. It's a mean night to ask you out, Doctor, but our Betty is pretty sick.

STRANGER. Weather doesn't bother me. I've been out in all sorts.

MARK. None worse than this storm, I'll bet.

STRANGER. In a way, yes; much worse.

JENNIE. I'm Mrs. Elliot, as you probably guessed.

MARK. 'Scuse me, Doctor. I'm forgetting my manners. I'm Mark Elliot. (*They shake hands.*)

STRANGER. I once had a great champion named Mark. Fine young fellow.

JENNIE. I don't know how much Mrs. Martin told you about Betty, but she . . .

STRANGER. I think I know all I need to know, Mrs. Elliot.

(*There is an atmosphere of peace and calm about the* STRANGER *that somehow is transferred to the sick-room.*)

JENNIE. And I'm sure Dr. Martin wouldn't ask you to come if he didn't have every confidence in you.

MARK. Jennie!

JENNIE. I'm sorry! I guess that did sound funny. I'm just upset I guess.

STRANGER. Naturally. And I assure you I have somewhat of a reputation as a physician.

JENNIE. I'm sure you have. Please forgive me.

STRANGER. I learned to forgive long ago. So forget it.

(*During this conversation the* STRANGER *has been removing his coat, gloves, scarf, etc.* MARK *takes them and places them on the chair near the door. The* STRANGER *seems in no hurry, nor disturbed about the patient. Nor do* JENNIE *and* MARK, *for some reason, seem anxious.*)

MARK (*looking about*). Did you bring in your bag, Doctor?

STRANGER. My bag? Why—er-r, no. Let's see the patient first.

BETTY. Mommy!

JENNIE. Coming, Betty. (*She hurries to the bed.*)

(*The* STRANGER *follows her, unhurried.* MARK *goes to the foot of the bed where he can see.*)

STRANGER. I wonder if the psalmist didn't get his inspiration from a mother answering the voice of her child: "He shall call upon Me and I will answer him."

MARK. We read that just a few minutes ago.

STRANGER. It's worth reading and remembering. (*At the bed.*) Hello, Betty. (*To* JENNIE.) How old is she?

JENNIE. Eight.

STRANGER. Too young to suffer.

MARK. That's what I told Jennie. But she sure has, poor little tyke. We did all we could for her. Then we—we prayed.

STRANGER. Yes, I know.

(BETTY *tosses and moans. The* STRANGER *has been somewhat in the background. Now he draws near the bed as* JENNIE *steps back to make room for him.*)

JENNIE. Oh, Doctor, she's so sick!

STRANGER. Why don't you sit down and relax a bit, Mrs. Elliot? You've done your part.

JENNIE. If there's anything more I want to do it. (*She goes to the chair at the left of the table and sits down, but on the edge of the chair, alertly watching the* STRANGER. MARK *is still at the foot of the bed. The* STRANGER *takes* BETTY'S *hand. She has been restless and moaning. Now she grows quiet. The* STRANGER *seems not at all perturbed at any time. Nor does he do anything a doctor might be expected to do. He simply—takes her hand in his.*) Her pulse—it—it's been so weak and fluttery. Can you—feel it—stronger?

STRANGER. I wasn't feeling her pulse.

JENNIE. But I thought . . .

STRANGER. I was just holding her hand. (*He places his hand on* BETTY'S *forehead.*)

MARK. Is she—she still burning up, Doc?

STRANGER (*almost casually*). Burning up? No, I don't believe so.

MARK. Her temperature must have been at least 104, wasn't it, Jennie?

STRANGER. Very likely, but not now. She's sleeping very comfortably. (*He puts* BETTY'S *arms under the covers, smooths her hair and straightens the bed-clothes.*)

JENNIE. Sleeping!

STRANGER (*kindly*). Sleeping. Better have some broth ready. She'll be hungry when she wakes up.

MARK. Hungry? But, Doc, she hasn't wanted anything. . . .

JENNIE. I tried some milk and some broth before. . . .

STRANGER. And she wouldn't take any?

JENNIE. No. Just a little while before you came I tried to give her some orange juice and she wouldn't take even a spoonful.

STRANGER. Probably she was too sick to want any.

JENNIE. She was, Doctor, she was. We did everything we could but it didn't seem to help a bit.

STRANGER. Then you prayed, didn't you?

JENNIE. Why—why, yes. Then we prayed.

(*The* STRANGER *has come down by* JENNIE'S *chair. He puts his hand on her shoulder.*)

STRANGER. Have the broth ready. She'll be wanting it.

(JENNIE *rises and goes to* BETTY. MARK *comes over to the* STRANGER.)

MARK. Doctor, we can't thank you enough.

STRANGER. Don't try, Mark. If children can't come to me, why I like to go to them.

MARK. You sure have a way with them. Even as sick as Betty is . . . was, she looked up at you and smiled.

STRANGER (*chuckling*). And then fell asleep.

JENNIE. She *is* sleeping, peacefully and naturally. Thank God!

STRANGER. Yes, thank God.

MARK. Sit down, Doc. and Jennie'll have some coffee for us in a jiffy.

JENNIE (*coming down*). Indeed I will, with some hot toast.

STRANGER. Would you mind very much if I didn't stop? I appreciate your kindness but the storm seems to have died down and I feel I should be on my way.

JENNIE. Why, if you must go, of course it is all right.

STRANGER. Perhaps Dr. Martin will be able to get here now that the storm has let up.

MARK. We'll certainly thank him plenty for sending you.

JENNIE. How can we ever repay you, Doctor?

STRANGER. By keeping the fires of your faith burning bright.

(MARK *has been helping the* STRANGER *with his coat.*)

MARK. Sure you won't stop for a cup of coffee?

STRANGER. Thanks, but I mustn't take the time.

MARK. Where to now, Doc?

STRANGER. Down the road.

MARK. Toward Shelby?

STRANGER. Toward . . . to-morrow. Good-bye, Mark. (*He holds out his hand, which* MARK *takes. The* STRANGER *has the glove on his left hand by now.*)

MARK. Good-bye, Doctor. (*He notices the back of the* STRANGER'S *hand. Still holding it he says:*) Looks like you got quite a cut on that hand at some time or other.

(*Note:* MARK *should not turn the* STRANGER'S *hand with the obvious purpose of letting the audience see the scar. If they do, all right, but the suggestion is sufficient . . . for now.*)

STRANGER. Oh, that's an old scar; very old. (*Turning to* JENNIE.) Remember, Mrs. Elliot, no more worrying.

JENNIE (*shaking hands*). I haven't worried since you came in, Doctor.

STRANGER. Well, see that you don't after I'm gone.

JENNIE. I won't.

STRANGER. Good-bye. And may the love of God bless your faith.

JENNIE. Oh, He has blessed us to-night in sending you.

STRANGER. Thank you. There's great joy in being a blessing. I don't believe I know a greater.

(*This conversation has brought them near the door.*)

JENNIE. Good-bye.

MARK. Good-bye, Doc.

(*The* STRANGER *goes out.* MARK *closes the door after him, then goes down by the table where* JENNIE *is standing and puts an arm around her. Together they go to the bed and look down at* BETTY, *asleep.*)

JENNIE. Sound asleep. (*She puts a hand on* BETTY'S *forehead.*)

MARK. Any temperature?

JENNIE. Not a bit.

MARK. I wonder what Dr. Standish did? He didn't give her any medicine.

JENNIE. And he *didn't* get his bag, after all.

MARK. Didn't even take her temperature, did he?

(*Now that he has gone they realize that there was something unusual about the* STRANGER'S *visit.*)

JENNIE. One thing is sure, he came as the answer to our prayer.

MARK. I—I guess he did, Jennie. And he didn't seem a bit worried when he came in.

(*They have come down by the table again.*)

JENNIE. Yet he seemed to know about Betty.

MARK. Probably Mrs. Martin told him all he needed to know.

JENNIE. Of course. But I'll never forget him, and this night.

MARK. I guess neither of us will, my dear.

(*There is the noise of someone outside, a stamping of feet, then a knock at the door. Before either* MARK *or* JENNIE *can get to it,* DR. MARTIN *comes in, snow-covered and bustling.*)

JENNIE. Dr. Martin!

MARK. How did you get through?

DR. MARTIN. Well, they had the big rotary plow digging through the drifts at Taft's Corner so I stayed right behind it. I hope I .... How's Betty? (*He has been taking off his gloves, now rubs his hands briskly to get them warm. It is evident that he expects to have work to do.*)

JENNIE. She's . . . she's all right, Dr. Martin.

DR. MARTIN. All right? What do you mean?

JENNIE. I mean she's all right. She's better.

MARK (*he has gone to the bed*). Come here, Doc.

(*Puzzled,* DR. MARTIN *goes to the bed and places his hand on* BETTY's *forehead.*)

DR. MARTIN. Not a bit of temperature. Sure she had one?

JENNIE. Oh, Doctor, her whole body was on fire.

DR. MARTIN (*taking* BETTY's *pulse*). Why, she's sleeping like a baby now.

JENNIE. Yes, and I'm going to get some broth ready for when she wakes up. Dr. Standish said she'd be hungry.

DR. MARTIN (*puzzled*). Dr. Standish?

MARK. We were lucky Mrs. Martin got him. Thank her for us a million times.

JENNIE. If ever prayers were answered ours were.

MARK. Thank God!

JENNIE. We didn't expect you'd be able to make it for a couple of hours so we were mighty glad to see him.

MARK. He sure knew what to do for Betty.

DR. MARTIN. What are you talking about? What's this about Dr. Standish?

JENNIE. Why, he just left a few minutes ago.

MARK. You must have passed him on the hill.

DR. MARTIN. I didn't pass anyone. Let me get this straight. You say the doctor was here?

JENNIE. Not five minutes ago.

MARK. If he'd stayed for coffee the way we wanted him to, he'd be here now. But he said he was going to . . . (*Puzzled.*)

JENNIE (*also puzzled*). Toward to-morrow.

DR. MARTIN. Listen, the operator at Shelby called back and said Dr. Standish was tied up for at least a couple of hours with an emergency operation. (MARK *and* JENNIE *look at each other bewildered.*) And the road from here to Shelby is blocked solid this side of the mountain. Nothing can get through.

MARK. But he . . .

DR. MARTIN. Did this man say he was Dr. Standish?

MARK. No-o-o, come to think of it. He didn't.

JENNIE. We . . . we just took it for granted.

DR. MARTIN. What did he look like?

MARK. Why, he was a fairly husky chap, with a very pleasant voice and manner . . .

JENNIE. There was something about him that brought a feeling of peace; that even made the storm seem less wild.

MARK. With just the candle-light it was hard to see just what he looked like, but he wore a beard. . . .

DR. MARTIN. A beard? There's no doctor anywhere around here that wears a beard!

JENNIE. And all he did was place his hand on Betty's forehead, and hold her hand in his.

(MARK *suddenly remembers . . . or is it suddenly? With wonder in his face he lifts his right hand and looks at it, then touches the back of it with the fingers of his left in a gesture, unexaggerated but which the audience cannot fail to interpret. When* MARK *speaks again it is with awe and reverence and wonder in his voice.*)

MARK. And His hand . . . His hands were scarred!

(JENNIE, *too, now understands. Her face, her attitude show it.*)

JENNIE (*slowly, awesomely, understandingly*). " Suffer the little children to come unto Me . . ."
MARK. " He shall call upon Me and I will answer him."

(*Both look up on* MARK'S *speech, the light of a faith confirmed shining in glory from their faces.*)

SLOW CURTAIN

THEY THAT WALK IN DARKNESS

AN EASTER PLAY IN ONE ACT

By

WILLARD S. SMITH

PRODUCTION RIGHTS

Copies of this play are available in single pamphlet form. The right to produce this play by one group of amateur players is authorized only by the purchase of six copies (one copy for each speaking part) at the current price of 50c each.

It is dishonest and illegal to copy parts.

49

THEY THAT WALK IN DARKNESS

CAST OF CHARACTERS

(For eight men and two women)

ZADOK......................*the "good man of the house"*
HANNAH ....*his wife*
RACHEL...................*their blind daughter, about 12*
JUDAS
A BEGGAR
JAMES
JOHN
JESUS
THOMAS, PHILIP *and the other disciples*

TIME—*The evening of the Passover.*

PLACE—*Outside the Upper Room, Jerusalem.*

SUGGESTIONS FOR STAGING

The "upper room" is easily constructed since it is square with a flat roof. The end opposite the door may be extended beyond the stage proper, thus providing more room for the disciples, some of whom may sit on the floor by the front wall.

The parapet, about eighteen inches in height, and the walls of the room may be covered with gray building paper, or with the gray paper used under linoleum. Use black crayon or charcoal for drawing a few cracks, the ends of the rafters and the broad border around the window. The "window" is but an opening cut in the wall about five feet from the floor. The roof must be covered with opaque material so no light can shine out.

A distant landscape scene for the space between the room and the side wall by the stairs may be drawn on large sheets of paper with artists' crayon. In lieu of this a dark blue cloth should be fastened smoothly over this space. Chalk spots for stars will lend realism to the sky effect.

It is not necessary to have a table in the upper room but it should be thought of as there. That is, the disciples, and Hannah and Rachel, must go around rather than directly across the room.

The disciples seated in line with the window and the audience must remember to act at *all* times and register properly even though they have little or nothing to say. They will, of course, join in the murmuring and exclamations where indicated in the script. Their attention will be directed mainly toward Jesus who is seated at the head of the table, which is the place farthest from the door.

Though there are, of course, supposed to be twelve disciples, ten will suffice as the audience does not have a chance to count them. While a cast of fifteen or sixteen is necessary, only four have any amount of memorizing to do: Zadok, Hannah, Judas, and the Beggar. Most of the disciples have little or nothing to say. The words of Jesus, all spoken from within the upper room, can be read, as can the speeches of the disciples spoken from there. All characters should be thoroughly familiar with their parts, however, so that their lines will sound conversational and natural.

The entrance and exit of Jesus and the disciples—their crossing from the stairs to the upper room and later their return—should be carefully rehearsed for position and timing. The murmuring by the disciples and the confusion when they speak more or less together also should be carefully rehearsed for naturalness.

The author is fully aware that he has taken liberties with the gospel order of Jesus' words spoken on the night of the Last Supper. But, kept in their general setting, they may take on a new and deeper meaning as we see them move a vengeful heart to forgiveness and bring sight to the eyes of a blind child.

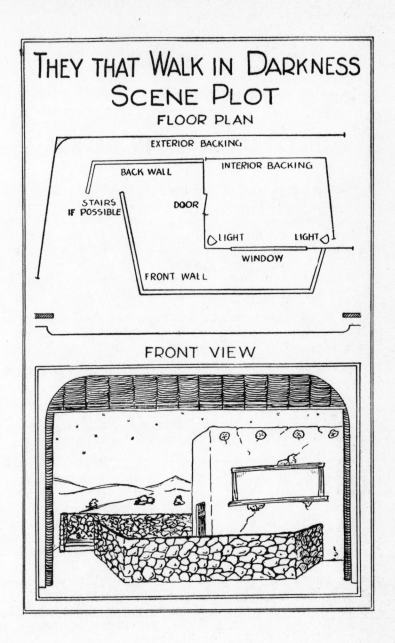

They that Walk in Darkness
Scene Plot
FLOOR PLAN

EXTERIOR BACKING

INTERIOR BACKING

BACK WALL

STAIRS
IF POSSIBLE

DOOR

LIGHT   LIGHT

WINDOW

FRONT WALL

FRONT VIEW

THEY THAT WALK IN DARKNESS

SCENE: *A parapet, the customary protecting wall, encloses the scene which is the roof of the house. At Right rear are the usual outside stairs to the street below. The "upper room," built on the roof, occupies about half the scene. It has a door on the right side and a "window" in the center of the front wall. The room should be thought of as ready for the Passover feast with a table (imaginary) in the center of the room and benches around the table.*

It is late afternoon with waning light which fades as the scene progresses until at about the time the BEGGAR *enters it is night. The room is light throughout the play.*

HANNAH *is heard singing to herself as the curtain rises and she is glimpsed through the window as she moves about the room, probably setting the table.*

ZADOK *comes up the outside stairs. He pauses to look across to the city, Right, and speaks to himself.*

ZADOK. Crowds, crowds everywhere. It takes more than the legions of Rome to quench the fire that burns in the heart of Israel. Yet I wonder—is it a fire that has nearly burned itself out, burning so low as to give no light?—The Passover will be kept tonight as it has been kept for generations, but the Lord God of our fathers seems far away. (*Pause. Then he continues thoughtfully.*) The Messiah. Can he be? . . . Ah, but how can he hope to deliver Israel with only words and promises, even though they be words to stir one's soul and promises to lift one's faith?

HANNAH (*she has come to the door which has been partly open*). Speaking to the stars, Zadok?

ZADOK (*whirling quickly*). Hannah! You startled me!

HANNAH. Keep thy thoughts to thyself and there will be no need to be startled. What holds thy interest in the city that makes thee talk into the empty night?

ZADOK (*looking off to the city, Right*). I was but watching the crowds that swirl along like leaves in the brook Kidron, carried along with no desire to change their course because it is so easy to let the waters bear them where they will.

HANNAH. The leaves cannot help their fate.

ZADOK. But the people can! Yet the Pharisees continue to feed them on lies, and the high priests grow rich from their sacrifices, and the great truths of the prophets are forgotten!

HANNAH. Hush! Men are in prison for saying as much!

ZADOK. And men who love the Lord their God can say no less. (*More quietly.*) Hannah, hast thou heard of one Jesus?

HANNAH. Jesus of Nazareth, the carpenter? (ZADOK *nods.*) Yea, I have heard of him. Is it—is it true that he heals the sick? Rebecca spoke of a woman healed of some grievous ailment but I thought it only an idle tale.

ZADOK. Yea, Hannah, he has healed many; men and women and—and children too.

HANNAH. Has—has he made the blind to see?

ZADOK. Hannah, Hannah! Dost thou expect miracles?

HANNAH (*sighing*). Of course. Only the Lord God himself could do that. But—oh! If only it could be!

ZADOK (*placing an arm around her*). Perhaps some day our little Rachel shall see again. That is my constant prayer.

HANNAH. And mine. (*Pause.*) Tell me, Zadok, why do the multitudes follow this Jesus?

ZADOK. He draws men to him as the sea draws the river. He attracts the evil and the sinful as the dawn attracts the darkness,—to dispel it.

HANNAH. Well, it is certain he has drawn out thy thoughts. But see that thy heart is not drawn away from me.

ZADOK. Dost thou fear that, my beloved?

HANNAH. Nay, my husband; but I have watched the change that recent weeks, days even, have wrought in thee. Since thy return from Jericho, and then last Sabbath when the crowds hailed this Jesus as one who came in the name of the Lord.

ZADOK. And the cries have died away so soon! Ah, but since first I saw him, first heard his words, I have felt the glow of his message and the power of his love.

HANNAH. His love?

ZADOK. Yea, that burned into my heart and set it on fire, that opened my eyes to the needs of others and the needs of my own soul; a love that Israel has lost, and suffered much in losing.

HANNAH. But if he brings it again, will not Israel rise in newness of love and glory?

ZADOK. It could, and with it lift up all mankind so that as long as men live on the earth they could live together as brothers. But—they will not listen.

HANNAH. But Zadok, if he is the Messiah, they *must* listen.

ZADOK. Must they? And what if they do listen with their ears when their hearts are hardened to anything but the lure of gold, and the goodness of Jehovah only stirs them to grasp for more? Sometime the world may listen, and heed,—when other ways have failed.

HANNAH. Then it may be too late.

ZADOK. It will never be too late to turn to Jesus of Nazareth. (*Rousing himself.*) But come! See that the table is ready and the room prepared. They should be here soon.

HANNAH (*turning toward the room*). It will be ready for . . . (*Turns back.*) Zadok! Is—is *he* coming here tonight?

ZADOK (*half laughing at her*). Yea, Hannah, thy woman's curiosity hath found its answer. Two men met me at the pool this afternoon. One said unto me: Where is thy guest-chamber that the Master may eat the Passover with his disciples? So I showed them this upper room, furnished.

HANNAH (*close to him*). 'Tis like thee, the good man of the house, as always. But with a strange, new light in thine eyes.

ZADOK. Perhaps because of the new fire burning in my heart. Now to thy place before the company arrives.

HANNAH. The Messiah! In our house! Oh, if only he might make our Rachel to see again! (*Exits into the room.*)

ZADOK (*to himself as he looks after her*). Yea, if that tale of the once blind man by the pool of Siloam is true. Ah, but I cannot arouse her hope on the strength of a beggar's tale. My poor, blind little Rachel! (*He sighs, then goes and looks out over the city, Right, so his back is partly turned toward the stairs.*) The Messiah! At times I almost know he is, but—but how can he deliver Israel with no army, no power with which to defeat the Roman legions? "Render unto Cæsar the things that are Cæsar's" . . . no thought of crushing Rome there. (*Sighs.*) I wish I knew. (*He turns and starts toward the room as* JUDAS *comes up the stairs.*)

JUDAS. Hail to thee!

ZADOK (*turning quickly*). Peace to thee! But ——

JUDAS. Art thou the master of the house?

ZADOK (*on guard*). I am Zadok, and this is my house.

JUDAS (*indicating*). This is the upper room?

ZADOK. Is it not plain?

JUDAS. There is to be a gathering here tonight?

ZADOK (*suspicious*). A gathering?

JUDAS. Yea. Did not two men meet thee and bid thee prepare the upper room for the Passover?

ZADOK. And who art thou?

JUDAS. Judas, of Kerioth. It is I who must guard the little silver and the still scarcer gold with which to buy food for the others and for my Master.

ZADOK. And thy Master is—Jesus of Nazareth?

JUDAS (*with a strained confusion, not too obvious*). Yea, yea, he is—he is my Master.

ZADOK (*deeply interested*). Thou art close to him daily. Thou hast followed him to Galilee and Judea.

JUDAS. Yea, I have followed him, though no man gets close to him, not close enough to know his thoughts and his plans.

ZADOK. But did he not once announce in the synagogue that he had come to give sight to the blind, to set at liberty them that are bruised, and release the captive?

JUDAS. And for nearly three years we have waited for that liberation, that freedom from tyranny.

ZADOK (*intently, eagerly*). I have heard that he *has* restored sight to the blind. Is it true?

JUDAS (*casually, almost as though exasperated at* ZADOK's *questioning*). He can do all things, and the lame and the lepers dog his footsteps day and night. But if he seeks to fulfill the prophecy of Isaiah he needs soldiers, arms, generals . . .

ZADOK (*innocently*). And money, I suppose, to turn the heads of some who might . . .

JUDAS (*startled*). What meanest thou?

ZADOK (*not noticing the interruption*) . . . place money above all else. Yet did he not say, "My kingdom is not of this world"?

JUDAS. Our suffering, our humiliation are of this world.

ZADOK. "Ye shall know the truth," he said, "and the truth shall make you free."

JUDAS. Yea, he said that when . . . Thou seemest well acquainted with his sayings.

ZADOK. The man holds a strange fascination for me. And sometimes I think I can almost catch a glimpse of his dream.

JUDAS (*with suppressed excitement*). But soon we shall see what . . . (*He catches himself and speaks more calmly.*) Come, come, what is the price of thy room, furnished? And remember we are not like the priests in the temple who become rich on the offerings of the poor.

ZADOK (*with pretended seriousness*). Well, let me see. The room should be worth five pieces of silver. . . .

JUDAS. Five pieces of silver! I doubt if that would leave money enough to buy food for another day. (*He takes a money-bag from his girdle and fumbles at the draw-string. It is evident that Judas is ill at ease.*)

ZADOK (*rather enjoying* JUDAS' *discomfort*). But it is a fine room, clean and well-tended. And for the meal for twelve—aye! for thirteen!—well, the price for all should be twenty-five or thirty pieces of silver.

(JUDAS *has opened the bag and just before the end of* ZADOK'S *speech he has poured the contents into his hand. At the mention of "thirty pieces of silver" he is startled into immobility. Though* ZADOK *speaks the words in all innocence, they pierce the mind of* JUDAS, *if not his heart.*)

JUDAS (*startled*). Thirty—pieces—of silver!

ZADOK (*noticing the money in* JUDAS' *hand*). See, thou hast it there; ten, twenty, thirty pieces. All new money and all of the Roman mint here in Jerusalem. (ZADOK *really thinks nothing strange about the fact as he pokes the money with his finger.*)

JUDAS (*arousing himself*). Nay! Nay! (*He hastily replaces the money.*) 'Tis the wrong bag. Those pieces . . . that silver . . . I was given them for . . . (*With an effort he regains part of his composure. He replaces the bag in his girdle and takes out another.*) How much, now, for the room and meal?

ZADOK (*no longer jocular*). Nothing. Thy Master is welcome. It is little I can do. Tell him the upper room is ready and is his in which to keep the Passover this night with his disciples.

JUDAS (*lifting his eyebrows*). Nothing? Good! There is little to spend and I must use it wisely. I shall go and tell him. (*He replaces the bag.* HANNAH *has come to the doorway and listens, unobserved.*)

ZADOK. Yea, go to him—and tell him. (*There should be a slight emphasis on "and tell him," though* ZADOK *has no suspicions.*)

JUDAS (*disturbed*). That . . . the room is ready?

ZADOK. What else wouldst thou have to tell him?

JUDAS. Nothing. Nothing. (*He turns and starts out.*)

ZADOK. I think I envy thee.

JUDAS (*he stops and half turns*). Envy—me? Thou dost envy *me?*

ZADOK. Thou art so near to him.

JUDAS. Yea . . . yea, I am near to him. But—why envy *me?* (*Exits down the stairs. ZADOK looks after him as HANNAH steps out.*)

HANNAH. Who is that man, Zadok, and what evil purpose hath he?

ZADOK. Not so hasty, my Hannah. Though he *did* act strangely, as though he were afraid.

HANNAH. As though he were afraid of himself. Who is he?

ZADOK. He did tell me his name but I have forgotten.

HANNAH. It is well that it should be forgotten. Is he a friend of Jesus?

ZADOK. One of his disciples. And soon the others will be here. Is the room ready?

HANNAH. Yea, the places are prepared and the unleavened bread is on the table.

ZADOK. The wine! Has not old Eli sent it?

HANNAH. Nay, but he promised to have it here in time.

ZADOK. He promised to have it here by sun-down. Go thou and fetch it. And tell him he had better tend his business or he will lose it. (*HANNAH exits by the stairs. ZADOK, after thinking a moment.*) Judas! That was his name. Judas of Kerioth. Somehow he did seem different from the others. But then, we all are different. (*He has turned toward the center of the stage and walks slowly, Left. Up the stairs slinks a ragged beggar. He is crippled and one hand is twisted. As ZADOK says, "We are all different" the beggar stumbles over a stick or some object by the rear wall. ZADOK whirls around.*) Who is there? (*The beggar starts back toward the stairs.*) Stop! What art thou doing here? (ZADOK *goes to the* BEGGAR *but does not deign to touch him.*)

BEGGAR. I—I—nothing. I only want—I came that I might . . .

ZADOK. That thou might steal from my table!

BEGGAR. Nay! Nay! I am but a poor beggar! I am no thief!

ZADOK. Well, thou art here for no good, that is certain, slinking into my house like a wolf sneaking up on the fold. I have a mind to call the Roman guard and let him take care of thee. (*He steps to the wall as if to call the guard.*)

BEGGAR. Nay! I tell thee I meant no harm! I will go!

ZADOK. Ah no, not until thou hast explained why a ragged beggar dare steal into the house of Zadok on this night.

BEGGAR. It is because of this night I dared to come.

ZADOK. What meanest thou? Why *this* house on *this* night? What dost thou know?

BEGGAR. Patience, I beg, and I will tell thee! I seek him who can straighten these crooked limbs. (*They have moved down Center.*)

ZADOK. "The sins of the fathers shall be visited upon the children."

BEGGAR. Nay, I was not always a crippled beggar. Once I owned as fine a fishing boat as any on Genesaret. (*Bitterly.*) Three years ago it was, one Reuben, son of Joel, made me as you see me now.

ZADOK. And why did he beat thee until thy body was crooked?

BEGGAR. He did not beat me. The stupid blunderer was with me on a fishing trip. He was at the helm. A sudden storm came down from over Mt. Hermon and tossed our boat about like a chip. Suddenly the mast snapped off and all Reuben did to keep it from crushing me was to shout as he leaped to safety.

ZADOK. And what more could he do?

BEGGAR. He might have swung the boat so that the wind would have carried the broken mast away from me. He might have leaped to my side and pushed me out of the way. He might have . . .

ZADOK (*somewhat amused*). But he did nothing *to* thee?

BEGGAR. Nay, but because of his cowardice, his blundering, I am—thus. But some day Reuben will pay!

ZADOK. And thou wouldst be made straight to avenge thyself upon this Reuben?

BEGGAR. An eye for an eye and a tooth for a tooth, saith the law.

ZADOK. Thou art sure of the law! And who is it thou seekest to straighten that crooked back of thine?

BEGGAR. A healer I heard of in Capernaum. He has power to cure all manner of diseases. When I reached there he had gone. But one who had been lame since childhood and who walked straight at the healer's touch told me he had gone to Jericho. So I . . .

ZADOK (*interested*). And this healer was . . . ?

BEGGAR (*matter-of-factly*). Jesus of Nazareth. I followed him to Jericho, only to lose him in the throng that pressed him when he restored the sight of a blind beggar.

ZADOK. Sight to the blind! What art thou saying?

BEGGAR. I knew the beggar. One Bartimeus, blind from the day he was born. And now he can see.

ZADOK. How can these things be?

BEGGAR. I know not how. I only know that they are.

ZADOK. Dost thou think this Jesus to be the Messiah of Israel? I would know the mind of a beggar as well as—as that of a member of the Sanhedrin.

BEGGAR. Messiah or not, I cannot say. I only know that he has healed the blind and the lame. I seek him that my body may be made whole again. (*Darkly.*) I'll settle my score with Reuben once I can straighten this crooked back he so nearly broke in two.

ZADOK. Well, thou canst not see him tonight. As his host I must see that he is not disturbed.

BEGGAR (*excited*). Then he *will* be here? They have not yet seized him?

ZADOK. Not yet seized him? What meanest thou?

BEGGAR. Nothing. I only heard . . .

ZADOK. Heard what? Speak, man, or I *will* call the guard!

BEGGAR. Nay! Nay! I will tell thee! Out near the cave of the lepers last night three men talked. I was resting nearby and they could not see me in the shadows. I did not mean to listen. I had been there——

ZADOK. Never mind the excuses! Go on! Couldst thou see them?

BEGGAR. At times, plainly.

ZADOK. Who were they?

BEGGAR. I know not. How could a beggar know the priests of the temple?

ZADOK. Priests?

BEGGAR. Two of them were. The other was a rough-bearded fellow who argued much over money for something. I heard him demand that he be paid more than thirty pieces of silver.

ZADOK (*he almost realizes the connection*). Thirty pieces of—— (*Voices are heard approaching.*) They come! Now you will have to stay. But keep out of sight else they who come as my guests will condemn me for harboring such as thee. (*The beggar slips into the shadows by the front of the room.* JAMES *and* JOHN *enter by the stairs.*)

JAMES (*speaking to* JOHN). If we are not to merit places of honor in his kingdom, pray tell who will?

JOHN (*as perturbed as* JAMES). It is not given him to say who shall sit on his right hand and on his left!

JAMES. Yea, those were the very words he spoke to our mother. (*He sees* ZADOK.) Is it here the Passover is to be kept?

ZADOK (*cautiously*). The Passover will be kept in every home tonight where the blood of Abraham has not been thinned by intermingling with Samaritans and Romans.

JOHN. Our Master bade us come hither.

ZADOK. And thy Master is . . . ?

JOHN. Jesus of Nazareth, the chosen one of Israel.

ZADOK. The Messiah, I have been told.

JAMES. And dost thou not believe?

ZADOK. Dost thou?

JOHN. Surely! Are we not members of his band of disciples?

ZADOK. Why?

JAMES. Why?

ZADOK. Because he works miracles? Because he heals the sick and (*Glancing toward the hidden beggar*) because he straightens crooked limbs so the lame can walk?

JOHN. Nay! It is for love!

ZADOK. Of him? Or of thyself?

JAMES. Thou art an impudent fellow. It is true we have seen him heal the sick and cleanse the lepers. But his power is revealed most when the sinner, one like that Magadelene wench, is born again into newness of life. He heals the diseased soul as well as the sick body.

ZADOK (*slyly*). And the places—the one on the right and the one on the left?

JAMES. Must the guest be questioned by his host?

ZADOK. Pray forgive me. The room is ready. (*He motions to it and* JAMES *and* JOHN *start toward it as* ZADOK *speaks again.*) Can—can thy Master give sight to the blind?

JOHN (*matter-of-factly*). Of a certainty! Ask Bartimeus, the beggar blind from birth. (*He and* JAMES *enter the room.*)

BEGGAR (*coming out of the shadows*). He has power! Did I not tell thee?

ZADOK. Power to heal sick souls, to redeem lost souls, to—to give sight to the blind!

BEGGAR. Did I not tell thee of Bartimeus? And he *can* make me upright!

ZADOK. Upright in body—or in spirit?

BEGGAR. Why—why, in body so that I can . . . ?

ZADOK. So that thou may have thy revenge on Reuben?

BEGGAR. Nay, not that alone. I—I walk uprightly in the law.

ZADOK. So do the Pharisees whom he called hypocrites, whited sepulchres, blind fools! (*The beggar backs away at*

ZADOK'S *vehemence. As* ZADOK *turns away from the beggar* HANNAH *comes up the stairs with a jug of wine.*)

HANNAH. Old Eli is like a gossipy old woman. Almost I had to give him the names of our guests before he would give me the wine.

ZADOK. Thou didst not tell him?

HANNAH. Nay. Only that there would be special guests.

ZADOK. Didst thou see anyone else?

HANNAH. Why, Zadok, the streets are full of people.

ZADOK. I mean any who might seek out our guests, with no good purpose?

HANNAH. I saw two who I think are disciples of his. And close behind them two Roman soldiers.

ZADOK. Soldiers?

HANNAH. Oh, Zadok, I cannot rid my heart of a strange heaviness. I feel as though there were shadows deepening across life as well as across the skies.

ZADOK (*an arm around her*). Let not the sight of Roman soldiers frighten thee, Hannah. Perchance the excitement of this night hath unnerved thee.

HANNAH. Nay, Zadok. The truth is—I am afraid.

ZADOK. There is naught to fear. Only Jesus and the twelve near him will be our guests tonight. No one else knows they are keeping the Passover here.

HANNAH. But if his enemies should find him . . .

ZADOK. Thou art much concerned for this Jesus, Hannah?

HANNAH. Yea. And I know not why. Only that deep within me I know—or do I know?—that he is not like others who have urged Israel to repentance. Yet I have never seen him.

ZADOK. He told the people that day that he had been sent to heal the broken-hearted, to preach deliverance to the captives . . .

HANNAH. To give sight to the blind! Oh, if he would!

ZADOK. Perhaps we shall know before this night is over. Now take the wine to the table. And it might be well if thou didst leave the room by the inner door. (HANNAH *goes into the room.* ZADOK *speaks to himself.*) " The acceptable year of the Lord." I wonder —— But what if one of the twelve should tell that he is to be here?

BEGGAR (*coming from hiding*). Surely none would be so base as to betray his trust.

ZADOK (*turning*). Thou eavesdropper! Must I flog thee to keep thee out of sight?

BEGGAR. But I would see Jesus!

ZADOK. Away, I tell thee! (*Motions toward the stairs.*) Get thee gone, and quickly, before the others come. I will not have thee . . . (*Voices are heard below.*) Now it is too late. Keep out of sight. (*The beggar again retreats into the shadows, going to the left of the window.*)

FIRST DISCIPLE (*offstage*). This is the house. Here we will find an upper room furnished as thou didst direct.

(*Two disciples enter, a little ahead of the others.*)

SECOND DISCIPLE (*to* ZADOK). The room is prepared?

ZADOK. Yea. Welcome to the humble home of Zadok. (*He motions to the room.*)

(*The other disciples enter and without pause, though not hurriedly, they cross and enter the room. As* ZADOK *finishes the above speech a soft light glows in the midst of the group, shining on One who is partly concealed by the others. He is dressed in a white or light-colored garment which distinguishes him from the disciples. The audience has just time to grasp the fact that it is* JESUS *in the moment or two taken by the following speeches, spoken as the disciples move across the stage. This scene should be carefully rehearsed for timing, placing and lighting. Movement across the stage should be natural with no suggestion that the disciples are trying to hide* JESUS. *The light shining on* JESUS *should not be bright.*)

A DISCIPLE. I tell thee it would have been better to call down fire from heaven rather than wait for thy enemies to strike.

ANOTHER DISCIPLE. How long, Lord, before thy kingdom shall come to pass? Already the high priests and Pharisees plot and scheme.

(JESUS *goes into the room on the above speech, the others standing aside to let him enter. When he answers it is from within the room while going to his place. The audience will glimpse him through the window as he goes to the head of the table, assumed to be the place opposite the door. Thus he is out of sight of the audience.*)

JESUS. The kingdom of God cometh not with observation, neither shall they say, Lo here! or Lo there! for behold, the kingdom of God is within you.

(*As soon as* JESUS *has entered the others jostle each other to get through the door. Do not exaggerate this, and at first, while* JESUS *is speaking it must not be conspicuous lest it detract from his words. As soon as he finishes speaking, the crowding becomes more obvious.* JUDAS *hangs back and is the last to enter. He looks back furtively, then goes in. The door closes. The audience can see the men as they take their places, but note that they do not go directly to them. There is apparent confusion as to where they will sit.*)

BEGGAR (*he has slipped out of the shadow*). I have seen him! I have seen him! I have seen Jesus!

ZADOK. And thy hand—canst thou straighten it? Or canst thou now walk upright, to face Reuben?

BEGGAR. Nay, I am not healed. But he does not know that I am here.

ZADOK. And he will not. (*He goes to the right of the window, the* BEGGAR *to the left. They watch and listen.*)

VOICES FROM THE ROOM (*confused*). I tell thee the place should be mine!

—Nay, mine!

—I tell thee I am older!

—Yea, and more blind and stubborn!

—Shall I sit at the lower end of the board as a servant?
—And what of I?

(*The voices die down as* JESUS *speaks.*)

JESUS. He that is greater among you, let him become as the younger; and he that is chief among you as he that doth serve. For which is greater, he that sitteth at meat, or he that serveth? I am in the midst of you as he that serveth.

(*There is a murmuring as the disciples take their places. Suddenly the* BEGGAR *seizes* ZADOK.)

BEGGAR. There *he* is! What is he doing here?
ZADOK. Be still, thou fool! They who come here this night are guests of the Nazarene and of mine. See that thy idle tongue casts no slur on any of them.
BEGGAR. But he comes for no good. It was he . . .
ZADOK. Silence, I tell thee! I wonder why Hannah does not bring the wine?
JESUS. With desire have I desired to eat this Passover with you before I suffer. For I say unto you, I will not eat thereof until it be fulfilled in the kingdom of God.

(*Murmur of voices among the disciples. While no set speech need be memorized each disciple should have a definite sentence in mind which he repeats two or three times so that the audience will get the effect of conversation, even though confused. The disciples seen by the audience through the window must be sure to act. The murmuring should not stop abruptly and at no time must it be carried over into the speeches of* JESUS, *or anyone else.*)

BEGGAR. Look! He girdeth himself with a towel.
ZADOK. And pours water into a basin. (*Slight pause.*) He is—he is going to wash their feet! Why did I not think of that? Surely he will judge me a poor host and ungracious to have neglected it.

BEGGAR. He goes first to the one with the money-bag, the one I saw. . . .

ZADOK. Judas. Of Kerioth. It was he who came to pay for the room. And seemed surprised that a friend of his Master's should take no pay for his hospitality.

BEGGAR. See! He cringes from the touch of Jesus.

ZADOK. Yea, so he doth. Strange!

BEGGAR. 'Twould be stranger if he did not.

ZADOK. Hush!—He goes to the one called Peter.

BEGGAR. Simon Peter. I have fished with him and his brother Andrew many times. They were in the boat the day Reuben let this happen to me.

ZADOK. I must ask their account of the accident.

BEGGAR. If this Jesus will but straighten my back I promise thou wilt see. . . .

ZADOK. Peter draws away from him.

PETER. Nay, Master, thou shalt not wash my feet!

JESUS. If I wash thee not, thou hast no part of me.

PETER (*penitently*). Lord, not my feet only but also my hands and my head.

BEGGAR. Peter himself called Reuben a bungling fool that day.

ZADOK. I care not! Be still!

JESUS. He that is washed needeth not save to wash his feet, but is clean every whit, and ye are clean, but not all.

(*Murmuring among the disciples.*)

ZADOK. He condemneth one as unclean. (*Puzzled.*)

BEGGAR. He hath power to make the lame walk—and he washes his disciples' feet!

JESUS. Know ye not what I have done to you? Verily, verily, I say unto you, the servant is not greater than his master; neither is he that is sent greater than he that sent him.

(*During this scene* JESUS *must naturally move about the room. He must remember that there is supposed to be a*

*table in the center of the room. For the sake of a change in
the position from which* JESUS *speaks,* PETER *might be seated
near the door. JESUS' last speech, above, might then be
spoken as he returns to his place at the head of the table.*
HANNAH *comes up the stairs. Hearing her,* ZADOK *crosses
hurriedly, fearing eavesdroppers. The* BEGGAR *remains at
the window.*)

ZADOK. What is it, Hannah? Why art thou not serving
our guests?

HANNAH. They are all served. Zadok, that man is at the
table who—who came to pay for the room; he who acted
so strangely.

ZADOK. True. Did he not say that he was one of Jesus'
disciples?

HANNAH. I—I do not like him. I—I think . . .

ZADOK (*reproachfully*). Hannah! Hannah! Thy dislike
of this—this Judas must not alter our part as hosts. They
who are gathered here tonight with Jesus are his friends.
(*Going to the wall, Right, he looks off.*) There are his
enemies. And I cannot help but wonder which will triumph,
the love of the one or the hate of the other.

HANNAH (*coming up to* ZADOK). Can anything defeat
love, my husband?

ZADOK. I know, my beloved. But hatred can distort a
life; it can kill generosity, forgiveness, pity, kindness.

HANNAH. But in the end love will conquer.

ZADOK (*turning to the* BEGGAR *who has edged out of the
shadows*). Can thy faith match that, thou vengeance-seeking
beggar?

HANNAH (*startled*). Zadok! Who is this?

ZADOK. An eavesdropper who would be made whole that
vengeance might be made easier.

BEGGAR. Nay! Not so! I—I seek . . .

ZADOK. Oh-ho! So thy mind is beginning to waver?
Good!

HANNAH. But who is he? And what is he doing here—
tonight?

ZADOK. He claims to know for a certainty that Jesus can heal the lame and halt.

BEGGAR. Yea, I know he can!

HANNAH. I have heard others tell of being made whole at his touch.

BEGGAR. His touch, yea, that is all. I have talked with those who can see because he touched their blind eyes.

(HANNAH *gives a little gasp.*)

ZADOK. And those, I suppose, who now walk straight that they may seek revenge.

HANNAH. Oh, but Zadok, if he can! If he has this power from God surely he would not hesitate to use it for the sake of a little child.

ZADOK. He loves children. When his disciples would have sent them away he once said, " Suffer the little children to come unto me and forbid them not for of such is the kingdom of heaven." But tonight—it seems as if this night were his own.

HANNAH. And because it is his own he shares it with others.

ZADOK. As he has shared all of his days, all of his years. As he will always share with those who love him, never failing those who truly seek him.

HANNAH. I cannot believe he would deny the plea of a blind child. Let me bring our Rachel to him.

ZADOK (*hesitatingly*). I dislike to disturb him at the Passover.—I know! Wait until the meal is over, just as they are ready to leave! Then it will not interrupt this meal that seems to mean so much to him.

HANNAH. All right, my husband. Oh, if only our child can be made to see again!

BEGGAR (*at the window*). He breaks the pascal bread.

HANNAH (*she and* ZADOK *have moved over to the window*). Behold the light in his eyes!

ZADOK. His whole face is aglow!

JESUS. This bread is my body, broken for you. This do in remembrance of me.

VOICES OF DISCIPLES. Thy body, broken?

—Nay, Master, it shall not be.

—What meanest thou, thy body?

—It is the pascal bread that is broken.

(These speeches spoken more or less together.)

JESUS. Greater love hath no man than this, that a man lay down his life for his friends. Ye are my friends if ye do the things which I command you.

THOMAS. Lord, thou knowest that we love thee.

JESUS. Yea. Yet verily I say unto you that one of'you shall betray me.

VOICES OF DISCIPLES *(in consternation)*. Nay, Lord!

—Betray thee?

—It shall not be!

—Who is it, Lord?

—Is it I?

—Or I?

—Is it I?

(Again, these speeches should be spoken more or less together, each repeating his lines two or three times, to give the effect of confused consternation. But the confusion should die down so that the " Is it I? " is distinguishable as coming from several of the disciples. ZADOK, HANNAH and the BEGGAR are aghast.)

ZADOK. Can he mean there is a traitor among them?

HANNAH. How can it be? Have they not all been with him since first he began to teach and preach?

BEGGAR. Yea, but some souls are shriveled by the light.

ZADOK. True, beggar. Remember thine own words.

BEGGAR. I mean that . .

ZADOK. Hush! He is dipping the bread!

JESUS. He it is for whom I shall dip the bread and give it.

HANNAH. He gives it to—to *that* man!

BEGGAR. The man I saw with the two priests by the cave of the lepers!

ZADOK. It is Judas. Judas with his thirty pieces of silver. I wonder . . .

BEGGAR. I know!

HANNAH. Hush!

JESUS. What thou doest, do quickly. For the Son of Man indeed goeth, as it hath been determined; but woe unto that man through whom he is betrayed!

(*There is talking and confusion in the room. Through the window* JUDAS *is seen as he leaves the table.* HANNAH, ZADOK *and the* BEGGAR *remain out of sight against the wall of the room as* JUDAS *opens the door and comes out.*)

JUDAS (*closing the door*). Soon they shall know whether his kingdom shall stand or not. Enough of this nonsense of loving all men. He would even love Rome! Yea, I go! To the garden on the Mount of Olives! That is where they shall find him. (*He moves toward the stairs.*) Soon, now, we shall see! (*Exits down the stairs.*)

BEGGAR (*starting toward the stairs*). I know not what evil thing he plans to do, but it shall not be if . . .

ZADOK (*stopping him*). Stay, thou fool! He is but one of the twelve, and better gone than remaining to spoil the Feast of the Passover for the others.

BEGGAR. But I heard him say that . . .

ZADOK. Be still!

JESUS. Now is the Son of Man glorified, and God is glorified in him.

HANNAH. He takes the cup!

JESUS. Our Father who art in heaven, we thank thee for the cup of blessing and for the cup of sacrifice. May we drink both to the glory of thy holy name. Amen.—This cup is the new covenant in my blood which is shed for many for the remission of sins. Drink ye all of it. Verily I say unto you, I will drink no more of the fruit of the vine until I drink it new in the kingdom of God.

DISCIPLE. But Master, we shall drink it with thee.

JESUS. Yet a little while I am with you. Ye shall seek me, and as I said unto the Jews, whither I go, ye cannot go.

ZADOK. He is going? Leaving Jerusalem?

HANNAH. And he has not seen Rachel!

ZADOK. Go, Hannah, down the outer stairs and into Rachel's room. Awaken her gently and lead her to the upper room by the inner stairs. I—I cannot believe he will mind.

(NOTE: *If there is no entrance into the room from backstage, have* ZADOK *omit " down the outer stairs."* HANNAH *will then go into the upper room and presumably down the stairs inside. She will remain out of sight of the audience, staying near the door.* RACHEL *will have been there all the time.*)

HANNAH. I will beg his forgiveness, for I *must* try. (*Exits.*)

BEGGAR (*calling after her*). And say a word for a crippled beggar!

ZADOK. Hold thy tongue! Is there no difference between a gentle child whose eyes cannot behold the beauty of earth and sky, and a life like thine, embittered with thought of revenge?

BEGGAR (*the light is beginning to penetrate*). He—he said something once about a child and the kingdom of heaven.

ZADOK. It were well for thee to heed his words. Listen!

JESUS. A new commandment I give unto you, that ye love one another, even as I have loved you.

ZADOK. Hear that? Let those words sink into thy heart.

BEGGAR. But he does not know Reuben and what he did to me.

ZADOK. Nay, but he knows all the hatred of man and how it can rise up against the goodness of God.

JESUS. By this shall all men know that ye are my disciples, if ye love one another.

74

PETER. Yea, Lord, thou knowest that we love thee. (*Murmuring of approval from the others.*) Gladly would I lay down my life for thee. I would follow thee to prison, to death! I would . . .

JESUS. Peter, Peter! Verily I say unto you, before the cock crows, thou shalt deny me thrice.

PETER. Nay, Lord! Nay!

DISCIPLES. Peter deny him?

—It could not be.

—Not Peter!

—Nay, not he!

ZADOK. Peter too! Oh, God, will they all forsake him?

JESUS. Peace I leave with you, my peace I give unto you. Let not your heart be troubled, neither let it be afraid. These things I have spoken unto you that your joy might be full. I go to prepare a place for you. And if I go and prepare a place for you, I will come again and receive you unto myself that where I am there ye may be also. And whither I go ye know, and the way ye know.

THOMAS. Lord, we know not whither thou goest, and how can we know the way?

BEGGAR. That is Thomas, called Didymus. I knew his twin brother in Galilee.

ZADOK. Hush!

JESUS. I am the way, the truth and the life; no man cometh unto the Father but by me.

PHILIP. Lord, show us the way and it sufficeth us.

BEGGAR. That is Philip of Bethsaida. Once he followed John the Baptist . . .

ZADOK. Be still, I tell thee!

JESUS. Have I been so long a time with you, and yet thou hast not known me, Philip? Believest thou not that I am in the Father and the Father in me?

PHILIP. Yea, Lord, I believe.

JESUS. The words that I speak unto you I speak not of myself but the Father that dwelleth in me, he doeth the works. Yet a little while and the world seeth me no more, but ye see me; because I live ye shall live also. He that loveth me keepeth my commandments, and he that loveth me shall be loved of my Father, and I will manifest myself to him.

JUDAS (*"not Iscariot"*). Lord, how is it thou wilt manifest thyself unto us and not unto the world?

JESUS. If a man love me he will keep my words; and my Father will love him, and we will come unto him and make our abode with him.

ZADOK. If only Jew and Roman and Samaritan would heed that command!

BEGGAR (*beginning to understand*). But surely he would not expect a man to love one who had crippled his body and his life.

ZADOK. I think, my poor blind friend, that is just what he does mean.

BEGGAR (*less bitterly*). But Reuben . . .

ZADOK. Hush!

JESUS. Abide in me and I in you. As the branch cannot bear fruit of itself except it abide in the vine, no more can ye except ye abide in me. I am the vine, ye are the branches. He that abideth in me bringeth forth much fruit; for without me ye can do nothing.

BEGGAR. Nothing—without him ——

ZADOK. Not even forgive.

JESUS. Herein is my Father glorified, that ye bear much fruit; so shall ye be my disciples. These things have I spoken unto you that my joy might remain in you, and that your joy might be full. Ye have not chosen me, but I have chosen you, and appointed you, that ye should go forth and bring forth much fruit, and that your fruit shall abide, that whatsoever ye shall ask of the Father in my name, he may give it you.

ZADOK (*fervently*). Oh, heavenly Father, in his name bring sight to the blind eyes of my child!

JESUS. Behold, the hour cometh, yea, is now come, that ye shall be scattered, every man to his own, and ye shall leave me alone. And yet I am not alone, because the Father is with me. These things have I spoken unto you, that in me ye might have peace. In the world ye shall have tribulation ; but be of good cheer; I have overcome the world.—Let us arise and go hence.

(DISCIPLES *rise.*)

FIRST DISCIPLE. Whither shall we go?
SECOND DISCIPLE. Where but to the garden on the Mount of Olives?
THIRD DISCIPLE. Let us sing a hymn before we depart.

(*Approval from the others. They join in singing a psalm, such as the following:*)

" O give thanks unto the Lord!
For he is good.
O give thanks unto the Lord of heaven,
For his mercy endureth forever."

(*As the singing finishes there is a difference in the murmuring and indications that* HANNAH *has come in. She can be glimpsed by the audience as she comes from around the back of the room and faces toward* JESUS. *She and* RACHEL *stop by the window, thus plainly visible to the audience.*)

HANNAH. Forgive me, I pray, but a mother's love knows no restraint. Oh, thou Jesus of Nazareth! If it be true that thy touch can restore the sight of the blind, have mercy on this little child and open her eyes that she may see!
DISCIPLE (*he is seen to step up to* HANNAH). But canst thou not wait until the morrow? The hour is late and the Master . . .
JESUS. Again I say unto you, Suffer this little child to come unto me, and forbid her not for of such is the kingdom of heaven. (*Murmuring among the* DISCIPLES.) Come here, my child.

(RACHEL, *who has been in front of* HANNAH, *takes a step*

forward, or moves so that she is framed by the window, yet within reach of JESUS' hand. As she moves forward the hand of JESUS is seen to reach forward. Gently he places his fingers on the child's eyes, leaving them there as he speaks.)

JESUS. Verily I say unto you, it is not the will of our heavenly Father that one of these little ones should suffer.— Open thine eyes, my child.

(His hand is slowly withdrawn. Slowly, hesitatingly, RACHEL'S eyes flutter open. She blinks them, passes her hand over them, registers amazement and joy as she turns to HANNAH.)

RACHEL. Mother! I can see!
HANNAH. Her eyes are open! May God be praised!
ZADOK. May God be praised!
BEGGAR. He—he opened her blind eyes!
JESUS. Now let us go hence. For behold, the hour cometh, yea, is now here.

(HANNAH and RACHEL have withdrawn from sight. The door opens, the DISCIPLES come out and go toward the stairs. As when they entered, JESUS is partly hidden by the others. The glow again shines on him from the time he leaves the room. The audience is now aware that the figure in the white robe is JESUS so especial care is needed to make his partial concealment natural.)

FIRST DISCIPLE. If we only had the faith of a child.
SECOND DISCIPLE. Yea, we too need such faith and love.
THIRD DISCIPLE. And humility. May God forgive me my blindness.
FOURTH DISCIPLE. Blindness of heart is as black as the blindness of that child's eyes before the Master touched them.

FIRST DISCIPLE. Tis good to see her joy on this night when the weight of sadness is heavy.

SECOND DISCIPLE. Was it sadness he felt?

(JESUS *has gone by now.*)

THIRD DISCIPLE. Perhaps. Over the stubbornness of the people.

(*The distance from the door to the stairs will determine how much of the above conversation can be used. It should be natural, as the group moves toward the stairs. The last two or three speeches can be given by disciples who casually linger behind the others.*

As the last of the disciples leave the room, the BEGGAR, *not too obtrusively, seeks to get close to* JESUS *or at least to attract his attention. But the disciples either pay him no heed, or one may shove him to one side.* JESUS *does not seem particularly aware of the* BEGGAR'S *presence, but at least once he almost pauses as he looks toward the* BEGGAR.

HANNAH *and* RACHEL *follow the last of the disciples through the doorway, leaving it open so that the light floods out.*)

HANNAH (*as soon as the disciples have gone*). Oh, Zadok! He did! Our child can see again! He healed her!

ZADOK. I know. I watched through the window. May God be thanked! (*His arm goes around* RACHEL *as he looks into her eyes. The natural joy of the parents is evident.*)

BEGGAR (*he has gone to the stairs to look after the departing guests. Now he turns back*). Surely he *is* the Messiah, the chosen one of God!

HANNAH. Yea, for our daughter sees again!

BEGGAR. But more than that he brings light to dark, blind souls. He speaks of forgiveness and love so that one *wants* to forgive even those whom he has hated. (*The change within the soul of the* BEGGAR *can be felt in his words.*)

ZADOK. Even—Reuben?

BEGGAR (*penitently*). Yea, even Reuben. He did all he could that day. He shouted to warn me. I must ask his forgiveness.

HANNAH. He said, " This commandment I give unto you, that ye love one another as I have loved you."

BEGGAR. He loved me! I could feel it when he looked at me—at me, a crippled beggar! Oh, Master, help me to love thee! I will seek out Reuben and beg that he forgive *my* blindness and forget my hatred! Then, then, oh thou Jesus of Nazareth, I will seek after thee and follow thee whithersoever thou goest! Surely in thy kingdom there is a place for the heart of a repentant beggar as well as for the heart of a child! Take mine, Oh Christ, and use it for thy glory!

(*About the time he says, " I will seek out* REUBEN " *his twisted hand begins to assume a natural position. As he continues speaking his crippled body straightens until, as he finishes speaking, he is standing upright, his arms extended, his head thrown back. He is healed. Swept away by the depth of his emotion he is not conscious of the physical change. The transformation should be so gradual that the audience should barely be aware of it until* HANNAH *speaks. As the* BEGGAR *speaks he moves into the path of light from the room which floods him.*)

HANNAH (*aware of the* BEGGAR'S *transformation*). Zadok! Look!

ZADOK. Thou—thou art well again! Thy faith and his love have made thee whole!

(*The* BEGGAR *looks at his hands, bewildered. He flexes them and feels his body, scarcely able to believe.*)

BEGGAR. I—I—I am healed! I can stand upright! He— Jesus—he healed me! (*Slight pause. Then he turns and hurries out calling.*) Reuben! Reuben!

ZADOK. Now surely we know he is the Messiah, for he doth heal men's hearts as well as their bodies.

HANNAH. " He hath brought relief to the captives—and sight to the blind."

ZADOK (*he has gone to the wall, looking after the disciples, Right*). Hannah!

HANNAH (*going to the wall with* RACHEL). What is it?

ZADOK (*pointing off Right*). Canst thou see a goodly number of Roman soldiers off there?

HANNAH. Yea, but—but what of that?

ZADOK. Nothing—I just wondered why so many were abroad—at this hour—on this night—and going toward the Mount of Olives.

HANNAH (*frightened*). Oh!

ZADOK (*looking off*). Jesus and his disciples have taken the path that leads to the brook Kidron.

HANNAH. That is not strange. I have been told he often goes that way and up to the garden called Gethsemane.

ZADOK. I know. But—but the night is dark——

HANNAH. Yea, *it is night.* And tomorrow . . .

ZADOK. Tomorrow this night, Gethsemane, the Passover kept here in the upper room, all will be history.

HANNAH. And dost thou think the world will remember?

ZADOK. How can the world ever forget?

(*They stand, looking across the city to the brook Kidron—and beyond.*)

SLOW CURTAIN

THE KINDLED FLAME

A DRAMA OF THE FIRST EASTER
IN ONE ACT

By

ESTHER BALDWIN YORK

THE KINDLED FLAME

CAST OF CHARACTERS

(For two men, two women, extras)

CYNTHIA, *a young Roman Christian.*

MARCUS, *her lover.*

LYDIA, *mother of Cynthia.*

ALPHENOR, *brother of Cynthia.*

PEOPLE WHO PASS BY OUTSIDE.

AN ANGEL.

———

SCENE: A room in a Roman house in Jerusalem.

TIME: *Scene* 1. A week before the Crucifixion. Evening.

Scene 2. Day of the Crucifixion. Midday.

Scene 3. Resurrection morning.

TIME IN PERFORMANCE: Approximately forty minutes.

NOTES ON PRODUCTION

The costumes of the main characters are of simple Roman design. The women wear flowing dresses of some soft material, such as cheesecloth or voile, tied at the waist with cords. Colors should not be too gaudy, but overdrapes of darker shades than the dresses may be used. Marcus wears a Roman soldier outfit with sword and helmet. Alphenor should have two short tunic costumes, the first drab and ragged for the scene of his homecoming. The passersby in the street may use bright colored tapestries and bits of material for head-dresses. The angel is in flowing white.

The cross carried in the procession may be easily con-structed of light wood or cardboard stained brown.

Dishes should be pottery if possible, with bowls or goblets in place of cups. The food may be bread, fruit, and grape juice or water.

Lights should be regulated according to the time of day in each scene. Colored spotlights, colored bulbs in the footlights, or the use of gelatine paper over lights will achieve the desired effects. Blue crepe paper covered with silver stars used in back of the window adds to the illusion of night in the first scene. The household gods may be represented by any small figurines or statuettes arranged on a table at one side.

THE KINDLED FLAME

SCENE ONE

SCENE: *A room in the home of a Roman family in Jerusalem. Furnishings are simple—a table, a bench or two, a small table at one side upon which are small statuettes representing household gods, a large urn or vase. The room has straight lines, simplicity, and not much richness or color. At Center back is a window with empty frames which open outward and back. A door at Right leads out into the street, a door at Left to another part of the house. Lights are dim. It is evening.*

CYNTHIA *enters, lights a candle on each table from a taper in her hand, and makes motions of tidying up the room. She is humming to herself.* LYDIA *enters with dishes for the evening meal. She looks sharply at the girl and then shrugs a resigned, tired sigh. The girl glances up and goes over to put an arm about her mother.*

CYNTHIA. Mother, you look very tired. Here, let me set the table. Is anything the matter? (*She takes the dishes and lays places for three.*)

LYDIA. Matter! Is not everything the matter? When I think back on the time before we left Rome two years ago, and then consider all the trials we've had since we made this hated city our home, I wonder what evil gods brought us to this place. First of all, it was your father's getting killed in a skirmish with the Jews. They are not our people; they did not want us here. Oh, his

86

death was so useless! (*She bows her head in her hands.*)

CYNTHIA (*Comforting her.*) Yes, I know, Mother. It has been very hard. But would you go back to Rome?

LYDIA (*Ignores her question.*) And then two months ago—your brother Alphenor with that white spot on his hand—leprosy. He could not live with us any longer, they said. He could not serve in Caesar's legions. *My boy*—forced to spend his days among the living dead, in a leper colony!

CYNTHIA (*Turns her face away. Then looks up with a brave smile.*) Ah, but Mother, had we never come to Jerusalem, how should I have heard about Jesus, the Prophet, the Galilean, whose words hold a promise of life?

LYDIA (*Bitterly.*) Enough of this Jesus. What does He know of our sorrows? What can He, a Jew, understand about Romans? There is no hope anywhere. We are but playthings of the gods, travelling through the world in obedience to their whims—until that blessed day when death shall send us all into oblivion.

CYNTHIA (*Eagerly.*) Oh, no, Mother, it isn't true! This man Jesus says it is not. I myself heard Him telling the people one day recently that whosoever will believe His words about the true God, the Heavenly Father, will have eternal life. He said so.

LYDIA. Idle words, child, meant to capture the crowd. If there were that hope, don't you suppose the world would be happier?

CYNTHIA. But I have been happier—so much happier since I have become His follower. There is an unexplainable, inner peace which makes me feel that all will turn out for the best. It is like a flame kindled. You can have it too, if you only will. Do you not know this?

LYDIA (*Shaking her head.*) I only know that turning away from the gods of our ancestors will but bring more troubles upon our heads. (*A knock is heard.*) See who that is at the door. (MARCUS *enters.*)

MARCUS (*Holding out his arms.*) Cynthia!

CYNTHIA (*Goes and puts her hands in his.*) **Marcus,** come eat with us. See, I have laid a place for you.

LYDIA. Yes, do, my boy. It gets lonesome without a man in the house. Come, take a chair.

MARCUS (*Removes his helmet and sits on a bench at the table opposite* LYDIA, *while* CYNTHIA *goes out for more food.*) Well, it feels good to sit down. There is no rest for Rome's guards in a place like Jerusalem. The feeling is none too cordial at best. (CYNTHIA *returns with a plate of bread and sits down.*) Any luck today, Cynthia?

CYNTHIA. Oh, yes. I sold that pallium, the cloak I was weaving last week. Latona, a wealthy matron, bought it. It looked very fine on her. And I have a tunic in the making. We have enough to live on.

LYDIA. Let us continue our conversation later. The rites are still to be performed. (MARCUS *glances quickly at* CYNTHIA, *who looks away and becomes suddenly silent.* LYDIA *places a cup before each of them and pours into the cups from an urn or pitcher. She then picks up her cup, goes over to the table at the side of the room, and pours out a libation to the gods, bowing with one arm outstretched before her as a gesture of worship.* MARCUS *rises to do likewise, again looks at* CYNTHIA. *She has not moved. He goes and follows* LYDIA'S *example.* CYNTHIA *folds her hands and bows her head over her plate as though in prayer. In a moment they return to the table and all resume the meal.*)

MARCUS (*Reprovingly to* CYNTHIA.) So you persist in taking seriously the teachings of this alien Prophet. Forget it, my dear. You give Him too much importance.

CYNTHIA (*Humbly.*) If I gave Him ten times the importance that I do, it would still be far too little.

MARCUS. The Man has bewitched you. His is an attractive personality capable of swaying the people. That is all. I have heard a little about Him, but I am not interested in seeing Him. Oh, Cynthia, forget all this and say you will marry me soon!

CYNTHIA. Please. Let's not talk about it right now. But you, Marc, tell us of the things you did today. What did you see that would interest us?

MARCUS. I saw merchants just arrived from Damascus with rare perfumes and silks such as I hope to buy for you some day. There were jewels red like drops of blood, blue like segments of the sky, and green like the sea. There were gold necklaces and bracelets shining in the sun. And there were little white doves with soft eyes like yours, Cynthia.

CYNTHIA. And what of the marketplace? Was it crowded with people?

LYDIA. Why so many questions, daughter? We cannot afford to buy their wares.

CYNTHIA. Oh, but it is so colorful and exciting when strangers come here from far away! Did they bring any news, Marcus?

MARCUS. Only tales of their trading along the way. Oh, and some said something about expecting the Galilean any day now.

CYNTHIA. The Galilean! Then He is coming back. Oh, if He could just see Alphenor! I know He could help him. (*Enthusiastically.*) I have seen Him do such wonderful things—heal the lame and the blind and those afflicted with all sorts of diseases—and I have even heard that He has been known to raise the dead.

MARCUS. People often fancy themselves healed when they are not, and as for the dead being raised—well, you know how stories often grow with the telling. But if it makes you feel any better to believe these things, my little Cynthia, I suppose there is not overly much harm in it.

LYDIA (*Rises to clear the table.*) I'll take the dishes out. You two may remain here if you like. (*Goes out.*)

MARCUS (*Earnestly.*) Cynthia, when will you marry me? I have prayed to Venus daily that you will consent. Do you not love me?

CYNTHIA. It is not a question of loving, Marc. If it

were, I would say yes with all my heart. But if we cannot agree on important issues, surely we are not fit to be mated. I have found a living faith in the true God, something so vital as to change my whole life and the way I feel about things. You do not understand because you do not know Him. If you did, you would see why I can never again serve the gods of our fathers.

MARCUS. Gods are all alike, though called by a number of names. But we have life to live. Some day they will take that from us and there will be nothing left. That is why we must take our happiness while we can, while we still have youth and dreams and each other. It is just that I don't want to see us cheated out of that which rightfully belongs to us. Would you even deprive us of this?

CYNTHIA. Gods are not the same. I used to pray to Jupiter, to Diana, to Venus. They could not answer prayer. Now I pray to a God who does. He is called Jehovah, the Holy One, the Heavenly Father. He does not wreak vengeance upon mortals. His is a gospel of Love, and that is what Jesus is here to tell us about. He also teaches that this life is not all, and that if we live His life here on earth, we are promised eternal life hereafter. You see, there are greater things at stake than merely our immediate happiness.

MARCUS (*Thoughtfully.*) I wish I could believe that.

CYNTHIA (*Eagerly.*) You can, Marc; you can! Won't you come with me to see the Galilean when He returns? You must hear His words, the things He says. Then you cannot help believing. You will know that what He says is true.

MARCUS. I am a Roman and a soldier. I cannot afford to listen to strange sentimental creeds. (LYDIA *enters and removes the rest of the dishes from the room.*)

CYNTHIA. My life was once like this candle before it was lighted. (*She idly fingers the candle on the table.*) But now there is a bright little flame like that one glowing inside of me. (*Smiles.*) Some day you, too, will understand. The Romans, our people, are groping for that Light. How I hope they find it! (LYDIA *re-enters and seats herself. She is occupied with a piece of cloth on which she is sewing.*)

LYDIA. When night comes like this, I miss Alphenor so much more. We used to gather around and hear the events of the day from him—(*To* MARCUS.) from both of you, when you were here, too.

MARCUS. But his accounts were far better told than mine. Your son had a rare gift of seeing more deeply into life than most people.

CYNTHIA. If only he were here now! We should be so happy!

LYDIA. Tomorrow you must take a basket of cakes and leave them for him, Cynthia. He always liked my meal cakes. (*A knock is heard. All face the door silently.* CYNTHIA *rises and goes forward.*)

CYNTHIA. Who can that be at this time? (ALPHENOR *enters, somewhat ragged. He is eager and excited.*)

ALPHENOR. Cynthia! Mother! It is I—*healed!* And you, Marc, come and see! The leprosy is gone! (*He holds out his hand.*)

LYDIA. Alphenor! My son! (*She and* CYNTHIA *embrace the boy.* MARCUS *grips his hand cordially.*)

CYNTHIA. You are whole again! Tell us quickly! How?

MARCUS. By Jupiter, it is good to see you! Tell us more, friend. How did this happen?

ALPHENOR. Haven't you heard? The Galilean is back in the city. Jesus, His name is. A great crowd welcomed Him with palm branches and hosannas. I heard the shouting and wanted to see Him.

CYNTHIA (*Breathlessly.*) Yes, and what else?

ALPHENOR. I crept up as near as I dared. Suddenly, someone noticing me gave a shrill cry, "Unclean!" The people drew away and left an open space before me. Then I saw Him coming riding on a donkey. His face was kind and compassionate, like none I have ever seen before.

LYDIA. And did He see you?

ALPHENOR. Yes, He saw me. Just as He passed, His look rested on me. I think He saw my hand, for He called me to Him and stopped the procession to speak to me.

CYNTHIA. What did He say?

ALPHENOR. He reached out and touched my hand gently with His fingers and said, "Go, my son, and tell others what the Lord hath done for you." I shall never forget that look. Then He rode on. When I looked down, my hand was healed.

LYDIA. It is wonderful beyond belief!

CYNTHIA. Now do you see what Jesus can do? I knew He could! I knew it!

MARCUS. It is very strange. Are you sure it was leprosy, Alphenor? This Prophet may be a mixer of magic to deceive the people.

ALPHENOR. Deceive? Not Jesus! I was sick and now I am well. I know, because it happened to *me*. I'm going to follow Him now. I am going out and preach to others about Him. Did you know that the people want to crown Him king?

CYNTHIA. King! Oh, Alphenor, He will rule wisely.

MARCUS. Just so long as He bows to Caesar.

ALPHENOR. I must go now. But I will return home soon.

LYDIA. Go? Tonight? Where are you going?

ALPHENOR. To tell my former fellow lepers about Jesus.

CYNTHIA (*Quietly.*) Yes, that is what He would want you to do.

MARCUS. Well, I am leaving now also. I will walk a little way with you, if you don't mind.

ALPHENOR. Fine, Marc. (ALPHENOR *bids his family good-bye and the two men go out.*)

CYNTHIA. Could anything be more wonderful than

having him back? You had better go to bed now, Mother. You need the rest. (*She kisses her mother and goes out softly.* LYDIA *picks up the candle and looks off into space, her face showing wonder.*)

LYDIA. My son alive from the dead! Almost *I* am persuaded to follow the Galilean.

CURTAIN

SCENE TWO

SCENE: *Same as before. It is midday. Lights are brighter.*

ALPHENOR *is discovered seated on a bench, apparently absorbed in thought. Presently* CYNTHIA *enters, opens the window at back Center, and suddenly notices* ALPHENOR. *She goes over to him.*

CYNTHIA. You seem to be thinking deeply, brother. What about?

ALPHENOR (*Looks up, reaches for her hand, and draws her down on the bench beside him.*) Cynthia, I want to talk to you.

CYNTHIA. Is it about Him?

ALPHENOR. The Galilean, yes. I am puzzled. I know not what to think. So much has happened in these last few days. A week ago the people were spreading garlands in His path. But now—He is being tried. I do not understand it.

CYNTHIA. Nor I. Could we doubt that He has the power to free Himself from all this unpleasantness if He chose? Why doesn't He? Last week I'm sure the people would have crowned Him king.

ALPHENOR. But you notice they didn't. He didn't want them to. It wasn't in His plan, I guess.

CYNTHIA. Not in His plan! Why, Alphenor, how

strangely you speak! If He were king, surely He would have more power over the people. Think of the good He could do.

ALPHENOR. It wasn't that kind of power He wanted—not a temporal kingdom. He wants a spiritual kingdom made up of all those who believe in Him with all their hearts.

CYNTHIA. Why—why that includes us, Alphenor—you and me.

ALPHENOR. Yes, and now that He's in trouble, I despise myself for having so little faith in Him.

CYNTHIA. We must believe! We must! (MARCUS *enters.* CYNTHIA *turns to him quickly and rises.*) What news, Marcus?

MARCUS (*Shakes his head.*) It looks bad for this man Jesus. He is being accused by His own people, the Jews. They are quite vehement.

CYNTHIA. But of what is He accused? What charges do they dare to bring against one so good as He?

MARCUS. They couldn't seem to arrive at anything definite at first. But there has been trouble brewing for some time among the Jewish high priests over this man. They've just been waiting to find something against Him. These rumors have passed around from time to time. I've heard them.

ALPHENOR. But what did they find against Him, Marc? Tell us all you know.

MARCUS. Well, Judas, one of the Galilean's close followers, turned on Him and got in with the Jewish leaders. He made a bargain with them to reveal his Master's whereabouts for thirty pieces of silver.

CYNTHIA. What a traitor! And after that?

MARCUS. Well, first He was taken to Annas and then Caiaphas, the Jewish high priests and the Sanhedrin. A lot of witnesses came in, but no two had the same story, until finally two mentioned having heard Him say that if they destroyed the Temple, He would restore it in three days.

ALPHENOR. I believe He could, too.

MARCUS. Why, that's madness! Naturally they mocked Him after that. They even asked Him if He were the Son of God.

CYNTHIA (*Eagerly.*) And what did He answer to that?

MARCUS (*Scornfully.*) He said He was. So you see they needed no further witnesses. They had Him on the count of blasphemy against their religion.

ALPHENOR. Nevertheless, they couldn't do much to Him, could they? They haven't the authority—

MARCUS. Oh, don't you think it! They immediately delivered Him over to Pilate, the governor. That's where He is now, being tried. Whatever Pilate says will decide His fate.

ALPHENOR. Pilate is a just man. He will not be moved by the jealousies that stir the Jewish priests. Surely, he will discover that Jesus is innocent of any wrong.

CYNTHIA (*Confidently.*) When he hears Jesus speak and looks upon His face, then he will know that there is, and can be, no evil in Him. Maybe He will show Pilate some of His miracles.

MARCUS. His magic made a big impression on you, didn't it, my little Cynthia? If He has such power, why hasn't He used it to effect His rescue before this?

CYNTHIA. Oh, I don't know! I don't know! I wish there were something I could do to help Him.

ALPHENOR. And I.

MARCUS. Well, there isn't. Down there where He is now, there is a crowd so large outside that you could never hope to get anywhere near the place.

CYNTHIA (*Resignedly.*) There is really nothing we can do but wait. It must come out right. Surely something will happen. (*A clamoring is heard outside.* MARCUS *motions toward the street.*)

MARCUS. It *has* happened! Look! (*Through the open window people are seen going by. A part of a wooden cross goes by. It is being carried by someone hidden by the others. Cries of "Crucify Him!" are heard.* ALPHENOR *and* CYNTHIA *watch in surprise and sorrow as the procession moves slowly and haltingly past.* LYDIA *enters at the first sound but does not go over to the others. She also stands looking. When they are past,* ALPHENOR *walks quickly to the window and stands silently looking after the procession, remaining thus for a long time.* CYNTHIA *bows her head in her hands and turns away.* MARCUS *takes a step or two toward her as if to speak, holds his hand out to her, thinks better of it, and drops it at his side.*)

LYDIA (*In a low, bitter tone.*) Where is your Galilean now, your Prophet of the true God? On His way to Golgotha. How wrong I was to entertain the thought that He might be what He claimed to be, what He seemed to be! All that is over now. May the gods forgive me for my momentary disallegiance! (*She goes to the altar, bows before it, and leaves the room.* ALPHENOR *still stands by the window.*)

MARCUS (*To* CYNTHIA.) I am sorry to see you hurt like this. But now you know and you must accept it. (CYNTHIA *does not answer, turns even farther away from him.*)

MARCUS. You had to find it out sometime. It is better to discover it now. Did I not tell you that you gave Him too much importance? Naturally it has made you disillusioned. The best thing to do now is to forget Him.

ALPHENOR. If you had known Him, you could not forget Him. What could Pilate have been thinking of? (*Pauses for a moment as if deciding.*) I am going out there. Perhaps there is something I can do for Him— a cup of cold water— (*Goes out.*)

CYNTHIA (*Turns desperately to* MARCUS.) Marc! Perhaps *you* can do something to save Him!

MARCUS. No, I cannot. I would be glad to help the poor fellow if I could. But Pilate has spoken. Crucifixion is a hard death. But evidently His own people have wished it so. We soldiers can do no more than obey the commands of our superiors. Even now I must leave you to go on duty.

CYNTHIA (*Horrified.*) There?

MARCUS. Yes, to keep the crowds back. To maintain order.

CYNTHIA. Order! Have you no heart, Marcus, that you can calmly discuss law and order, when He is dying?

MARCUS (*Gently.*) You are unjust, Cynthia. I do not like to see any man die, but a soldier can't have feelings in such matters. I do not go there from choice.

CYNTHIA. I had hoped that you would hear His words, that you would love Him, too. And now—it is too late.

MARCUS. Cynthia, these teachings—this belief has separated us long enough. Now you must realize that it is worthless and unworthy of keeping us apart any longer. Let it be buried when He is buried. Why should we wait?

CYNTHIA (*Turns away and goes over to the table. She picks up the candle.*) And put the flame out? No, Marc. Never. I can't.

MARCUS (*Angrily.*) Foolish symbolism! Mad philosophies! I cannot understand you. I cannot make you realize anything, even in the face of this complete collapse of your hopes. I am convinced that nothing I can say will make any difference. I leave now, and in the meantime may you come to your senses! (*He goes out.*)

CYNTHIA (*Turns sorrowfully and impulsively calls after him, but he is out of hearing.*) Marc!

CURTAIN

SCENE THREE

SCENE: *Same as before. It is the morning of the Resurrection.*

97

LYDIA *comes in busily, tidies the table, puts things in order.* CYNTHIA *enters more slowly from the outdoors with some flowers, which she proceeds to arrange on the table.*

CYNTHIA (*Looks out the window.*) It is a beautiful morning. All the air seems fresh and joyous with new life—not as though He were lying in His grave. (*Sighs.*)

LYDIA (*Attempts to cheer her.*) Yes, it is a lovely morning. One is meant to be glad on such a day. Remember, dear, no matter what of joy or sorrow happens on this old earth, life must go on. I have found it true from experience. Always the long parade marches on and leaves tragedy to dull itself with the years. It is fortunate for us that it is so.

CYNTHIA. See, already the people are going about their accustomed tasks as though nothing had happened— (*While she speaks, one or two persons pass by the window.*)—as though a man had not died out there on that lonely hill two days ago. Some of them will go to the Temple to worship the father of the One they have slain.

LYDIA. I hope Marcus will come back soon. He has not been here since day before yesterday. I fear you were too harsh with him, Cynthia. I know you were upset over this event. Surely Marc will realize that.

CYNTHIA. He has been on duty constantly.

LYDIA (*Cheerfully.*) Naturally. Well, we shall probably see him in the near future. Where is your brother? Doesn't he want any breakfast? (ALPHENOR *enters somewhat sleepily.*)

ALPHENOR. Did I hear someone mention my name?

CYNTHIA. Yes, it is time you were coming. Would you mind bringing in the bread? (ALPHENOR *goes out and returns with plate of bread.* CYNTHIA *goes out for some other articles for the table.*)

LYDIA. Do you plan to go back into Caesar's legion, son?

ALPHENOR. I don't know. I shall have to think it over.

LYDIA. Your father was proud to bear the arms of Rome and so is Marcus. It is well for you to do likewise.

ALPHENOR. I am thankful I was not bearing them these last few days. I could not have been a part of the deed they sanctioned.

LYDIA. Then you saw it?

ALPHENOR. Yes. (CYNTHIA *enters and walks around the table, serving the other two as they talk.*)

LYDIA. A horrible sight, it must have been!

ALPHENOR. It *was* horrible, yes. But He made it somehow beautiful. Do you know what He said on the cross? He looked up, and as though He were speaking to Someone near, said, "Father, forgive them, for they know not what they do."

CYNTHIA. He said *that?* (*She takes her place at the table.*)

ALPHENOR. Yes, and there was a radiant look on His face when He uttered the words. I knew He must be praying. *That,* after the way they had treated Him.

CYNTHIA. Don't, Alphenor! I can't bear to hear any more!

LYDIA. Where is He buried?

ALPHENOR. In a tomb in Gethsemane. The sepulchre is one belonging to Joseph of Arimathea.

LYDIA. Had He no relatives, no persons who were close to Him?

ALPHENOR. His mother, Mary, was there. And a young man whom He addressed as John. I took him to be a close friend or disciple. At the last, Jesus turned and commended His mother to the care of this youth, as to someone He trusted implicitly.

CYNTHIA. It is like Him. (MARCUS *enters suddenly, very much excited.*)

MARCUS. He is not there! He is risen! I saw it with my own eyes! Things you would never dream! The tomb is empty!

CYNTHIA. What, Marc? What do you say?

MARCUS. Jesus is not there! He is risen!

LYDIA. Someone has stolen His body.

MARCUS. Oh, no! I saw it. I was on duty in the garden. They put a guard of us around the vicinity for that very reason—to prevent anyone from stealing His body and saying He had risen. You see, they were afraid of that.

ALPHENOR. Where were you, Marc, and what did you see?

MARCUS. I was stationed halfway between the sepulchre and the road. Some other guards watched close beside the tomb. It was my duty to keep away prowlers.

CYNTHIA. Go on, Marc! What then?

MARCUS. Well, the first night nothing happened. It was so still that I had a lot of time to think. It was terrible! I kept seeing His face on the Cross.

ALPHENOR. When did it occur, this miracle?

MARCUS. It was early morning. Most of the men were getting pretty sleepy. But I was wide awake. I had rather an uneasy feeling that something was about to happen. Suddenly there was a rumbling of the earth, terrifying after the stillness, and a blinding light surrounding the sepulchre. Against it I could see the silhouettes of the guards start up and then fall as though dead.

ALPHENOR. What did you do?

MARCUS. Nothing. I have never been so frightened in my life. I just stood there rooted to the ground, watching.

CYNTHIA. And then?

MARCUS. I felt dazed. The light was very bright. When I could see clearly again, the stone was rolled away and an angel was standing in the opening saying, "He is risen." My first thought after my terrible fear was the realization that burned itself across my mind again and again. *He was* the *Son of God!*

CYNTHIA. Yes, Marc, He was.

ALPHENOR. And *is.*

LYDIA. How blind I have been!

ALPHENOR. How unbelieving we have all been!

CYNTHIA (*Wonderingly.*) He said He would raise the Temple in three days. He spoke of His resurrection. To think that I should have doubted Him even for a moment! (*Bows her head.*)

MARCUS (*Looks at them all in turn.*) *You* blind, unbelieving, and doubtful! Mine is the greater sin. I scorned and shunned Him. I refused to have anything to do with Him. I helped carry out His crucifixion. I jeered at those who did believe. (*He turns to* CYNTHIA.) Oh, Cynthia, can you and your brother ever forgive me? (*She puts out a hand and nods silent assent.*) After I left the garden, I followed the rest of the terror-stricken guards to the high priests. I had nothing but contempt for those dignitaries who had plotted His death, and for myself who had aided their designs. But I wanted them to know the truth as I had found it out.

ALPHENOR. How did they receive the news?

MARCUS. They were afraid; we could see it. The face of Caiaphas turned white. But he tried not to show it. Then they offered us gold to keep quiet what we had seen. The people must not hear it, they said.

LYDIA (*Fearfully.*) Did the soldiers accept the money?

MARCUS (*Bitterly.*) Yes, most of them, I am sorry to say. They excused their greed by saying that peace and order must be preserved at any cost. It was "their duty." Duty! What an empty word it has become!

LYDIA. You were right, my son. I perceive that there are greater things than one's duty as a soldier. A lot of things have been changed this morning. It is as though a burden had been lifted from my heart. Death, then, can't be the end of life!

CYNTHIA. Is it not wonderful? Somehow I have a feeling that this event will make a difference to all the future years. He suffered for us, but He is still a living Lord.

ALPHENOR. His work will continue to go on.

MARCUS. I wish I could rejoice with you. True, my

eyes have been opened and I believe in Him now. But He would not accept *me*. I shunned Him so long. I helped put Him to death.

CYNTHIA (*Goes quickly to him and lays a hand gently on his arm.*) Marc, you *do* believe?

MARCUS. With all my soul!

CYNTHIA. Then He will accept you. Don't you remember His words on the Cross—"Father, *forgive* them, for they know not what they do"? He wasn't leaving out anyone then, Marc.

MARCUS (*Slowly, as if he is just remembering and comprehending it.*) "Father, forgive—them—" Yes—yes, I remember! Oh, thank God! Then it is mine, too—the kindled flame! (CYNTHIA *smilingly stands near to him. He puts an arm about her. Softly from backstage several voices are heard singing "Christ Arose." The stage lights dim out, as an angel, spotlighted, appears in the open window with a lighted cross. The four face the window and kneel reverently.*)

CURTAIN

THE PROMISED ONES

A BIBLICAL PLAY IN ONE ACT
AND THREE SCENES

By

ROBERT ST. CLAIR

PRODUCTION RIGHTS

THE PROMISED ONES

CAST OF CHARACTERS

(For three women, four men, and narrator)

JOACHIM ....*A man of Nazareth*

ANN ....*His wife*

MARY ....*Their daughter*

JOSEPH ....*Mary's suitor*

ELIZABETH ....*A relative*

ZACHARY ....*An elderly priest; Elizabeth's husband*

THE ANGEL GABRIEL

NARRATOR (*Either male or female*)

SYNOPSIS OF SCENES

SCENE ONE: *Joachim's house in Nazareth.*

SCENE TWO: *Zachary's home in Ain Karim.*

SCENE THREE: *Joachim's house again.*

PRODUCTION NOTE

Although there are three scenes in the play, no actual change of scenery is necessary because the entire action is performed in draperies with only a few pieces of furniture. Therefore, the play may be given on any size stage or platform, or in a church, where it is most effective. In the latter instance, the church altar is used for the scene between Zachary and Gabriel. If produced on a stage, the altar will be hidden behind the back drapery, which will open in the middle to display the "Tabernacle." Outside of three or four spotlights, no special lighting is required. The musical background that is used for some of the scenes may be records played on a record player offstage. But where the play is produced in a church, the church organ will be used.

THE PROMISED ONES

AT THE BEGINNING, *a* NARRATOR, *dressed in Biblical garments, appears at one side, bathed in a soft light, and addresses the audience. The* NARRATOR *may be male or female. Soft, religious music fades in as a background while he or she is speaking.*

NARRATOR. Many long years ago there lived in the town of Nazareth, in Galilee, a happy little family of three. There was Joachim, a good man; his wife, Ann, a devout woman; and their daughter, Mary, who was loved by all who knew her because of her sweet, gentle disposition and her remarkable serenity of soul. Joachim's family could trace their ancestry back to the House of David, and they were very proud of their illustrious forebears. Now there also lived in Nazareth at that time a carpenter by the name of Joseph. Joseph was a bachelor, and like most bachelors who have passed the age of maturity, he was lonely and longed for a good wife. Then he met Mary at the well one day, and although he didn't speak to her, he knew that he had at last fallen in love. He saw her often after that, but still he never spoke. Then he sought out her father and they had a long and serious talk. Afterwards, Joachim invited Joseph to go home with him, and Joseph was only too eager to follow. (*The music rises, the light on the* NARRATOR *goes out, he disappears in the darkness, and the lights come up for . . .*)

SCENE ONE

(*This is Joachim's house, which is sparsely furnished with only a rough table, a bench and a few three-legged stools. The table and bench are over on the Right, and it is here that* ANN *is sitting to arrange some dates and figs in a large earthen bowl. The background doesn't matter. We must imagine the rough-dressed stones of the walls.*

The music fades out as the lights come up, and at once
JOACHIM *enters from the Left, with the handsome, muscular* JOSEPH *at his heels.* JOACHIM'S *manner is good-naturedly amused.* JOSEPH, *however, is nervously self-conscious. He is afraid of the reception he will receive.*)

JOACHIM (*speaking as he enters*). Come in, young man. There is nothing to be frightened of. We have a visitor, Ann—— (*Pauses at Center.*)

ANN (*smiling. Placing the bowl on the table*). So I see.

JOACHIM. His name is Joseph. Joseph, this is my wife.

JOSEPH. Peace be unto you, good woman.

ANN (*gently smiling*). And unto *you*, my son.

JOACHIM. Joseph is a carpenter, Ann; a good one too, I've heard.

ANN. Yes, I know. I have seen him in the village, working in his shop.

JOACHIM (*extolling* JOSEPH'S *virtues*). He is thrifty, industrious, sober and reliable——

ANN (*interrupting*). How do you know all this, my husband?

JOACHIM (*wisely*). Oh, I have a way of finding out the things I want to know. (*To* JOSEPH. *Indicating the stool over Left.*) Sit down, Joseph.

JOSEPH. Thank you—— (*Sits, nervously.*)

ANN. You are well acquainted with my husband, Joseph?

JOSEPH. No. I have seen him in the synagogue many times, as I have also seen you, and—and your daughter, Mary—— (*Hesitates and swallows, his throat feeling suddenly dry.*)

ANN (*suddenly understanding*). Mary? Ah! (*Looks at* JOACHIM, *who looks quickly away.* JOSEPH *fails to notice her frown as he goes on talking.*)

JOSEPH. But—but I have never spoken to him until this morning.

JOACHIM. I was passing his shop and he called out to me——

107

JOSEPH (*quickly*). To pass the time of day——
(*Gulps and looks to* JOACHIM *for help.*)

JOACHIM (*to* ANN. *Continuing*). We spoke of the weather and the crops——

JOSEPH (*to* ANN. *Taking up the story*). And King Herod, who has lately murdered more of his family——

ANN (*interrupting*). Every day he kills our *own* innocent people. What are we going to do about it? We are nothing better than slaves to Rome!

JOACHIM (*seriously*). Peace, Ann! Joseph did not come here for a political discussion. (*His manner lightening again.*) As I was saying, we talked about all these things until I was ready to leave. Then the truth came out. What Joseph really wanted to talk to me about was Mary. (*Grins at* JOSEPH, *who clears his throat again and lowers his eyes.*)

ANN. I had guessed as much. (JOACHIM *and* JOSEPH *are surprised.*)

JOACHIM. You had?

ANN (*nodding a smiling affirmative*). Mothers can always *feel* these things, Joachim. And Mary has been *talking* about the handsome, bashful young carpenter who always seems to be in front of his shop, pretending to be busy, whenever she passes that way to and from the *well*.

JOSEPH (*bending eagerly forward*). She has?

JOACHIM (*to* ANN). You haven't told *me* this.

ANN. I did not think it necessary. (JOACHIM *looks rather hurt. Moves upstage as* ANN *leans forward to address* JOSEPH *again, her manner quite serious now.*) You are in love with her, Joseph?

JOSEPH (*feelingly*). So much in love that I ask only to be near her—to protect and watch over her for the rest of my life. (*Rises and moves closer to her as he goes on talking.* JOACHIM *moves down Left to watch and listen.*) There is something strange about my feeling for Mary, and I find it rather difficult to describe. It is a tender and gentle sort of feeling—almost like that of an older brother instead of a lover. And yet I wish to marry her.

ANN (*softly. Folding her hands in her lap and looking down at them*). What—is your background, Joseph?

JOACHIM (*quickly. Before* JOSEPH *has an opportunity to answer*). I meant to tell you about that, Ann. Joseph belongs to the House of David——

ANN (*quickly looking up*). So?

JOACHIM (*continuing*). He can trace his ancestry back as far as Abraham. It is all in the scrolls in the synagogue.

ANN (*to* JOSEPH. *Unconsciously straightening*). We are also of the House of David, Joseph.

JOSEPH. Yes. I know.

ANN (*smiling again. Now all warmth and friendliness*). Mary is up on the roof, putting out dates and figs to dry in the hot sun——

JOACHIM (*chuckling*). And listening to every word we say, I'll wager.

ANN (*rising*). I'll call her down. (*Goes Right, calling offstage.*) Mary, will you come down? A young man with a handsome golden beard is here to see you. (*Smiles around at* JOSEPH, *who instantly becomes nervous again.*) She has admired the beard, Joseph, and the goodness in your eyes. (*Soft music fades in as* MARY *quietly appears over Right. She is serene and smiling, entirely self-possessed although she knows what* JOSEPH *is here for.*)

ANN (*waits until* MARY *has paused beside her, then indicates* JOSEPH). Mary, this is Joseph.

MARY (*quietly*). Peace be unto you, Joseph.

JOSEPH (*lowly. Almost worshipfully*). And to you, Mary.

JOACHIM (*to* MARY). You were listening from above, my child?

MARY (*simply*). Yes, Father. I could not help but overhear.

ANN. Joseph loves you——

MARY (*softly. Without taking her eyes from his*). I know.

JOSEPH. I have loved you since the first day I saw you drawing water from the well.

MARY. I know that also. I could see it in your eyes.

Ever since, I have walked past your shop—waiting for you to speak. (*The music dies away.*)

ANN (*a trifle shocked by her simple frankness*). Mary! This is boldness.

JOACHIM. No, Ann—not when Mary says it.

MARY (*still looking at* JOSEPH, *whose expression is one of incredulous, though happy, relief*). It was meant to be.

ANN (*surprised by the strange remark*). What did you say, Mary?

MARY (*going closer to* JOSEPH). I am glad you love me, Joseph, for I love you. And it shall make me very happy to be your wife. (*Holds out her hand.*)

JOSEPH (*lowly. Almost reverently taking her hand*). Mary! (*There is a short pause during which they all hold their positions, then* ELIZABETH *enters quickly down Left.* ELIZABETH *is a sixty-year-old woman, but one who walks with dignity and strength. Sorrow and suffering have left their marks on her courtenance, but she carries her load with fortitude and abiding faith. Her hair is white and her garments are travel-stained.*)

ELIZABETH (*speaking as she enters and pauses down Left*). Peace be unto you, my relatives.

ANN. Elizabeth!

JOACHIM (*greatly surprised*). What brings you to Nazareth?

ANN (*hurrying toward* ELIZABETH *to embrace her, going in front of the others*). Is Zachary with you?

ELIZABETH. No. I came alone. Zachary could not get away from his duties at the synagogue.

MARY (*to* JOSEPH. *Explaining*). Elizabeth is my mother's niece, although older than she is. She is the daughter of my mother's older sister. (*To* ELIZABETH, *moving to Left Center, via the front of* JOSEPH.) It is good to see you again, cousin.

ELIZABETH. And it is always a joy for me to see *you*, Mary. (*Goes closer to* MARY *to embrace her.*)

JOACHIM. But what brings you at *this* season of the year, Elizabeth? It must be something important for you to come alone—all the way from Ain Karim?

ELIZABETH (*talking rapidly*). It isn't so far, Joachim.

(*To* ANN.) Zachary has had wonderful news and I couldn't wait to tell you about it. At last—after all these years of praying for the honor—he has been chosen to officiate in the ceremony at the Great Temple in Jerusalem!

ANN (*astonished*). In the Tabernacle?

JOACHIM. The Holy of Holies?

MARY. How wonderful! (*Going closer to* JOSEPH, *who has now moved down Right.*) Zachary is a poor priest at the synagogue in Ain Karim, Joseph.

ANN. Oh, Elizabeth! We are all so happy for him.

JOACHIM (*to* ELIZABETH). When does he go?

ELIZABETH. Within a few days now. I have yet to make his robe. He is like a child, he is so happy over it. We should like you to make the journey with us, so you —our beloved relatives—can be present to see his triumph.

JOACHIM. We shall be glad to go——

MARY. I have never been to Jerusalem——

JOSEPH. Nor I.

JOACHIM. Perhaps you can go *also,* Joseph?

JOSEPH. It would be an honor——

ANN. Elizabeth, this is Joseph, a carpenter. He belongs to the House of David.

ELIZABETH. Peace be unto you, Joseph.

JOSEPH. And to you, good woman.

JOACHIM (*to* ELIZABETH). And now that you have told us your good news, Elizabeth, it is time for us to tell you ours. Joseph and Mary are betrothed.

ELIZABETH. *Mary!*

ANN. It was settled just before you arrived.

ELIZABETH (*hurrying closer to* MARY *to embrace her again*). May Jehovah bless you, gentle cousin, and give you great happiness. *This* will be something for *me* to take back to *Zachary.* Have you named the happy day?

MARY. No——

JOSEPH. I have much to do before then, I'm afraid. I must save more shekels, build another room onto the back of my shop, buy a goat and chickens——

JOACHIM (*chuckling*). And *I* must have time to accumulate more shekels for Mary's *dowry*——

JOSEPH (*to* ELIZABETH. *Changing the subject*). Will your children go with you to Jerusalem? (*Instantly,* ELIZABETH's *face clouds over, and the others turn serious.*)

ELIZABETH (*lowly*). Zachary and I have no children, Joseph.

MARY (*to* JOSEPH). It is the one great sorrow of their lives——

JOSEPH. I am sorry I spoke. (*Looks greatly embarrassed.*)

ANN. Sit down, Elizabeth. (*Goes closer to her.*)

ELIZABETH (*to* JOSEPH *as she sits on the bench beside the table.* JOACHIM *sits on the stool down Left*). We are old, Zachary and I, and the Lord has seen fit to make me barren. But Zachary is a man of great and simple faith, and he continues to pray—day and night—that he shall be blest with a son before he dies. (*Sighs, then smiles.*) But I must not cast a shadow of sorrow over this happy gathering. God has been more than good to us and we must give Him proper thanks. (*Looking from one to the other.*) Is it all settled then—that you will accompany us to Jerusalem so that we can worship in the Great Temple together while Zachary prays in the Tabernacle?

JOACHIM. Of course——

ANN. Oh, yes. *Such* an honor is only given to a man in a *lifetime.*

ELIZABETH (*rising*). Then I must go back to Ain Karim and tell Zachary at once. (*Moves down Left.*)

JOACHIM (*rising*). Today?

ANN. Stay and eat with us first, Elizabeth?

MARY. You will be too weary if you go now, cousin.

ELIZABETH. No. I am too excited to think of weariness, and I must start work on Zachary's robe if I am to have it finished in time. It must be yellow with blue tassels, such as the High Priests wear. It will be beautiful, and he will look so imposing in it, with his white hair and long white beard. (*Lifting her hand.*) Peace be unto you, my loved ones, and to *you,* Joseph, until we meet again. (*Exits.*)

OMNES (*together*). Peace be unto you, Elizabeth.

ANN (*calling after* ELIZABETH *as she too exits, followed by* JOACHIM. *The music fades in.* MARY *gives* JOSEPH *her hand, and they move to follow the others*). Will you not take some dates and figs?

ELIZABETH (*off Left*). No. Nothing. I do not wish to eat until I get back home. (*The music rises,* MARY *and* JOSEPH *are nearing the exit down Left, and the lights go out. If the play is being performed on a stage, the curtain will now come down. If not, the lights will remain out until Scene Two.*)

END OF SCENE ONE

(*As soon as the lights go out, the* NARRATOR *enters down Left. As soon as he—or she—is in position, the soft light comes on to cover him,—or her—then the music softens for the narration.*)

NARRATOR. And so it was that two families were made happy that day. Joseph was going to wed Mary, and the seventy-year-old Zachary was to have his moment of greatness in Jerusalem. The robe was finished in time, and the two families met in the tiny village of Ain Karim, which was only a few miles from Nazareth. Then they mounted their donkeys and set off for the great city, where Zachary parted company from the others and left them in the outer court while he went into the inner temple and was given his censer and instructed what to do. Everything went well until he had performed the first part of the ceremony and had entered the Inner Sanctuary. But there something mysterious happened, and when he came out again, Zachary had been stricken dumb! The family were humiliated for all felt that the venerable old man had been a failure. It was a sad and perplexed group who returned to Ain Karim the following day. That is, all but Zachary were sad, and he was strangely *excited* all the way. (*The music rises, the* NARRATOR'S *light goes out, he—or she—disappears in the darkness, and the lights come up for . . .*)

SCENE TWO

(This is supposed to be a large room in ZACHARY'S *house, but the only changes are in the furniture, which is now rearranged. The table stands down Left and there are backless benches on either side of it. On the table are a candle and several pottery bowls. A smaller table is down Right, with stools on either side of it. As the music fades out . . .)*

ELIZABETH *(entering down Right with the nervously excited* ZACHARY, *who continually mouths words that no one hears.* ELIZABETH *is weak and spent, but in spite of this her concern is all for her aged husband.* ZACHARY *is an imposing sight with his white hair and flowing beard, his weathered features and his white-and-yellow priestly robe with blue tassels.* ELIZABETH *leads him to Center stage as she speaks).* Oh, thank Jehovah—home at last. Poor Zachary. Oh, my husband, what a great misfortune to come upon you. All your life you have longed to celebrate a sacrifice in the Great Temple, and now—in the twilight of your days—when you can never have another such opportunity—you are mysteriously unable to speak! *(A little sob escapes her, but she is quick to control her emotion as she gently urges him to sit on the bench, right of the table down Left. He tries desperately to tell her something.)* No. Do not try, Zachary. Sit down and rest yourself. So much excitement is not good for you. I beg you to be calm while I invite the family in. Then I shall cook you something to eat and put you to bed. *(He shakes his head. She pats his shoulder.)* You *must* eat, Zachary, to give you strength. And you must sleep. It has been a wearisome journey—home. *(Moves to Right a few steps, calling offstage.* ZACHARY *looks around on the table, then rises and exits quickly down Left.)* Come in, people. Come in and rest yourselves. He seems to be more quiet now. *(Turns to see* ZACHARY *leaving the room. Moves a few, quick steps to the Left.)* Zachary! What are you doing, my husband? *(Her voice breaking.)* Oh, merciful Jehovah! What has come over the man to make him act so strangely?

JOACHIM (*entering Right, quite slowly. He is talking to* ANN, *evidently continuing a conversation begun off-stage*). I cannot understand it, Ann. He was well and happy when he went up the twelve steps that are for the twelve tribes of Israel——

ANN (*as they pause at Center*). And we were all so proud of him as he lifted the censer and prayed——

JOACHIM. There was nothing wrong when he lifted the veil at the opening to the Inner Sanctuary——

ANN. I know, Joachim. But when he was in there so long and the worshippers grew restless——

MARY. (*quietly. She has entered Right with* JOSEPH *during the above*). Mother——

ANN. Yes, Mary?

MARY. I have been thinking—it could be that he suddenly contracted some strange disease of the throat from one of the beggars in that vast crowd.

ANN. Maybe so, child. Maybe so. (*Sighs, twists her fingers together and moves up Center.*)

JOSEPH (*who has paused down Right*). I could hardly believe my eyes when he rushed out of the Tabernacle with that wild look about him——

JOACHIM. I can still see Annas, the High Priest, hurrying up to him to demand an explanation of his strange conduct.

JOSEPH. But he could give none. That was when everyone first realized he could no longer talk.

ANN (*moving closer to* ELIZABETH, *who is down Left, looking offstage*). What is he doing, Elizabeth?

ELIZABETH. He went into the inner room—perhaps to lie down. (*Hurries closer to* JOACHIM.) Oh, Joachim, do you think he has become possessed by evil spirits? Surely the living God would not inflict *that* misery upon us?

ANN (*moving closer to* ELIZABETH *so that the three of them are standing at Center*). Oh, no, Elizabeth. There is a reason behind this. We must wait with patience and humility for the Lord to reveal it to us in His own good time. (ZACHARY *enters down Left, with a quill, parch-*

ment and an ink pot which he quickly places on the left side of the table and sits on the bench beside it.)

JOSEPH. Here he comes——

MARY. With parchment and quill!

JOACHIM. All the way back from Jerusalem he has been trying to tell us something, but none of us could understand his signs. Now, I think, he is going to *write* what he wishes us to know.

ANN (*eagerly. Moving closer to the right side of the table*). Are you, Zachary? (*He nods an emphatic affirmative.* ANN *sucks in her breath and moves quickly to the upstage end of the table.*)

MARY (*to* JOSEPH). Now perhaps we shall know what is behind the mystery, beloved. (*Goes closer to him down Right.*)

JOSEPH (*lowly*). Beloved. It is like music to my ears when you call me that, Mary. (*Takes her hand and gently urges her to sit on the stool. By this time,* ZACHARY *has dipped the quill into the ink pot, and now he begins to write in feverish haste.*)

ANN. See? He is beginning to write.

JOACHIM. Read it, Elizabeth, so that we all may hear.

ELIZABETH (*leaning over the table. Narrowing her eyes*). I—my eyes are dim. The words are blurred——

JOACHIM (*putting his hand on* ANN'S *shoulder*). Help her, Ann. (ZACHARY *continues writing as* ANN *joins* ELIZABETH *behind the table and puts her arm around the woman as she leans over to read aloud.* JOACHIM *goes closer to* MARY *and* JOSEPH *down Right.*)

ANN. "I—have been listening to an—(*Gasps.*)—an angel!" (*She and the others react in horrified disbelief.*)

ELIZABETH. An—angel?

JOSEPH. That is blasphemy!

ANN (*moving quickly down Left so that she is behind* ZACHARY). Oh, Zachary! Tear it up, quickly, before someone else reads what you have written and reports it to the High Priest! (ZACHARY *frowns and shakes his head and continues writing.*)

JOSEPH (*to* JOACHIM). A man could be put to death for writing such dangerous thoughts!

ELIZABETH (*wailing and wringing her hands together as she moves via the front of the table, toward the group over Right*). Aie! Alas, my poor husband! He has gone completely mad! Oh, what shall I do? What shall I do! (*Sobs and buries her face in her hands as* MARY *rises and takes her in her arms, comfortingly.*)

MARY. Be comforted, Elizabeth. Let him continue. Men have listened to angels before.

JOACHIM (*nodding an affirmative*). In our own family. There isn't anything so strange about *that*.

MARY. All we have to do is read the Scriptures of Moses——

ANN (*getting control of herself*). I—I had forgotten. (*To* JOACHIM.) I am sorry, my husband. Forgive me.

ELIZABETH. He has written *more*——

JOACHIM. Read it to us, Ann.

ANN (*going closer to* ZACHARY *so she can read over his shoulder*). "As I entered the sanctuary I saw a figure standing there——"

ELIZABETH. A figure of flesh and blood?

MARY (*softly*). Do not interrupt her, cousin—— (*Sits on the stool again. Lovely, religious music fades in.*)

JOACHIM. Go on, Ann. Read.

ANN (*continuing. Slowly—distinctly, so that every word will be heard*). "He stood with folded wings and looked at me. I was so frightened I almost dropped the censer. My body grew cold and my brain whirled. My knees were shaking as if with a nervous chill. Then he spoke to me in a voice that was strangely sweet——" (*The music rises. The lights go out. There is a short pause, during which the curtains are parted at the back and* ZACHARY *hurries up Center to assume his position in front of the altar. Then a rose-colored spotlight comes on to reveal* ZACHARY *and the majestic, white-robed figure of the angel. It will be dark on the forepart of the stage, and the other characters hold their positions. N. B. Where the play is performed in a church, the angel will merely appear from behind a screen where he has been*

hidden, and this scene will be enacted in front of the real
altar. The music lowers, but continues to play.)

ANGEL. Fear not, Zachary. I have been sent to this
holy place to bring you glad tidings. Your prayers have
been heard. Your wife, Elizabeth, shall bear you a son.

ZACHARY (*awed*). A—son? After all these years, I
am to have a—child?

ANGEL. You shall call his name *John,* which means
the gracious gift of God. And you shall have joy and
gladness. Many shall rejoice in his nativity and he shall
be great before the Lord. He shall drink no wine or
strong drink and he shall be filled with the Holy Ghost.
He shall grow up to bring many of the people of the
country to the worship of the Lord their God. He shall
have the spirit and the power of the ancient prophet Elias.

ZACHARY (*lowly. Almost doubtingly*). My son—a
prophet!

ANGEL. He shall turn the hearts of fathers unto their
children, and the incredulous to the wisdom of the just,
to prepare unto the Lord a perfect people.

ZACHARY. Whereby shall I know this? For I am an
old man and my wife is advanced in years.

ANGEL (*simply*). I am—Gabriel.

ZACHARY (*gaspingly. Backing away a step*). Gabriel!
One of the four archangels of the Heavenly Host?
Gabriel, who visited the prophet Daniel?

GABRIEL. The same. (*With sudden sternness.*) But
I like not your doubting manner, Zachary. And for this
you must be punished. (*His voice rings out.*) Behold—
you are dumb! (*The music rises to a high, dramatic
pitch.* ZACHARY *gasps again, attempts to say something,
finds that his voice will not come. The angel regards him
silently as he clutches at his throat. Then the light goes
out, the music dies away and* ANN'S *voice is heard reading
in the darkness. The curtains close out the view of the
altar,* ZACHARY *hurries to sit in his former position at
the table, then the lights come on to show him finishing
the writing, and the other characters in the same positions
as before.*)

ANN (*her voice loud while she is reading in the dark-*

ness, then softening as the lights come on and the music fades). "I closed my eyes and prayed as never before. When I opened them again the angel was gone. It was a miracle and I had doubted. But as I staggered out of the holy place I found that his words were already proved true; I was dumb. I could not speak. I could not make anyone understand what had happened to me." (ZACHARY *lays down his quill.*)

JOACHIM (*to* ELIZABETH. *Jubilantly*). A son! Elizabeth, you are to have a *son!* (ZACHARY *nods an affirmative.*)

ANN (*overawed*). A prophet!

JOSEPH (*excitedly*). And you must call him John!

JOACHIM (*to* JOSEPH. *Indicating* ZACHARY). His dumbness must be a sign!

MARY (*to* JOSEPH). Perhaps his voice will return when the child is born.

ELIZABETH (*sobbing with joy as she hurries closer to* ZACHARY, *who rises and takes her in his arms*). A miracle! Zachary, you have seen a miracle!

ANN (*going closer to* JOACHIM). God has indeed answered their prayers.

JOSEPH (*to* MARY). No wonder he behaved so strangely.

ANN. He has been under a terrible strain——

ELIZABETH (*to* ZACHARY. *Smiling through her tears*). Ever since we left Jerusalem I have been weeping tears of sorrow and humiliation. Now they are tears of joy. (ZACHARY *smiles and nods his understanding.*) But enough of tears. We must celebrate this wonderful mystery with a feast of thanksgiving. Ann, you and I will prepare it. Will you lay the fire, Joachim? Afterwards, we shall talk.

JOACHIM. But we must return to Nazareth bright and early in the morning, Elizabeth. I have my work to do.

JOSEPH. And I must get back to my shop.

ELIZABETH. So be it. (*Taking* ZACHARY'S *arm. Leading him to the Left.*) Oh, Zachary. Zachary! We are to have a son—at last. (*They exit down Left.*)

ANN (*to* JOACHIM, *as he puts his arm around her*

shoulder and they start slowly over Left). Those were strange words the angel spoke to him, Joachim. He said the child shall be "filled with the Holy Ghost." What does that mean, do you think?

JOACHIM (*they pause near the exit, Left*). I do not know, Ann. I only know that a great miracle has come upon Zachary and Elizabeth, and we must wait for the Lord to fulfill His promise to them. (*They exit. Soft organ music fades in.*)

JOSEPH. Do you believe it will come true, Mary?

MARY (*thoughtfully. Moving to Center*). Zachary is a good man. He would not lie. Either he is possessed by evil spirits or he and Elizabeth are to have a child. (*Turns to face him.*) And I do not think him possessed.

JOSEPH (*moving closer to her*). Nor I. And no man in his right senses would place himself in such a position with his wife and relatives, unless he believed the truth of what he had written with all his heart and soul.

MARY. And there are his friends and neighbors—people who go to the synagogue. They will be watching—waiting for the miracle to come to pass. Zachary is now committed by a prophecy to *prove* his statements, or be branded as a liar and a madman. (*Smiling.*) Yes, Joseph. I—believe.

JOSEPH. And I. (*Slowly taking her in his arms. With great tenderness.*) Mayhap some day you and I shall be blessed with a son, Mary.

MARY (*softly. Wistfully*). We must *pray* for one, Joseph—as cousin Elizabeth and Zachary prayed. (*The music swells as he leads her slowly off Left. Then the lights go out, the NARRATOR enters, and the soft light to illuminate him—or her—comes on. The music softens as he—or she—begins to speak.*)

END OF SCENE TWO

NARRATOR (*speaking as soon as the spotlight comes on*). The next morning, there was not much said about the miracle of the priest and the angel, and soon it was time for the ones who lived in Nazareth to return to their homes and work. For a while, none of them could think of much except Zachary's amazing experience. But as the months passed by, the memory became dim and almost dream-like. As a matter of fact, the episode had almost been forgotten entirely, when one day a message from Elizabeth arrived. She had written to Ann——

ELIZABETH'S VOICE (*loudly. Clearly. Coming out of the darkness down Left, offstage. The* NARRATOR *remains immovable while she speaks*). Peace be unto you, my beloved aunt and family. God has heard our prayers indeed, and the promise of the holy angel has been fulfilled. *At my age I am going to have a child!*

NARRATOR (*to the audience*). The astounding news was like another miracle to Joachim, Ann and Joseph, and they all sent return messages to the happy Elizabeth and Zachary—messages of congratulations and great rejoicing. Then, in the balmy month of April, with the sweet smells of spring in the air, Joseph finally decided that he had saved enough money for his marriage. So after his work one balmy evening, he bathed and dressed with unusual carefulness, and set out for Joachim's house to tell the family that he was now prepared to make Mary his wife. (*The music swells, the* NARRATOR'S *light goes out, he— or she—exits in the darkness, and we are ready for . . .*)

SCENE THREE

(*This is Joachim's house again, and the furniture is just the way we saw it at the beginning.* ANN *sits at the table over Right, working on some embroidery.* MARY *is at the entrance down Left, smiling sweetly as she sees* JOSEPH *outside. The music slowly fades away.*)

MARY. Oh, it is you, Joseph? Come in. (*Moves a step or two toward the Center as he enters, carrying a lighted lantern.*)

JOSEPH. Peace be unto you this beautiful spring evening, Mary. And unto *you,* my mother-soon-to-be. (*Blows out the lantern and sets it on the floor.*)

121

MARY and ANN. Peace, Joseph.

JOACHIM (*entering down Right*). Ah, Joseph, my son. It is good to see you.

ANN. Fetch him a stool, Mary. (MARY *gets one from upstage. Brings it down to Left Center.*)

JOACHIM (*moving closer to* JOSEPH). How is it in the town today?

JOSEPH. I had a talk with a traveller whose broken wheel I mended. Thank you, Mary. (*Sits on the stool.*) He told me how the people in Jerusalem look down upon us countrified Nazarenes and call us yokels with uncouth Northern accents. He says that the actors in the stadium often imitate our ways and manners, and that one of their favorite jokes about us is the question, "Can anything good come out of Nazareth?"

JOACHIM (*frowning*). Ill-mannered sophisticates!

ANN. Little do they know how *we* feel about *them*. Unnatural, overcivilized, immoral——

JOACHIM (*gently reproving*). Peace, Ann. It is the city and their unbelief that has done that to them.

JOSEPH (*getting down to the real reason for his coming*). I—I was counting up my savings today—— (JOACHIM *and* ANN *exchange quick, knowing glances.* JOSEPH *looks down at the floor as he continues.*) I am ready to buy my goat and chickens——

MARY (*now standing down Left*). Are you, Joseph? How wonderful!

JOACHIM (*clearing his throat*). A-hem! Go on, Joseph. (*Sits beside the table, Right.*)

JOSEPH. I have added another room behind my shop. I shall make furniture for it soon. (*Smiling at* MARY.) I do not want *my* wife to have to skimp and scrape.

MARY (*gently*). I am not worried about that, Joseph.

JOACHIM. *Well*, then, if all this has been accomplished, what makes the delay?

ANN (*gently reproving*). Joachim! (*Rises. Goes closer to* JOSEPH.) Mary's father and I shall not stand in the way of an early marriage, Joseph. And there is really no reason to wait any longer. Have you fixed a day in your mind?

JOSEPH. No. I must talk to Mary about that. (*Rises.*)

JOACHIM (*rising*). Er—Ann. Shouldn't you and I go up on the roof to collect the dates and figs?

ANN (*taking the hint*). Yes, Joachim. They should be well-dried after the heat of today's sun. (*Starts down Right.*)

MARY (*blushingly*). Mother!

ANN. When you get everything settled, Joseph, you can let us know. (*To* JOACHIM, *as she exits down Right.*) There was no cause for you to be so *brazen* about it!

JOACHIM (*chuckles, follows her down Right, pauses and turns to* JOSEPH). Have you eaten, Joseph?

JOSEPH. Yes. Before I decided to come.

JOACHIM. Then peace be upon you, my son. And may the Lord bless your union as I shall. (*Exits.* MARY *goes closer to the table, passing in front of* JOSEPH.)

JOSEPH (*softly*). Mary——

MARY (*as he hesitates*). Yes, Joseph?

JOSEPH. When shall it be?

MARY. Within three months I shall be your wife.

JOSEPH (*surprised*). Three months? When, at last, I am ready to——?

MARY (*interrupting. Going closer to him. Placing a gentle hand on his arm*). Do not look so disappointed, my love. There is much sewing to be done, and my father wishes to accumulate more shekels to fill out my dowry. Three months will not seem so long after the date is fixed.

JOSEPH (*smiling. Taking both her hands in his*). So be it, Mary. I would wait many years if that was *your* pleasure. (*Seriously.*) Sometimes you frighten me, Mary. Have I told you that before?

MARY. No, Joseph.

JOSEPH. You are so quiet, so tranquil. Nothing ever seems to disturb you.

MARY. Why should it, Joseph?

JOSEPH (*continuing*). You are so different from all the other girls of Nazareth. Somehow—I find it difficult to put into words—but there is something about you that makes me feel very humble. What can it be that sets you so apart?

MARY. I'm sure I do not know, Joseph. *I* am not conscious of this difference you speak of. But *I* have realized a great difference in *you.*

JOSEPH (*surprised*). In—me?

MARY (*nodding a slow, smiling affirmative. Going to sit on the bench beside the table*). From the other men of the village, most of whom are rough and sinful.

JOSEPH. Yes. The Nazarenes are generally a rowdy lot. My friends call *me* a *visionary*—

MARY. Because you do not gamble or drink with them or the men in the caravans. Nor do you associate with tavern women.

JOSEPH (*smiling*). I find *my* pleasures in talking to my neighbors, working at my trade, reading the Scriptures and worshipping my God.

MARY (*softly*). I am proud of you, Joseph. You do credit to your ancestors. (*Rising.*) But it grows late and you must be up at daybreak tomorrow. Will you see my parents again before you leave? (*Takes his arm.*)

JOSEPH (*they start walking toward the exit down Left*). No, I think not. There is no need for further talk. You have set the date and I am content. The Lord be with you, Mary, 'til we meet again tomorrow. (*Picks up the lantern.*)

MARY (*softly. With half-closed eyes. The organ music fades in again*). The Lord will be with us all our lives, Joseph, so long as *we* are with the *Lord.* (*He kisses her gently on the forehead and exits. The music rises—swells climactically, and as she stands watching after him the lights go out—just long enough for GABRIEL to appear at the back. Then the rose-colored spotlight comes on to cover him, and the music dies down as a background to the Annunciation.*)

GABRIEL (*in ringing tones*). Hail, Mary, full of grace! (*She whirls and stiffens in astonished wonder upon seeing the apparition. GABRIEL moves a step down Center as he continues.*) The Lord is with you. Blessed are you among women. You have found grace with God.

MARY (*lowly. Tremblingly*). I—have found grace with——?

GABRIEL. Fear not, Mary. You will conceive in your womb and bring forth a son. And you shall call his name *Jesus,* who shall have kingdom over all the earth. And of His kingdom there shall be no end.

MARY (*awed. Speaking like one in a trance*). I shall have a son? How shall this be done, seeing I know not a man?

GABRIEL (*taking a step closer. His eyes full of compassion*). The Holy Ghost shall come upon you. The power of the Most High shall overshadow you and therefore also the Holy one which shall be born of you shall be called the *Son of God.*

MARY (*lowly. In a loud, half-whisper*). The—Son of —God!

GABRIEL. Your cousin Elizabeth has also conceived a son. This is the sixth month with her that was called barren. Because with God nothing is impossible. *He* shall be called *John*—by some, John the Baptist. He shall proclaim Jesus the *Messiah.*

MARY (*stands immovable for a slow count of five, then sinks to her knees, bows her head and clasps her hands prayerfully*). Behold the handmaid of the Lord. Be it done to me according to your word. (*The music swells, the angel stretches forth his arms in blessing and backs slowly up Center, and the lights go out.*)

THE END

NOTE: Where the play is performed on a stage, *the curtain will come down.* In a church, however, the lights will remain out until Mary and Gabriel have disappeared. Then the music comes to a climax of rejoicing and the lights come up again.

THE PRODIGAL COMES HOME

A BIBLICAL DRAMA IN ONE ACT

By

MARY MONCURE PARKER

PRODUCTION RIGHTS

Copies of this play are available in single pamphlet form. The right to produce this play by one group of amateur players is authorized only by the purchase of eight copies (one copy for each speaking part) at the current price of 50c each.

It is dishonest and illegal to copy parts.

THE PRODIGAL COMES HOME

FOR FIVE MEN AND THREE WOMEN

CHARACTERS
(In the order of their first appearance)

NAOMI...........................*The prodigal's mother*
LABAN ....*Her elder son*
DEBORAH ....*Laban's betrothed*
MANASSEH ....*The prodigal's father*
SERVANT ....*In Manasseh's household*
LEAH ....*Deborah's mother*
EZRA ....*Manasseh's neighbor*
JOEL..............*Manasseh's younger son, the prodigal*

TIME—*Between 30 and 33* A. D.

PLACE—*Manasseh's house in a city of ancient Palestine.*

TIME OF PLAYING—*Twenty minutes.*

COSTUMES AND CHARACTERISTICS

The costumes are the long, loose robes worn by the Jews in Bible times, consisting of the tunic and the mantle. They may be made of cheesecloth and designed in different bright colors in order to make a pleasing stage picture. There is neither time nor necessity for a change of costume, except for Joel. The feast prepared by Manasseh is an impromptu affair and the guests are supposed to come in everyday dress. The women may add gayly colored silk scarfs or veils to their costumes, on appearing for the feast, if desired. Both men and women wear sandals, preferably in brown or some other dark color.

NAOMI—A middle-aged, motherly soul, of dignified and matronly appearance. Wears a gray robe with a veil of dull rose color enveloping her head and shoulders. She has a golden chain about her neck and wears long golden earrings.

LABAN—A serious but rather prosy young man in his late twenties. Wears a loose, light brown robe extending nearly to his ankles, neat and well made.

DEBORAH—A lovely young girl of twenty, romantic of disposition and loyal to her first love. Her long black hair falls unbound on her shoulders. Wears a sleeveless white robe, with a delicate blue veil floating from a silver band fastened around her forehead. Her only ornaments are a golden chain about her waist and several golden bracelets on her arms.

MANASSEH—A big, dark, bearded man in his late forties, with a prosperous air. He wears a dark green robe reaching to his ankles, with a yellow scarf about his head bound with a dark green band and falling to his shoulders.

SERVANT—A man of about thirty-five. Wears a neat, dark brown robe of coarse material.

LEAH—A middle-aged woman of great decision of character, inclined to be a trifle sharp. Wears a dark maroon robe, with a purple veil falling from the gold band around her forehead.

EZRA—An elderly man, wearing a dark blue robe, over

which is draped a traveler's brown cape, very plain and simple, hanging loose from his shoulders. On his head he wears a turban of blue cloth, arranged in folds.

JOEL—A fine-looking young man of twenty-four or so, dark, smooth-faced, and of a strongly fascinating personality, as befits a prodigal son, who is to be forgiven everything chiefly on account of his charming and lovable qualities. At his first entrance he wears a soiled and ragged gray tunic reaching a little below the knees, with a rope about his waist, bare legs, and shabby sandals. Later he makes a quick change to a handsome bright red robe, with a heavy golden chain about his neck and a gold ring on his finger.

PROPERTIES

For Naomi, a small child's garment of a deep rose color. For Joel, a rough wooden staff of the type used by oriental travelers.

STAGE DIRECTIONS

Up stage means away from footlights; *down stage,* near ɩ .otlights. In the use of *right* and *left,* the actor is supposed to be facing the audience.

THE PRODIGAL COMES HOME

SCENE: *Living room in the home of* MANASSEH *in a city in Palestine, about the period of 30 to 33* A. D. *It is obviously the home of a wealthy householder living in comfort. The room has three doors: one at left leading to the street, a second one at left leading to the servants' quarters, and a third in the center of the back drop leading to the living quarters of the family off up right and to the hall of feasting off up left. The room has no windows, being lighted, like many oriental homes, presumably from a skylight. None of the furniture is upholstered or modern in appearance. A heavy wooden bench, large enough to seat two persons, is well up center, a little right of the center door, with a rug of subdued oriental design thrown across it. A plain wooden chair is down right, and a wooden table is down left, with a chair having no back placed at right of it. On the table is a brass bowl. The floor is heavily marked with black crayon, to represent tiling. At each of the doorways are heavy dark curtains, which part in the middle. If desired, the play may be given without any front curtain.*

At rise of curtain, NAOMI *is seated in the chair down right, alone on the stage, with a small rose-colored garment in her hands. If no curtain is used, she may enter, up center, from right, and come down center to the chair at right, with the child's garment in her hands. She looks at it, holds it out in front of her, and caresses it tenderly, then speaks aloud, as if to some one.*

NAOMI (*sadly*). My dearest, my best beloved. My Joel! Where are you? Where are you? (*Lets the garment fall into her lap.*)

Enter LABAN, *left.*

LABAN. Mother, did you speak?

NAOMI (*tries to hide the small garment*). I was talking to myself, Laban, my son—a habit, I fear, that grows with age.

LABAN. Mother, you are grieving again. I see Joel's small garment that he wore as a child.

NAOMI (*catches up the garment and kisses it*). I do not mean to grieve; but where is Joel? Where is my son?

LABAN (*comes to her and puts his hand on her shoulder*). Far be it from me to chide you, my dear mother. Joel is alive and well.

NAOMI. And you did not tell me?

LABAN. My father forbade me, lest it sadden you that Joel had sent no word. We heard some months since, from a traveler journeying from Cæsarea to Jerusalem by caravan. Joel is well and living in magnificence in Cæsarea—like a prince, they say, with daily feasting and merriment. His table groans with rare foods and choicest wines, and many sit with him at meat.

NAOMI. And he has sent no word to me, his mother, of his welfare?

LABAN. Mother, that is the reason my father forbade me to speak, lest you grieve. I tell you, that you may not be in constant doubt.

NAOMI. This knowledge gives me greater sadness, my son. Yet I rejoice that he is well and prosperous.

LABAN (*bitterly*). What cares he for any of us? (*Walks to center and pauses.*) When he left home, Joel took his portion of our father's substance. It was his choice. He lives as he desires. We are nothing to him.

NAOMI. But Deborah, the damsel that he loved—the child of our friends—what of Deborah?

LABAN. My mother, Deborah knows of this. (*Hesitates.*) I have ever loved her, but until recently, I have kept silent. Now I have spoken, and she has promised to become my betrothed. Deborah tarries timidly at the door. (*Crosses to left door.*) I will fetch her. (*Opens door.*) **Here** she is.

Enter DEBORAH, *left. She pauses shyly just inside the doorway.*

DEBORAH (*to* NAOMI). My mother was detained by her household duties. She will come to greet you and even now is on the way hither. Laban grew impatient to bring me to his home, and so I came. I trust I am not overbold.

(LABAN *takes her hand and leads her to his mother.*)

NAOMI. Dear Deborah, you are ever sweet and gentle. Laban tells me he has asked your hand in marriage.

DEBORAH. Yes, dear Naomi.

NAOMI. I thought your heart was otherwise engaged. (*Sighs.*) It is better thus, perchance—although— (*Pauses.*) But, nay, I will not sadden you. Come closer to me. (LABAN *and* DEBORAH *kneel before* NAOMI.) My blessing go with you, dear children, all through life.

Enter MANASSEH, *left.*

MANASSEH. What is this I behold? (*Comes down right of center.*)

(LABAN *and* DEBORAH *rise and* LABAN *leads* DEBORAH *to his father.*)

LABAN. Your blessing, my father. Deborah has promised to be my betrothed one. Her mother and mine have bidden us Godspeed.

(NAOMI *slips out at center, turning right.*)

MANASSEH. It is well, my children. (LABAN *and* DEBORAH *kneel before him a moment, and* MANASSEH *touches their heads. Then they arise.*) You, my son Laban, have been to me a treasure. For hours have you toiled in the fields with the hired servants, to save me from labor. The plow, the winnowing fork, the threshing sledge, in turn, beneath your wise direction have doubled my substance, and I have prospered. (*Bitterly.*) My son Joel has forgotten us. My substance was all he desired. His portion! His portion! And it was not of his earning! (*Sits in chair down right.*)

LABAN (*puts a warning finger to his lips, then notices his mother has gone*). Ah, my mother has gone. I feared she would be sad if you spoke thus of Joel.

Enter SERVANT *at right.*

SERVANT. Master Laban, a yoke of oxen has fallen in the field. One is ill unto death.

MANASSEH (*to* SERVANT). Go to your mistress Naomi for some of the bitter herbs she has brewed.

(*Exit* SERVANT, *up center, turning right.*)

LABAN. Even in my hour of rejoicing, must I be called to service. Forgive me, my father. I meant not to complain. Deborah, I must leave you for a time. They have need of me in the field. (*Exit at right.*)

MANASSEH. Laban is my mainstay.

Enter LEAH *at left.*

MANASSEH (*rises*). We welcome you, Leah. It is a happy day that we learn our children are to be united in marriage at a later time.

LEAH. I am content, Manasseh, and all is well.

Enter SERVANT, *up center, from right.*

SERVANT. I have the brewing of herbs, master.

MANASSEH. I will take it to Laban. Go summon your mistress and tell her our neighbor Leah awaits her.

SERVANT. Yes, master. (*Exit, up center, going right.*)

MANASSEH. I will go to Laban in the field. Naomi will be with you soon. (*Exit at right.*)

LEAH (*sits in chair, left*). You are indeed fortunate, Deborah, that Laban desires you for a wife. His lands are rich and fertile, and his many fields yield in abundance. His father's portion, too, will be his. Glad, indeed, would many maidens be at such good fortune. You are favored above the rest. Yet well I know that you still long for Joel, and it angers me.

DEBORAH (*sits in chair, right, and speaks longingly*). Joel was fair and yet ruddy, and his hair was as black as a raven's wing. He told me I looked forth as the morning, with eyes that overcame him.

LEAH (*sharply*). Words, mere fanciful words, without meaning! Long since has he forgotten you. What of your duty to me? Am I not a widow? What shall I do in my old age? Would you remain unwed, a thing of scorn, pointed at as the cast-off plaything of a wild youth? Where is your pride?

DEBORAH (*dreamily*). We wandered in the groves and danced the hours away. Laban talks only of the fields and grain and oxen. Joel talked of the sun, the moon, the stars, and of his love for me.

LEAH (*impatiently*). Deborah, you shame me. You act like a child. Joel idled the hours away while Laban worked with the servants. Will grain grow where no seed is sown? How think you Laban's land and Manasseh's have a goodly yield? 'Tis by toil! I have no patience with you! (*Rises and walks up stage, and then comes back.*)

DEBORAH (*wearily*). My mother, I pray you cease your chiding. I have yielded to your desires! (*Rises and stands, clasping her hands together.*)

LEAH. Hush! Say no more. I hear some one coming.

Enter NAOMI, *up center, coming from right.* LEAH *turns as* NAOMI *comes to her.*

NAOMI. I greet you, Leah, my neighbor. Forgive my delay. I had brewed some bitter herbs, and I sent the lotion to the field for the oxen that were ill.

LEAH. Naomi, I have come at Laban's request. He asked

me to bring Deborah to you for your blessing, and for Manasseh's.

NAOMI. We both love Deborah sincerely and have given them our blessing.

LEAH. Deborah, my child, will you go into the courtyard and await Laban's return? I desire a word with Naomi.

DEBORAH. Yes, my mother. (*Exit at right.*)

NAOMI. I seem remiss in my hospitality. Will you be seated, Leah?

LEAH (*sits at right*). Naomi, I know your heart is with Joel.

NAOMI (*standing at center*). Do you feel that Deborah loves Laban, Leah?

LEAH. Naomi, my friend, a young girl does not know her own mind. Her wiser elders must decide for her.

NAOMI (*sorrowfully, with a far-away look*). She and Joel were two beautiful young things in the garden of life, as carefree as butterflies flitting in the sun. Joel loved her.

LEAH (*energetically*). I am amazed at you, Naomi. Has Joel ever sent my child a message? Long since has he forgotten her.

NAOMI. Perhaps not. (*Crosses to chair down left and sits.*)

LEAH. Naomi, your eyes are blind with love for your younger son. I have heard that he lives as a prince in a far-off country; and yet has he ever sent a message of greeting, even to you, his mother?

NAOMI (*rises*). Love is not so easily cast off. I sometimes think my heart is breaking. Joel was so young, so beautiful, so full of youth and joy! (*Pauses and wipes her eyes.*) Yet—heed not my plaints, Leah. They are both my sons, and Laban has been ever faithful. It is better that Deborah and he shall wed. I gave them my blessing, as I have said. (*Goes up center and pauses by bench with bowed head, as if overcome.*)

Enter LABAN *and* MANASSEH *at right.*

LABAN. We have saved the oxen with the bitter herbs. It was like unto a magic potion.

(NAOMI *crosses left and faces* LABAN *and* MANASSEH. LABAN *crosses to center.*)

LEAH. You are provident and thoughtful, Laban. Well may your parents take pride in you.

LABAN. Your words are kind, Leah. Where is Deborah?

LEAH. Did you not see her in the courtyard? Then she must have started home along the highway. I, too, must return.

LABAN. We will follow her. I will walk with you, if I may.

LEAH (*bowing graciously to him and turning to the others*). Farewell, my friends, for a time.

NAOMI. Farewell.

MANASSEH. Farewell. (*Exeunt* LABAN *and* LEAH *at left.* NAOMI *goes to bench up center and sits.* MANASSEH *sits beside her.*) Naomi, you are distrait, and your countenance has fallen. Let not your mind dwell upon a son who has no thought for you.

Enter SERVANT *at left.*

SERVANT. Master, your neighbor Ezra the merchant man has returned from his travels and comes to greet you. (*Pulls curtains of door aside to let* EZRA *pass in.*)

Enter EZRA *at left. The* SERVANT *crosses to right and goes out, right.*

EZRA. Greetings, Friend Manasseh! Greetings, Naomi!

(NAOMI *bows.*)

MANASSEH. Welcome, Ezra, my neighbor. You are welcome, indeed. It is many months since I have seen you.

NAOMI. I will leave you for a time, my husband, to attend to my household tasks. Well I know how pleased you are to hold converse with Ezra. (*Exit, up center, going right.*)

MANASSEH. Come; lay aside your cloak, Ezra, and tell me of your travels in foreign lands. (*Takes* EZRA's *cloak and lays it on the bench up center.*) Sit you down. (EZRA *sits at left.*) How found you the marts of trade? (MANASSEH *sits at right.*)

EZRA. Egypt is a wondrous land where caravans are as numerous as the sands of the desert and where gold is a thing of plenty. Before I journeyed to Egypt, I was in far Cæsarea.

MANASSEH. In Cæsarea? Saw you aught of my son Joel?

EZRA. Yes, Friend Manasseh, I saw him.

MANASSEH. I hear he lives in a manner befitting one of high degree, if the rumors that come to us be true.

EZRA. Such tidings are the truth, Manasseh. At least it was so when I was first in Cæsarea. Daily feasts, rivaling those of the wealthiest did your son Joel spread. His house was of marble, with fountains and costly hangings.

MANASSEH. I have heard that he has prospered.

EZRA. My friend Manasseh, you do not understand. His substance is spent in riotous living. Dancing girls, mad music, flowing wine make his guests merry, but his guests are of the worst, not the best. They fawn upon him, but they make sport of him when he is not nigh to hear. At least, so I learned on my first visit to Cæsarea.

MANASSEH (*rising and pacing the floor*). Thus is my hard-earned substance thrown away in sinful living!

EZRA. It will not last long, methinks, Friend Manasseh. His pace is swifter than that of the chariots of the arena, for Cæsarea has an arena like unto that of Rome.

MANASSEH (*pauses at center*). When at home, Joel grew restless. Never would he labor in the fields. While Laban toiled, Joel wandered in the cool groves. Even the maiden Deborah could not hold him, nor could his mother's love. As the war horse scents the battle from afar, so Joel felt the call of other lands. He demanded his portion, and I in my weakness gave it to him.

EZRA. I desire not to be the bearer of ill tidings, yet it is right to tell you, my friend, what I have learned. Again I went to Cæsarea, and Joel had gone. None knew of his whereabouts. He may be living in grandeur in some other land, and yet there were rumors—

MANASSEH (*alarmed*). What rumors, my friend? Out with it. I must know!

EZRA. That his substance was spent and his so-called friends had deserted him.

MANASSEH. So I feared. Hush! (*Puts his finger to his lips.*) Naomi comes! (*Crosses to right.*)

Enter NAOMI, up center, coming from right. She comes down center.

NAOMI. You have returned but lately from Cæsarea, Friend Ezra? My heart yearns for news of Joel, my son. I alone, it seems, remember him as Laban and Deborah have plighted their troth. A few short months ago it was, that Deborah and Joel desired to wed. Youth changes, alas!

MANASSEH. Naomi, dear one, speak not in bitterness. Deborah's mother has consented. She, too, desires that Deborah should become Laban's wife. Joel sent no word, and we heard he prospered.

NAOMI. Perchance I am harsh. Come, Friend Ezra; tell me of Joel.

(NAOMI *sits, down right.* MANASSEH *goes up stage and stands by bench, up center.*)

EZRA (*embarrassed*). It is some months since I heard of him. I have journeyed later to many places and have just returned here to my own province, Naomi.

(MANASSEH *stands as if in deep thought.*)

NAOMI. You have seen my son Joel. Is it well with him?

EZRA. Yes, Naomi, I saw him. (*Hesitates, then evasively*). It is well with him—your son Joel! (*Rises nervously as though eager to leave.*)

NAOMI (*looking at him keenly*). Your speech is halting. Is there aught to fear?

EZRA. Why—I—I—

MANASSEH (*coming down stage and interrupting, speaks excitedly*). What shall he tell you, my wife? The truth? It is this: Our son spends my hard-earned substance in wicked living with those who are steeped in sin. It was for this that Joel demanded his portion—for this!

EZRA. I must not tarry, my friends. I am sad to have brought ill tidings. (*Crosses to bench up center and gets his cloak, then goes to door at left.*) Farewell, my friends.

MANASSEH. Farewell!

(MANASSEH *crosses to left of center as* EZRA *exits, left.* NAOMI *is too absorbed to heed* EZRA'S *departure. She comes to* MANASSEH *and stands by him.*)

NAOMI. Manasseh, my husband, perchance they are not true—these tales that Ezra brings.

MANASSEH (*gloomily*). They are all too true. I feared it when word came to me of his manner of living some months since. No longer is Joel a son of mine. I renounce him!

NAOMI (*in a pleading tone*). For my sake, my husband, speak not thus; for the sake of the tiny one who lay in my arms as I sat on the housetop in the cool of the evening; for the sake of the little boy who played at your knee. He may return to us.

MANASSEH. I will not forgive him! (*Sits with head leaning on hand in chair down left, his arm resting on the table in an attitude of despair.*)

NAOMI (*comes to him*). Oh, my husband, it is a wonderful thing to forgive. He is ours; we cannot forget that. Our own flesh and blood—our son.

MANASSEH (*after a painful pause*). Wife of my heart, I cannot resist your pleading. In spite of all, I love him!

NAOMI. I will attend to my household tasks with a lighter heart, that you speak thus, my husband. (*Exit, up center, going right.*)

MANASSEH (*aloud, speaking to himself in anguish*). My son Joel, my son Joel! My burden is great! (*Bows his head.*)

Enter SERVANT *at right.* MANASSEH *looks up at him.*

SERVANT. Master, a beggar is without. I saw him afar off, and when he came closer I bade him begone, but he still remains there outside the quarters of your hired servants. He is a creature of rags with a staff.

MANASSEH. Give him food and let him begone.

Enter JOEL *at right, leaning on his staff. He comes slowly to center.*

MANASSEH (*glancing at him inattentively*). Do not enter here. The servants will give you food.

SERVANT (*to* JOEL). Come with me. (*Exit at right.* JOEL *pays no attention to him.*)

JOEL (*in despair*). Father! (*Totters and then steadies himself.*)

MANASSEH (*rises*). Who are you? (*Gazes at him and cries out.*) Joel! Joel—my son! (*Pauses in amazement.*)

JOEL (*puts up his hand in protest*). I am no longer worthy to be your son. Make me as one of your hired servants. My substance is spent. I have sinned against Heaven and in your sight.

MANASSEH (*bitterly*). When all was gone, then you thought of your father and your mother!

JOEL (*bows his head*). I deserve your reproaches, my father. Yes, it is too true. Then I thought of my home, and I said, "I will arise and go to my father, not as his son, but as a hired servant, if he will have me thus." (*Drops on one knee.*)

MANASSEH (*sadly*). My boy—like this! Rise. Sit there at the table. Tell me what this means. (*JOEL rises, sits at the table, and lays his staff on table.*) I almost doubt my eyes. Tell me your story. (*Crosses and stands at right.*)

JOEL (*with emotion*). I threw away all my substance in mad, wild living. When it was gone, my so-called friends laughed me to scorn. Not a hand was lifted to my aid. My riches melted as the mist before the sun. My former friends —what a word!—drove me from their doors when there was no more to be obtained from me. Lower and lower I fell. Oh, I cannot tell you, my father, the depths of my degradation. I am not worthy to remain here in your house! (*Rises and tries to take a step, but drops back in the chair as if too weak to go on.*)

MANASSEH. I would hear your story, Joel. Tell it to me. (*His tone is kindly, but he speaks with authority. Sits at right.*)

JOEL. I became a swineherd and did eat of the husks I threw to the swine. Day by day, I sat thus watching these creatures until I could no longer endure the agony. I said, "I will arise and go to my father." But father, I sit in your presence—I, who am sinful and defiled. (*Totters to his feet.*) Make me one of your hired servants—just a servant —not your son. (*Picks up his staff.*) But I will go again.

MANASSEH (*comes center and holds out his arms*). Joel, Joel—my son, come to me!

JOEL. Father! (*Goes to* MANASSEH, *and they embrace.*)

MANASSEH (*calls*). Naomi! Naomi! (*Takes* JOEL's *staff from him.*)

NAOMI *appears at the door up center, coming from right.*

NAOMI. Yes, my husband.

MANASSEH. Joel, our son, has returned!

(JOEL *goes left of center and stands with head down in shame.* NAOMI *hurries to him, then pauses, bewildered.*)

NAOMI (*in amazement*). Joel? It is my little lad! (*Starts to touch him. He draws back.*)

JOEL. Oh, my mother, do not touch me. I am sinful and defiled. My rags will soil you.

NAOMI (*tenderly*). I do not see the rags, beloved. I see

only you. My son—my younger son—my baby! (*She holds out her arms to him. They embrace.* NAOMI *leads him to bench and they sit.*)

MANASSEH (*going to right door and calling off right*). What, ho! Without, there!

Enter SERVANT *at right.*

MANASSEH. Prepare the best robe. My son, my son Joel, has returned. Get a ring for his finger and a chain for his neck. Prepare a feast and bid them kill the fatted calf. This, my son, is alive and with us again. He was lost and is found. Go assemble the servants and bid them make ready. (*Hands* JOEL'S *staff to* SERVANT.)

SERVANT. Master, I hasten to obey! (*Exit, right, carrying staff.*)

(NAOMI *rises and takes* JOEL *by the hand.*)

NAOMI. Come with me, my son, and put on seemly garments for the feast.

JOEL. Yes, my mother. I will come, but I am not worthy of your love and my father's.

(*Exeunt* NAOMI *and* JOEL, *up center, going right. Here* JOEL *makes a quick change of costume.*)

MANASSEH (*calling off right*). What, ho! Without, there!

Enter SERVANT *at right.*

MANASSEH. Bid Laban, my son, come to me!

SERVANT. Yes, master. Laban, your son, has returned from the gracious Leah's and even now is at the door inquiring about the preparations for the feast. I will summon him. (*Turns to exit at right when—*)

LABAN *enters at right.*

MANASSEH. Laban, rejoice with us. Your brother Joel has returned.

(Exit SERVANT *at right.)*

LABAN *(angrily)*. My father! This feast for Joel—the waster, the spendthrift, who has forgotten us until his substance is spent?

MANASSEH *(joyously)*. But he has returned unto us again. It was as though he were lost and now he is found. My son is found—

LABAN *(interrupting, still in anger and scorn)*. He came to us in tatters, with his portion spent, it is said.

MANASSEH. Aye, but we will clothe him in purple and fine linen, for he has returned to us.

LABAN *(crosses left to table, speaking bitterly)*. This Joel, your son, spends his portion in riotous living, and lo, he is treated as some great personage when he wishes to return! What have I gained by my loyalty to you, my father, for my years of faithful service? Never have I transgressed your counsels; yet when have you made a feast for me, that I make merry with my friends?

MANASSEH *(crosses to* LABAN *and speaks earnestly)*. My son, you have been my mainstay. For you there has been no need for repentance. As age approaches, I lean on you. Yet may I say this, my boy? Your mother and I did not ask for praise that we nourished your tender years. The sun does not ask praise, nor the rain that falls upon the thirsty soil, nor do the seeds that grow, when they fulfill their mission. Your brother Joel has sinned, but he has repented. Conquer your bitterness, my son Laban. *(Puts his hands on* LABAN'S *shoulders.)*

LABAN *(after a moment's struggle)*. My father, because it is your wish, I will welcome Joel.

MANASSEH. Laban, my son, you are a true man, and I love you.

LABAN. Your words mean much to me, my father. *(Turns and goes to door up center, then pauses.)* I will go to greet my brother Joel. *(Exit, up center, turning right.)*

Enter SERVANT *at right.*

SERVANT. Master, the maiden Deborah is here. She has returned by the rear and is yonder in the courtyard. (*Points right.*)

MANASSEH. Bid her enter.

The SERVANT *goes to right door and brings in* DEBORAH, *then exit at right.*

DEBORAH. I waited not your bidding, Manasseh, father of Laban. My mother paused to greet a neighbor. (*Comes to center.*) I could not wait in my eagerness to learn of the sudden cause for rejoicing. We were bidden to a feast.

MANASSEH. Our son Joel has returned.

DEBORAH (*in amazement*). Joel!

MANASSEH. I will summon him. (*Exit, up center, going right.*)

DEBORAH (*stands as if dazed and presses her hands to her hair and exclaiming aloud*). Joel! Joel! (*Moves to left center.*)

Enter JOEL, *up center, coming from right. He wears a red robe with a chain of gold about his neck and a ring on his finger.*

JOEL. Deborah! (*Comes quickly down to her. She looks at him, and then turns slowly from him.*) Deborah—it is gracious of you to come to greet me.

DEBORAH (*turning toward* JOEL). Joel, I did not know for whom the feast was being prepared. You sent no word.

JOEL (*eagerly*). Oh, Deborah, how lovely you are! How I have longed for you! How often have I thought of the hours when we wandered together through the groves!

DEBORAH (*turns from him in sorrow*). Mock me not, Joel. I had no message from you. I was forgotten.

JOEL. Deborah! I am unworthy to touch you, but I have always adored you. All through my absence, when it seemed that I must plunge into the madness of the world, ever would your beautiful face come before me. Oh, Deborah, I know not why I went—except that I longed for life. The plow and the winnowing fork sickened me. I was weary of the fields and grain. Like some bird with bound wings, I wanted to fly away to lands I had not known.

DEBORAH (*goes to chair at left*). You went away. You say you loved me, and yet I could not hold you. (*She sits sadly, with bowed head a moment, then lifts her face in pride.*)

JOEL (*comes nearer but does not touch her*). You did hold me. Through it all there was your lovely self, and yet I dared not think of you. I was mad with joy at the freedom from restraint. I was drunk with adulation and the money that ran like water through my hands; yet I have never ceased to love you.

DEBORAH. Does real love forget, even for a time? Not even a message did you send to me.

(JOEL *goes to chair down right and sits dejectedly.*)

JOEL. I cannot blame you for feeling I had forgotten. Alas! The world that called to me with cries I could not still flattered me in my prosperity and mocked me in my degradation! It was not real life; it was but the will o' the wisp, luring me to the swamp of misery. Yet—you were there before me when I dared think of you—in your loveliness and purity. I cannot hope for your forgiveness. And I still dare to love you.

DEBORAH (*sadly*). Joel, it is too late. I am pledged to Laban.

JOEL (*in amazement, rises and goes to center*). To Laban? My brother Laban? Do you love him?

DEBORAH (*rises*). Do not ask me, Joel!

JOEL (*goes to her and kneels at her feet and lifts her garment to his lips with emotion*). No! No! You do not love him. I can see it in your face. You still love me, Deborah!

LABAN *enters, up center, in time to hear* JOEL'S *last speech. He comes down right and pauses.*

DEBORAH (*exclaiming nervously*). Laban!

(JOEL *rises and comes between them.*)

LABAN (*sadly*). I have heard. I would not wed Deborah against her will.

JOEL (*distressed*). Laban—I did not know at first. I will go away again—

DEBORAH (*crying out*). No—no! (*Then she turns partly away and goes up stage.*)

LABAN. Think not I took advantage of your absence, my brother. (*Resentfully.*) I have always loved Deborah. Word came to us of you only through travelers. It was her mother who consented, and she desired to see us wed; and so I spoke, thinking you had perchance forgotten.

Enter NAOMI *and* LEAH, *up center from right, followed by* MANASSEH.

LABAN (*turning to* NAOMI). My mother, the love that Deborah and Joel had for one another still holds them. I say this not in bitterness. Love is not a thing of barter.

LEAH (*in surprise, coming to center*). What is this I hear?

DEBORAH. Oh, my mother, chide me not, I pray you. (*Goes to* LEAH, *and they go up stage together, left of center, talking in pantomime.*)

JOEL (*goes to* LABAN). Laban, you are more worthy of Deborah than am I.

NAOMI (*comes down to center*). In a matter of the heart, Deborah must be allowed to choose.

DEBORAH (*coming down center to* NAOMI). What of me? Must I be counted fickle, that I forget Joel when he is out of sight, even though he sends no word to me? Must I be cruel to Laban and forget my promise to him when his brother has returned? How can I choose without wounding one or the other?

NAOMI. Consult your own heart, my child. Neither of my sons would desire that you wed without love.

DEBORAH. Oh, how can I say it? I love—Joel! (*Drops her head on* NAOMI'S *shoulder.*)

JOEL (*wistfully*). Laban, do you forgive me? (*Holds out his hand.* LABAN *hesitates, then takes it.*)

DEBORAH (*turns to* LEAH). My mother!

LEAH (*putting her arms about* DEBORAH). I love you, Deborah. I am content if you are happy.

Enter the SERVANT, *up center, coming from right.*

SERVANT (*to* MANASSEH). Master, the feast is in preparation in the great hall beyond. Your guests have been summoned and will soon arrive.

MANASSEH. Come, my beloved ones, to the hall of rejoicing.

(*Exit* SERVANT *at right. Exeunt* NAOMI *and* LEAH, *up center, going left.* JOEL *takes* DEBORAH'S *hand in his, then pauses as they reach the center door.* JOEL *comes a few steps down center.*)

JOEL. My father and Laban, we await you.

MANASSEH. Go to the hall to greet our friends, Joel. We are coming. (*Exeunt* JOEL *and* DEBORAH, *up center.* LABAN *stands at right center as if in thought.* MANASSEH *comes to him and puts his hands on* LABAN'S *shoulders.*) My son, you forgave your brother. In a moment, in the twinkling of an eye, have you grown great, for you have become the captain of your own soul.

(*If there is no curtain,* MANASSEH *and* LABAN *go slowly off up center, turning left.*)

CURTAIN

THE SILVERED ROPE

A BIBLICAL DRAMA IN ONE ACT

By

JAY G. SIGMUND

and

BETTY SMITH

PRODUCTION RIGHTS

Copies of this play are available in single pamphlet form. The right to produce this play by one group of amateur players is authorized only by the purchase of five copies (one copy for each speaking part) at the current price of 50c each.

It is dishonest and illegal to copy parts.

THE SILVERED ROPE

FOR THREE MEN AND TWO WOMEN

CHARACTERS
(In the order of their first appearance)

DORCAS ....*Lazar's wife*
SAPPHIRA...............................*His daughter*
LAZAR ....*A goat breeder*
PHILIP ....*His son*
STRANGER ....*A wayfaring guest*

TIME—*Nearly twilight of the first Good Friday.*

PLACE—*Lazar's hill cottage on a slope near Jerusalem.*

TIME OF PLAYING—*Fifteen minutes.*

COSTUMES AND CHARACTERISTICS

The costumes are the long, loose robes worn by the Jews in Bible times, consisting of the tunic and the mantle. They may be made of cheesecloth and designed in various bright colors to make a pleasing stage picture. Both men and women wear sandals, preferably in brown or some other dark color.

DORCAS—A quiet, gentle woman of forty, with dark, fading beauty and hair neatly bound. She wears a dull crimson robe.

SAPPHIRA—A beautiful, dark-haired, dark-eyed girl of eighteen, with unbound hair. She wears a bright-colored orange robe.

LAZAR—A great, black-haired, black-bearded, middle-aged man, wearing a red and yellow tunic, with a knife thrust into the belt, and a pouch hanging from the belt.

PHILIP—A beardless lad of twenty, resembling his father. Like his father, he is strong, assured, knowing, and free-speaking. He wears a brightly striped tunic.

STRANGER—A tall, thin, dark, bearded man in his late thirties, gaunt and emaciated. He wears a worn brown robe, and around his waist a much-spliced and frayed girdle of rope, from which is suspended a great leather wallet.

PROPERTIES

For Dorcas, hand carder and bunch of raw wool. For Sapphira, small jug, round loaf of bread, three large earthenware cups, two small moulds of cheese in a dish, bowl of dates. For Lazar, knife, pouch. For Stranger, thirty silver coins in leather wallet, the coins being metal washers the size of a half dollar, covered with tinfoil; or bottle caps, hammered flat, may be substituted for the washers and covered with tinfoil.

NOTE.—A wool carder is a kind of crude wooden comb with wide teeth projecting from a very wide ridge. It may be made of beaverboard, thin wood, or several pieces of cardboard pasted together. A piece of the board twelve inches square should be notched along one side with a row of twelve wide teeth, each about two inches long, one tooth to each inch of linear measurement. At the end opposite the teeth, a handle five inches long and two inches wide should be cut out and rounded off, leaving a ridge about five inches wide between the teeth and the handle. If raw wool is unobtainable, a good substitute for it is a two-foot piece of new hemp rope unraveled at one end. Several two-foot lengths tied together at one end and unraveled at the other will look like raw wool across the footlights. Or a long, thick piece of cotton batting may be used, with pieces of twine tied tightly around it at top and bottom and at intervals of six inches in between.

STORM EFFECTS

In the thunderstorm scene, the effect of lightning may be secured by flashing the house lights rapidly on and off. Thunder may be produced by beating a bass drum with a rolling noise or by means of a thunder sheet, a piece of sheet iron suspended by one end and shaken at the free end, or by sinking a vacuum cleaner in an ashcan, covering it with the lid, and turning on the electricity. Wind for the storm may be simulated by having a shrill whistle blown and letting the sound die away gradually.

STAGE DIRECTIONS

Up stage means away from footlights; *down stage,* near footlights. In the use of *right* and *left,* the actor is supposed to be facing the audience.

THE SILVERED ROPE

SCENE: *The living room of* LAZAR's *home, a plain cottage with rough, whitewashed walls. It has two doors: one in center of left wall leading outdoors, and a smaller door a little up right, leading to the rear of the house. Two small, deep-set windows are at right and left of left-hand door respectively. Against the wall down right stands a crudely made bench. Down left is a rough plank table crudely made, around which are gathered three three-legged stools, of the same rough workmanship. A jug and several rough drinking cups are on the table. A small, bright-colored rug lies on the floor up center, with a large water jug beside it. On a nail in the wall up center hangs a coil of new rope about ten feet long, neatly looped. Two shepherd's crooks stand in the upper right-hand corner. As it is about the time of twilight on the first Good Friday, orange and rose bulbs predominate in the stage lights, which are much subdued and keep growing dimmer throughout the play until, near the end, the lights are almost extinguished, leaving the stage in semi-darkness for the thunderstorm. After the storm, the former dimmed lighting prevails until the end.*

At rise of curtain, DORCAS *is seated on the bench carding a pile of wool in her lap with a hand carder, while* SAPPHIRA *is leaning against the door jamb of the left door, gazing off left.*

DORCAS. Seest thou thy father?
SAPPHIRA. Nay.
DORCAS. Eventide is close upon us, and thy father and thy brother are not returned from the city.
SAPPHIRA. Crowded is the city road and black with people

and beasts. (*Turning to* DORCAS.) Mother, is it not time for food?

DORCAS. We wait on their returning ere we break the bread.

SAPPHIRA. But hold! Even now I discern them. Pressed out from the crowd, they come this way.

DORCAS (*rises and places wool and carder on bench*). Fetch ye then the wine and bread. Hungry are they, and have great thirst.

SAPPHIRA (*as she moves to right door*). I pray this day was profitable, else my father find the food sore lacking. (*Exit at right.*)

(DORCAS *takes jug and cups from table and places them on bench.*)

DORCAS (*calling to off right*). Make haste. They come— our men.

Enter SAPPHIRA *at right, carrying a smaller jug, presumably containing wine, a round loaf of bread, and two large earthenware cups. These she places on table with* DORCAS' *help.*

SAPPHIRA (*a little sullenly*). 'Tis done.

DORCAS. The new cheese, this morning made. Hasten!

As SAPPHIRA *hurries off at right,* LAZAR *and* PHILIP *enter at left.*

LAZAR. How now, wife?

PHILIP (*in greeting*). My mother.

DORCAS. The board is spread.

SAPPHIRA *enters at right, carrying a cheese in a dish.*

SAPPHIRA. Ye delayed. We feared for you.

(LAZAR *moves up stage, holding out his hands.* DORCAS

lifts jug from the floor up center and allows a trickle of water to run over his hands. He seats himself at table while PHILIP *holds out his hands for water, and* DORCAS *pours it.*)

LAZAR. Jerusalem did hold more excitement to-day than e'er saw I before. (*Pours wine from smaller jug into cups.*)

PHILIP (*sitting at table*). Aye.

SAPPHIRA (*as she arranges food and dishes on table*). But why? Hast not heard, nor hast seen?

LAZAR. Hast not heard, nor hast seen?

DORCAS. Always to wait to hear is the lot of women.

LAZAR (*as he and* PHILIP *break off pieces of bread and eat and drink*). This day have they crucified the half-mad poet-teacher, who was called Jesus.

SAPPHIRA (*turning away*). Oh, wicked shame that they turned beasts and did this thing! (*Sits on bench.*)

PHILIP (*eating*). What carest thou? His death was just, methinks.

LAZAR (*musingly*). Why is it that women always have sympathy for any queer dreamer who comes with strange doctrine?

DORCAS. And why is it that men can turn wolves and slay one who is gentle and good, just because the words from his mouth are not like unto those that spill from the mouths of camel drivers? (*She goes to window and stands with elbow on ledge, looking out.*)

LAZAR (*smiles good-naturedly and nods knowingly at his son*). Aha! Methinks, son, that thy mother, though she only heard this wand'ring, mad poet but once, was coming under his spell. 'Tis strange the way he had with women!

(*During the pause that follows,* SAPPHIRA *picks up the wool and carder and cards the wool.*)

DORCAS (*shading her eyes as she looks off left*). A stranger comes down the road toward our house.

PHILIP. A neighbor come to sit awhile and muse with my father.

LAZAR (*pushing the food away and leaning back from the table*). Aye. To muse on the crucifixion. (*Pauses a moment.*) What fools people may make of themselves! Simon of Cyrene, whom oft I met in Jerusalem taking goats to market, followed the throng. And when this Jesus did stumble to the ground, Simon allowed the soldiers to place the cross on his own shoulders. He did carry it a great distance. I saw him afterwards. He sat by the roadside sore weeping, whilst a manservant picked a broken splinter from his shoulder.

SAPPHIRA (*clearly*). Blest be this Simon of whom you speak.

DORCAS. No neighbor is this who arrives. (PHILIP *hurries to the window and looks over his mother's shoulder.*) A stranger stands on our threshold.

PHILIP. An odd-looking man with matted beard and tattered tunic.

LAZAR. Bid him enter.

PHILIP *throws open left door.* SAPPHIRA *rises and stands near right door. Enter* STRANGER *at left. He looks terrified and breathes heavily as though he had been pursued. The family look at him, half frightened and half glad. The* STRANGER *looks at each one questioningly. Then he speaks in a low and musical voice.*

STRANGER. Ah, good man and family, I am a traveler who has grown weary and hungry. Wilt allow me to rest here? (*Fingers his wallet nervously as he talks.*)

LAZAR. Welcome, thrice welcome, stranger. All there is in this poor place is thine. Come, wife; fix a place that this stranger may eat and rest.

SAPPHIRA *slips off at right and returns at once with another cup, more cheese, and a bowl of dates.* DORCAS *clears a place at the table. The* STRANGER *sits at left of table.* LAZAR *sits behind table, and* PHILIP *stands behind his father.* DORCAS *stands off to one side waiting to serve. When* SAP-

PHIRA *returns and places the food on the table, she stands near right door.*

STRANGER (*nervously fingering his wallet*). Ah, good folk, ye are indeed kind. I could not have gone much farther.

PHILIP. From whence comest thou?

STRANGER. Jerusalem. (*He shudders.*)

LAZAR (*pouring wine into his cup*). Aha! And why comest thou to this quiet neighborhood when in Jerusalem is much going on, this day?

STRANGER. Ah, I look on Jerusalem only with loathing.

DORCAS. Who would not despise Jerusalem now after what was done there this day?

STRANGER (*spills the wine he is trying to drink*). Dost know, then, what happened there this day?

LAZAR. Yea. I had gone there to market goats; and would I had gone another day. The buyers were too many away from the stalls, trailing behind a mob to see a vagabond carpenter nailed to a beam.

STRANGER (*shudders and nervously fingers his pouch*). My friend, didst ever hear the words of this carpenter?

LAZAR. Nay.

DORCAS. I did, and his voice was as water running over the pebbles of a clear stream when one thirsts. He told a parable. I was charmed by the lesson he gave. (*Pauses.*) I feel a great loss has come to me. The world has gone gray because a light which shone there has been snuffed.

LAZAR. See, stranger, how a head may be turned by a few jeweled words chanted by a roadside?

STRANGER (*sadly*). Ah, well I know how she listened and was held in deep thrall. I, too, have oft heard him. And would I might again! I am in great torment, and he could comfort me, were he but here again.

PHILIP. Oho! So thou, too, stranger, art one who has fallen under his spell?

STRANGER. I once followed his teachings. (*Pauses.*) Now here am I, miserable and lonely. No more may I harken to the cadence of his voice. (*Sighs.*) Ah, friends, question me not, but only believe one who now knows misery because he had not enough faith in songs and dreams—because he thought the stuff of earth was greater than soul need.

LAZAR (*suspiciously*). Even thou speakest in the manner of a poet. But thou art welcome under my roof for a brief resting place, stranger. I like not those who use silken poet words. But thou seemest an honest fellow, so I will overlook the fact that thou hast been listening to idle talk; and again I say to thee, "Welcome!"

(*The* STRANGER *pays no attention to* LAZAR, *but half rises from his chair and fastens his eyes on the rope hanging on the wall.*)

PHILIP. Stranger, I notice that thou hast looked at the coil of rope on yonder pin. Why doth it claim thine interest?

STRANGER (*disturbed, sits down, ill at ease*). Ah, I know not why except (*furtively*) I need a new girdle. I think my pouch should be more tightly bound about its mouth with a bit of stronger cord.

PHILIP. If thy wallet holds gold or silver, surely should it more be tightly bound. There are thieves hereabouts, and one should guard one's wealth.

STRANGER (*sadly, staring at rope again*). Ah 'tis no doubt true. Still, what is silver?

LAZAR. Many would think otherwise.

STRANGER. I have thirty pieces of silver, but I have no rest or contentment.

LAZAR. Well, if that strand of rope seems to be of some worth to thee, and thy silver so irksome, mayhap we can help thee. Stranger, how much for this length of rope?

(*The* STRANGER *shudders, pauses, hangs his head, then gestures toward the rope.*)

STRANGER. Take it down, that I may see its length.

(PHILIP *takes rope from nail and uncoils it. He whips*

it out and causes it to wriggle about the floor like a snake.)

LAZAR. See! A fine rope of pure hemp, which I used but the once—new, strong, and clean. How much for a girdle length of it?

STRANGER (*impulsively*). Ten pieces of silver. It is too much, but I will gladly give it.

LAZAR. Done! (*The* STRANGER *nervously removes his old girdle, while* LAZAR *cuts rope into two pieces with knife which he takes from his belt.* STRANGER *opens wallet and counts out ten pieces of silver, which he hands to* LAZAR. *He puts the new girdle about his waist and ties the other piece of rope about his wallet.* LAZAR *puts the silver in his pouch.*) That was a good bargain for thee.

STRANGER. Yea. I fear I have more use for rope than for money.

(*Meanwhile* DORCAS *and* SAPPHIRA *are seated on bench, listening.*)

LAZAR. Thou art strange. Thy words are poet words. True, thou lookest not too well with thy torn robe. But I wonder, couldst not be a man who has seen better days?

STRANGER (*sadly*). Aye, aye. Better days have I seen indeed.

LAZAR. Of course thou hast said naught of thy calling. But it is evident that thou art a man of some learning, perhaps a teacher; not a soil tiller.

STRANGER. Not a teacher but one taught by a great teacher. I love these slopes, yet I cannot remain here. There is no spot where I can fare and be at peace. The world, great as it is, cannot hold a tortured spirit like mine. I am not to know such a thing as happiness again.

LAZAR (*confidentially, to* PHILIP). Hark, hark to the man! What a play of words! What strange hint of tragedy in his talk! Listen well, Philip; 'tis good that a lad hear such jeweled words.

PHILIP (*contemptuously*). Words! What are they?

STRANGER. And now, my friends, I must be on my way.

It is not well for me to tarry too long in one spot.   My thanks to you all.

(*He bows low to each one.   All bow low in return, the women rising from the bench.   He moves toward left door.*)

LAZAR.   A safe journey, poet-stranger.   We are charmed by thy words and mystified about thee.   May the roadway be clear this night, for darkness will soon come upon thee. May thy words charm others on the morrow as they have charmed us.   A good journey to thee.

(*The* STRANGER *is at left door.   Unexpectedly his manner becomes animated.   He hurriedly unfastens the rope which ties his wallet to his girdle.   With trembling hands he holds out the wallet.*)

STRANGER.   I still have twenty pieces of silver left in this wallet.   It grows dark.   I can journey no further.   Thou art crowded and have no room for guests.   I saw a great cypress near to thine house.   Here, take the twenty pieces of silver. Allow me to rest under this great tree.   Is it well?   Wilt do it?

(LAZAR *and* PHILIP *exchange glances.   They are pleased with the offer but craftily dissemble.*)

PHILIP.   Oh, well, the price is not great; but if it is all thou hast, we will take it.   We have been glad to listen to thy talk and hence do not want to quibble.

(*He holds out his hands.   The* STRANGER *pours the silver into them.*)

STRANGER.   Now thou hast all the coins that have burned and burned like a living fire.
DORCAS.   Stranger, wouldst thou have a rug for thy bed under the cypress?
STRANGER.   Nay.   The dark wind shall wrap my body, and the softness of the night mists shall be enough.

SAPPHIRA. Ere thou goest forth, stranger, give us the gift of thy name.

STRANGER (*after a pause*). Judas Iscariot. (*Exit at left.*)

LAZAR. Of all the strange vagabonds that have come this way, this man is strangest. Did the fool not realize that the silver he gave us would buy rope enough to girdle him an hundred times? Did he not also realize that gladly would we let him sleep under the cypress without price?

DORCAS. His name should be full of portent, placed by the side of his manner. Yet I only recall him as a stranger.

PHILIP (*fondling money*). Would some conscience-crazed poet passed this way each blessed day!

SAPPHIRA. I wonder what this stranger is now doing? Did he, after all, lie under the great tree?

LAZAR. What concerneth me is whether this stranger hath yet more silver. (*Pauses.*) Sapphira, thou art young. Words from thee will fall soft on the stranger's ear. Go thou to the cypress tree and ask him if he would purchase dates to take on his journey.

(SAPPHIRA *goes to doorway at left and is about to exit. Suddenly she stops, puts her hand to her mouth, and stifles a scream.*)

DORCAS. What spell hath clutched the world to-day?

(SAPPHIRA *frantically clutches the door post and tries to support herself. Her knees give way, and she starts to sink to the floor.*)

LAZAR. Speak! Speak!

PHILIP. What now, my sister?

SAPPHIRA. There—under the cypress tree. The stranger! He hangs!

(*She sinks to the floor. The other three rush to left door and look off left.*)

DORCAS (*screams*). I can see plainly from here. His face is horrible!

(*She lifts* SAPPHIRA *and, both supporting each other and sobbing quietly, they exeunt at right.* LAZAR *and* PHILIP *stare off left.*)

PHILIP. His body hangs by the rope his silver bought! (*Shudders.*)

LAZAR (*fearfully*). Go quickly, Philip. Cut the body down, lest it attract vultures. (*The stage suddenly grows dark.*) Give me the silver. Let me hide it.

There is a flash of lightning, followed by the roar of wind. LAZAR *is seen hiding the silver beneath the rug. It grows darker. Terrific lightning flashes, followed by thunder. The two women run on at right, screaming. The lightning flashes reveal all the family huddled in a corner.*

PHILIP. I cannot go to the cypress tree.

(*There is a terrific roar, followed by a loud crash, then a lull. During the lull,* LAZAR *screams.*)

LAZAR. Take the accursed silver, Philip, and cast it out the door.

(PHILIP *gets silver from under rug and throws it off left. Immediately the storm stops, the light grows brighter, and the darkness disappears.*)

PHILIP (*standing in doorway and looking off left*). Look, father! The great tree has been leveled to the earth by the storm. I can see the brown tunic of the stranger showing through the twisted branches.

LAZAR (*coming down stage and speaking with dignity*) Son, go dig a clean grave near the clump of olive trees. He shall have a good burial. He was a strange man, and I understood him not. But yet he had flaming power. Mayhap it was because somewhere, sometime, he had talked with prophets. I know not. But he shall have a clean grave in my own burial lot. Go, Philip. Go quickly. I shall follow soon and aid thee.

(*Exit* PHILIP *at left, with bowed head.*)

CURTAIN

OUT OF THE DARKNESS

A BIBLICAL DRAMA IN ONE ACT

By

JOHN McGREEVEY

PRODUCTION RIGHTS

Copies of this play are available in single pamphlet form. The right to produce this play by one group of amateur players is authorized only by the purchase of seven copies (one copy for each speaking part) at the current price of 50c each.

It is dishonest and illegal to copy parts.

CAST OF CHARACTERS

((For three women, four men, and extras)

BERNICE—An old woman with a gossipy tongue and an untiring interest in other people's lives.

URIAS—A former high priest of the Jews; now a suspicious, unhappy old man seeking to justify his hypocrisy.

DRUSILLA—A lovely woman in her middle forties. She is the completely devoted wife and mother, sharing her affection with Titus and Cornelius.

RUTH—A charming and unspoiled girl of seventeen or eighteen. She is very sincere and straightforward and much in love with . . .

TITUS—A blind boy of nineteen. The son of Drusilla and Cornelius, he is not tainted with bitterness and is only bewildered by the strange behavior of . . .

CORNELIUS—A former Roman soldier, who carries a secret with him always . . . a dark secret that has destroyed his hope for happiness.

SILAS—A follower of the Nazarene and disciple of Paul. About the same age as Cornelius, he is gentle, reverent and above all, humble.

Townspeople, Followers of Silas, Etc.

PLACE

The garden of Cornelius' home in Bethsaida, near the Sea of Galilee.

TIME

A spring morning in the year 54 A.D.

PROLOGUE

(To Be Spoken or Read before the Curtain)

From the Book of St. Matthew, Chapter 28, Verses 11 to 15. Now, when they were going, behold, some of the Guard came into the city, and showed unto the High Priests all the things that were done. And when they were assembled with the elders and had taken counsel, they gave much money to the soldiers.

Saying, say ye that His disciples came by night and stole Him away while we slept. And if this comes to the Governor's ears, we will persuade him and secure you. So, they took the money and did as they were taught; and this saying is commonly reported among the Jews, until this day.

OUT OF THE DARKNESS

SCENE: *The courtyard of a prosperous home in Bethsaida by the Sea of Galilee. The year is 54 A.D. A gate, which leads to the street, is set in the downstage Right wall. From the gate the wall slants Left upstage to the house door which is up Left. The Left wall is perpendicular to the audience. Up Right, not far from the gate is a large fig tree, and beneath it, a rustic bench. Down Left is a long table, with benches on either side. Centered in the upper Left wall of the house is a door.*

AT THE RISE OF THE CURTAIN: *It is early morning, the first day of the week, after the Feast of the Passover. For a moment the stage is deserted. Then there is a vigorous knocking at the gate at Right. A pause, and then as the knocking is repeated,* BERNICE *enters from the house and crosses to the gate. She is an old woman in her seventies. She walks with difficulty, but her mind and tongue are always active, and she thrives on morsels from other people's lives. Her voice is shrill and excitable. She is muttering incoherently as she hobbles across the stage and opens the gate.*

URIAS *(Offstage at Right.)* Good morning, good morning! Is your master in, old woman?

BERNICE *(Moving toward Center, haughtily.)* If you mean Cornelius, he's not my master but my nephew, and he is *not* here, old man.

URIAS *(Following her onstage. He is a former High Priest of the Jews — crafty and quick-witted. For years he has plotted and schemed to keep himself in favor with the people and the Romans. Now he is an old man, entering his dotage, and fears and misgivings assail him. He finds himself constantly compelled to justify his past mis-deeds. At the moment he is visibly nervous. His old hands tremble and his eyes dart worriedly about the court-yard.)* A thousand pardons. I spoke in haste. Your forgiveness.

BERNICE *(Sharply.)* You are too old a man to be hasty in your speech.

URIAS. It is only that in my anxiety to speak with your nephew . . .

BERNICE. And *he* is anxious to speak with no one.

URIAS. Is he ill?

BERNICE. He has been a sick man for twenty years and more.

URIAS *(Coming closer to her at Center.)* What do you mean by that?

BERNICE *(Slowly.)* With his sudden wealth came unhappiness.

URIAS *(Quickly.)* It is often so. But, if I could see him now . . .

BERNICE. I have told you he is not here.

URIAS *(Apprehensively.)* Gone from Bethsaida?

BERNICE. No. He walks by the sea. Night and day, for twenty years and more, he walks and stares out across the Sea of Galilee.

URIAS. And that is where he has gone this morning?

BERNICE. I suppose, though we never question him. His temper is quick.

URIAS. Perhaps if I went down to the shore, I might meet him?

BERNICE *(Indifferently, moving Left.)* Perhaps.

DRUSILLA *(From the house at Left.)* Bernice — who was it?

BERNICE *(At the table down Left.)* A man to see Cornelius.

URIAS *(Looking toward the house.)* His wife?

BERNICE *(Nods.)* My niece, and a woman with a great heart to have stayed with him in all this.

DRUSILLA *(Appears in the house door. She is a lovely woman in her middle forties. She is completely, devoted to her husband and son. A woman of intuition rather than conviction, she is at times frightened by her Roman husband.)* A man? What man, Bernice?

URIAS *(Moving up toward DRUSILLA.)* Urias is my name. I need to speak with Cornelius the Centurion.

DRUSILLA *(Moving down toward Center to meet URIAS.)* My husband is not well. He suffers greatly at this time. I — I couldn't tell you when you might see him.

URIAS *(Prying.)* Why is he grief-stricken? Illness in the family, perhaps?

DRUSILLA *(Tiredly.)* No new illness.

BERNICE. But an old one that lingers.

URIAS. I don't understand.

BERNICE *(Sharply.)* And why should you? It's no concern of yours.

DRUSILLA. Gently, Bernice.

URIAS. Perhaps I have more reason to be concerned than you think.

DRUSILLA. There is an inn where this street meets the sea. Sometimes my husband goes there at times like this.

URIAS. I know the place. I'll look for him there. *(Starts to Right.)*

DRUSILLA *(Following URIAS.)* He is not a well man. You don't mean to trouble him further?

URIAS. Only to give him a word of warning. *(He is at the gate.)*

DRUSILLA *(Worriedly.)* A warning?

URIAS *(Opening the gate.)* To save himself and all of us new trouble. You've both been very kind. Good morning to you. *(He exits Right.)*

DRUSILLA *(Stands at the gate, looking after URIAS for*

a moment.) That man, Bernice. His face — I know that face . . .

BERNICE *(Moving toward Center.)* Of course. He was one of the high priests in Jerusalem who gave Cornelius the money that morning.

DRUSILLA *(Back toward* BERNICE.*)* Bernice — don't!

BERNICE *(Laughing shortly.)* Don't speak that which we all think?

DRUSILLA *(Tiredly.)* It doesn't help to speak of it.

BERNICE. And it doesn't help *not* to speak of it; or if it does, why can't Cornelius sleep? Why does he wander like a madman along the seashore?

DRUSILLA *(Wearily.)* If only a thing could be finished — forgotten. But, no. The memory of the deed must live with us forever.

BERNICE. Each year as the Passover draws close I've seen this happen.

DRUSILLA. And this year it's so much worse because *they* are preaching here.

BERNICE. His followers. You hear them on every side.

DRUSILLA. It's a torment for Cornelius. He feels that he must argue with them — shout them down.

BERNICE. He argues only with himself — trying to shout down memories.

DRUSILLA *(Crosses to the table down Left.)* Perhaps you're right. I don't know, Bernice. I know nothing except that I'm tired of living in that shadow.

BERNICE *(Following her.)* And now this high priest comes here to make new trouble.

DRUSILLA *(Sitting tiredly.)* Just twenty years ago this morning Cornelius came home to me . . . *(She shakes her head at the memory.)*

BERNICE *(Nods.)* Well do I remember — and there's been unhappiness ever since! *(Sighs.)* Will they be eating here this morning?

DRUSILLA. I don't know. Titus has gone with Ruth.

BERNICE. That girl! She's not for a boy like Titus.

DRUSILLA. She loves him. She understands him.

BERNICE. Her people have nothing.

DRUSILLA. They have no money. There are other things.

BERNICE. So you and I are left alone in the house!

DRUSILLA. You and I, Bernice — and I have no hunger for food.

BERNICE. Well, I have. I'm done with fasting. (TITUS *and* RUTH *are heard off Right, laughing and talking.)*

DRUSILLA *(Rising.)* I think that's Titus I hear now.

BERNICE. And Ruth with him! *(Going to the house door.)* I'll start the meal.

TITUS *(As the gate swings open.)* Home already, Ruth? I can hardly believe it.

RUTH *(Off Right.)* Time goes too quickly when we're together.

DRUSILLA *(Calling to them.)* You were out early this morning, children.

TITUS *(Enters through the gate. He is a handsome young man of nineteen. His voice, his manner, his outlook give no clue to the fact that he is blind. There isn't a single grain of bitterness in his attitude. He holds* RUTH's *arm as he comes through the gate.)* What a morning it is, Mother!

RUTH *(Leading* TITUS. *She is a girl of seventeen whose beauty is not external, but from within. She deeply loves* TITUS *and is willing to build her life on his. There is no martyrdom in her love and no pity for* TITUS' *blindness.)* We've been to the marketplace.

DRUSILLA. Bernice is preparing the morning meal. You must break your fast with us, Ruth.

RUTH *(As she leads* TITUS *to Center.)* I shouldn't. My mother . . .

DRUSILLA. She won't mind.

TITUS. And I *want* you to stay. I want you to help me tell Mother what we heard in the marketplace.

DRUSILLA *(Taking his arm and helping him sit at the table.)* Sit down and rest, son. That's a long walk before you've broken your fast.

RUTH. It's my fault. I've been telling him of these men . . .

TITUS *(Excitedly.)* And so I made her promise to let me hear them.

DRUSILLA. What men is it you've listened to?

RUTH. The one is named Paul.

DRUSILLA *(Sharply.)* Paul! You mean he who *was* Saul of Tarsus?

RUTH. Yes. That was before his conversion.

DRUSILLA. But — he is a follower of the Nazarene.

TITUS. Of course, Mother! And when he speaks, it's as though you heard Jesus of Nazareth Himself.

DRUSILLA *(Crossing to Right, attempting to hide her agitation.)* Is this the first time you have gone to listen to this man?

TITUS. Yes, but it won't be the last.

DRUSILLA *(Looking away.)* Titus — your father doesn't believe . . .

TITUS. Father has never heard Paul — or Silas.

DRUSILLA. You know your father is very much opposed to those who follow the Nazarene.

RUTH. I hope that I haven't caused trouble.

DRUSILLA *(Quickly moving back toward them.)* No. Of course not. It's just that — well — right now, Titus, I wouldn't mention these men to your father.

TITUS. Father is out?

DRUSILLA. Yes. He went out early.

TITUS. Mother, you and father were living in Jerusalem then, weren't you?

DRUSILLA. Then? What do you mean?

RUTH. He means when Jesus was alive.

TITUS. Father never talks about it, but he was stationed in Jerusalem then I know. Aunt Bernice told me.

DRUSILLA. Your father was a centurion in the Roman garrison there.

TITUS *(Excitedly.)* And did you know Jesus?

DRUSILLA. No. And you must never mention that name to your father.

TITUS. But why? If Father didn't know Him . . .

DRUSILLA. Don't ask me "why," Titus. Just don't mention the Nazarene in this house ever.

TITUS. But after hearing Paul and his friend Silas today, I've been thinking, Mother.

RUTH. Titus, your mother is upset. Tell her later.

DRUSILLA. Thinking what, Titus?

TITUS *(Boldly.)* That I might like to go with them.

DRUSILLA. Go with them! You — you mean — be a follower of — of the Nazarene?

TITUS. The things they said, Mother! His teachings — things I've always felt but could never put into words. *(Remembering.)* Blessed are the poor in spirit: for theirs is the Kingdom of Heaven. And, blessed are the pure in heart: for they shall see God. (BERNICE *enters from the house door, carrying two dishes. She stops as she hears* TITUS *and* RUTH *and listens warily.)*

RUTH *(Softly.)* Blessed are the merciful: for they shall obtain mercy.

TITUS. And, blessed are they that suffer persecution for justice' sake: for theirs is the Kingdom of Heaven.

DRUSILLA *(Forcing a smile.)* Words — lovely words — but, Titus . . .

TITUS. No, Mother. More than that. Words that are the keys to love for one another.

BERNICE *(Suddenly speaking out.)* You've been listening to those that preach the gospel of the Nazarene.

TITUS *(Turning toward the sound of her voice.)* Bernice?

BERNICE *(Coming down to the table with the dishes.)* That's where this girl has taken him, Drusilla.

174

RUTH. He asked to go.

BERNICE. Because the idea was put in his mind.

DRUSILLA. Peace, peace. He has gone, and he has listened.

TITUS. And I've learned, Mother. I learned more in one hour listening to Silas than in all these nineteen dark years.

BERNICE. Silas! Yes. He and his friend Paul are the rabble rousers.

RUTH *(Defiantly.)* Not rabble rousers. They merely preach the truth, and those who wish may listen.

BERNICE. The truth! No one but prophets and fools seek the truth!

DRUSILLA. Is the meal ready?

BERNICE *(Not to be diverted.)* Titus has too much idle time. He should be given work to do with his hands. I know a blind man in Capernaum who does marvelous work with leather.

DRUSILLA *(Sharply.)* Bernice!

BERNICE *(Moving toward the house door.)* I know, I know. My advice isn't wanted. But you'll see. Such visits to the marketplace will mean more sorrow for this house. *(She exits into the house.)* More unhappiness . . .

RUTH *(Going to* DRUSILLA.*)* I'm sorry, I didn't think . . .

DRUSILLA. Bernice is an old woman, Ruth. She says much she doesn't mean.

TITUS *(Rising with some difficulty.)* And whatever she meant, Ruth, I'll never forget this morning.

DRUSILLA. Be careful, son.

TITUS. Yes. *(Feeling his way back to the bench.)* I must *always* be careful. Perhaps they wouldn't want me. I'm so helpless.

DRUSILLA *(Crossing past* RUTH *and putting her hand on* TITUS' *shoulder.)* It would be no life for you. They must travel always — with no home . . .

TITUS. The earth is their home.

DRUSILLA It's exciting to listen, but listening day after day and the excitement wears off.

TITUS. I would never lose my enthusiasm for Him and what He said. Think of it, Mother. You and Father lived in Jerusalem when He was there — walking in the streets — speaking in the Temple. And yet you never heard Him.

DRUSILLA *(Slowly.)* No. I never heard Him.

TITUS. And Father?

DRUSILLA. I don't know, and you mustn't ask him.

TITUS. Twenty years ago they killed Him, and yet He's only now beginning to live. *(Softly.)* I should say they *tried* to kill Him.

RUTH. They crucified Him, but He rose from the dead.

DRUSILLA. So his followers said.

BERNICE *(Re-entering from the house.)* The meal is ready for those who have time for simple food. *(Puts two more dishes on the table.)*

RUTH *(Moving toward the gate.)* I'd better go. I'll come back later, Titus.

TITUS. You won't forget? There's so much for us to talk about, Ruth.

RUTH *(Softly.)* No, Titus. I won't forget. *(She goes.)*

DRUSILLA *(Helping TITUS to face the table.)* Ruth is a fine girl, Titus.

TITUS *(Simply.)* I love her very much.

DRUSILLA. But she has strange ways.

BERNICE *(Serving from the dishes.)* Brazen ways. Taking Titus to the marketplace to listen to those men.

TITUS. Aunt Bernice, Ruth took me only because I begged her to. She tried to tell me what the men said, but she confused them — and so, I made her promise to take me that I might hear for myself.

DRUSILLA. You must never go again.

TITUS. But why? I'm almost twenty, Mother. There's

little for me here. To go out and hear such things makes life seem a little closer to me.

DRUSILLA. I can't tell you why, Titus. I can only beg you if you have any love for me or respect for your father not to go there again. Forget what you heard today. There's no happiness in it.

TITUS. Forget what Silas said about Jesus? Mother — you don't meant that.

BERNICE *(Sitting.)* Cornelius should tell the boy. It's time he knew.

DRUSILLA. Be quiet, Bernice. That is for Cornelius to say.

TITUS. Tell me what, Mother? What is it I should be told?

CORNELIUS *(Off Right.)* Titus! Titus!

DRUSILLA. It's your father.

BERNICE. And in a nice temper by the sound of him.

CORNELIUS *(Enters through the gate, Right. He is a well-built man of fifty. He carries himself well, a hangover from his military training. But he moves like a man with a weight on his shoulders. His once handsome face is pale and drawn and he looks old beyond his years. As he enters the garden, he is greatly agitated.)* Titus!

TITUS *(Standing with some difficulty.)* Yes, Father?

DRUSILLA *(Crossing toward* CORNELIUS.*)* Cornelius — what is it?

CORNELIUS *(Brushing his wife aside and going to the boy.)* Titus, were you in the marketplace this morning?

TITUS *(Bewildered.)* Yes, Father. I went with Ruth.

BERNICE. That brazen girl!

CORNELIUS *(Taking* TITUS' *arm roughly.)* What were you doing there?

DRUSILLA *(Coming to her husband's side.)* Cornelius— you're upset. You don't know what you're saying.

CORNELIUS *(Shaking* TITUS.*)* Tell me — what were you doing? Were you listening to those liars? Answer me!

TITUS (*Frightened and bewildered.*) Father, what is it? What have I done?

DRUSILLA (*Sharply.*) Cornelius! You're hurting him. Stop it. (*Louder.*) Stop it.

CORNELIUS (*Dazedly.*) I — I'm sorry. (*Releases the boy.*) Titus — I didn't mean to . . .

TITUS: I only went with Ruth, Father. I didn't mean any harm.

CORNELIUS (*Crossing to Right.*) No peace. Never any peace. It wasn't enough that my only son was born blind! Now they're poisoning his mind.

DRUSILLA (*Following him.*) Cornelius! Not in front of Bernice and the boy!

TITUS. No one is poisoning my mind, Father.

CORNELIUS. It's the money. Why did I ever take the money?

DRUSILLA. Did the high priest find you?

CORNELIUS (*Turning quickly, frightened.*) High priest? What high priest?

BERNICE. An old man — he said his name was Urias.

CORNELIUS Urias! What does he want?

BERNICE. He said he wanted to warn you.

CORNELIUS (*Distractedly.*) They're bringing it all back again. First that Paul and his rabble shouting in the marketplace — and now Urias — like a skeleton from the grave.

DRUSILLA (*Taking his arm.*) You're trembling. Sit down, Cornelius. I'll bring you a little wine. Here . . . (*She takes him to the bench under the tree.*)

CORNELIUS (*As he sits, looks up at her brokenly.*) You've been a good wife to me, Drusilla, and I've given you nothing but sorrow.

DRUSILLA. I'll be back with the wine in just a minute. (*Crossing to* TITUS.) Come with me, son.

TITUS (*Uncertainly.*) If — if Father thinks that I . . .

178

DRUSILLA *(With gentle firmness, taking his arm.)* Come with me.

TITUS *(As they move up to the house door.)* I didn't think Father would mind.

DRUSILLA *(Softly, as they enter the house.)* Your father isn't well, Titus. *(Pause.)*

BERNICE *(Coming Right.)* It was just twenty years ago this morning, wasn't it, Cornelius.

CORNELIUS *(Dreamily.)* Yes. Twenty years ago.

BERNICE. You came running in to the garden of our house in Jerusalem. Never have I seen a man so frightened!

CORNELIUS *(Only partially aware of her.)* It was like a dream that doesn't end but goes on and on and you keep telling yourself that it's only a dream — but you never wake up.

BERNICE *(Drawing closer to him.)* You were telling us — Drusilla and me — telling us of the wonderful thing that had happened, and then, they came — the high priest and his followers. They took you away, Cornelius — and when you came back, you said that you had made a mistake — that nothing you had told us was true.

CORNELIUS *(Rising in agitation.)* Lies! All of it was lies. They did steal His body. They did, they did, they did!

BERNICE. And then we left Jerusalem and moved here.

CORNELIUS *(Moving Right, aimlessly.)* Here to this forgotten corner of the earth where no one will listen to a madman if he happens to forget that he was well paid for silence.

BERNICE *(Following him.)* I always wondered, Cornelius. I always wondered what *did* happen that morning.

CORNELIUS. Who knows? It's been so long. I've told so many stories and heard so many.

BERNICE. But if what Paul and the others say is true ...

CORNELIUS *(Turning on her.)* Well, it *not* true. He was dead. Do you understand? Dead! I saw the body myself before the tomb was sealed. It was a trick. They did it. Peter and the others . . . *(Sinking back onto the bench.)* It *must* have been a trick.

BERNICE *(Slyly.)* Titus doesn't believe it was a trick.

CORNELIUS *(Coldly.)* What do you mean? What does Titus know about it?

BERNICE. You know where he was this morning. He admitted it.

CORNELIUS. He only went because of Ruth.

BERNICE. I heard him tell his mother he wanted to go with Paul and Silas.

CORNELIUS. No. I won't listen to you. You just want to torture me.

BERNICE. They've taken everything else away from you — your peace of mind, your future — your pride. Now, it's your son.

CORNELIUS *(Rising and moving toward the house.)* I won't listen to you. *(Calling.)* Drusilla — Drusilla.

BERNICE *(Following him.)* Oh, she'll shield the boy. But I heard them.

DRUSILLA *(In the doorway with a wine glass.)* I'm sorry I was so long . . .

CORNELIUS *(Going to DRUSILLA up Left.)* Bernice says that Titus means to go away.

DRUSILLA *(Looking at the old woman.)* Bernice . . .

CORNELIUS. Does he? She said he told you . . .

DRUSILLA. He mentioned it — but it's nothing.

CORNELIUS. It's everything!

DRUSILLA. Drink this wine, Cornelius. It will calm you.

BERNICE. There's no wine in the world to calm him.

CORNELIUS. He — he wants to go with Paul and Silas.

BERNICE. I heard him say it.

DRUSILLA. A boyish whim.

CORNELIUS. Surely it's enough that he was born blind. They won't take him away from us all together.

DRUSILLA *(Giving him the wine.)* Here. Drink this.

BERNICE *(Crossing Left to the house.)* I know what you're thinking, Drusilla. I told Cornelius because it's his right to know.

DRUSILLA *(Quietly.)* I've said nothing, Bernice. You reproach yourself.

BERNICE *(As she goes into the house.)* More grief for this house — more sorrow.

DRUSILLA *(Moving down Left away from Center.)* You mustn't let Bernice upset you. Her tongue finds occupation in gossip, but her brain has long been idle.

CORNELIUS. You're sure there's no danger?

DRUSILLA. None — unless you provoke him. He's young and impressionable. Life has given him little and in the words of the Nazarene he finds a legend that gives him strength he's never known.

CORNELIUS *(Away.)* Perhaps I should tell him.

DRUSILLA *(Moving back toward Center.)* What purpose would that serve?

CORNELIUS. I think he has a right to know.

DRUSILLA. Not now. Later, perhaps. You're in no mood to tell him calmly, reasonably — as you must.

CORNELIUS. You're right. But he must be told. *(Bitter laugh.)* It's the only legacy I have to leave him.

DRUSILLA *(Back to the table.)* The food is cold. I'll warm it for you and you must eat a little.

CORNELIUS. I'm not hungry.

DRUSILLA *(Taking two dishes from the table.)* We'll all eat a little together. The four of us. Just rest. I'll get the others. *(She exits through the house door.)*

CORNELIUS *(Stands down Right and stares for a long moment after his wife. Then he paces restlessly Left. There is a knocking at the gate. Whirling around, he calls.)* Who is it?

URIAS *(Off Right.)* Urias. I have come again looking for Cornelius the Centurion.

CORNELIUS *(Having crossed to the gate, hoarsely.)* What do you want with me?

URIAS *(Off Right.)* I must speak to you, Cornelius. At once. Open the gate.

CORNELIUS *(Opens the gate and* URIAS *enters.)* Can't you leave me in peace?

URIAS *(Crossing toward Center.)* I was here earlier, but you were out.

CORNELIUS *(Following him to Center.)* What is it? What new trouble? Or maybe you've come to observe the twentieth anniversary of our deceit.

URIAS. That is precisely the kind of talk you must stop.

CORNELIUS. Perhaps it would be better if I stopped talking altogether.

URIAS. You were well paid for your silence.

CORNELIUS. And I've earned every silver piece you gave me.

URIAS. These followers of His . . .

CORNELIUS. Paul and Silas?

URIAS. Yes. They know that you are here in Bethsaida.

CORNELIUS *(Panicky.)* Why should *they* know that? Why should they care that an obscure Roman centurion has retired with his family?

URIAS. They know that you were one of the guards at the tomb.

CORNELIUS. How could they know? Who told them?

URIAS. Who can say how these people know things? They do — and they intend to talk with you.

CORNELIUS *(Violently.)* No.

URIAS. They mean to make you deny your story.

CORNELIUS. They have no right to question me. I won't speak to them.

URIAS. Yes, you will. To refuse to see them is to admit your fear of them.

CORNELIUS. Urias, I can't. Haven't I suffered enough? Can't you spare me this final agony?

URIAS. You have only to say that your story is true.

CORNELIUS. They're coming here?

URIAS. So we are told and you must be ready for them. If you're clever, we can turn this trick of theirs in *our* favor.

CORNELIUS *(Wearily.)* How?

URIAS. A crowd will follow them here. When those people hear you tell your story, they'll be lost to the Nazarene forever.

CORNELIUS *(Stricken.)* A crowd — no — I — I can't face them.

URIAS *(Harshly.)* You must. There's too much at stake for you to weaken now. *(Taking a leather pouch from his robe.)* I've brought you more money . . .

CORNELIUS. I don't ask for money, Urias. Only a little peace.

URIAS. And you shall have it. Don't you see? This is your chance to silence all the doubts and misgivings forever?

CORNELIUS *(Back toward* URIAS.*)* You'll stay?

URIAS. I don't know — it — it might appear suspicious.

CORNELIUS. You must! I can't face them alone.

DRUSILLA *(In the house door.)* Cornelius — who is it? *(Coming onstage and seeing* URIAS.*)* Oh! I heard voices . . .

URIAS. I found your husband at last.

DRUSILLA *(Going to* CORNELIUS.*)* Cornelius! What is it? You look ill.

CORNELIUS. They're coming here — to our house.

DRUSILLA. Who is?

CORNELIUS. The followers of the Nazarene — Silas and the others.

DRUSILLA. But why? Why should they come here?

CORNELIUS. To question me.

DRUSILLA. No. We won't let them. They can't come in.

URIAS. They must.

DRUSILLA *(Back to* URIAS.*)* I knew when you came here this morning that there would be trouble, just as there has been every day of our lives since that morning you first came to our house in Jerusalem . . .

CORNELIUS. Drusilla . . .

URIAS. There'll be no trouble. Your husband simply silences these ridiculous rumors forever.

DRUSILLA. You and the others—with your money . . .

CORNELIUS. Don't listen to her!

DRUSILLA. And what has the money brought us? Unhappiness, fear, despair — and blindness for our son!

CORNELIUS *(Furiously.)* Don't say that! Do you hear me, woman? Don't ever say that.

DRUSILLA *(Goaded almost to hysteria.)* He was born blind. Why? Do you know why? *(Back to* URIAS.*)* Or maybe you do? Why was he born blind?

URIAS. It was the will of God.

DRUSILLA. It was a punishment — a punishment for our sin — our lie!

CORNELIUS. Stop! Stop! I won't listen.

DRUSILLA *(Pleading.)* Send them away, Cornelius. Don't talk to them. Let us have the raveled ends of our lives at least.

CORNELIUS *(Torn with indecision.)* I don't know. I don't know.

URIAS. He must see them. There's no choice.

RUTH *(Off Right, calling.)* Titus! Titus!

CORNELIUS *(Startled.)* Who's that?

DRUSILLA. It's Ruth.

RUTH *(Outside the gate.)* Titus — Titus, can you hear me?

DRUSILLA *(Going to the gate.)* Ruth, what's the matter? What's happened?

RUTH *(Excitedly, off Right.)* They're coming here. They're on their way here now.

DRUSILLA *(Opening the gate.)* What is it you're saying, Ruth?

RUTH *(Entering and crossing* DRUSILLA *toward Center.)* Where's Titus? I must tell him.

DRUSILLA *(Puzzled.)* He's in the house. Ruth, why are you so excited?

RUTH. Silas and the others are coming here.

URIAS *(Stepping down to her.)* How do you know this?

RUTH. Rachel told me. She heard them talking of it in the marketplace. Paul has crossed the sea to preach in Capernaum and Silas is to join him there — after he has talked with Cornelius the Centurion.

CORNELIUS. Why are they coming? Did Rachel hear?

RUTH. She didn't know — only that they were coming to the house of Cornelius the Centurion. Maybe they're going to help Titus.

DRUSILLA. Help Titus?

RUTH *(Simply.)* Make him see.

URIAS. Don't talk nonsense, child.

RUTH *(Very directly.)* There was once another blind man in Bethsaida and Jesus made him see.

TITUS *(Groping in the house door.)* Is that Ruth's voice?

RUTH *(Running to him.)* Titus, Titus! They're coming here — to your house — Silas and the others. Maybe they can help you.

TITUS *(As* RUTH *leads him downstage.)* Coming here— to this house?

RUTH. They're on the way· now. They'll be here any minute.

CORNELIUS *(Shakily.)* Titus, you're to go back in the house at once.

TITUS. You mean I'm not to be here when Silas . . . ?

CORNELIUS *(Abruptly.)* They aren't coming here to see you.

RUTH. Then *why* are they coming?

CORNELIUS. They're coming to question me.

DRUSILLA (*At his side.*) Cornelius, are you sure?

CORNELIUS (*To* TITUS.) Titus, when I was a Roman soldier stationed in Jerusalem, the year before you were born, I was assigned one night to guard a tomb . . .

TITUS (*Slowly.*) To guard a tomb . . .

CORNELIUS (*With difficulty.*) It was the tomb of the Man who called Himself Jesus of Nazareth.

TITUS (*Excitedly.*) Then you *did* know Him? Mother said . . .

CORNELIUS (*Topping him.*) The high priest knew that the Nazarene's followers would try to steal His body because He said that on the third day He would rise from the dead . . .

URIAS (*Joining in.*) And so we asked Pilate that a guard be placed on the tomb.

CORNELIUS. And I was one of those soldiers that kept the vigil by the tomb of the Nazarene.

RUTH. But — if — if you were there — you — you *must* believe in Him!

CORNELIUS. Why should I? His followers — Peter, James, John — all the others — they *did* steal His body — while we slept. He didn't rise . . .

TITUS (*Fiercely.*) No. I don't believe you!

DRUSILLA. Titus — your father . . .

CORNELIUS (*Quickly.*) That's why they're coming here this morning — to make me say that I lied. Well, I didn't.

RUTH. You were asleep — you don't *know* . . .

URIAS. He knows. We *all* know. It was nothing but a hoax.

CORNELIUS (*Tiredly.*) And that's what I'm going to tell Silas and all of them when they come here.

TITUS (*Brokenly.*) You were there — you — you saw His body . . .

CORNELIUS. Twenty years ago . . . (*Off Right there is the growing noise of a crowd.*)

URIAS. Listen! That must be Silas. I'll stay in the background, Cornelius.

RUTH. Titus . . . *(Going to him.)* . . . Titus, this is your chance.

TITUS *(Dazedly.)* My chance, Ruth?

RUTH. Silas will be here — here in your garden — if you could tell him about your eyes . . .

TITUS. But Ruth — if what Father says is true . . .

CORNELIUS. And it is. It is. Could I live a lie for twenty years? *(Knocking on the gate.)*

URIAS. Remember, Cornelius . . .

DRUSILLA *(As they all stare at the gate.)* Shall I go, Cornelius? *(BERNICE enters from the house and stands up Left, watching.)*

CORNELIUS *(Slowly.)* No, Drusilla. They're looking for me. *(He crosses to the gate.)* Who is it?

SILAS *(Outside the gate.)* We come seeking him who is known as Cornelius the Centurion.

CORNELIUS. What do you want of him?

SILAS. Only a few words.

CORNELIUS *(Opening the gate.)* Enter. I am the man you seek.

SILAS *(Enters through the gate. He is a man of the same age as CORNELIUS, but everything about him is simple and gentle. His voice radiates kindness and sincerity. He enters the garden humbly and stands watching CORNELIUS. A part of the crowd presses in behind him.)* I am he they call Silas — a friend of Paul.

CORNELIUS *(Moving to Center, abruptly.)* I have heard you in the marketplace. What is it you want with me?

SILAS *(Moving onstage. More of the crowd follows him in.)* I am sorry to disturb you here in your home . . .

CORNELIUS *(With exaggerated ease.)* These people are only members of my family — my wife, my son, my aunt, a neighbor's child. Speak your mind.

SILAS. You were at one time a Roman soldier.

CORNELIUS. I was a Centurion.

SILAS. Stationed, I believe, in Jerusalem.

CORNELIUS I was.

SILAS. This was many years ago?

CORNELIUS More than twenty.

SILAS. You resigned and came here to Bethsaida shortly after the crucifixion?

CORNELIUS *(Coldly.)* Which crucifixion? There were so many.

SILAS. Of course. Forgive me. I meant the crucifixion of Jesus — the Nazarene.

CORNELIUS. I believe it *was* soon after His death that we came here.

SILAS. After Jesus was crucified, He was placed in a tomb that belonged to Joseph of Arimathea — and the high priest insisted on a guard.

CORNELIUS. They feared what His followers might do.

SILAS. You were one of the guards appointed.

CORNELIUS. I was.

SILAS. And after — after Jesus had risen from the dead — you told everyone that His body had been, stolen . . .

CORNELIUS. I told the truth.

SILAS. This story which you told is still heard in many places . . .

CORNELIUS. The truth has a way of spreading.

SILAS. The truth is what we want, Cornelius.

CORNELIUS *(Stubbornly.)* While we slept, Peter and the others stole His body.

SILAS *(Slowly.)* If what you say were true, it would mean that Paul, Luke . . . all of us are wrong . . . are preaching untruths. *(The crowd stirs and mutters angrily.)*

CORNELIUS. It is what I have always said.

SILAS. For twenty years you've lived and remembered that morning when you came into Jerusalem . . .

CORNELIUS. Why shouldn't I remember it?

SILAS *(Softly.)* The memories were too black for Judas Iscariot. He hanged himself.

CORNELIUS. Iscariot, the traitor? What is he to me?

SILAS. They paid *him* thirty pieces of silver.

CORNELIUS *(Unnerved.)* I've answered your questions. Now you must go.

SILAS. A man's life is soon over. In twenty *more* years at best, you will be dead — but what you have said, whether it be true or false, will survive you. Can you think of all the millions yet to live whose faith your word will murder and still insist that your story is true?

CORNELIUS *(Slight pause.)* You have my answer.

SILAS. Yes, I have your answer, Cornelius, but I had hoped that you would find it in your heart to repent. We won't keep you longer. *(The crowd mutters angrily as SILAS turns to go.)*

RUTH *(Calling.)* If you please, holy Silas . . .

BERNICE *(Moving up.)* Be quiet, girl.

SILAS *(Stopping and turning.)* What is it, my child?

DRUSILLA. Ruth — no! Let him go.

SILAS. You called to me. What was it you wanted to ask?

RUTH *(Coming to him.)* Forgive me for calling out so rudely — but — I — I have a favor to ask . . .

SILAS. Ask it, my child.

RUTH *(Goes to TITUS and takes his hand.)* Come, Titus. You must tell him . . .

SILAS *(As RUTH and TITUS approach him.)* This is the son of the Centurion?

CORNELIUS *(Hollowly.)* He is my son.

DRUSILLA. Blind from birth.

SILAS *(To RUTH.)* And you wish me to pray for him, that God in His infinite mercy might restore his sight?

RUTH. If you would, holy Silas.

SILAS *(To TITUS.)* And you — what is your name, my son?

TITUS. I am called Titus.

SILAS. Do you have the faith, young Titus?

TITUS. The faith?

SILAS. Do you believe in the Nazarene as the Son of God?

TITUS *(Slowly.)* This morning — when I listened to you and Paul in the marketplace — I could believe — but now . . .

SILAS *(Gently.)* There can be no life, no light without faith, my son. If you could believe, there might be hope . . .

DRUSILLA. Hope that he might see?

URIAS. Cornelius, can't you stop this mockery?

RUTH. Titus, didn't you hear? If you can believe — your faith may make you see . . .

SILAS. If you could kneel, my son, and find it in your heart to declare your faith in Jesus. He has infinite mercy and understanding. Here in your own town of Bethsaida He made a blind man see — because that man had faith . . .

RUTH. Titus — I'll kneel with you . . .

TITUS. I wanted to believe — all my life I've been searching through the dark for something — anything that I could hold — and now I thought I had found it. But — if what Father says is true . . .

DRUSILLA *(Sharply.)* Cornelius . . .

RUTH. Titus, our life together is before us. Your father's life is past — it's over and done. Don't let the shadow of his unhappiness cloud our future . . .

SILAS. Faith is such a hard-won treasure, young Titus — and so easily forfeited — a chance remark, an unthinking slur — and it's gone.

TITUS. I know — but I couldn't kneel and *not* believe. It — it would be the blackest sin I could commit.

DRUSILLA *(To* CORNELIUS.*)* I've asked little of you in our life together, Cornelius.

URIAS *(At the other side.)* Don't listen to her. The boy is blind because God willed it so, and only followers of the devil would try to change it . . .

SILAS *(To* TITUS.*)* The decision must be yours, my son . . .

RUTH. Titus — as you love me — can't you find it in your heart to know the truth . . .?

TITUS. The truth? What is the truth?

DRUSILLA *(With terrible intensity.)* Cornelius — the truth! Tell Titus the truth. He must know it. Do you hear me? He must.

TITUS *(Groping toward his father.)* What is it, Father? Can I believe? Only *you* can tell me? What is your answer? What's the truth, Father? Won't you tell me?

CORNELIUS *(Stands out from the group and for a long, agonizing moment searches each face in turn for an answer.* SILAS, URIAS, DRUSILLA, BERNICE, RUTH — *and then, like a man collapsing, he takes* TITUS' *outstretched hands and pulls the boy with him to his knees at Center stage. He says in a horrified whisper.)* I lied—Titus. I lied. For twenty long, dark years I've lived a lie. You've walked in darkness and so have I. God forgive me for my sin. God forgive me.

URIAS *(Standing at* CORNELIUS' *side.)* You cheat! You traitor! You promised me — you promised me . . .

CORNELIUS *(Lifting his face from his hands.)* All these years I haven't dared remember it as it was that morning — a morning just like this. We were sitting there — Marcus, Tiberius and me — and we saw that first streak of silvered dawn in the East. The birds were beginning to waken in the olive trees and I was thinking of Drusilla and home . . .

SILAS *(Softly.)* Dawn — the dawn of a new day and a new hope.

CORNELIUS. And then, as the light spread, there was a

growing sound, as though ten thousand hands struck ten thousand lyres at once and the music enveloped us until we could hardly breathe. With the music, there was a blinding light — a thousand times brighter than the summer sun at noon. I fell forward and as I fell, I heard the great stone that covered the entrance to the tomb rolling back — and then, the music grew even louder — and the light was like a pain — and then — I think I must have fainted. *(He stops and passes his hand over his eyes.)*

URIAS *(Shrilly.)* You took our money and tricked us . . .

CORNELIUS *(Rising.)* You'll have your money back — all of it.

URIAS *(Shouldering his way through the crowd toward the gate.)* You've ruined us — ruined us all. *(He exits Right.)*

TITUS *(Rising at his father's side, groping.)* We'll pay him back, Father — together — you and I — we . . . *(He stops and shakes his head — and then covers his face with his hands. All eyes are on him. The crowd scarcely breathes. Slowly, he lowers his hands. His shoulders straighten. He turns and goes up to the fig tree and looks hungrily at it for a long moment and then.)* So this is a tree.

RUTH *(Excitedly.)* Titus . . .

SILAS. My boy — what is it?

CORNELIUS. Titus — Titus — tell us . . .

TITUS *(Taking them all in.)* This beauty — all this beauty in God's world — and I'm to see it . . .

DRUSILLA. He can see. *(Coming to CORNELIUS' side.)* Did you hear, Cornelius? After all these aching years — our son can see.

TITUS *(Moving downstage.)* Mother . . . *(He looks at her with love and devotion, then moving on.)* Ruth . . .

RUTH. Your faith, Titus — your faith worked the miracle . . .

TITUS *(To* CORNELIUS.*)* Father, you gave me the faith to see.

CORNELIUS. I only returned what I had stolen. *(The crowd excitedly exclaims "It's a Miracle." Gradually, all are kneeling.)*

RUTH *(Taking* TITUS' *hand and leading him down Left.)* I knew He would help you . . .

TITUS *(Gently helping* RUTH *to kneel.)* Sky — and grass — and birds — and the faces of the people I love — to see them all . . .

CORNELIUS *(Holding* DRUSILLA'S *hand.)* If this holy man would pray for us . . . *(The crowd agrees.)*

DRUSILLA *(As she kneels at* CORNELIUS' *side.)* We're free. After twenty years — free to love one another, Cornelius — no fear — no suspicion — just love. *(All are kneeling.)*

SILAS *(Softly.)* As Jesus said: "Because thou hast believed, thy faith hath made thee whole."

CORNELIUS. Could you pray for us, holy Silas?

SILAS. We'll pray together and to express our thanks, we have the most beautiful prayer in the words of man, because the Nazarene Himself gave it to us. *(He bows his head and begins softly.)* Our Father, which art in heaven, hallowed be Thy name. *(Slowly, one by one, the crowd joins him, until all are praying.)* Thy kingdom come, Thy will be done, on earth, as it is in heaven. Give us this day our daily bread and forgive us our trespasses as we forgive those who trespass against us. And lead us not into temptation, but deliver us from evil. Amen. *(Slow curtain — down at the prayer's end.)*

CURTAIN

PRODUCTION NOTES

This play can be very effectively produced with an absolute minimum of equipment. Draperies or curtains will suffice, since the playing area at no time is spotlighted more than the action. If you use a realistic set, the fig tree can be easily fabricated with a quantity of chicken wire as the base of the trunk and ordinary paper toweling as the bark. A detailed floor plan is included for your convenience, but you needn't feel restricted to that arrangement. Whatever your personal staging problem may be, this play will readily adapt itself. The only danger to be avoided is "overproducing" — losing the story and the simplicity of the effect in a welter of costumes, staging and music. A chorus can be used very effectively *in the background,* but it should *never* obtrude.

PROPERTIES

ON STAGE: Tree; three benches; table.

PERSONAL: Purse (Urias); dishes (Bernice); wine-glass (Drusilla).

LIGHTING

The entire action of the play occurs on an early spring morning, outdoors, so the light should be warm, with a predominance of straws and ambers. Little change is necessary, unless the director wishes to arrange a special spot for Cornelius at Center.

COSTUMES

The play can best be costumed in standard biblical attire, though it may be played in stylized costumes. Completely simple costumes are recommended.

THE ANGEL IN THE WINDOW

A DRAMA IN ONE ACT

By

Effa E. Preston

PRODUCTION RIGHTS

Copies of this play are available in single pamphlet form. The right to produce this play by one group of amateur players is authorized only by the purchase of eight copies (one copy for each speaking part) at the current price of 50c each.

It is dishonest and illegal to copy parts.

CHARACTERS

MR. HOLMAN .... *Chairman of the music committee*

MISS OVERTON .... *The church accompanist*

MONA
GLORIA
KATHY
LORA   } *Members of the double quartet choir*
NORMAN
HAL
GENE
KEITH

MARTHA WAYNE .... *An unhappy church member*

JOHN MARTIN .... *A member with a problem*

MR. GEORGE GRAYSON....*The donor of a new church window*

ANGEL .... *Whose image is in the old window*

TIME: *An evening in summer.*

PLACE: *A Sunday school and entertainment room in a small church.*

TIME OF PLAYING: *Twenty-five minutes.*

198

COSTUMES AND CHARACTERISTICS

MR. HOLMAN is a pleasant and amiable man in his early thirties. He wears a conservative business suit.

MISS OVERTON is a wholesome-looking young woman in her late twenties. She wears a simple dark tailored suit.

The eight members of the choir, MONA, GLORIA, KATHY, LORA, NORMAN, HAL, GENE, *and* KEITH, are young people in their late teens. All are good singers and wear white choir robes.

MARTHA WAYNE is a dark-haired, dark-eyed girl of eighteen, with a strained, worried expression. She wears rather shabby street clothes.

JOHN MARTIN is an ambitious young man of twenty, very eager and impatient of restraint, yet he looks downcast and frustrated. He wears a well-fitting light suit.

GEORGE GRAYSON is a middle-aged businessman, very successful and well-to-do, yet his riches have not spoiled him. He is rather short and stout, with a ready smile and an affable manner and wears a dark, expensive-looking suit.

THE ANGEL is a pretty blond girl with a sweet voice and a pleasing manner. She wears a long, pale blue robe, silver slippers, and a pair of folded wings attached to her shoulders and made of white net and feathers. Two of the small feathers should be easily detachable.

PROPERTIES

For Miss Overton, a wrist watch. For Norman, a long roll of paper, on which is a list of names like a petition.

MUSIC

The songs used in the play will be found in the following books: "Softly Now the Light of Day" in Denison's "Songs Worth While," and Handel's "Largo," "Sound the Loud Timbrel," and "Nearer, My God, to Thee" in "The Golden Book of Favorite Songs." The last number will also be found in any hymnal. For the incidental music, "Panis Angelicus," a phonograph record may be used—Victor RCA Record 13589, played by the Boston Pops Orchestra.

STAGE DIRECTIONS

Up stage means away from footlights; *down stage*, near footlights. In the use of *right* and *left*, the actor is supposed to be facing the audience.

THE ANGEL IN THE WINDOW

SCENE: *A Sunday school room, often used for entertainments and rehearsals. It has a single door, in the middle of the left wall, opening into a hallway that leads to the front door. Along the right wall stands a piano and stool. Alongside the piano on the up-stage side are two rows of benches for the choir. Along the left wall on both sides of the door are several rows of benches and chairs for the audience. The side walls are covered with dark curtains, and the back drop is a dark curtain, opening at the center to reveal a large stained glass window. This window may be painted on thin paper in bright colors outlined in black. In the center is a picture showing the head and shoulders of an angel resembling as closely as possible the girl who plays the part of the* ANGEL. *The face of the* ANGEL *is turned toward the benches on which the choir sit. Off stage behind the window there should be a bright flood light, to be turned on whenever it is necessary for the* ANGEL's *face to be seen. As it is an evening in summer, the light over the piano and the ceiling chandelier in the middle of the room are lighted and the stage lights are full up.*

AT THE RISE OF THE CURTAIN: *The members of the choir,* MONA, GLORIA, KATHY, LORA, NORMAN, HAL, GENE, *and* KEITH *are seated on the benches beside the piano, singing "Softly Now the Light of Day."* MISS OVETTON *accompanies them at the piano, while* MR. HOLMAN *stands up center listening to the rehearsal. The flood light back of the window is shining brightly during the singing. As the hymn ends, the light is dimmed and the window is no longer clearly seen.*

MR. HOLMAN *(Coming down stage and joining the singers.)* You sang very well.

MISS OVERTON. But they must put more expression into their singing tomorrow evening. *(To the choir.)* Remember, boys and girls, we shall have guests, and one of them is very distinguished.

MR. HOLMAN. Yes, indeed. It's very important that you sing well tomorrow evening. Not that you don't always do your best.

GLORIA. I always sing better when the lights are on back of the window. I guess I need to see the Angel.

KATHY. It's queer, but I feel the same way, Gloria. When I see the smile on her face I just naturally want to sing my very best. It sounds silly, but it's true.

MR. HOLMAN. What on earth are you two girls talking about?

LORA. They're talking about the Angel in the window, Mr. Holman. I think we all feel the same way.

MR. HOLMAN. Oh, *that* window? *(Indicates the window up center.)*

HAL. Of course. It's the only one with an angel in it.

MR. HOLMAN. Oh, yes, that window. But we're going to have that taken out.

GENE *(In dismay.)* Taken out?

MR. HOLMAN. Oh, we'll have a new one put in.

GLORIA *(Blankly.)* Why have it taken out?

MR. HOLMAN. It's rather old-fashioned. We'll have a modern one with complicated designs and scrolls and things.

KEITH *(Shrugging.)* That's the first time I ever heard that church windows become old-fashioned.

GENE. I always thought the older they were the more valuable they were.

MONA *(Firmly.)* Mr. Holman, I'd like to know who started this silly idea of a new window, and why.

MISS OVERTON. Don't be rude, Mona.

MONA *(Apologetically.)* I'm sorry, Miss Overton, but we really want to know.

KEITH. Tell us, Mr. Holman.

MR. HOLMAN (*Unruffled and smiling.*) All right, Keith. I'll tell you all I know about it.

GLORIA. I think we'd better sit down.

(*All sit and gaze accusingly at* MR. HOLMAN.)

MR. HOLMAN. Now don't look at me like that. It wasn't my idea. It seems this window was given to the church— really not given—bought by money solicited from the small congregation when the church was first built and consisted of two rooms, this being one of them. The window doesn't harmonize with the others, now that we have a much larger church, since all the additions have been made. All the other windows are very modern and this one just— er—er—doesn't harmonize.

MONA. I think all that is very silly, Mr. Holman. We folks in the choir like to look at that window when we sing. Maybe the Angel likes to look at us.

NORMAN (*To the other singers.*) Let's send a petition to the executive board or whatever they call themselves, asking that we keep the window. We'll start early tomorrow morning, and I feel sure we'll get plenty of signatures.

KATHY. That's a fine idea, Norman.

MONA (*Turning to* MR. HOLMAN.) You still haven't told us who started this idea.

MR. HOLMAN. A Mr. Grayson who used to live here. He's very rich, and he wanted to do something for the church.

MISS OVERTON. You see, he lived here when he was a little boy, and there wasn't much of a church then, so he wants to make this one more beautiful.

LORA. Taking away the Angel is no way to do that.

MR. HOLMAN. I had no idea there was such a feeling about the window. I don't mind telling you boys and girls that if you get a sufficient number of signatures on your petition you may save the window. All Mr. Grayson wants to do is to help us in some way. He will be at your concert tomorrow evening, so you'd better get busy with that petition.

HAL. So he's the distinguished visitor.

MISS OVERTON. Norman, come to me first with your petition. I have a very imposing way of writing my name.

NORMAN. Thank you, Miss Overton. I'll be around at eight in the morning.

MR. HOLMAN. If you really feel that way, I'll sign, too. You'll get plenty of signers. By the way, has anyone heard how little Jimmy Wayne is? Do you know, Lora? You live over in his neighborhood.

LORA. He's no better, Mr. Holman, and the doctor still isn't sure what is the matter with him. I saw Martha this morning, and she told me.

MISS OVERTON. Those poor people! It's a shame, and there's nothing anyone can do except pray for Jimmy. The church is paying all the medical expenses.

GENE. So long as we're telling bad news this evening, let me add my bit. I hear John Martin is going into Morrison's shop as a mechanic instead of finishing college. His mother is terribly unhappy about it.

MR. HOLMAN. And very likely some poor boy really needs that mechanic's job. It isn't fair.

MISS OVERTON (Glancing at her wrist watch.) Come on, folks. It's late. Maybe the janitor wants to lock up.

KATHY. Haven't you heard, Miss Overton? This room is to be left unlocked from now on, so those who wish to do so may come to rest or pray or meditate.

MR. HOLMAN. Now that's a fine idea. I hope many will take advantage of it. Certainly every church should have an open door.

KATHY. And an angel in the window.

NORMAN. Mr. Holman, I still can't see why that Mr. Grayson had to pick on a window as his gift:

MR. HOLMAN. My dear boy, it was all he could think of.

KEITH (To the other singers.) Come on; we need a good sleep. There's a hard day ahead of us.

OTHER CHOIR MEMBERS (In confused chorus.) Good night, Miss Overton. Good night, Mr. Holman.

MISS OVERTON AND MR. HOLMAN (In concert.) Good night.

(The eight singers exeunt at left.)

MISS OVERTON. Poor things! They're terribly worried.

MR. HOLMAN. I know.

Miss OVERTON. Mr. Holman, you're really in charge of the music in the church, so you must have some influence with the powers that be. Couldn't you talk Mr. Grayson into doing something else with his money?

MR. HOLMAN. I couldn't, but perhaps the petition will.

Miss OVERTON. Do you know, I like that old window myself.

MR. HOLMAN. So do I.

(They go off at left, and the church is empty. The lights are now very dim. Soft sweet music is heard—"Panis Angelicus," played on a phonograph off stage, near the window or back of the piano. As is grows softer, MARTHA WAYNE enters, sits up left and weeps. The ANGEL slips through the opening in the dark curtain beside the picture up center and enters. The window is now quite dark. The music continues pianissimo throught the ensuing scene.)

ANGEL. Why do you weep?

MARTHA *(Looking up and recognizing the ANGEL.)* You are the Angel in the window!

ANGEL. Yes.

MARTHA *(Bewildered.)* But . . . but how did you get down? Are you real?

ANGEL. I will tell you a secret. Every night when all is dark and still, I slip down from the window. I look to see if there is anyone whom I can help, but no one ever comes.

MARTHA. That is because the church has always been locked. Just last evening the pastor decided to leave this room always open.

ANGEL. I am glad. The doors of a church should never be closed. But I fear I shall not be here much longer.

MARTHA *(Timidly.)* Why, Angel?

ANGEL *(Dejectedly.)* My window is to be replaced by a new, more modern one very soon.

MARTHA. I am sorry, and many others will feel the same way.

ANGEL. I can't go back without having done one good deed. I shall have visited the earth in vain if I do that, and if I go back, I may never return.

MARTHA *(Shaking her head.)* I don't understand.

ANGEL. I know what you are wondering. Back of the pictured angel in the window, in every church window, is the spirit of a real angel. Sometimes this spirit takes on an earthly form, as I do tonight and as I have done every night for years. But let us talk no more of me, my dear. You were weeping. What troubles you?

MARTHA *(With a sob.)* My little brother Jimmy has been ill for nearly a year and he is growing steadily worse. The doctor has given him up.

ANGEL *(Surveying her thoughtfully.)* You are Martha Wayne. I heard the choir children speaking of you and your brother Jimmy often. Martha, go home to your brother and play. I, too, shall pray. Take this tiny feather from my wing. *(Takes a feather from her wing and hands it to* MARTHA.*)* Brush your brother's lips and forehead with it. Tomorrow night at this same time return to tell me your brother is better. Do not fear. He will not die for many years to come.

MARTHA *(Gratefully.)* Thank you, Angel. *(Wipes her eyes.)*

ANGEL *(With gentle gravity.)* Do not thank me, Martha. I am but the instrument of One far greater than we can comprehend.

MARTHA *goes off quietly at left. The music, which has been very soft during the conversation, swells more loudly, and the stage lights are extinguished. In the darkness the* ANGEL *makes a noiseless exit through the curtains up center. In a few second the music again grows soft and the lights begin to burn dimly, though the window is still in darkness. At this point,* JOHN MARTIN *enters at left, sits on one of the benches up left, and closes his eyes as if to listen to the music. He apparently goes to sleep. As before, the* ANGEL *enters up center through the curtains and appears in a spotlight while the rest of the room is dark.*

ANGEL. Are you in trouble, my friend? Can I be of help to you?

JOHN *(Startled.)* Who are you? You look like the Angel in the old window.

ANGEL. I am. I just came down to see if I could help

206

you. I do want to help somebody before I have to go back.

JOHN. Go back? Go back where? To the window?

ANGEL *(Sadly.)* To heaven. This church is to have a new, more modern window, with no angel in it.

JOHN. Oh! I'm sorry.

ANGEL. Don't be sorry for me. Let's talk about you. I know what you were thinking as you sat there almost asleep.

JOHN *(Staggered.)* You do? What was it?

ANGEL *(With a kindly smile.)* You were thinking that you don't want to go back to college for two more long years. You want to work with you hands. You want to be a mechanic in a big plant where you can get a huge salary and perhaps, in time, be an inventor. You were thinking you didn't need a degree to become an inventor. Then you remembered how anxious your parents are for you to be graduated. You knew they have saved for it ever since you were a baby.

JOHN *(Amazed.)* Yes, that is exactly what I was thinking. I can't make up my mind.

ANGEL. Don't you think it would be a shame to disappoint your parents? You're halfway through college now. You'll have all the rest of your life to be a mechanic and invent things and make money.

JOHN. But two years sounds like such a long time.

ANGEL. Merely a moment in Eternity.

JOHN. It's a wonderful position. It has to be filled right away. I can have it if I say the word, but I must decide this week.

ANGEL. Perhaps someone else really needs this wonderful job—needs it to support himself or his family. Think of that.

JOHN. Carl Crane would like the job, and he needs it. He's a very good mechanic, as good as, if not better than I am. I could get the job for him.

ANGEL. If you return to college you will make your parents happy, if you get that job for him you'll make Carl Crane happy, and, in making others happy you, yourself, will be doubly blessed. To help others is the very best thing in life.

JOHN *(Troubled.)* But . . . *(Hesitates.)*

ANGEL. Think it over, John, and if you decide to return to college, let me know. I shall be ashamed to leave Earth without one good deed to be written in the Golden Book. Think it over. *(The ANGEL drops a tiny feather near JOHN as, during her conversation, she has moved closer to him. As she speaks again, her voice grows faint. The lights grow very dim and she exits through the curtains in a moment of darkness. As light shows faintly again JOHN stands, looks about, shakes his head, and rubs his eyes as if still half asleep, and goes off at left. The ANGEL re-enters up center, where the spotlight shines on her. She prays.)* Dear Lord, please make the young man choose the right way. Please make little Jimmy well again. Let my poor efforts not have been in vain. And, if it but be Thy will, allow me to remain here in this window and in my small way be of help to those who come in here to worship Thee and to sing Thy praises. But, whatever Thy will, I shall obey it gladly. Amen.

(The curtain is lowered for a few minutes to signify the passing of twenty-four hours. When it rises, the scene is unchanged. The stage lights are full up and the window shows plainly. The singers are seated in their places beside the piano, with MISS OVERTON on the stool. MR. HOLMAN and MR. GRAYSON sit on the front bench of the seats up left listening while the choir sings two selections. These songs may be "Sound the Loud Timbrel" and Handel's "Largo," though their use is optional. At the close of the last song, the singers leave their seats and drift over to where the two men sit. MISS OVERTON rises and joins them.)

MR. GRAYSON. That was the best musical program I've heard in a long time, Holman. That choir sings well.

MR. HOLMAN. I thought you'd enjoy it, Mr. Grayson.

MISS OVERTON. Thanks for your kind words, Mr. Grayson. I think they sang well, too.

GLORIA. The Angel was smiling at us. We had to sing well.

GENE. Of course we did.

MISS OVERTON. I was very much pleased with you.

KATHY. Excuse the interruption, Mr. Holman, but did you know that little Jimmy Wayne has improved so much the doctor thinks he'll be well in a few months?

MR. HOLMAN. That's wonderful.

NORMAN. Mr. Grayson, we hope you won't be offended, and we don't wish to seem rude, but we know why you came to our little concert tonight. You came to see where the new window could be placed.

MR. GRAYSON *(Surprised.)* Why, yes, I did.

NORMAN. We don't like the idea of a new window. We're more than satisfied with the old one.

(The other singers nod vigorously in agreement.)

MR. GRAYSON. I've heard rumors to that effect.

NORMAN. We took a petition around this morning asking that the old window remain. Look at this, sir.

(NORMAN takes from under his robe a sheet of paper on which is a long roll of names and hands it to MR. GRAYSON, who looks at it with interest. The choir members watch him anxiously.)

MR. GRAYSON. Well, well. Quite a list of names, my boy.

KEITH. You see, Mr. Grayson, we're sort of superstitious about the Angel in the window.

HAL. We think we sing better when she's smiling at us.

MR. GRAYSON. Was she smiling at you tonight?

GENE. Yes, she was.

GLORIA. Sometimes the light isn't lit by the window. Then we can't see her, and . . .

LORA *(Interrupts.)* And then we don't sing so well.

KATHY. Maybe we're foolish, but that's the way we feel, Mr. Grayson.

MR. GRAYSON. I'm not so sure you're foolish. I sort of liked the angel myself tonight. *(Puts the petition in his pocket.)*

MR. HOLMAN. Go on and tell them. Mr. Grayson. Why keep them in suspense?

MR. GRAYSON. Mr. Holman told me about the way you felt before he brought me here to listen to you sing. I have decided to do as you wish. I shall not give the church a new window. The old one remains. You will not lose your angel.

ALL THE CHOIR MEMBERS *(Fervently in concert.)* Oh, thank you, Mr. Grayson.

MR. GRAYSON *(Amused.)* This is the first time I've been thanked for not giving somebody something.

MISS OVERTON. Yes, it's certainly something new to have a gift refused. Isn't it?

MR. GRAYSON. Oh, but I'm going to give your church something, anyway.

MONA. What, Mr. Grayson?

MR. GRAYSON. A check for the amount the window would have cost me, to be used for whatever your executive board deems best, so long as it isn't a new window.

NORMAN. That's fine!

LORA. I feel so happy.

(All the singers beam.)

MR. GRAYSON. Well, I'm glad everybody's happy. I don't feel too sad myself.

MISS OVERTON. Boys and girls—excuse me—ladies and gentlemen of the quartet, let's sing one more hymn for Mr. Grayson, to show our appreciation. What is your favorite hymn, Mr. Grayson?

MR. GRAYSON. I hardly know. "Nearer, My God, to Thee," I think.

MISS OVERTON. We'll sing it for you.

(The choir members and MISS OVERTON return to the piano and sing the hymn. At the close a few linger in their seats, while the others, with MISS OVERTON, cross to left and rejoin the two men.)

MR. GRAYSON. Thank you very much.

MISS OVERTON. Did we tell you, Mr. Grayson, this room is open all the time so that those who wish to may enter at any hour?

MR. GRAYSON. An excellent idea.

MR. HOLMAN. We'd better go, so some same people have a chance to come in if they wish.

MISS OVERTON. It's growing late, anyway.

LORA *(Finding feather dropped by* ANGEL.*)* Look, a feather!

GLORIA. It looks like a feather from an angel's wing.

(All look toward the window, where the ANGEL *is smiling.)*

MONA. Let it be where you found it, Lora. Maybe the Angel will want it back.

*(*LORA *drops the feather on the floor.)*

MISS OVERTON. Come on. We must go.

(All the company go off at left, leaving the stage unoccupied. The lights grow dim, and the window is dark. The music of "Panis Angelicus" comes very softly from off up center and continues pianissimo throughout the ensuing scene. JOHN *enters at left, sees the feather, and picks it up, then looks up at the window.)*

JOHN. Angel, if it wasn't a dream I had last night, if you really talked to me, please come down from your window again.

(The ANGEL *enters through the curtains up center and appears in the spotlight.)*

ANGEL. Here I am, John.

JOHN. Then it wasn't a dream. Angel, I took your advice. I'm going back to college. Carl got the job as the mechanic today. He's happy; my parents are happy. Strange to say, so am I. I thank you, Angel. From the bottom of my heart I thank you. Look. I found this feather when I came in.

ANGEL. I meant you to keep it. Whenever you look at it, remember me and these words, "He shall give His angels charge over thee to keep thee in all thy ways."

JOHN. I shall never forget you, Angel.

(Exit JOHN *at left. The spotlight is turned off, the lights grow dimmer, and the music swells, as the* ANGEL *slips off through the curtains up center. After a moment,* MARTHA *enters at left and looks up at the window. As she speaks, the music drops to pianissimo.)*

MARTHA. Angel, Angel in the window, please come down. I wish to speak to you.

(Under cover of the darkness the ANGEL *enters through the curtains up center, and the spotlight is trained on her.*

The stage lights come up a little and the music continues very softly throughout the scene.)

ANGEL. Here I am, Martha.

MARTHA *(Looking radiantly happy.)* My brother is better. The doctor says he is going to get well.

ANGEL. I am very glad.

MARTHA. The instant I touched his lips and his forehead with the feather from your wing he fell asleep, and when he awoke his pain was gone. He was smiling and happy, thanks to the magic of your wing.

ANGEL. No, Martha, thanks to your faith and to your prayers.

MARTHA. And the old window is to stay. The choir members took a petition to the people. Dear Angel, you will always be in our window now.

ANGEL. Yes, I know, and it makes me very happy. But, had I been called back to heaven, I should at least not have been ashamed to go, as I feared I should be. Two people have had faith in me so I could help them. And the choir singers have always liked me to smile at them when they sang. I feel now that my presence here is not entirely in vain, although many times I have feared it was.

MARTHA *(Earnestly.)* But no angel could live in vain.

ANGEL. And no human being, either, my dear.

MARTHA. May I keep the feather, Angel? It will serve to remind me how necessary it is to have faith. I had faith in you, and Jimmy is getting well.

ANGEL. Keep the feather if you wish, Martha, and always remember the words in the Bible: "Faith is the substance of things hoped for, the evidence of things not seen."

MARTHA. I shall never forget, Angel. Thank you, and good-bye.

ANGEL. Good-bye, Martha. *(MARTHA goes off at left. The spotlight grows faint but still shines on the ANGEL, who again prays.)* Dear Lord, I thank Thee that the young man has chosen the right way. I thank Thee that little Jimmy is going to be well. I thank Thee that I am to remain here, the Angel in the window. In my small way, may

I be of help to the peope who come here to worship, and may their faith and my efforts never falter. Amen.

(The music of "Panis Angelicus" grows loud. All lights fade.)

CURTAIN

GREATER THAN ANY MAN

A DRAMA OF THE CHRISTIAN CHURCH
IN ONE ACT

By

ALBERT CROTHERS SMITH

PRODUCTION RIGHTS

Copies of this play are available in single pamphlet form. The right to produce this play by one group of amateur players is authorized only by the purchase of six copies (one copy for each speaking part) at the current price of 50c each.

It is dishonest and illegal to copy parts.

A WORSHIP PERIOD

(Below is printed a short devotional program which may precede the offering of the play—"Greater Than Any Man.")

MEDITATION *(Soft music)*—"The Church"
"O Lord of life, and truth, and grace,
Ere Nature was begun!
Make welcome to our erring race
Thy Spirit and Thy Son.

We hail the Church, built high o'er all
The heathen's rage and scoff;
Thy Providence its fenced wall,
'The Lamb the light thereof.'

Thy Christ has reached his heavenly seat
Through sorrows and through scars;
The golden lamps are at His feet,
And in His hand the stars.

Oh, may He walk among us here,
With His rebuke and love,—
A brightness o'er this lower sphere,
A ray from worlds above!"
—By Nathaniel Langdon Frothingham.

HYMN—"Dear Lord, We give Our Youth to Thee"—*Laufer*

PRAYER:
Our Heavenly Father, we thank Thee for this great institution: the Christian Church. Teach us, we pray, the deep significance of such a trust that we may make of it something more than a structure of bricks, of wood, of stained-glass windows.

Here may we find a more intimate association with our Lord Jesus that His steadfastness in the face of sin, His tenderness and sympathy to all classes and in every condition, His glorious capacity for sacrifice—even to the Cross, may guide us in our efforts toward the establishment of Thy Kingdom here on earth.

Reveal in us a capacity for love and for understanding that every man may be our brother; every burden of another, our cross to bear; every sinner, a soul to save. And may we here and now resolve to dedicate our thoughts, our lives and our fortunes to the fulfillment of the Greater Church. Amen.

HYMN—"The Church's One Foundation"...................*Stone*

PSALM 100:
"Make a joyful noise unto Jehovah, all ye lands.
Serve Jehovah with gladness:
    Come before his presence with singing.
Know ye that Jehovah, he is God:
    It is he that hath made us, and we are his;
    We are his people, and the sheep of his pasture.
Enter into his gates with thanksgiving,
    And into his courts with praise:
    Give thanks unto him, and bless his name.
For Jehovah is good; his loving kindness endureth
        forever,
    And his faithfulness unto all generations."

HYMN—"When I Survey the Wondrous Cross"..........*Watts*

GREATER THAN ANY MAN

CAST OF CHARACTERS

(Six men, three women, several boys)

SILAS GROVER ....an influential church officer.

FRANK GROVER ....his son.

ERIC ....the always agreeable sexton of Trinity church.

REV. HUGH FOSTER...................youthful pastor of Trinity.

JOHNNIE WALKER ....a boy's boy.

CHARLES WALKER ....his father.

BETSY LIVERMORE ....gushy director of dramatics.

GIRLS ....two soloists or a duet.

BOYS ....several in baseball togs.

PROPERTIES

A small piece of glass which may be broken behind the scenes.

A baseball, gloves, and a bat.

Some pieces of scenery.

THE SCENE *is the front of the sanctuary of Trinity Church. All of the action takes place around or near the altar.*

The front pews should be vacant. It is late afternoon on a Saturday. Several sections of scenery are scattered about just as they have been brought in, preparatory to being set up for the pageant to be presented on Sunday. As the play begins, MR. GROVER *and* ERIC *enter from a side door at the Right of the altar. A small single light makes their forms barely visible.*

MR. GROVER *(Gloating.)* Well, Eric, I'm glad we arranged a meeting for this hour, very glad. And not a soul around to bother us.

ERIC *(Meekly.)* Yes, Mr. Grover.

MR. GROVER. As president of the Men's club and as the largest contributor to this church, I think it's my duty to keep an eye on the doings around here.

ERIC. You're right, Mr. Grover.

MR. GROVER. The oil tanks downstairs were filled just two days ago. Now they're almost empty. It's just as I thought—we are burning a lot more oil in this church than is necessary.

ERIC. Shall I turn on more lights, Mr. Grover?

MR. GROVER. No. We won't need them. Besides, the church can use the saving.

ERIC. Yes, Mr. Grover.

MR. GROVER. I'm not one to interfere with the normal run of events, Eric, but the upkeep of this church is altogether too high. Why, there are meetings here every night in the week. When I was a boy, we never had all of these do-fangled clubs and socials. And who ever heard tell of young adult groups or church libraries? *(Sarcastically.)* And Rev. Foster says, "It's the New Church." Well, maybe he can find a New Way to pay the bills. These things all take fuel and light. *(Excitedly.)* Do you hear me, Eric? Fuel and light! Believe me, the trustees are going to hear about this.

ERIC. Just as you say, Mr. Grover.

MR. GROVER. And another thing, Eric. Those young hoodlums must stop playing ball in our vacant lot next door. That is church property, and they have no right to be there. It's a wonder that every window in the church hasn't been broken by this time. *(A loud crash of glass is heard from the next room. Excitedly.)* What was that, Eric?

ERIC *(Calmly.)* Must be a baseball, sir. They were playing out there when I came in this afternoon.

MR. GROVER *(Enraged.)* Great Heavens! After them, then! Why are you standing there like a dunce? But wait. Perhaps they'll come in to get the ball. I just remembered that I left the door ajar as I came in. Come, let's hide here in the shadow. We'll grab them as they go by. *(The men wait quietly for several seconds. Then the figure of a youth emerges from the door at the Right. As he approaches the spot where the men are hiding, they leap out at him.)*

MR. GROVER *(Triumphantly.)* Hah, there, you young rascal! Not so fast. *(BOY struggles.)* I have him, Eric.

JOHNNIE WALKER. Ow-w. Pl-please, Mister. I didn't do it, honest I didn't. Don't hurt, me, Mister.

MR. GROVER *(Tauntingly.)* Thought you could break the church window and get away with it, didn't you? Thought it would be a smart trick to sneak in here and get your ball too, didn't you? Well, we've caught you, and, by Harry, you are going to pay for your mischief! Who are you, anyway? Turn on some more lights, Eric. I guess it will be worth it to get a good look at this culprit. *(ERIC goes out.)*

JOHNNIE *(Struggling all the while.)* Let me go. I said I didn't do it.

MR. GROVER. Don't try to lie your way out of this. The idea of wrecking church property! What kind of folks have you? My Frank would never think of doing such a thing.

Baseball! Bah! Frank has no use for it. *(Lights go on. Surprised.)* So! You are the Walker boy, aren't you? *(*JOHNNIE *nods.)* Your father used to come to men's class. Hasn't been out lately. *(Sneering.)* Suppose he is too good for us.

JOHNNIE *(Quavering.)* We-ell, sir, he used to come quite often, but he got sick of it. He told Mom that most of the men were old crabs who didn't want to have any fun for themselves, and didn't want anyone else to have any either. He said that the most they ever did was to squawk about expenses and criticise everything the minister was trying to do. And I—I guess that's why he doesn't come any more. And he said sis and I had better not come because those old fogies didn't want the young folks to enjoy themselves.

MR. GROVER *(Angrily.)* Oh, so he said that, did he? Humph! A fine example of fatherhood he is. At least you don't find our sons smashing the church windows. If I had my . . .

REV. FOSTER *(Entering from a side door.)* What's all this noise about? Why, hello, Mr. Grover. Is something wrong here?

MR. GROVER *(Surprised and startled.)* Hello, Rev. Foster. I—er—er hardly expected that you would be here at this hour.

REV. FOSTER. I wouldn't have been but for the fact that the Sunday School is rehearsing its pageant now rather than later this evening. But you haven't told me what all the shouting was about. *(Turning.)* You're Johnnie Walker, aren't you?

JOHNNIE. Yes, sir.

MR. GROVER *(Bursting in.)* And he just batted a baseball through the church window. More expense for the members to share. It's about time this thing was stopped.

I propose to go to the police if these boys persist in playing baseball on church property.

REV. FOSTER (Soothingly.) Just a minute now, Mr. Grover. Perhaps Johnnie will tell us his side of the story. Will you, Johnnie?

JOHNNIE. I tried to tell him, sir, but he wouldn't believe me. You see it was really not me who batted that ball.

REV. FOSTER. Who was it, Johnnie?

JOHNNIE (Gazing shyly at MR. GROVER.) I—I can't tell, sir. Usually the fellow who breaks a window has to go after the ball himself, but this time I was doing it for someone who was afraid to come in here. But I can't tell his name, sir. I promised I wouldn't. If you will just give me the ball, sir, we'll see that the window is paid for. Honest we will, sir.

MR. GROVER (Indignantly.) What kind of bosh is this? Don't give him the ball. We would never see him again. I never heard such a story. Come here, young man, (Grabbing JOHNNIE by the arm.) I think I'll take you home right now and settle this thing with your folks.

JOHNNIE (Frantically.) Oh, please let go of my arm. Don't take me home. I said we'd pay for the window. Please let me go.

REV. FOSTER (Interceding.) Perhaps you had better let me handle this, Mr. Grover. I will be responsible for him.

MR. GROVER (Impatiently.) You ministers are too easy. This boy needs a little discipline. He should be taught more respect for the church.

REV. FOSTER (Unheeding.) Listen, Johnnie, you go out now and round up your friends and come back in a few minutes. We'll see if we can't work out some arrangement to take care of the damage. Will you? (JOHNNIE nods.) That's fine. Remember now. Come back in a few minutes.

JOHNNIE. Okay, sir, don't worry. I'll be back. (Exits.)

MR. GROVER *(Severely.)* It seems to me, Brother Foster, that you're much too easy in this matter. Those young scoundrels are always getting into some kind of mischief. The Lord only knows what they will do next.

REV. FOSTER *(Laughingly.)* Come now, Mr. Grover. They wouldn't be boys if they weren't getting into something. Were you such a perfect child?

MR. GROVER *(Unyieldingly.)* I don't claim to be perfect, Parson, but I certainly shouldn't want to be classified with that young reprobate who broke the church window. Why aren't his parents more responsible? Why, take my son Frank, for instance. There's a boy who has been brought up to respect the rights of others.

REV. FOSTER *(Yawning.)* Yes, we know. Frank is a fine boy. But how did you happen to be at the church today? Did you wish to see me?

MR. GROVER *(Slightly embarrassed.)* We-el—er—not exactly, *(Becoming braver.)* but I guess I might as well discuss the matter with you now as later. As er—you know, Rev. Foster, I am not a man to be critical of the action of others, but during these past few months I have felt it my duty to keep a pretty close watch over the church program and *(Ahem.)* I can't say that I have found things particularly satisfactory.

REV. FOSTER *(Somewhat shocked.)* Why, what is the matter? Have my sermons offended you?

MR. GROVER *(Hesitating.)* No-o, er—in fact they have been fine.

REV. FOSTER. Have I neglected some of the sick or the shut-ins?

MR. GROVER. No. I haven't any complaint in that direction.

REV. FOSTER. Well, what is it then? Are the people dissatisfied with the leadership I have offered?

MR. GROVER. You are a good leader, I guess, but it's

something else which I am complaining about. This church is running up too much expense. The building is open practically every night in the week. We are using up too much heat and light. There's no need of all these organizations that have been formed. *(Warming up to his subject.)* Boys' clubs, girls' clubs, young adult groups, a library. When I was a boy, we didn't have these things, and I haven't suffered for the lack of them. Why, that costs money. What are we trying to make our church, a nursemaid for the whole community?

REV. FOSTER *(Calmly.)* Shouldn't it be, Mr. Grover?

MR. GROVER *(Heatedly.)* Of course it shouldn't! Let the parents bring up their children themselves. Why should we take care of their children for them? What does it get us but a lot of debt?

REV. FOSTER *(Slowly.)* What does it get us, you ask. Is that the most important consideration? We like to call our church the house of God. Is there a limit to the service we can do in His name? I came to this church because I saw here an opportunity to do God's work. I didn't come for the salary—that is hardly enough to live on, but I won't complain about that. When I arrived here at Trinity, this church like many others all over the country had ceased to grow, its program was not suited to its needs, it was not abreast of the times. It had refused to acknowledge serious rivals in the field of human interest. This competition soon began to make itself felt, and church attendance began to slump. Sunday movies and Sunday sports, and every imaginable sort of entertainment that could be thought up by money-hungry promoters, reared their ugly hulks on every side to lure both old and young from places of worship. This was a serious struggle. And the church lost out. Yes, I have formed clubs and groups which you have never had here before. Yes, I have attempted to keep these church doors open to all our parishioners at all times. Why, you ask? Because I believe that Jesus Christ brought us a religion for everyday in the week. I believe that He wanted us to be Christian in every way of life. I believe that folks of the same age and the same interests can derive through their clubs and groups what amounts to a spiritual refuelling when they meet in the atmosphere of church surroundings. I believe that these results cannot be measured in dollars and cents or in heat and light.

MR. GROVER *(Still unwon.)* That all sounds very well, Rev. Foster, but bills are bills no matter which way you look at it, and a church which can't pay its bills cannot exist. You know the old saying, "A church debt is the devil's salary."

REV. FOSTER *(With much feeling.)* Brother Grover, believe me, I'm just as much interested in keeping this church out of debt as you are—but spiritually as well as materially out of debt. I have faith in human beings. I have faith that our boys and our girls—these young men and young women to whom we are devoting so much of the time and the money of the church today—will make a very healthy church of tomorrow. Of course they have failings. We have them, too. But, with the grace of God and the love and understanding of his son Jesus Christ, these failings will not hold back the progress of a growing church.

MR. GROVER *(Edging away towards the door.)* We will see. We will see. But I have my doubts. I'll be back. *(Exits through rear door of church. The minister gazes after him, then suddenly thinking of something walks through the door on the Left of the altar. Returns in a few minutes. Carefully looks at the baseball he has in his hand. Then chuckles. Starts up as four boys enter through the door on the Right of the altar.)*

REV. FOSTER *(Cheerfully.)* Hello, boys. So you did come, eh?

JOHNNIE. All but one, sir.

REV. FOSTER. What is the matter with him? Is he sick?

JOHNNIE *(Hesitating.)* No. He just didn't come.

REV. FOSTER *(Laughing.)* Who is he? What's his name? Why, there's nothing to be afraid of.

JOHNNIE. We really can't tell his name, sir. We promised.

REV. FOSTER. Come now, boys, can't you trust me?

JOHNNIE. We-ll, maybe. Is Mr. Grover coming back?

REV. FOSTER. No, not right away.

JOHNNIE. Will you promise not to tell him?

REV. FOSTER. I'll do what I think is best.

JOHNNIE. Okay, then. It is Frank Grover, Mr. Grover's son. He hit the ball through the window, but he didn't dare come in here because his father would whale him if he found that he was playing ball with us fellows. He wanted us to be sure to get the ball before his father looked at it because it was a present from his uncle and it had the uncle's autograph on it. Have you got it, sir?

REV. FOSTER. Yes, I have it, Johnnie, and I had an idea as to who owned it. But perhaps we should introduce ourselves. You know we have some pretty important business to handle here.

JOHNNIE *(Pointing out the boys who are togged out in various degrees of baseball uniforms and equipment.)* This is Bob. That's Charlie. And that one over there is Bill.

REV. FOSTER. I am glad to know you, fellows. Now don't you think we can all be good friends if we try? I haven't been at this church very long and that's probably why I don't know you better. But really I don't bite and there isn't any reason in the world why any of you should be afraid of me. What do you say, shall we be friends? *(Boys look at each other and then back at the minister and grin.)* Well, that's fine. Now I should like to ask you a question. Do any of you come to our Sunday School?

JOHNNIE. We used to, sir, but it was too tame. Then everybody glared at us when we laughed or made a noise.

We never had any fun. They just wanted us to sit still and look straight ahead during the service. And I guess they never cared what happened to us after we went out.

REV. FOSTER. Perhaps they didn't understand the kind of a program young people need, Johnnie. We have tried to change things a little bit lately. Do you boys like to hike? *(Boys nod.)* Do you like gym games? *(Nod.)* Do you like to read adventure books? *(Nod.)* And I suppose you don't like parties, and games and ice-cream? *(Boys show much interest in what has been said.)* Then if you like all of these things I have mentioned, I am sure you would enjoy coming out to our Sunday School affairs. We have our clubs which take care of all the sports and socials you would want. All that we ask is faithful attendance and proper attention at our Sunday School and church services. You fellows are smart enough to know that there are times for fun and laughter and that there are other times when it is best to be serious. In Sunday School we all try to learn more about God and His son Jesus. Outside of church we try to practice what we have learned inside. You boys want to grow up to be real he-men who will be respected by everyone, don't you? Well, that is just what the church can help you to become. The church teaches you to be fair to others, to be good sports, to play the game of life like real men. At the socials you will meet other boys and girls like yourselves who are trying to lead good lives. And all that it will cost you, fellows, is a little time and a little effort on your part.

JOHNNIE. You mean we don't have to pay to belong to the clubs.

REV. FOSTER. It won't cost you any money, Johnnie; just a real try at leading better lives and at helping other people. Does it sound all right to you, boys?

BOYS. Gosh, you bet it does.

JOHNNIE. We didn't know you had a gym fixed up, and club rooms, and a library.

REV. FOSTER. I am going to make a proposition to you, boys. Your baseball broke one of the windows here. That damage must be made good in some way. Now I happen to know that your folks haven't any money to spare for a thing like that. Supposing we forget about the bill if you will promise to attend church and Sunday School for a month, just to see how you like it? Does that sound fair?

BOYS. Gee, yes, if you let us in the clubs too.

REV. FOSTER. Now it happens we are needing some good men right now to help set up the scenery for the Sunday School pageant we are staging tomorrow. How about helping with the lights and stage?

BOY *(CHARLIE.)* I'll take care of the lights. My father is an electrician.

BOY *(BILL.)* I'll work on the scenery. I can build things.

BOY *(BOB.)* I'll do anything you want me to, sir.

REV. FOSTER. Good. Stay right here, fellows. I'll come right back and tell you where to start in. *(Exits Right.)*

CHARLIE. He's a swell guy, isn't he?

BILL. You bet! Nothing like the old geezer they used to have here.

BOB. Gee, we can have a lot of fun belonging here. I hope they collect stamps. *(Another boy—FRANK GROVER—enters cautiously from the door at the Right and moves toward the group.)*

FRANK *(Whispering.)* Hey, Johnnie, where's my ball?

JOHNNIE. Gosh, I forgot all about it. But we won't have to pay for the window. We're going to come here to Sunday School. The minister is tops. He's coming right back. Why don't you get him to fix it up with your dad?

FRANK. Nobody can fix it up with my dad. Boy! I hope he doesn't find out about it. *(There is a bustle at the back of the church. Presently the high-pitched, nervous voice of BETSY LIVERMORE is heard as she and the girls pick their way down from the rear of the church. She hasn't noticed the boys who are seated down front.)*

MISS LIVERMORE. Come, girls. We can't wait any longer. The rest of the cast will be in later. O-O-Oh, you boys frightened me. What are you doing here? Ah-ha, so someone told you there were girls in the play—and so you want parts. Well, we can use you, hmmmmm, we can use you. Take your places, girls. *(Girls walk up on the altar and stand in the background—an organist or pianist accompanies.)* Ready with the music. *(REV. FOSTER has returned.)* Oh, how do you do, Mr. Foster? Can you imagine it? The pageant will be presented tomorrow and only half the cast is here. I do hope they come. All right, Ann *(A soloist.)* Ann, all right. Music, please. *(ANN attempts to rehearse her part as a noise is heard at the rear of the church. The music may be the hymn, "The Way Of The Cross Leads Home". Pounds. MR. GROVER and MR. WALKER make their way down the aisle, GROVER leading.)*

MR. WALKER. Maybe you're right, Grover. But I can't believe that my boy would tell a falsehood about it.

MR. GROVER. Of course he did it. He can't deny it. We caught him in the act. There he is now, running behind that seat. *(JOHNNIE WALKER has been standing in the background and hasn't yet been observed by MR. GROVER. It was FRANK GROVER who tried to hide from his father.)* Come out of there, you. Ahh. Why—why, Frank. What are you doing here? *(REV. FOSTER steps forward quickly and hands MR. GROVER the baseball.)*

REV. FOSTER. By the way, Mr. Grover, do you recognize this?

MR. GROVER. Why, that is Frank's ball. *(Severely.)* Frank, how did that get here?

FRANK *(Badly frightened.)* Oh, Dad, it was all my fault. I hit the ball through the window, but I was too much of a coward to come in after it, so Johnnie said he would.

MR. WALKER *(Moving threateningly toward* MR. GROVER.*)*
I guess you have a bit of explaining to do yourself, Grover.
So you were trying to cover up your own son by dragging
my Johnnie's name into it? Why, I have half a . . .

MR. GROVER *(Stunned by the turn of events.)* B-but I
thought . . .

MR. WALKER. Never mind what you thought. I . . .
*(*MISS LIVERMORE *who has all the while been trying to rehearse her pageant comes toward the men in search of as-
sistance. She breaks into the conversation.)*

MISS LIVERMORE *(Pleadingly.)* Oh, gentlemen, gentlemen.
May I interrupt? Hmmmm. We just haven't enough folks
to practice this scene, and I must get an idea of the timing
and the positions. Won't you please read these parts until
the children come? Please, gentlemen? *(The men are upset
at this development, but are unable to gracefully refuse*
MISS LIVERMORE'S *request. So they follow her directions
rather reluctantly.)* Now boys *(She beckons to the boys.)*
you gather around in a semi-circle in the background of the
altar. Mr. Foster, will you please stand in center stage?
And Mr. Grover, you stand on the right. Mr. Walker, you
stand on the left facing Mr. Grover. There, that's fine.
Now here are the parts for you to read, gentlemen. Watch
your cues. Mr. Walker, you are the Voice of Youth. Mr.
Grover, you are the Voice of Maturity. And Mr. Foster,
you are the Voice of the Cross. Everybody ready now. Remember, bright cheery faces. Triumph is the feeling we are
trying to convey. *(*MR. WALKER *and* MR. GROVER *are uneasy, facing each other.* REV. FOSTER *does not seem to mind.
The soloist proceeds with her piece after which the* VOICES
speak.)

YOUTH.

I am the Voice of Youth
A church does not live that refuses to grow.
Youth is growth.

Jesus said, "Suffer the little children to come unto me; forbid them not; for to such belongeth the kingdom of God." (Mark 10:13,14)

Laughter, optimism, purity, life . . .

These things give I to the church.

MATURITY.

I am the Voice of Maturity.

Jesus said, "Who then is the faithful and wise servant, whom his lord has set over his household, to give them their food in due season? Blessed is that servant, whom his lord when he cometh shall find so doing." (Matthew 24:45,46)

The strong church rises from a strong foundation.

Faith, judgment, the wisdom of years . . .

These are my boast.

THE CROSS.

I am the Voice of the Cross.

Christ had but one challenge to all who would follow Him:

"Take up thy cross and follow me."

Mine is the story of suffering, death and resurrection.

"Come unto me all ye that labor and are heavy laden, and I will give you rest." (Matthew 11:28)

The shadow of the Cross reaches out to both old and young.

It is a kindly harbor in every storm, a stalwart friend in every woe.

Sympathy, friendship, peace—His love

Are your home in me.

MUSIC. Soloist may sing here the hymn, "In The Cross Of Christ I Glory." By Bowring.

MISS LIVERMORE *(After the music has ceased.)* Wonderful, gentlemen, wonderful. You made such good children. Hmmmm.

MR. GROVER *(Offering his hand to* WALKER.*)* I am afraid I have been childish. Our petty quarrels seem so small here in the light of the Cross. A new vision came to me just now. Material things have blinded me so in the past. I guess I have always made the mistake of placing a price tag on religion, and by doing it have lost so much that is good and beautiful in life. Funny how such things hit you all at once, isn't it?

MR. WALKER. I have been wrong, too, Grover. I feel like a slacker who has deserted his post in a time of grave danger. I should have known that running away from the church would not assist in improving it. Criticising won't help without some definite Christian action to accompany it. The fault isn't with the church, or with the minister. And it isn't with us because we haven't tried. We did try, each in our own way, but we were trying in the wrong direction.

MR. GROVER. How true that is. But I never would have believed it last week, or this morning. Christ said that a little child shall lead them. Walker, we have really found ourselves—our Christian selves—here at this Sunday School pageant. *(Turning to* REV. FOSTER.*)* I wonder if you can forgive my wrongs, Rev. Foster? I see now that the church doesn't belong to me alone, or to the official board, or to the trustees. It is just an instrument that God has placed in our hands temporarily to use for the benefit of all of His people. And God's house it will surely be from now on, if my influence can accomplish it. Fuel and light. How stupid I have been! Fuel to kindle the spark of Christian love in the hearts of our people. Light to show them the road to the Master. What a wonderful return for such a small cost! And the secret of it all is in discovering that GREATER THAN ANY MAN is the Church of the Master! *(*REV. FOSTER *places his arms about* MR. GROVER *and* MR. WALKER *and pronounces the benediction.)*

THE VOICE THAT FAILED

A DRAMA IN ONE ACT

By

EFFA E. PRESTON

PRODUCTION RIGHTS

Copies of this play are available in single pamphlet form. The right to produce this play by one group of amateur players is authorized only by the purchase of eight copies (one copy for each speaking part) at the current price of 50c each.

It is dishonest and illegal to copy parts.

CAST OF CHARACTERS

Mr. Holmes
Miss Diana Dale
Mr. Niles
Mr. Garth
Mrs. Garth
Mr. Morris
} *members of the church committee*

Miss Mary Girard .... *church organist and member of the committee*

Solinda Sayers .... *a former choir singer*

Miss Grace Hadley .... *a visiting social worker*

Time: *A summer evening.*

Place: *A committee room in the church.*

Time of Playing: *Twenty minutes.*

COSTUMES AND CHARACTERISTICS

All the characters wear everyday costumes, suitable for summer. Solinda dresses in white. She is the youngest, being about twenty-five. Miss Hadley, Miss Dale, and Miss Gerard are in their late twenties. The rest of the cast are in their middle thirties and forties. All should be good singers. Mr. Holmes is a thin, dyspeptic type, without enthusiasm, who takes a pessimistic view of things and seldom agrees with anyone. Mr. and Mrs. Garth are a cheerful, wholesome couple, who always agree with each other. Miss Dale is a positive young woman, with the courage of her convictions. Miss Hadley is a young woman of force and decision, who can be aggressive in support of her principles. Mr. Morris is a portly, well-groomed businessman, conspicuous for his poise and executive ability. Solinda is an attractive girl, of a naturally sunny and hopeful disposition. Misfortune, however, has given her a sad expression. Mr. Niles is a brisk, lively little man, who gets along well with everybody. Miss Gerard is of stylish stout build, neatly tailored, and is very efficient and businesslike.

MUSIC

The songs, "Abide With Me" and "Praise God From Whom All Blessings Flow," may be found in any hymnal. "The Lord's Prayer," by Malnotte, may be sung by Solinda herself, or a phonograph record of the song may be used. It will be found in Victor Record Album No. M-679, being a Red Seal record of the song as sung by Gladys Swarthout to piano accompaniment. If preferred, other sacred songs, equally suitable, may be substituted by the director.

STAGE DIRECTIONS

Up stage means away from footlights; *down stage*, near footlights. In the use of *right* and *left*, the actor is supposed to be facing the audience.

THE VOICE THAT FAILED

SCENE: *A committee room in a small church on a summer evening. It has two doors—one at right leading to the outer hall and the street and the other at left opening into the assembly room. The only furnishings are about a dozen straight-backed chairs scattered around the upstage end of the room. Throughout the play the stage lights are full up.*

A short time before the curtain is raised, the sound of singing comes from off left, where a prayer meeting is closing with a stanza from the hymn, "Abide With Me," sung by the congregation. Toward the end of the song, the curtain rises on an empty stage. As the music ceases, the door at left opens and the following members of the cast enter: MR. HOLMES, SOLINDA SAYERS, MISS DALE, MR. NILES, MISS HADLEY, *and* MR. *and* MRS. GARTH. *They leave the door open behind them.*

MR. HOLMES *(Turning and addressing the others.)* Now, friends, if you'll be seated for a few minutes we can hold our committee meeting in a very short time. The pastor is sorry he can't be present. Mr. Morris is evidently delayed, but I'm sure he'll soon be here.

SOLINDA *(Deprecatingly.)* I'm not on the committee, Mr. Holmes, so I'll leave.

MR. HOLMES. No need to, Solinda. No need to go at all.

MISS DALE. No, sit down, Solinda, and wait for me, please. I want to talk to you after the meeting. We won't be long.

(All find seats on the chairs up stage. SOLINDA *sits near the front beside* MISS DALE.*)*

MISS GERARD *(Calling from off left through the open doorway.)* Solinda, please come in here a minute and help me with the music for Sunday.

SOLINDA. Of course, Mary. *(Rises, crosses, and goes off left, shutting the door behind her.)*

MR. NILES. Is this meeting about the money, Holmes?

MR. HOLMES. Certainly. As you all know, Miss Carson, who worshipped here for years, left the church five thousand dollars in her will, and we've got to decide what to do with it soon or, according to her will, it goes elsewhere. Jane Carson always was set in her ways.

MISS HADLEY *(Making an uneasy movement as if about to rise.)* I shouldn't be here. I'm not even a member of your church. I'm just a visitor in town.

MRS. GARTH *(With good-natured authority.)* You stay right here, Grace Hadley. I may need you later.

MISS HADLEY *(Sinking back into her seat.)* All right, if I'm not intruding.

MR. NILES. Goodness knows there are plenty of ways we can use the money.

MISS DALE. I still say Solinda's idea was the best. Poor girl! She looks so sad all the time.

MR. GARTH *(Trying to change the subject.)* The music was good tonight, wasn't it?

MRS. GARTH. Very good, but nobody can sing the way Solinda used to.

MR. GARTH. You're right, my dear.

MR. HOLMES. Oh, I wouldn't say that.

MISS DALE *(Bursting out in exasperation.)* Harvey Holmes, sometime you're going to agree with somebody, purely by error, and it's going to be just too bad.

MR. NILES *(Reminiscently.)* Solinda used to sing a solo nearly every Sunday.

MISS DALE. And at least every six weeks she was asked to sing our favorite.

MISS HADLEY *(Interested.)* What was that?

237

MRS. GARTH *(Interposing eagerly.)* "The Lord's Prayer." Nobody ever sang it like Solinda.

MISS HADLEY. But I don't understand. Why doesn't she sing now?

MRS. GARTH. Maybe I'd better tell you before she returns. She had a beautiful voice. She intended to be a concert singer, and then just as she was ready to begin her career, something awful happened.

MISS HADLEY *(Curiously.)* What? Did she lose her voice?

MRS. GARTH *(Nodding solemnly.)* She surely did!

MISS DALE. Let's begin at the beginning. She was all alone in the world except for her little sister Martha, whom she loved very much. She had great plans for Martha, who was really a talented child. She played the piano remarkably well. Solinda was studying voice and the lessons for two took nearly all their money, but they managed to struggle along and were very happy.

MRS. GARTH. Solinda was a wonderful manager.

MISS HADLEY *(A little impatiently.)* She must have been! But what happened?

MRS. GARTH. She was ready to give her first concert, here in this church. Her teacher had arranged a series of good concerts for her. With the money she would receive she was going to send Martha to a musical institute and pay for vocal lessons for a poor little girl, Elsa March, who has a truly remarkable voice, but whose family is practically penniless. Solinda planned to have her own instructor take Elsa as a pupil.

MISS HADLEY. Elsa's family couldn't do anything?

MISS DALE. The father is a helpless cripple. The mother takes in washing and does the best she can. There are two other children besides Elsa, both very bright.

MR. HOLMES *(Coldly.)* Still not geniuses.

MISS DALE *(Dramatically.)* The day of Solinda's first concert, which never came off, Martha became very ill— polio. It was the only case in town, though the surrounding country had many cases.

MR. GARTH. The hospital here was full. Every hospital for miles around was full—private rooms, wards, everything.

MRS. GARTH *(With a sigh.)* We all were going to help with the expenses, but we couldn't do anything. There wasn't any ambulance available, but we finally made arrangements to take her to a city hospital on a plane.

MR. GARTH. The day she was to be flown to the city Martha died.

MISS HADLEY. But what about Solinda's voice?

MISS DALE. She was brave as always, and after Martha's death she planned to continue her work and assist Elsa, the little girl with the voice. The first time Solinda tried to practice she found that her voice was absolutely gone. She couldn't sing a note. She had lost her voice from the shock and it is very doubtful if she ever recovers it.

MR. HOLMES. Doctors said another shock or some violent stimulus might help.

MISS DALE *(Shrugging.)* If there were anything in this town to give anybody a stimulus, violent or otherwise!

MR. GARTH. So poor Elsa never got her lessons.

MR. NILES. Solinda teaches piano. She has to make a living somehow—poor girl! She seldom goes out. I was surprised to see her tonight.

MRS. GARTH *(Thoughtfully.)* When Solinda sang, her voice seemed to come from a world far from ours—a world of tenderness and love. She may never sing again, but there is still music in her soul.

MR. GARTH. I heard the child Elsa sing. The girl is poor and undernourished, but she sings with remarkable feeling and understanding. I can't understand how it is possible.

MISS HADLEY. Why hasn't someone else done something for Elsa?

MR. HOLMES. There are so many cases needing attention.

MISS HADLEY. But now you have some money.

MISS DALE. Solinda was planning to endow a bed in the

hospital, too. But she didn't get much cooperation. People are so indifferent. Just the same, I believe I'll start something tonight.

MR. GARTH *(Grinning at her.)* Good for you, Diana. I'll back you up.

MRS. GARTH. So will I, Diana.

MISS HADLEY *(Energetically.)* Count on me, too.

MR. NILES *(Jocularly.)* When Helen Hadley speaks, folks listen. I went to school with her. I know.

(SOLINDA and MISS GERARD enter at left, cross, and take seats near the front.)

MISS GERARD *(Speaking as they enter.)* Solinda, I could never manage this choir business without your help. *(Pats her shoulder gratefully.)*

SOLINDA *(Earnestly, with a smile.)* If you only knew how glad I am there is something I can do to help, Mary.

MR. NILES. Say, if that Morris chap doesn't get here soon I'm going home. *(Rises and takes a restless turn or two at right up and down stage.)*

MR. HOLMES. He'll be here any minute and the meeting won't take long.

MISS DALE. You never know, Mr. Holmes.

(MR. MORRIS enters briskly at right. MR. NILES returns to his chair.)

MR. MORRIS *(Apologetically.)* I'm very sorry to be so late, folks, but I've been stopped on the street at least twenty times by people with wonderful suggestions about what to do with that money. You'd think it was ten million, at least.

MR. HOLMES *(Peevishly.)* I guess this committee can do its own thinking.

MR. MORRIS *(Crossing down left, where he stands looking up stage, while the others turn to face him.)* As you know, friends, our faithful member, Jane Carson . . .

MRS. GARTH *(Interrupting.)* Excuse me, Mr. Morris, but we have here two ladies not on the committee, Miss Solinda Sayers and Miss Grace Hadley. We urged them to remain, feeling sure you would have no objections.

MR. MORRIS *(Heartily.)* Certainly not, Mrs. Garth. We are all, I am sure, very glad you have them with us. As I was saying, Miss Carson who passed away last month had left our church about five thousand dollars to be used as we, the committee appointed by the governing body of the church, see fit. The matter must be definitely decided by one week from today or the money reverts to a distant cousin of Miss Carson's in Idaho.

MR. HOLMES *(Emphatically.)* And it's up to us not to let it revert.

MR. MORRIS. The meeting is now open for suggestions.

MISS DALE *(Rising.)* I think it would be a wonderful thing if we used the money to endow a bed in the hospital. *(Looks around defiantly and sits.)*

MR. MORRIS. It is true the charity ward cannot accommodate all the patients who need care, or the private rooms, either.

MR. NILES *(Curiously.)* What suggestions did you get on your way here?

MR. MORRIS *(Smiling reminiscently.)* One man wanted to put the money in the bank to draw interest until we have a definite use for it.

MISS GERARD. When do we not have a definite use for money?

MR. MORRIS. We couldn't do it if we wished, Miss Gerard. Miss Carson stipulated a definite use of the money at once. We just aren't permitted to wait for an emergency.

MR. NILES. That's right.

MR. MORRIS. Then a lady stopped me and asked why didn't we have a paid quartet and buy robes for the junior choir.

MISS GERARD *(Dryly.)* What we need in our choir is a few good voices. Even one would be a big help.

MISS DALE. You've got something there.

MR. MORRIS. A businessman suggested chimes, but I told him we hadn't enough money. He thought we had fifty thousand to spend. That reminds me of a letter I have received from Mr. Green, the absent member of our committee, suggesting that we build a monument to the memory of Miss Carson or give the money to the chamber of commerce. I wrote him that the living need charity more than the dead do monuments, that the chamber of commerce can take care of itself, and anyway we haven't that much money.

Miss Gerard. How about that hospital bed?

Miss Dale. And how about Elsa Marsh and her music lessons? She could pay us back some day maybe, if we must be mercenary.

Mr. Holmes *(Didactically.)* "Practical" is the word, Miss Dale. Practical, not mercenary.

Miss Dale *(Paying no attention to him.)* When I think that a year—just one year today, has passed since Solinda planned those wonderful things, and we've just sat here like bumps on a log and done nothing about them!

Mr. Holmes *(Rebukingly.)* But, after all, Miss Dale, weren't those ideas, beautiful as they were, a bit sentimental and impractical?

Solinda *(Speaking in hurt tones.)* Oh, no, Mr. Holmes! Elsa has a wonderful voice. The world should hear it. And you know how greatly in need of added facilities our hospital is. Even one extra bed in a ward may save many lives.

Miss Hadley *(Rising and interposing vigorously.)* I know I have no business to speak. I am merely a summer visitor. But, as a trained and experienced social worker, I am shocked and disgusted at what that—er—gentleman just said. As a human being, I am just plain mad. What's sentimental about helping the poor and needy? Isn't there authority in the Bible for that? Or isn't the gentleman familiar with the Bible? What's impractical about providing aid for a sick child or helping a poor girl get proper training in order that she may earn a good living and provide heartwarming entertainment for her listeners? Remember you can't make good citizens out of boys and girls who are pushed around during their childhood, who feel friendless and unwanted, or who become ill because of the unsanitary conditions in which they live. It's a wonder to me they grow up as respectable as some of them do. As for the hospital, what better use could the money be put to that more beds or an extra ambulance? I appeal to your reason as well as your hearts. *(Sits.)*

MR. MORRIS. Very well said, Miss Hadley.

MISS HADLEY *(Rising again.)* I've had ten years' experience in the slums of a big city, and I have never seen a family more in need of aid than the Marsh family. I visited them yesterday.

MR. MORRIS. It is kind of you to be so interested, Miss Hadley.

MISS HADLEY. Not at all. I have what we all have—the interest of a person who believes that God blesses the generous thought. *(Sits.)*

MISS DALE *(Rising.)* I feel that Helen Hadley knows what she's talking about. She is considered an extremely capable social worker. *(Resumes her seat.)*

MR. MORRIS *(Smiling.)* Of course she is; but how did we get of the subject of social workers, anyway? Will the committee members please retire? No, you might not come back. Just confer for a moment, then we'll put the matter to a vote.

(MISS DALE, MISS GERARD, MR. NILES, MR. HOLMES, and MR. and MRS. GARTH gather in a group at the rear of the stage and talk in whispers. Looking tired and bored. MR. MORRIS remains at the front of the stage.)

MISS HADLEY *(Heatedly in a low tone. To SOLINDA.)* Talk about one-way minds in a one-way street! How can they even hesitate?

SOLINDA *(In a conciliatory tone.)* At heart they are really very kind. I trust them to do the generous thing.

MISS HADLEY. I hope you're right.

(MR. MORRIS watches the conference at the back of the room, then, after a pause, he calls to the committee members.)

MR. MORRIS. Any time the committee is ready, we will proceed with the meeting. *(The six committee members return to their seats. MR. MORRIS continues.)* Attention please. The following suggestions have been made: endowment of a hospital bed; a paid quartet and robes for the Junior choir; and providing educational and financial help for the Marsh family, particularly Elsa. The meeting is again open for discussion.

MRS. GARTH. We simply must have a hospital bed.

MR. NILES *(Briskly.)* Of course that quartet and robe business is silly. What do we think we are? A cathedral on Fifth Avenue? I vote for the bed in the ward.

MISS GERARD *(With emphasis.)* So do I.

MISS DALE. We can easily keep up the expenses of the bed if we once get it. And we don't have to save a cent of the money so let's look after the Marsh family—Elsa, anyway. When I think of the way Solinda worked and planned and dreamed of all this! We could have the greatest choir in the world with robes of velvet, but to the people of this church it would never equal Solinda's singing "The Lord's Prayer." Not to those of us who know and love her.

MRS. GARTH *(Enthusiastically.)* My sentiments exactly!

MR. GARTH. I agree with my wife, as usual.

MISS GERARD *(Warmly.)* You know darned well I do, too.

SOLINDA *(Touched.)* Thank you, my friends. You are very kind. I am sure you will decide upon the best possible use for the money.

MISS GERARD. We can if we put our minds and our hearts into it. Remember last Sunday's text: "Though I have all faith, so that I could remove mountains, and have not charity, I am nothing."

SOLINDA *(Wistfully.)* If only I could sing again, just for one tour of concerts, then we would have money enough for everything. We could put two-thirds of what I earned with Miss Carson's money.

MR. NILES. I'm in favor of trying both schemes—endowing the hospital bed and helping Elsa Marsh. We can raise money somehow to carry them on.

MISS HADLEY *(Rising and addressing the meeting earnestly.)* May I interrupt again? If you do both, you will have benefited not only the sick and the poor, but the town and the entire county. And most of all you will have benefited yourselves. You will have proved that you really do believe that the greatest thing in the world is charity and that it does begin at home. Of course you can raise needed additional money somehow. *(Resumes her seat.)*

MR. HOLMES *(Querulously.)* It's quite a responsibility.

MISS DALE *(To* MISS GERARD.*)* Mary, please go in and play Solinda's song.

*(*MISS GERARD *hurries off at left, and a moment later the music of "The Lord's Prayer" is heard very softly off left.)*

MR. MORRIS. We'll put it to a vote. All in favor of the hospital bed and a musical education for Elsa Marsh and helping the rest of the family if possible, stand. (*MISS DALE, MISS GERARD, MR. NILES, and MR. and MRS. GARTH rise. MISS HADLEY and SOLINDA remain seated. MR. HOLMES is the last to rise, but he smiles as he does so. MR. MORRIS looks around and continues.)* Miss Gerard is not here.

MISS DALE. She votes yes.

MR. MORRIS. We have a majority, anyway. According to our bylaws, the vote is decided in the affirmative. We carry out Solinda's wishes. And may we extend our profound gratitude to Solinda, who has never wavered in her effort to help others and whose shining example has shown us the way? From now on, I am sure we shall all understand more clearly the words, "Inasmuch as ye have done unto one of the least of these my brethren, ye have done it unto me."

(Suddenly the music off stage grows louder. SOLINDA *rises and sings "The Lord's Prayer" to the music. If a record is used,* SOLINDA *should move her lips in accord with the singing of the soloist. This effect will require much practice.* MISS GERARD *may turn on the phonograph off stage.*

All those on the stage listen in awed amazement. As the song ends, SOLINDA *smiles happily at them.)*

MISS DALE *(Incredulously.)* You sang! You sang, Solinda!

MR. NILES. It's a miracle.

MRS. GARTH. It's what the doctor said—a stimulus!

MR. GARTH. It's wonderful!

MISS GERARD *enters at left.*

MISS GERARD *(Crying out in joy.)* Solinda, you sang!

SOLINDA *(Beaming.)* Now we need have no fear. We shall have beds in the hospital and education for the Marsh children. I shall give my concerts this year. I know it. I sang for joy because you remembered my plans. I am sure I shall always sing now, with my voice and my heart. Thank you, my friends. Through you, God has answered my prayers.

MISS GERARD. It's too good to be true.

SOLINDA. When Martha died I felt that at least she was safe and happy. Then Elsa, with no one to help her, filled my mind and heart, as did the poor sick children with no care. Now, when you know our hospital can have room for at least one more needy one, when you hear Elsa sing a song you can't forget, you will feel happier than ever before.

MRS. GARTH *(Almost tearfully.)* It's hearing you sing again that makes us happier than ever before, Solinda!

SOLINDA *(Glowing with joy.)* Before we go, let us sing "Praise God From Whom All Blessings Flow."

(All sing the long meter doxology. The grouping is as follows.)

Back row—MR. *and* MRS. GARTH, MISS GERARD, MR. HOLMES, MR. NILES.

Front row—MISS HADLEY, SOLINDA, MISS DALE, MR. MORRIS.

CURTAIN

DEADWOOD

A DRAMA IN ONE ACT

By
WAYNE C. LEE

PRODUCTION RIGHTS

Copies of this play are available in single pamphlet form. The right to produce this play by one group of amateur players is authorized only by the purchase of five copies (one copy for each speaking part) at the current price of 50c each.

It is dishonest and illegal to copy parts.

CAST OF CHARACTERS
(For Four Women and One Man)

GRANDMA LARSON ....about 70

ETHEL GARRY ....about 50

CORA FREMONT ....about 50

GEORGE TOLIFF 35

JEAN RAMBER ....about 21

SETTING: The living room of Grandma Larson's tiny two-room house.

PLAYING TIME: 30 minutes.

LIGHTING: *No special effects.*

COSTUMES: *Grandma wears a good, though old-fashioned, dress. She wears glasses that sit far down on her nose and she looks over them at anything beyond arm's length. Cora and Ethel wear spring coats and hats and carry purses. George wears a matched work shirt and pants. There are spots of mud on the pants. Jean wears an old dress that has spots of mud on it.*

PROPERTIES: *Kettle and ladle, soup plate and spoon, blanket and quilt, match in cupboard, purses for Cora and Ethel, each with dollar bill, water bucket and dipper, small clock.*

SETTING: *Grandma's small living room. There are two entrances, one at Right and one at Left. Right leads outside and Left goes into Grandma's bedroom. Against the upstage wall at Right is a narrow upright cupboard. Next to it on the Left is a small one-burner kerosene stove with a kettle sitting on the back of it. To the left of it is a table with two kitchen chairs pushed up to it. Against the upstage wall at Left is a wash stand with a bucket and wash basin sitting on it. A towel is hanging from one end of the stand. In the wall between the wash stand and the table is a small window. On a shelf beside the window is a clock showing two-thirty as the curtain rises. A rocking chair sits downstage from the wash stand.*

248

DEADWOOD

AT RISE: *Grandma Larson is moving across the stage. She goes to the stove, takes the lid off the kettle and looks inside.*

GRANDMA. This soup will make a fine supper. *(Puts the lid back on the kettle.)* Now let's see. *(Looks at the clock.)* Two-thirty. I've got half an hour to get to that meeting. I'll have to start pretty soon. I do hope there is something I can do. *(Knock is heard offstage Right.)* Oh, dear. Now who can that be? I hope it isn't someone who will make me late for the meeting. *(Crosses to Right and opens the door.)* Why, I do declare. Ethel and Cora. Come in. I haven't seen you two in a coon's age. *(Ethel Garry and Cora Fremont enter at Right. They cross to the center of the stage, looking over the room critically.)*

ETHEL. We were just passing by and thought we'd drop in for a minute.

CORA *(Shrugging in a careless manner.)* You know how it is? Old friends.

GRANDMA. Of course. Won't you sit down? *(Indicates the chairs and shakes her head sadly when her visitors aren't looking.)*

CORA *(Sitting in the rocker.)* My, this *is* a nice chair. *(Looks at Ethel.)*

ETHEL. I imagine it is. *(Pulls the chair out from the table and sits.)* It is used a lot. And it takes use to make a chair really comfortable.

GRANDMA *(Taking the other chair and pulling it over in front of the cupboard and sitting.)* A chair is like a house. A house isn't home unless it's really lived in and not just used for a stopping place.

ETHEL. This must be a home to you then. You're seldom out of it, are you?

GRANDMA. I go out when it's necessary. But the older you get, the smaller your world becomes. I spend much of my time writing letters and piecing quilts.

CORA. It must be an exciting life.

ETHEL *(Sarcastically.)* Useful, too.

GRANDMA. I have no complaints. I am so much better off than those poor people down along the river.

CORA *(Rocking slowly, folding her hands in comfort.)* Too bad about them. They shouldn't have built their homes so close to the river.

ETHEL. Floods come every so often. They should have known better than to build down there.

GRANDMA. We don't always have the choice of where we live.

CORA. How true! Is this where you want to live?

GRANDMA. I'm happy here. I've lived here so long, I wouldn't be satisfied anywhere else.

ETHEL. Nonsense- Of course you would be happy somewhere else.

GRANDMA. I imagine those people without homes would be glad to have anything, even a little shack like mine.

CORA. Maybe. But I say it's their own fault for building down there.

ETHEL. There was a man at my door this morning asking me to give something to help those made homeless by the flood.

GRANDMA. I suppose you gave him something.

ETHEL. Oh, yes. But the ingrate didn't seem to be satisfied. He wanted me to help with some kind of relief work.

CORA. The nerve of that man! I'll bet it was the same one who came to our house. He asked me the same thing.

GRANDMA. And you wouldn't help?

CORA. Why should I help people who deliberately ask for trouble by living down there along the river? I gave him a dollar and that was that.

ETHEL. That's just what I did. I thought my dollar would do them as much good as I· would.

GRANDMA. I imagine you're right about that.

CORA. I suppose that fellow didn't come here.

GRANDMA. No. At least, he hasn't yet. And I would like to help.

ETHEL. What could you do?

GRANDMA. I don't know. They are holding a meeting down

at the city hall this afternoon at three to tell people what they can do to help the flood victims. I thought I'd go down and see what I can do.

CORA. But you know without going down there that you can't do anything. You're not able to do any of the work they would ask you to do. They work like a slave at a place like that. I know. I volunteered once. I promised myself— never again! (Rocks more vigorously.)

ETHEL. That brazen man who came by this morning even asked me if I had a spare room where I could put some of those people from down along the river. I told him "no" in a way he understood it, believe me.

CORA (Throwing up her hands.) What woman would want one of those people from down on the river in her house?

GRANDMA. I would if I had room.

ETHEL. You couldn't squeeze a sparrow in here to spend the night. I don't see what you're worrying about. There's nothing you can do.

GRANDMA (Looking up at the clock.) I suppose there isn't. But in the morning paper it said everybody could do something. Maybe I'm just nobody. (Cora and Ethel exchange glances and nod. A knock is heard at Right.)

GEORGE (Offstage Right.) Say, Grandma, can I get a drink?

GRANDMA (Getting up and going to Right. Opens the door.) Of course, George. Come in. You don't have to knock.

GEORGE (Entering.) I figure a person is entitled to privacy in his own home. (Crosses to the wash stand.) I've been down along the river helping. Sure a lot of work to do there. I got pretty hot and dry. (Takes a dipper of water from the bucket and drinks.)

ETHEL. What can anybody do down there with the water so high?

GEORGE (Turning back from the wash stand.) Plenty! Rescue and salvage work, mostly. There are lots of things that we can get out of the houses. And not long ago we found a man and his wife marooned in the attic of their home.

GRANDMA. It was lucky you were there to get them out.

GEORGE. I reckon it was. That house was swept down the river just a few minutes after we got them out. I'm on my way now to see if I can find some warm blankets and clothes for them. They're wet and that wind is pretty chilly.

CORA. It certainly is too bad they didn't know enough to live somewhere else.

GEORGE. Those people didn't have money enough to rent anything up here on the hill. So they rented down along the river where it was cheaper. They figured that was better than depending on charity.

ETHEL *(Shrugging.)* And what did they gain by it? Now they'll really be on charity. Don't even have clothes.

GEORGE *(Moving around to face Ethel and Cora. Puts his hands on his hips and speaks angrily.)* I suppose if a fire burned you out, we should say it was too bad you didn't know better than to have a stove in your house?

CORA *(Leaning back in the rocker.)* Mercy me! We didn't say anything about a fire.

GEORGE. A fire or a flood. It's all the same when you're left without clothes to wear or a home to live in.

ETHEL. Of course, we feel sorry for them. Don't misunderstand us.

GEORGE *(Emphatically.)* I don't misunderstand you! Not a bit!

GRANDMA. Where are you going to get those blankets, George?

GEORGE. I don't know. I'm just going to hunt for someone who will donate some.

GRANDMA. You wait right here. I've got some in my bedroom I can spare. *(Starts to Left.)*

GEORGE. I can't wait, Grandma. I've got some other things to do. But if you can spare a blanket or two, it will really help. I'll be back in a few minutes and pick them up. *(Exits at Right.)*

GRANDMA. I must get those blankets for George. Excuse me. *(Exits at Left.)*

CORA. Well, Ethel, we're getting nowhere fast.

ETHEL. Do you think Grandma realizes how much she is in the way here?

CORA. I doubt it. I feel sorry for the old lady. But after all! This place! It's an eyesore to the whole block.

ETHEL. I should say it is. When this house was built it probably looked as nice as the rest. But all the others have been torn down or moved away. This is a nice respectable district now—except for this place.

CORA *(Rocking complacently.)* It isn't as if we were trying to hurt Grandma. We'll be doing her a great favor if we can convince her to sell this place and move to an old folks' home.

ETHEL. She would receive wonderful care there. I'll bet she doesn't half take care of herself here. *(Gets up. Goes to the cupboard. Opens it and looks inside.)* Doesn't have half enough dishes.

CORA *(Getting out of the rocker with effort.)* Look over here. *(Goes to the wash stand.)* Doesn't even have water in the house. There's that old pump and well out back. Been there for fifty years if it's a day. She has to carry all her water from there. Nothing, absolutely nothing modern. She lives a slave's life.

ETHEL. Such a tiny little stove! *(Lifts the lid on the kettle and looks in.)* Come here, Cora. Look at this.

CORA *(Hurrying over and looking in the kettle. Shocked.)* Soup! Of all things! And it isn't the nutritious soup you buy in the store, either. Just plain homemade soup. Probably all the leftovers she's had for the last week.

ETHEL. Maybe soup is all she ever has. *(Puts the lid back on the kettle and turns away, wrinkling her nose as if the smell was bad.)* It's a wonder she is still alive.

CORA. It's our duty, Ethel, to see to it she moves to some old folks' home.

ETHEL. She'll probably say she likes to live this way.

CORA. She doesn't know any better. But she's no good to society here and you know it. She's holding up the development of this entire block.

ETHEL. As far as society goes, she is just deadwood.

CORA. No good to anybody.

ETHEL. How are we going to approach the subject? *(Goes to Right and opens the door and looks out.)*

CORA. I thought you were going to do that. I just came along to back you up. What do you see out there? *(Comes over to stand behind Ethel and try to see around her.)*

ETHEL. I was just looking at all the people down close to the river. Mostly curiosity hounds, I suppose.

CORA. I was down there a while this morning. But they tried to get me to work in one of those emergency kitchens. Just what did they think I was, anyway?

ETHEL. I went down, too. Thought I might get some news. But they put me to feeding little kids. Half frozen and half starved. It nearly made me sick. I had to get away. What have we got nurses and doctors for?

CORA. Well, we'd better talk to Gandma about our business as soon as she comes back. We're missing out on too much by staying here. *(Turns away from the door.)*

ETHEL *(Shutting the door and turning back to center.)* You're right, Cora. No telling what might be happening down there. I want to know. *(Grandma enters at Left, carrying a big blanket and a quilt.)*

GRANDMA. These ought to help warm those youngsters. *(Drops the blanket and quilt on the floor.)*

CORA *(Flopping down in the rocker.)* Grandma, Ethel has some important things to talk over with you.

ETHEL *(Quickly.)* No more me than Cora, Grandma. *(Sits in the chair by the table.)*

GRANDMA. I'm ready to listen. *(Glances up at the clock.)* I wish George would come after these blankets. *(Sits in the chair at Left.)*

ETHEL. Well—you see— *(Shifts uncomfortably.)* Don't you get lonesome living here alone?

GRANDMA. Oh, yes, sometimes. If I had a little more room I'd take in some of those homeless people now. They would be wonderful company.

CORA. Wouldn't you like to live with a lot of other people?

GRANDMA. That depends on several things. Just being with people so we could sit and look at each other wouldn't be my idea of company. I have never been more lonesome than I was one time in a big crowd of strange people. There are lots worse things than living alone.

ETHEL. Wouldn't you like to live in a **modern** house? You'd have running water and a nice refrigerator.

GRANDMA. Maybe I would. I don't know. I've never had such things. I'm afraid I'm too old now to get used to new gadgets. Anyway, I don't have money enough to buy fancy things.

CORA. But they would be nice.

GRANDMA. I wonder. Used to be when John and I first bought this little place and he worked down in the railroad yards, everybody on the block had a house something like ours. Then John died and the railroad company gave me this pension that I've lived on ever since. Other people in the block either moved away or built new homes. They bought fancy things. But they have never been as happy as the old crowd who used to live here.

ETHEL. Maybe you don't know how happy they are.

GRANDMA. Maybe I don't. If they're happy at all, they certainly never show it. Used to be we were all neighbors. Now I hardly know that anybody lives in those other houses. If I didn't hear their television sets blaring or hear them quarreling, I might think I lived on a forgotten street. *(She tips her head back thoughtfully and closes her eyes while Cora and Ethel exchange glances, shaking their heads.)* Whenever anything happened to anyone along the street, we all heard about it. If it was good news, we all felt good. If it was bad news, we all felt bad and we helped the unfortunate ones if there was anything we could do. Now it takes a major tragedy like this flood to bring out the good in people. And even that can't always dig down deep enough to find any good.

CORA. Wouldn't you rather live in comfort than just exist with your memories?

GRANDMA. Comfort isn't altogether just having an easy chair to sit in or a soft bed to sleep in. Comfort is a state of the mind. I'm more comfortable than most of my neighbors. I know I am.

ETHEL. Comfortable in this—this shack?

GRANDMA *(Looking sharply at Ethel.)* Maybe it is a shack. But it's home. Some of these big houses are just buildings. But I've preached enough of a sermon. Just what important things did you want to talk about? *(George enters at Right.)*

GEORGE. Well, I'm ready for those blankets, Grandma.

GRANDMA *(Rising and pointing to the blanket and quilt on the floor.)* There they are, George. I do hope they will help.

GEORGE *(Crossing to pick up the blanket and quilt.)* They will, all right. Say, isn't this your best quilt, Grandma?

GRANDMA. Yes. But I don't need it now. It's the heaviest one I have. I thought it would do the most good.

GEORGE *(Fingering the quilt.)* This is the one you won the prize with at the fair, isn't it?

GRANDMA. That's it. But if it keeps some youngster from catching pneumonia, it will mean more than a prize at the fair.

GEORGE *(Picking up the blanket and quilt.)* I guess it would. They're sure going to need a lot of things.

ETHEL *(Looking at Cora.)* Maybe I ought to help a little more. *(Opens her purse and takes out a dollar bill.)* Here, George. Take this down to them. This makes twice I've contributed.

GEORGE *(Taking the money.)* I hope it doesn't bankrupt you.

CORA *(Opening the purse and taking out a dollar bill.)* Here. Take this, too.

GEORGE *(Taking the money.)* Thanks. *(Sarcastically.)* In spite of the generous good will behind these gifts, it will help feed some hungry kid. *(Turns to Grandma.)* I'll try to keep track of your quilt, Grandma, and get it back to you.

GRANDMA. That's all right, George. If you can, I'll appreciate it. But use it where it's needed and don't worry about losing it. Say, George, have they got plenty to eat down there?

GEORGE. There is never enough at a time like this. There are some who haven't had anything to eat since sometime yesterday.

GRANDMA. You send up one of them. I've got some soup here that I'll heat up.

GEORGE. All right, Grandma. I'll send up that woman we just rescued from her attic. *(Exits at Right.)*

ETHEL. Are you going to feed her your soup?

GRANDMA. *Of course. (Goes to the stove. Gets a match from the cupboard. Makes a pretense of lighting the burner. Pulls the kettle up over the burner.)* This soup will warm her up.

CORA. What about your supper?

GRANDMA. I'll have time enough to get more supper. Or if I don't, it won't hurt me to go without one meal. Those people down there have missed three or four already.

CORA. I certainly hate to miss a meal.

GRANDMA *(Looking at Cora.)* I can believe that.

ETHEL. I don't think it's necessary to deprive ourselves just to help some people who wouldn't help themselves.

GRANDMA. There are very few people so worthless they won't help themselves.

CORA. Did you ever think about trying to help yourself? *(Rocks leisurely.)*

GRANDMA. I always try to help myself. That way I'm not in anybody else's way.

ETHEL. It doesn't work out that way. Does it, Cora?

CORA *(Looking at Ethel and nodding.)* I should say not. There comes a time when we can't keep out of the way.

GRANDMA *(Turning away from the stove and facing Cora.)* I suppose you are referring to me, Cora. Do you think I'm not keeping up my end of things?

CORA *(Hastily.)* Now I didn't mean it just that way, Grandma.

GRANDMA. I suppose you would like to have me go to an old folks' home?

ETHEL. Now that you've put it so bluntly, you will have to admit there are a lot of advantages in it for you.

GRANDMA. More advantages for you, I imagine, getting me off this street.

CORA. Not at all. We'd like to have you stay here. But a home built especially for older people has so many advantages. Our modern way of living has ways of meeting every problem.

GRANDMA. Such as this flood, I suppose? *(Turns back to the stove. Lifts the lid off the kettle, looks in, and nods her head.)*

ETHEL *(Looking at Cora and shaking her head. Speaking to Grandma.)* Our modern methods will take care of all the homeless, all right.

GRANDMA. I'm sure it will. But only if we do it. None of our wonderful inventions are going to work any better than we do. *(Knock is heard at Right.)*

CORA. They can get here fast enough if there's something free being given away.

GRANDMA *(Crossing to Right and opening the door.)* Come in. Come in. You must be dead on your feet.

JEAN *(Entering.)* I am, almost. George said you had some hot soup. I haven't had anything to eat since yesterday noon. *(She follows Grandma into the room. Her steps are unsteady, her clothes are old. Her hair is disheveled and there is mud on her face.)*

GRANDMA *(Moving her chair up to the table.)* Here. Sit down. What's your name?

JEAN. Jean Ramber. *(Sits on the chair. Ethel gets up quickly as Jean comes close to her and moves her chair over beside Cora and sits down again.)* My husband and I just moved into our house a month ago. He is down at the river now helping salvage things from some of the homes.

GRANDMA. Did you lose many of your things? *(Takes a soup plate and a spoon from the cupboard and sets them before Jean.)*

JEAN. Everything. *(Suddenly breaking down and sobbing.)* We've just been married six weeks. We had so many beautiful wedding presents.

GRANDMA *(Taking the ladle and dipping some soup out for Jean.)* If your husband is safe, you have much to be thankful for.

JEAN *(Drying her eyes.)* Oh, I am thankful. There are others who suffered much more. The Mickols lost their little girl. At least, no one has seen her. *(Eats her soup hungrily.)*

CORA *(To Ethel.)* I hadn't heard about that. Ethel, we'd ought to go down and find out more.

ETHEL. You're right, Cora. That is really news.

GRANDMA. Is there anything I can do for the Mickols?

JEAN. I don't think there is anything that anyone can do now. They are trying to find the little girl.

CORA. Ethel, isn't Sam Mickols the one who had that terrific quarrel with his wife not long ago?

ETHEL *(Excitedly.)* I do believe you're right, Cora. He was working in one of the stores unpacking freight. They said he was being seen quite often with one of the clerks in the store.

CORA. I heard that, too. It's a wonder his wife stayed with him.

JEAN *(Looking at Grandma.)* Are they talking about Sam and Ruth Mickols?

GRANDMA. They're just talking to hear their heads rattle, Jean. Don't pay any attention to them.

JEAN. But Sam and Ruth are so much in love, they wouldn't fight. And right now they are having such awful trouble! It doesn't seem fair to talk about them.

ETHEL *(Indignantly.)* A lot a creature like that knows about what should or shouldn't be talked about.

CORA. If a man is going to gallivant around, he ought to be exposed.

GRANDMA. Right now Sam Mickols isn't gallivanting around, I can assure you.

ETHEL *(A little taken aback.)* Well, maybe not right now.

GRANDMA *(Ladling out more soup for Jean.)* Is this warming you, Jean?

JEAN. Oh, I feel so much better already. I wish my husband could have something like this. He hasn't had anything to eat, either.

GRANDMA. Didn't you get anything to eat at the emergency kitchens?

JEAN. We didn't get out of our house attic until just a little while ago. We didn't get to one of the kitchens. It seems they're having trouble finding people to help operate the kitchens. The Red Cross is doing most of it but they need help.

ETHEL *(Proudly.)* I helped a while this morning.

GRANDMA. There are still hungry people down there this afternoon.

CORA. Certainly you don't expect us to spend our whole lives down there helping creatures like—like this?

GRANDMA *(Emphatically.)* No. I wouldn't expect you to do anything like that. More soup, Jean?

JEAN. No, thank you. I—I'd like to have the rest for my husband, if you can spare it.

GRANDMA. That's what it's for. I don't know of anyone I'd rather have eat it.

JEAN *(Rising.)* Maybe he can come up here.

GRANDMA. Take it to him. *(Lifts the kettle off the stove and hands it to Jean.)*

JEAN *(Taking the kettle.)* Thank you, Grandma. Neither Bill nor I will forget this. And I'll bring back your kettle.

GRANDMA. Don't worry about that. Just get that soup to him while it's still hot.

JEAN *(Crossing to Right.)* I will and thanks again. *(Exits at Right.)*

CORA. I'll bet that's the last you'll ever see of your kettle, Grandma.

GRANDMA. It will come back. And if it doesn't, it's paid for. *(Turns out the fire in the stove.)*

ETHEL. It's no wonder you don't have anything if that's the way you take care of it.

GRANDMA. I take care of things. I just try to use them where they're needed most.

ETHEL *(Rising.)* It's no use, Cora. Grandma will never listen to reason.

CORA *(Rising.)* I suppose you're right, Ethel.

GRANDMA. That's according to what you mean by reason. *(George enters at Right with a kettle.)*

GEORGE. I was coming up here when I met Jean with a kettle of soup for her husband. I had a little bucket with me so she poured the soup in that and asked me to return this kettle.

GRANDMA *(Taking the kettle.)* Never is a short time after all, I guess.

GEORGE *(Perplexed.)* What do you mean, Grandma?

GRANDMA. Oh, I was told I'd never see this kettle again.

GEORGE *(Looking at Cora and Ethel.)* I can make a good guess who said that.

GRANDMA. Isn't there something I can do to help those poor people, George?

GEORGE. I'm afraid not, Grandma. You can't stand to work in the emergency kitchens. Let the younger women do that. You've served your day at it.

GRANDMA. But I feel so—so worthless. *(Cora and Ethel exchange glances and nod.)*

GEORGE *(Patting Grandma's shoulder.)* You're worth a lot to me, Grandma, just remembering all the good things you've done. Now you be good and don't over-do. I've got to get back to work. *(Exits at Right.)*

ETHEL. George has the right idea, Grandma. You shouldn't over-do.

CORA. That's right. You should relax and enjoy life at your age.

GRANDMA. Maybe so. *(Looks at the clock.)* Well, it's too late to go to the meeting now. I don't suppose there is a thing I could have done, anyway. But I did want to help. *(Sighs.)* Well, I'm going to go through my trunk again. Maybe I've got some old clothes that will help out those people. *(Exits at Left.)*

ETHEL *(Shrugging and sighing.)* We're not going to get her out, Cora. We might as well face it.

CORA. I suppose so. *(Sighs.)* Too bad, too. This block would look so much better with a decent house here. But Grandma just won't move. She's a drawback to everything and everybody. Just plain deadwood.

ETHEL *(Drawing herself up proudly.)* Well, at least we tried to do something for the community today.

CORA. But what can you do when you can't clear out the deadwood? *(Ethel and Cora look at each other and shrug, making a despairing gesture as the curtain falls.)*

(CURTAIN)

NOT WITHOUT HONOR

A RELIGIOUS DRAMA IN THREE SCENES

By

ELAINE WALKER GETZINGER

PRODUCTION RIGHTS

Copies of this play are available in single pamphlet form. The right to produce this play by one group of amateur players is authorized only by the purchase of ten copies (one copy for each speaking part) at the current price of 50c each.

It is dishonest and illegal to copy parts.

CAST OF CHARACTERS

(For Ten Women)

MARY.........................the mother of Jesus
JUDITH................................his sister
MIRIAM ....another sister
JOHANNA...........................another sister
TABITHA..........................a crippled girl
OFFSTAGE VOICE OF JESUS
HANNAH ....a neighbor
DORCAS................................a neighbor
REBECCA ....a neighbor
SARAH.................................a neighbor
RACHEL ....a neighbor

This play was written for a teen-age church school class when no suitable religious play could be found, and was successfully performed by them. It could be given by women or a combination of girls and women. The number of neighbors can vary with the group performing the play. One setting is used, simple props, and Biblical costumes are worn.

SETTING: Interior of the simple Nazareth home of the family of Jesus.

PLAYING TIME: 25 minutes.

SCENE ONE:
  Morning.

SCENE TWO:
  Late Afternoon.

SCENE THREE:
  Next day.

NOT WITHOUT HONOR

SCENE ONE

Time: *Morning.*

Mary (*Enters, busies herself around the kitchen a moment and then goes to the door and calls.*) Come, girls, we must start lunch or those hungry brothers of yours will be here before we're ready.

Judith. We're coming, Mother. I'm getting hungry myself.

Miriam. I am, too. What can we do to help?

Mary. Hasn't your sister come back from the well yet? I need the water for these meal cakes.

Miriam (*Goes to the door.*) I don't see her, Mother. I wonder what's keeping her?

Judith. Probably gossiping with the neighbors again. You ought to speak to her about that, Mother.

Mary. Oh, doubtless she'll be back shortly. I suppose they're asking her about your brother Jesus again.

Judith. I wouldn't doubt it. Old Sarah stays around that well to hear all the gossip that's going around, and she's always asking when Jesus will return.

Mary. You shouldn't speak about Old Sarah like that, child. She has a kindly heart in spite of her sharp tongue.

Miriam. She's always nice to me though she does pester me to know when we expect Jesus. She thinks that —

Johanna (*Rushing in.*) Oh, Mother, that awful old woman!

Mary. Why, Johanna! What a way to speak!

Johanna. Well, that's just what she is! Old Sarah! She says that Jesus is too good to come see us any more. Too set up by the crowds that follow him to bother with us. Why, she even said —

Mary. Quiet, my child. Repeating gossip does no one any good. Your brother is very busy with his work, and he is a long way from here. We can't expect him to come to see us very often.

JUDITH. But it's been such a long time since he was here last! It seems like he could spare us a little of his time.

MIRIAM. I'd certainly love to see him again. Whenever he's at home everything seems to go just right.

MARY. It would indeed be a pleasure to have him with us again. But his work must always come first.

JOHANNA. But what is his work, Mother? He's always going around and preaching to people. What does he have to say that's so important?

MARY. I'm not quite sure I understand it all, but ever since he was just a little boy he has had a dream of a better world which men themselves could make if they treated each other with mercy and kindness. He teaches of a kingdom of love where God is the father of all, and all men are brothers. He hopes to get people to follow him and to try out his plan in their lives.

JOHANNA. Why doesn't he talk about the kingdom of Israel instead? If our men had a leader, we might drive these cruel Romans out of our land and once more have a king in Jerusalem!

JUDITH. Just think! Our own brother might be king! King of all the Jews! He could do it too, for he has a way with people and could get them to follow him.

MARY. Girls! Be careful! What if a Roman spy heard you? We would be put to death for such words, or worse, sold into slavery! We can trust no one these days. Perhaps even our next-door neighbor —

MIRIAM. Jesus doesn't believe in war and bloodshed, anyway. He says that love, not hate, will rule the world, and if all men are brothers, there can be no war. Jesus says God loves all people, not just Jews alone. Jesus says —

HANNAH (*Coming in the door.*) Talking about that fine brother of yours again, I see. My, I'd certainly love to see him again! How is he, Mary?

MARY. Why, Hannah! I didn't hear you knock. Come on in! We were so busy talking away —

MIRIAM. We haven't heard from Jesus for a long time but he must be all right. He's so big and strong!

HANNAH. I should say so! My boys have always envied those fine strong shoulders of his. But he worked hard enough to earn them!

MARY. Yes, he did. Carpentry is hard work.

HANNAH. Well, Judith, Johanna, how are you? Anxious to see your brother, too, no doubt?

JUDITH. Indeed we are. I'm interested to hear all about the places he's visited. Jerusalem and Sydon and Tyre —

JOHANNA. I wish he would come home. The neighbors are always asking about him and we don't know anything to tell them.

TABITHA *(Tapping timidly on the door.)* May I come in, please?

MARY. Of course, my dear. Come right in.

JOHANNA. Let me help you, Tabitha. You look so tired.

TABITHA. I am tired. It is so hard for me to get around, but I did want to ask if your brother is coming home soon. I've heard so many stories about people he has healed and I'm sure he could heal me too. It would be like being born again to stand up straight and walk like other people do.

JUDITH. Poor Tabitha! It must be very hard for you. I wish I could help you in some way.

MIRIAM. Could I fix a little bowl of soup for Tabitha, Mother? She must be hungry.

MARY. Why, yes, of course, Miriam. Here is a bowl. *(Miriam fills the bowl and gives it to Tabitha who eats hungrily.)*

JUDITH *(Hands her a piece of bread.)* Here, eat this with your soup, Tabitha.

TABITHA. Oh, thank you. You are all so kind.

JUDITH. Would you like some more?

TABITHA. No, thank you. I must go now. I'm holding up your lunch. But what about Jesus? Will he come soon?

MARY. I don't know what to tell you, Tabitha. We haven't heard from him for a while, but I suppose he'll be home one of these days.

MIRIAM. We'll let you know as soon as he comes, don't worry.

OTHERS. Yes, we will!

TABITHA *(Goes painfully to the door.)* All right. Don't forget! *(Exits.)*

HANNAH. My, that poor child! I hope your son can help her. She's a sweet little thing, and deserves any help she can get.

MARY. Yes, she bears her pain bravely. Hardly a day goes by that she doesn't stop and ask about Jesus. I hope for her sake he comes soon.

HANNAH. Well, I'd better be going too. I have my own lunch to get. Tomorrow is the Sabbath so I'll see you all at the synagogue.

MARY. Yes, we'll all be there, of course. Goodbye, Hannah.

HANNAH. Goodbye.

GIRLS. Goodbye.

MARY. Now, girls, we'd better hurry. It's getting late. *(All work busily, and in silence for a few moments.)*

JOHANNA. Do you really think Jesus will come soon, Mother?

JUDITH. He certainly ought to. How long has it been, anyway?

MIRIAM. I don't know. I guess it's —

VOICE *(Offstage.)* Mother! Mother! I've come home!

MARY *(Hurries to greet him.)* Jesus! My son! Oh, my son!

GIRLS. It's Jesus! He's come home! *(They run offstage.)*

CURTAIN

SCENE TWO

TIME: *Later that same afternoon.*

JUDITH *(Entering with Johanna.)* Johanna! Aren't you just too thrilled for words? Our own brother the center of so much attention?

JOHANNA. Yes, and tomorrow he will stand up in the synagogue before all the elders and preach!

MIRIAM *(Entering.)* I wonder what he'll talk about?

JOHANNA. Oh, I don't know. It won't matter much. Everyone wants to hear him no matter what he says.

JUDITH. And no wonder! Hasn't he been traveling all over the countryside, talking to people everywhere and getting more and more followers?

JOHANNA. That's what I meant when I said I wished Jesus would gather all his followers together and lead an attack on the Roman officials at Jerusalem. He could end their power over us forever!

MIRIAM. It would be wonderful for our people if Jesus could do that. Why, the stories he told about the way our people are oppressed by the Romans were terrible!

JUDITH. I know. Did you hear him tell about how our people are thrown into prison when they can't pay those awful taxes the Romans demand? And the taxes get higher and higher.

JOHANNA. And then they're sold into slavery when they don't pay what they owe!

MIRIAM. How do they expect our people to earn any money in prison to pay their debts?

JOHANNA. What do the Romans care about that? They don't care about anything but power and money!

JUDITH. Our brother Simon said that it's getting harder and harder to make a living working in competition to free slave labor.

MIRIAM. It must be. Jesus says the slaves are treated very cruelly too. Why, they're tortured or put to death for just any slight offense.

JOHANNA. I know, isn't it horrible? And yet I suppose the Romans wouldn't be able to keep so many slaves

269

under control if they didn't use terror and force. There are almost as many slaves as free men, Jesus said.

MIRIAM. Jesus says he hopes to change all that some day. He hopes that men will accept his teachings and treat each other fairly and with mercy as brothers should.

JOHANNA. Jesus is an idealist! Too much so for his own good. He'll get nowhere with those ideas. The only way those wicked Romans can be made to change their ways is to conquer them by force. To think that our own Jewish people — God's chosen people — should be slaves to those pagan Romans!

JUDITH. Perhaps Jesus has come back to Nazareth to join his own people together first and then get others to join them to overthrow Caesar's legions!

MIRIAM. I'm sure he hasn't. He said nothing about it at lunch or when he talked to their neighbors who dropped in to see him.

MARY (Entering.) My, you're nearly through, aren't you? I'm sorry I didn't get in sooner to help you clear up the lunch things, but there were so many friends wanting to see Jesus. He was quite worn out, especially after his long journey, so I urged him to lie down and rest. I sent the folks away finally, and shut the front door, or they'd still be bothering him.

JUDITH. I don't know when I've seen so much excitement in our little town of Nazareth. Everyone is eager to see our famous brother.

MIRIAM. And he is eager to see them, too. He is as happy to be here with them and to talk in the synagogue as if it were the Temple in Jerusalem!

JOHANNA. Wouldn't you love to see the Temple, though? Jesus says it is the most beautiful building he ever saw. I could just sit for hours and listen to him tell about the things he has seen in Jerusalem.

MARY. He doesn't say much about his work except that everywhere he goes people are very kind to him and listen attentively to his message. I worry about him, though; whether he has enough to eat, a place to sleep, and if he is well. Does he look well to you girls?

JUDITH. He looks fine, Mother. Don't worry about him.

JOHANNA. You don't need to worry about him, Mother. He can take care of himself. Why, as big as Simon has grown, Jesus is still the tallest of all our brothers, and the strongest, too.

MIRIAM. And yet he's the gentlest and kindest.

MARY. I want to prepare some of his favorite dishes for tomorrow. Judith, get me a clean bowl, please. Am I in your way, Johanna?

JOHANNA. No, of course not. I'll make room for you here. *(Knock is heard at the door.)*

MARY. Come in. *(Neighbor enters with a bowl in her hand.)* Hello, Dorcas, how are you?

DORCAS. Fine, thank you, Mary. How is everyone at your house?

MARY. Very well, indeed, Dorcas. Won't you sit down? Judith, clear off a place on the bench for her.

DORCAS. Well, I can't stay but a minute. I just stopped in to borrow a little meal to make some cakes.

MARY. Why, certainly, Dorcas. You're welcome. Johanna, will you take Dorcas' bowl and fill it for her? *(Johanna takes the bowl and fills it.)*

DORCAS. Oh, thank you. Not so much, Johanna. Just a little will do. There. That's right. *(Johanna returns her bowl.)* Oh, Mary, I hear Jesus is at home again. Will he stay with you this time?

MARY *(Smiling.)* Yes, he's home for a little while at least, and we're very glad.

DORCAS. My, you must be proud of him! Every day or so word comes of someone he has healed, or some new place where he has preached, it seems like. And now he's home!

HANNAH *(Sticking her head in the door.)* Oh, Mary! He has come, hasn't he? My, I'm so anxious to see him! Is he busy now?

DORCAS *(Eagerly.)* I'd like to see Jesus, too! Where is — ?

HANNAH. Hello, there, Dorcas! I didn't see you —

MARY. I'm sorry, but Jesus was so tired I urged him to lie down and rest for a while. But you can see and hear him tomorrow. *(Knocking at the door.)*

MARY. More neighbors, I guess. Come in. *(Rebecca enters.)* Well, Rebecca, come join us, won't you? Dorcas and Hannah are already here.

REBECCA *(With a bowl in her hand.)* Thank you, Mary, but I really can't stay. *(Nods to the other women.)* I just stopped by to see if you could spare a little oil. I ran out just a little while ago —

MARY *(With a twinkle in her eye.)* Why, yes, certainly, Rebecca. Here, Judith. *(Hands the bowl to Judith.)*

REBECCA *(Looks around for Jesus and is startled when Judith returns her filled bowl.)* What? What's this for, child?

JUDITH *(Suppressing a laugh.)* This is the oil you came to borrow, Rebecca.

REBECCA. Oh — oh, yes, that's right. Stupid of me to forget what I came over for.

SARAH *(Entering abruptly.)* Doubtless you came over to see Jesus, just like the rest of us. And here comes another one. Come on, Rachel, join the crowd. *(Rachel enters with a bowl.)*

MARY. Come in, both of you. We're just sitting around talking.

RACHEL *(Looks around the room, embarrassed.)* Oh, why, you have quite a houseful, Mary. I guess I'd better go on. I just came —

SARAH. Yes, to borrow — I know, we all did.

RACHEL. I — I ran out of meal, and — see, here is my bowl.

HANNAH *(Laughs merrily.)* Well, Mary, looks like all your friends have come to see you today. I wonder what the attraction is? *(All laugh at this. Settle comfortably.)*

MARY. I'm sorry you can't see Jesus right now, but he is so tired that I felt he must rest. Miriam, go in and see if he is asleep and if he still has that cover over him. He said he didn't need it, but I thought he did. *(Miriam exits.)*

HANNAH. So you put a cover on him, eh, Mary? These mothers — no matter how grown-up or famous their sons get, their mothers have to fuss over them.

SARAH. Well, well, Mary, what did Jesus have to say? What's he going to talk about tomorrow at the synagogue? I suppose he'll try to tell us what we ought to do and think. I declare, I don't know what this younger generation is coming to, with all this talk about being modern, and up-to-date, and trying new ways. Why, my son, Nathaniel —

JOHANNA *(Patronizingly.)* Of course Jesus has been preaching in Jerusalem and all the big cities, so he knows all the latest ways.

JUDITH *(In the same tone.)* Why, he's just been everywhere and seen just everybody! And everywhere the people just lay down their work to follow him!

SARAH. Perhaps. Perhaps. Maybe he can fool the people in the big cities where they don't know he's just a plain carpenter, but we home folks have known him all his life. He can't put anything over on us.

MARY. Well, now, Sarah, you mustn't feel that way. Jesus just says what he believes is right. He —

MIRIAM *(Re-enters, assisting Tabitha, who is very excited.)* I met Tabitha out in front, Mother; she's heard that Jesus is home.

TABITHA. Oh, yes! Where is he? Can I see him right away? Oh, I'm so happy! Now I can be well again!

MARY. Sit down and rest, Tabitha. Jesus is sleeping now.

MIRIAM. I tried to tell her that, but she wanted to see him right away. *(Neighbors talk among themselves, ignoring Tabitha, Mary, and Miriam.)*

MARY. I'm sorry, Tabitha, but you'll have plenty of

273

time to see and talk to Jesus tomorrow. He'll stay with us for a little while this time, I hope.

TABITHA. But, Mary, I want to see him right away.

MIRIAM. Now, Tabitha, I'll help you home, and then you come back tomorrow when Jesus is awake and see him then.

TABITHA. Well, all right, if you say so —

MARY. Yes, I think that's best.

MIRIAM. Shall we go now?

TABITHA. All right. Goodbye, Mary. Tell Jesus I want to see him.

MARY. I will. Goodbye, Tabitha.

HANNAH. Well, we'd better go too. It's late.

MARY. Don't rush away. (*Business of general goodbyes, as all leave.*)

CURTAIN

SCENE THREE

TIME: *Next day.*

JOHANNA (*Bursts out.*) Oh, Mother, how could he say such things?

JUDITH. He's completely turned all our friends against him! They'll never follow him now!

JOHANNA. He's made us the laughing-stock of the whole town!

MARY. Now, now, girls, don't get all upset again. Jesus only spoke what he believes. Even though we don't understand him, he must have had his reasons.

JOHANNA. But to tell the people that he is the promised one — the Messiah that our prophet Isaiah foretold! It was blasphemy, Mother!

MARY. I don't think he meant it so. And then, perhaps he is right. Perhaps he is the Messiah. I remember so many things that have happened during his life that have puzzled me, things that marked him as unusual, different from the rest of us.

MIRIAM. Yes, I know. Although he has been more thoughtful and kind to us than our other brothers, he seemed to live a life apart from us, somehow. As though he felt and thought things beyond our everyday existence.

MARY. I've noticed that, too. But there were other things — even more unusual. You remember how I told you he was born in a stable in Bethlehem when your father and I had to go there for the census? How the shepherds came from the fields to see him and wise men from faraway lands brought him gifts?

GIRLS (*Eagerly.*) Yes, we remember!

MARY. They knelt before him — before my tiny, new-born son — and called him king! King of Israel! Your father and I were proud, but we were frightened too — afraid Herod might hear that our baby had been called king and have him put to death. So we hurried away and hid in Egypt for many years.

GIRLS. Yes! Yes! Go on!

MARY. We returned when we thought it was safe and Jesus grew up quietly here in Nazareth. Nothing more was said about kings though I often wondered about it, remembering the night when he was born. And when we took him to the Temple in Jerusalem, he was so interested in everything there that we thought he might become a rabbi. But the years passed and he worked on in the carpenter's shop, helping your father and then taking his place when he — he left us. It wasn't until your cousin John began to preach that Jesus became restless. Even then, although he followed John and became baptized by him, he returned to the shop.

JUDITH. Until our other brothers were old enough to take his place and take care of us.

JOHANNA. And then he went away to preach.

MIRIAM. And now the people have driven him away and he may never come back again! Oh, Mother, it's so terrible!

JOHANNA. The shepherds and the wise men called him king, and he could have been king of Israel, but now he'll

275

be almost a fugitive, unable to return to his own home town.

MARY. I heard Jesus say, "A prophet is not without honor save in his own country — "

JUDITH. A prophet — when he might have been king! *(Loud noises outside as of a crowd of people passing. Dorcas, Rebecca, Rachel, Sarah, Hannah enter the house, arguing and talking among themselves.)*

SARAH *(Belligerently.)* Well, Mary, I said your son couldn't fool us country folk! We've seen him in his true colors now!

REBECCA. Everybody making such a fuss over him as if he were somebody and then him getting up and telling us —

SARAH. He put on all the airs as if he were better than my boys, but none of my boys was ever stoned and run out of town!

DORCAS. Too good to see us yesterday when we came to see him, but not too good to take it on the run when we took after him!

REBECCA. What about all this healing we heard so much about? Old Jacob dared Jesus to cure him of the palsy, but he couldn't do a thing about it!

SARAH. Of course he couldn't! Nor Esther's blind girl! Nor old Reuben's crippled arm!

MARY. Well, really, Sarah, I don't know what to say —

HANNAH. Now, Mary, we don't blame you a bit. Of course, you couldn't help it. Don't be harsh with Mary, Sarah!

JOHANNA. Sarah is right! Jesus certainly made a fool of himself!

JUDITH. We're so ashamed!

SARAH *(More kindly.)* There, I'm sorry, Mary. I didn't mean to speak so harshly to you and the girls. Of course, it wasn't your fault. We should have known better than to have expected a carpenter to know about the scriptures.

TABITHA *(Enters in great excitement.)* Mary, Mary,

where is Jesus? What have they done to him? I tried to get to the synagogue, but the people crowded around Jesus so that I couldn't get near him. Where is he now?

DORCAS. He's left town! With half the town after him!

REBECCA. He spoke blasphemy in the synagogue!

SARAH. He said he is the Messiah! So the men stoned him and ran him out of town! The idea of him saying such a thing!

HANNAH *(More kindly.)* He couldn't have healed you anyway, child. He was unable to heal anyone.

TABITHA. What? No one was healed?

REBECCA. Of course not! He has no power to heal, or preach either. He'd best be back at his carpentry.

SARAH. He'll not come back to this town again to preach or anything else. Our men will see to that!

TABITHA. But Jesus could have healed me! I know he could!

MIRIAM. How could he? He couldn't heal anyone else.

NEIGHBORS. No, not one!

MARY. Jesus felt very badly about that. He wanted to heal everyone but he could not. He said they didn't believe in him; didn't believe he could heal them, so he could not. Jesus said he was powerless to help them unless they had faith in him and in his ability to heal.

SARAH. That's a poor excuse! Anyone could say that.

RACHEL. That's right. That doesn't mean a thing!

TABITHA. But he could heal anyone who did believe, who did have faith in him? Did he say that, Mary?

MARY. Yes, Tabitha. And he was very sad because no one did believe.

TABITHA. Oh, Mary! I believe in him! I know he could cure me! I have always believed it! If I could only see him and talk to him, I'd tell him I have faith that he could make me well!

REBECCA. A lot of good that would do!

JUDITH. He couldn't do a thing for old Jacob.

DORCAS. Nor for Leah.

SARAH. Nor for anyone! It wouldn't do you a bit of good to see him.

MIRIAM. But they didn't believe in him! Rebecca, you said yourself that old Jacob dared Jesus to cure him. That's not faith. Jesus is no cheap trickster or magician!

MARY. Indeed he is not! He heals people because he loves them so much he can't bear to see them suffer. Truly, Tabitha, such faith as yours deserves its fulfillment.

SARAH. Too bad she wastes her faith on a carpenter! Pray to God for release from your suffering, child. If it is His will, you will get well.

TABITHA. But my faith is not wasted! I believe in Jesus and I have faith that — (*She stops abruptly as a new sensation runs over her. Her body straightens, her face is alight with the radiance of her faith. In bewildered surprise she moves first one foot and then the other as she takes — very slowly — one step, then another. There is an awed silence during which the others watch her, first in disbelief, in surprise, and finally in awe, as they drop to their knees around the radiant girl.*)

VOICE (*Softly, yet clearly and confidently.*) "Thy faith, hath made thee whole."

CURTAIN

LET YOUR LIGHT SO SHINE

A DRAMA IN THREE SCENES

By

ELAINE WALKER GETZINGER

279

CAST OF CHARACTERS

(For two men and two women)

ROGER BARRETT
ALICE, HIS WIFE
TED ⎫
⎬ Their Teen-age Children
NANCY ⎭

SETTING: Living room of an average American home.
TIME: The present.

SYNOPSIS OF SCENES

SCENE ONE: Late evening.
SCENE TWO: The next evening.
SCENE THREE: The morning of the next day.

LET YOUR LIGHT SO SHINE

Setting: Living room of an average American home.
Time: Late evening.

SCENE ONE

(Nancy and Ted are tensely listening to the radio.)

Alice *(Entering.)* Why, Nancy, are you still up? It's so late.

Roger *(Coming in behind her.)* You shouldn't have waited up, kitten. Our bad news would have kept till morning.

Ted. Tough luck, Dad. We heard it on the radio. Not all the precincts are in yet, but . . . *(He snaps off the radio.)*

Nancy *(Running to Roger, puts her arms around him and bursts into tears.)* Oh, Daddy, I'm so sorry you lost. How can people be so mean?

Roger. Not mean, kitten. Just lazy. Too lazy to bother to vote. Or too busy with their everyday routine to take time.

Ted. Don't they realize their everyday routine could change pretty fast if they aren't careful who gets into office?

Roger *(Wearily.)* I know, I know. But they just can't see it. We tried our best to tell them, but it just didn't work. They didn't bother to vote, and Grimes is back in again.

Alice. Sit down, Roger. You look so tired. I'll go make some coffee.

Roger. No, thanks. I don't believe I want any, honey.

Ted. But Grimes is a crook, Dad. You proved that he got a rake-off on that street paving job. And that lighting contract went to his former real estate partner. I bet Grimes got a big cut out of that too. How could people be so blind? Don't they want honest men in government?

Roger. I'm afraid it isn't that simple, Ted. Of course most peopl don't want crooks running their cities, but they elect them just the same by staying away from the polls. Because you can be sure all the party workers got out to vote today. They want to keep their jobs.

•

281

NANCY. But why do people stay away from the polls, Daddy? They sure couldn't blame the weather today. It was perfect.

ROGER. I know, and we had counted on good weather bringing out a big vote. I don't know what happened. They just didn't turn out. I began to get the picture this morning when we went around to the various voting places and the clerks all told us the voting was very light. When the vote is light, the machine candidates usually go in.

ALICE. And it isn't even the fault of the machine, or the men back of it. It's the voters themselves who mean well, but who aren't interested enough to get out and vote.

ROGER. Like Jack Evans who was out watering his lawn tonight when I drove by. He hadn't voted. He said he got home late and decided not to bother changing clothes and going over to the polls. I took him, dressed as he was, and a neighbor who was out watering his lawn too. I'm not even sure the neighbor voted for me, but at least he did vote. And Jack voted for me anyway, in spite of himself.

TED. For Pat's sake, wasn't he passing out your cards on his block? I thought he took a stack of them home with him the other day.

ROGER. Yes, and yet he wasn't going to bother to vote because it was too late to change his clothes and go over. That's what gets me! You can't count on anybody! You can't trust anyone to do as they say. What good did it do for Jack to pass out my cards if he didn't vote for me? It's the votes that count.

NANCY. You'd think people would want honest men on the council. Why, last year in eighth grade we studied all about how the council regulates taxes and garbage disposal and street lighting and everything. Wouldn't you think they'd care who made their laws?

ROGER. Only when it hits their pocketbooks, honey. Only when taxes go up or a new bonding issue is floated. Then they yell their heads off. But the rest of the time they sit back and let the machine run things like they did today.

TED. How could they, after all the things you told them about Grimes and the rest of the machine?

ROGER. I don't know, Ted. I kept hammering away at the facts every time I spoke. And you know that big stack of letters we all stamped and addressed telling about that faked report Grimes gave the County Commissioners.

TED. Do I? My hand still aches!

ROGER. And look how your mother worked, talking to people all over the district, telling them what I hoped to do to improve Madison if they elected me councilman. And they all seemed interested, too, she said.

ALICE. Oh, yes, they all said they were glad to know about a fine man like you, active in Scouting and church work and all. They said you were just the type of man who should be holding public office. I just don't understand what happened.

NANCY. And golly, Mother talked to everybody! I know that Saturday when I went with her we went into every back alley shack and basement cubby hole. I didn't know there were places like that so close to home. And all those stairs! We didn't miss anybody!

ROGER. I've been hearing about what she did for me. Your mother's a great little salesman. Mr. Bergen said she could have a job selling cars on our lot any time she wanted it.

ALICE. It was a great deal of work, but it was interesting too. I met so many new people and saw a lot of things I'd like to do something about. Those poor little children growing up in some of those places would break your heart. We've got to do something about it, Roger, even if you didn't get elected. I'd like to look up the housing and zoning laws, and I'd like to find out who owns that property over on Haynes and River Street, too.

ROGER. Grimes, very likely; and he's probably making a fortune out of it. But if that's what the people want, why should we interfere? We tried to make it our business, but the people couldn't see it that way. They like the good old status quo. It's less bother.

ALICE. Don't let this make you bitter, Roger. We did the best we could . . .

ROGER. That's just it, don't you see? We did the best

we could, but it wasn't enough. We couldn't shake the voters out of their apathy. I'm not bitter, but I am very disappointed. Where were all the people who wished me well; who promised to vote for me; who said they were glad to know about an honest man running for office?

ALICE. I know, I'm disappointed too. Not only that you didn't get elected, but that the people didn't care enough to vote. And yet they seemed so appreciative that I had taken time to come and tell them about you. Why, they even waved after me as I went down the walk and said to tell you they hoped you got in. Where were they today?

ROGER. Going about their business as usual. Watering their lawns, going to their bridge clubs, or putting over a deal. What we should have been doing, if we'd had any sense. I'm disappointed for myself, naturally—the weather was just what we'd hoped for, and it seemed like the people were behind me. Yet I lost. And it would be the same for any man like me. That's what I feel the worst about: can any man, running alone and only on his own qualifications, ever beat the political machine? I don't think so.

TED. But, gee, Dad, you are going to run again, aren't you? Maybe next time . . .

ROGER. There isn't going to be any next time, Ted. This is the second time I've let Joe Anderson talk me into running for councilman against my better judgment. Not counting the time I ran for the school board two years ago. Politics aren't for little fellows like me. I don't have any political savvy or the stomach to swallow the double crossing and double dealing that goes on behind the scenes.

ALICE. Thank goodness! I wouldn't want you to be like that.

ROGER. From now on I'm sticking strictly to my own business—selling cars for Bergen Motors. The public wants men like Grimes, and that's all right with me. I won't put up any more arguments against him.

NANCY. But, Daddy, that isn't like you—to give up like that. If Mr. Grimes is cheating the people, aren't you going to keep on fighting him? When the Park Board was going to close down our playground on Maple Street you made them keep it open and even buy new equipment for it so the kids'd have some place to play.

ROGER. That was different, honey. Anyway, I can't do any more tonight. It's high time we were all in bed, and especially you. Run on now.

TED. Speaking of cars, Dad, I thought you said that red convertible was going to be junked. The one I was looking at on the lot the other day.

ROGER. That's right. It had been in a wreck. I told you that's why I wouldn't sell it to you. Mr. Bergen said it was out of line.

TED. Well, Larry Russell is driving it or its twin brother. And he said he bought it from Bill Warren at the Bergen lot. He had it at school today.

ALICE. Roger! Bill wouldn't have sold it against Mr. Bergen's orders, would he?

ROGER. He would if he could make money on it. He'd sell a broken-down taxi with a split block if he could talk somebody into buying it.

ALICE. What if this boy would have an accident with the car? Wouldn't Bill be responsible?

ROGER. Oh, Bill'd wriggle out of it some way. His kind always do. He goes right on, selling one junker after another, and making money hand over fist, while I try to be honest and what does it get me? Bill took his family to Florida last Christmas and we went to your brother's!

ALICE. Maybe so, but I bet we had a much better time, and with a clear conscience too. I wonder what Ann Warren thinks about Bill's deals?

ROGER. I don't imagine she knows much about them. They each go their separate ways. He earns the money and she and Kathy spend it. They don't make a team like we do at our house.

TED. I think Mom's right. I bet we did have a better time at Uncle Dan's. I'd hate to have some of Bill's rotten deals on my conscience. I'm glad Dad's honest. I can be proud of him. Why, when I was passing out his cards to my teachers you should have heard the swell things they said about him. And some of them had bought cars from Dad too.

ROGER. That's good to hear, Ted. Maybe we're on the right track after all. I don't know. But kind words and a clear conscience don't pay the grocery bills or win elections either, apparently. I did think they would have helped, though.

NANCY. You're still the most wonderful daddy in the world, even if the people were too dumb to vote for you!

ROGER *(Putting his arm around her shoulders.)* I'm glad you think so, kitten. But it's still way past your bedtime, and all your blarney won't stop the clock. Come on, Alice, I guess the only way we'll get these night owls of ours to bed will be to go to bed ourselves. We can't settle all the world's problems tonight, anyway.

SCENE TWO

(Next evening. Same setting.)

ROGER *(Entering.)* Hi, honey. Where's everybody? *(Kisses Alice.)*

ALICE. In bed. It's late, or hadn't you realized? Ted has to get to school early tomorrow to get out the Herald, and Nancy was in a mood, so I urged her to go to bed and sleep it off.

ROGER. A mood? What do you mean?

ALICE. You know—I guess she was counting a great deal on your winning the election and it was a little hard to face her friends today. She'd bragged so much about you and how you couldn't lose. And of course, she's so disappointed for you. She can't understand why everybody doesn't love you like she does. She thinks you're a pretty wonderful guy, and so do I.

ROGER. Thanks, honey, I can use a few kind words. I know what Nancy's been through today. I've had quite a day myself. Everybody calling and saying they were sorry. I even had an offer to run this fall as an independent on a coalition ticket. You know, appeal to the better element of both parties.

ALICE. That might work! Who made the offer?

ROGER. Ralph Colby. The fellow who put up that new subdivision out south.

ALICE. That sounds like a good idea. All those new people and all. I suppose you'd run for councilman-at-large then instead of from our district alone. What's the matter? Aren't you interested?

ROGER. I've had enough of politics. If yesterday hadn't been enough to make me decide against running again, today sure was. What with all the second-guessers and back-slappers coming into the office all day with their "Better luck next time," and all that. But I finally found a way to get rid of them.

ALICE. You weren't rude to them?

ROGER. No, I didn't have to be. All I did was to ask them if they had voted. That usually shut them up in a hurry. You'd be surprised how many had to back down and start making excuses. They didn't get around to it, or they were too busy to get away from the office. Intelligent men, who should realize what local government means to their own businesses, if nothing else. I don't get it. I've always thought that honesty and loyalty were more important than making money, but I guess I was wrong.

ALICE. You're all mixed up when you talk like that. They're the ones who are wrong, putting business first.

ROGER. No, I'm the one who's out of step. When it comes to a showdown like yesterday, you find out what people really think. I thought that the way I'd lived, the things I believed in, the service I'd given the community would recommend me for the job of councilman. Instead they reelect a crook like Grimes who's always out for all he can get. So what can I believe except that I was wrong?

ALICE. I know how you feel, Roger, but . . .

ROGER. But nothing! I've been a fool, that's all. I thought if I could convince people that Grimes wasn't fit to hold public office they'd get out and vote against him. But they don't care. You can't fight that. They just don't care. If there had been a good turn-out and Grimes had won by a big margin, I'd have accepted that. It would have been the decision of the people. But this way . . .

ALICE. I know, I just don't understand it.

ROGER. Well, I do. There wasn't anything in for them. It wasn't any "skin off their teeth," as we used to say when we were kids. It isn't any off mine, either, now. It was a jolt, but I know the score now. Everybody's out for all they can get for themselves and nobody else, and that's the way I'm going to be, too. Bill Warren's the smart one, and from now on he's going to have a star pupil. We'll go to Florida yet, wait and see!

ALICE. Roger, you don't mean that! Just because you're disappointed . . .

ROGER. Disappointed? No, just smart. I've learned something—the hard way—if you're smart, you look out for number one. Only a fool wastes his time doing anything for anybody else. Do you think they appreciate it? Do you think they thank you for it? Why, just last week I talked a fellow out of buying a flashy sport coupe we had on the lot and do you know what happened?

ALICE. He went somewhere else?

ROGER. Worse than that. Listen. This car he liked was no good. Not worth half what we were asking for it and I told him so. I tried to show him a four-door that was real clean, low mileage too, but he had his heart set on this coupe. I pointed out that the rods were noisy and it used a lot of oil. Besides, the brakes were bad. He thanked me for being so honest with him, but he didn't buy anything and finally he went away. But do you know what happened two days later?

ALICE. He came back?

ROGER. He came back all right, but not to me. He went over to Bill and when he left the lot he was driving the sport coupe.

ALICE. Why would he buy the car after all you'd told him about it? Didn't he realize you were only trying to help him?

ROGER. He didn't want to be helped. People don't. He wanted that car. And Bill made himself fifty dollars that I could have had just as easily. I cheated myself out of fifty dollars by being honest. How crazy can you get?

ALICE. But would you have felt right, selling that car?

ROGER. Sure, why not? It's what the customer wanted. I should have sold it to him.

ALICE. But that isn't the way to do business. To make money cheating people. That isn't like you. You always said it was good business to be honest as well as being the right thing to do. That if you were honest they'd be satisfied with their car and they'd come back and bring their friends in, too.

ROGER. Maybe. If they didn't see something they liked better on another lot. Besides, Bill gets repeat business, too. No matter how he rooks them, they still come back. I don't know why. So why should I bother telling them the truth about a car? I'm going to make money, too. Loads of it. So I can give you and the kids the things Bill's family have. Money's the only thing that counts in this world. Why, if I had enough money I might even have beaten old Grimes.

ALICE. Don't talk like that. You're tired and disappointed now. Disillusioned too, and I don't blame you. But you'll feel different tomorrow. It's late. Let's go to bed. It's been a long hard day for you. But it isn't the end of the world for us. We still have everything we had before—our family, our home, our friends. We haven't lost anything really.

ROGER. No, nothing important. It's high time I lost my illusions anyway. From now on, I'm through wasting my time on anything but making money, and the first thing I'm going to do is call Mr. Carlson and tell him he'll have to get another boy to head up the Community Chest this year. I've done it for so many years he just takes it for granted that I'll do it again. I saw him on the street the other day and he reminded me it's almost time to start making plans for it.

ALICE. But you've always done things like that, Roger. People expect it of you. Anyway it's too late to call him tonight. You'll have to call him in the morning. Maybe you'll change your mind by then.

ROGER. No, I've made up my mind. I used to think that service to the community was a man's first obligation after taking care of his own family. That's why I decided to run for councilman. I wanted to make Madison a better city for Nancy and Ted and the other kids to grow up in.

ALICE. I know what you mean. I felt the same way or I'd never have gone from house to house campaigning for you. But even if you didn't get elected to the council, you can still help in other ways.

ROGER. No, I'll be too busy. I'm spending all my time on the lot selling cars to anybody who wants one. No more free lectures on the bad points of a car. I'll sell them what they want. And if they want a big trade-in, I'll jack up the price, and give them whatever trade-in they want. That's what Bill does and he sells cars!

ALICE. But, Roger, how are you going to live with yourself, even if the customers don't know the difference?

ROGER. The same way Bill does—forgets about it. When you have enough money coming in, you can forget a lot of things. Take the Horton's for example—Mrs. Horton was in today to buy a car for their son—everybody conveniently forgets how he made his pile, but they all want a share of it. I got my cut today. I sold her that foreign sports car we've had on our hands for months. Bergen had even offered a bonus to the salesman who unloaded it, and I did, too.

ALICE. That's wonderful! Aren't you pleased?

ROGER. Not with this deal, honey. It's not much of a car. That's why we've had so much trouble selling it. It's about to fall apart under its shiny new coat of paint. It'll probably cost plenty to put it into shape, but they can afford it. A few more deals like that and we'll begin to have things, too—trips, nice clothes, and more advantages for the children.

ALICE. But at the expense of your personal integrity, Roger. Even if nothing else matters to you now, doesn't that matter?

ROGER. You can't buy trips to Florida with integrity. It isn't worth an Indian penny at the supermarket.

ALICE. Oh, Roger, you really have lost then. You've lost a great deal more than the election. You've lost yourself!

ROGER. Don't be so melodramatic, honey. On the contrary, I think I've found myself. At least I'm awake now to what's going on.

ALICE. Doesn't it mean anything to you that the children are proud of you, that their teachers speak well of you? It means a lot to them to know their father is respected and looked up to.

ROGER. Ted'll be a lot prouder when I get him that car he's been wanting. And I can get it too, if I do business Bill Warren's way.

ALICE. Roger, I just can't get through to you. It's like talking to a stranger. *(She is interrupted by the telephone ringing.)* Who could be calling at this hour?

ROGER. I'll get it. *(He lifts the phone.)* Hello. What? Take it easy, Bill. I can't understand you. Is she badly hurt? Sure, I'll be right over. Goodbye. *(He turns to Alice.)* Kathy Warren's been in an accident. Bill wants me to drive him and Ann over to the hospital. Kathy was driving their car. I'll be back as soon as I can.

ALICE. I'm coming with you. Maybe I can help Ann some way. I'll leave a note for the children. *(She scribbles a note hastily.)* Is Kathy badly hurt?

ROGER. Bill wasn't sure. The police had just called him. We'd better hurry. Bill sounded like he was falling apart. *(Exeunt.)*

SCENE THREE

(Morning the next day. Same setting. Enter Alice and Roger from outside. At the sound of the door, Nancy and Ted hurry in from the kitchen.)

ALICE. Mhm-m, it smells good in here! I could sure use a cup of that coffee. Couldn't you, Roger?

ROGER *(Dazed.)* Yes, I'd like some coffee.

NANCY. How is Kathy? Is she going to be all right?

TED. What happened? We got your note, but it didn't say much.

ALICE. Yes, Kathy's going to be all right, but she's badly injured. She'll be in the hospital a long time. The other young people are in a very critical condition and one boy is dead.

ROGER *(In the same tone.)* Did you ever see anything

like that car? I've seen some bad ones, but that convertible
was just torn in two!

TED. Convertible? Who was it that was killed, Dad?
Anybody I know?

ROGER. And Bill's face—when he realized that pile of
junk he'd sold that boy nearly killed his own daughter!
What if it had killed her? What would his big commission
mean then?

ALICE. It did kill someone else's child. Someone who
wasn't guilty of selling a defective car.

NANCY. Mother! Who was killed?

TED. Who *was* it, Dad? What's it all about?

ALICE. That boy—Larry Russell, I think you called him
—who bought a car from Mr. Warren. A car that was supposed to be junked. You were talking to your father about
it yesterday.

TED. Yes, I know. But what happened? Was Kathy with
him?

ROGER (*Rousing himself from his pre-occupation.*) No,
she was driving Bill's car, Ted. It's a wreck, too. Larry lost
control of his convertible when he made a sharp turn pulling into the Wagon Wheel just as Kathy was pulling out.
He couldn't stop. He was thrown out of the car and killed
instantly when his head struck the curb. His car hit Kathy's
broadside and turned over twice before it crashed against a
stone retaining wall. The whole front end was sheared off.
It was terrible!

ALICE. Fortunately he was alone in the car. The others
were all with Kathy.

NANCY. Larry Russell dead? Why, he was one of the
most popular boys in school! Everybody liked him.

TED. He was in a lot of my classes. Kind of a reckless
kid, especially when he was driving a car, but gee—dead . . .

ALICE. We've been with the Warrens at the hospital most
of the night. They're almost out of their minds with worry.
Kathy is a mighty lucky girl to be alive, and they know it.

ROGER. How can Bill face the Russells? Tell them he
sold their boy the car that killed him?

ALICE. Is he going over to talk to them today?

ROGER. He said he was. I guess he felt he owed them that much. But what can he say to them? What can he do? *(Bitterly.)* Refund their money?

TED. Take it easy, Dad. It was an accident. Larry drove like a crazy fool. He was bound to get into trouble sometime.

ROGER. But that car—it was out of line—he didn't have a chance!

NANCY. Did Mr. Warren know that when he sold it, Daddy?

ROGER. Yes, he knew it. But all he could think of was the commission. That's all he ever thought of.

ALICE. I imagine he's thinking about something else this morning. Perhaps that commission doesn't look quite so big now.

ROGER. It couldn't ever be big enough to make me sell a junker like that. I don't know how he could do it.

ALICE. But I thought you were going to be Bill's star pupil. Think of nothing but commissions, too. What does it matter if some poor fool gets gypped? Or hurt in a car wreck? You were going to forget everything but piling up money, remember?

ROGER. Not that way. There isn't enough money in the world to make me forget that my greed killed a boy, as Bill's has. What if it had been Ted? Or Nancy?

ALICE. And yet, just yesterday you took an order from Mrs. Horton for that worthless sport car because of the fat commission. A few more like that, you said, and we'd be going to Florida, too.

TED. What do you mean, Mom? What are you and Dad talking about?

NANCY. I'm surprised at you, Mother. You know Daddy wouldn't sell a car that wasn't any good.

ROGER. You're right, honey, I wouldn't. I guess I was a little mixed-up yesterday. Just for a little while it seemed like I'd been headed in the wrong direction all my life. That I'd been a fool to think it paid to do things for people. To think that honesty paid even if people didn't appreciate it. Just for a little while I thought that maybe making money was the most important thing after all. Money and the things money can buy.

ALICE. But money can't buy peace of mind for Bill, Roger. Not after last night.

TED. Nor life for Larry Russell.

ROGER. I know. It can't even buy the right words for Bill to say to Larry's parents. It can't buy anything really. Nothing that matters.

ALICE. Oh, Roger!

ROGER. If you folks'll excuse me now, I have a phone call to make.

ALICE. Roger, I was hoping you'd changed your mind about the Community·Chest by now.

ROGER. Community Chest? What do you mean?

ALICE. Aren't you going to call Mr. Carlson? You started to call him last night but it was too late.

ROGER. No, that wasn't who I was going to call. I *have* changed my mind about that, and a lot of other things, too. I don't know how I'll find time to head the drive, but I'll manage somehow, I always have. I want to do it.

ALICE. I'm glad.

ROGER. I'm going to call Mrs. Horton about that car she bought yesterday. I think I can find something a little better for her boy after all. She'll probably think I'm crazy, though.

ALICE. Probably. But who cares? *(She smiles happily.)* Welcome home, darling.

TED. Welcome home? Honestly, parents say the craziest things sometimes!

NANCY. What do you mean, Mother? Daddy hasn't been away, have you, Daddy?

ALICE. A long, long way. But he's back now. And while you're at the phone, Roger, why don't you call Mr. Colby and tell him you'll think his offer over seriously? About running for the council on that coalition ticket, I mean.

ROGER. I might do just that. It's worth considering, anyway. You know, I think I like the road I've traveled better than Bill's after all.

CURTAIN

BEFORE THE DAWN

A DRAMA IN ONE ACT

By
ALEXANDER BADGER

PRODUCTION RIGHTS

Copies of this play are available in single pamphlet form. The right to produce this play by one group of amateur players is authorized only by the purchase of five copies (one copy for each speaking part) at the current price of 50c each.

It is dishonest and illegal to copy parts.

CAST OF CHARACTERS
(For three men and two women)

BURKE .... The warden
JOE .... The guard
DIANA DAYTON .... A young newspaper woman
ELLEN BRADY .... A girl of eighteen
JIM CARSON .... The condemned man

TIME: The present—a winter morning, about five-thirty.

PLACE: The warden's office in a state's prison.

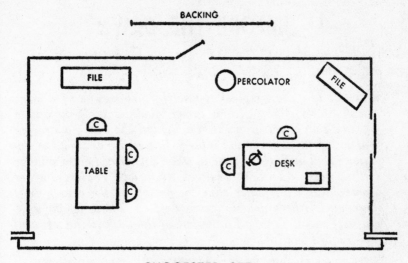

SUGGESTED SET

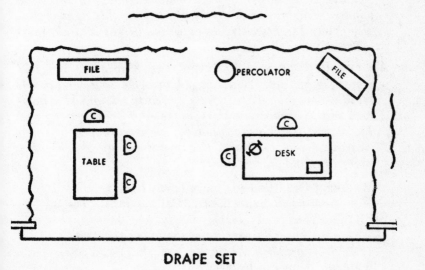

DRAPE SET

BEFORE THE DAWN

TIME: *The present. A winter morning, about five-thirty.*

PLACE: *The warden's office in a state's prison.*

SETTING: *Is quite simple, essential furnishings being a large desk down Right with a green shade desk lamp and a phone set; a swivel desk chair behind the desk; a straight office chair at its right; a large filing case against the upstage wall at Right; in the upstage corner at Left, a smaller filing case; a large table down Right with chairs; a water percolator with paper cups to the left of the center door upstage. Other furnishings as desired. There is one exit, upstage wall Center. To the left of the desk in the left wall is a large window.*

NOTE: *The set may be carried out with simple draperies.*

LIGHTING: *The lighting is not too bright, ostensibly coming from the lamp on the warden's desk. The only change in lighting is the growing light which streams in from the window. During the progress of the play this light gradually grows brighter, climaxing in the bright sunlight indicated at the play conclusion.*

AT THE RISE OF THE CURTAIN: *The Warden is revealed seated at his desk studying a letter. He is a kind-faced, middle-aged man with gray hair, wearing a dark blue business suit. In a moment, the upstage door opens quietly and Joe enters. He is a black-haired, muscular-appearing man wearing a blue uniform. Hearing the door, the Warden swings around in his chair.*

WARDEN. Oh! It's you, Joe. *(Turns back.)*

JOE *(Coming down to the right of the desk.)* Yes, sir . . . Everything is all ready, sir.

WARDEN *(Absently, staring at the letter.)* All set?

JOE *(At one end of the desk.)* Yes, sir . . . all set.

WARDEN. How did he sleep?

JOE. Like a baby. I left him eating breakfast.

WARDEN *(Glancing up.)* Oh? Anything special . . . for his breakfast?

298

JOE. No, sir. Just the usual. I told him—yesterday I told him he could have anything he wanted for breakfast. All he asked for was the usual. I told him . . .

WARDEN *(Absently, staring at the letter again.)* Just the usual, eh?

JOE. Yes, sir. Bacon and eggs was all he wanted.

WARDEN *(Lays the letter on the desk.)* H-m-m-m-m . . . Are the reporters all here?

JOE. All that signed up except one—from the Morning Post.

WARDEN. Who's that?

JOE. A woman—Diana something-or-other.

WARDEN. I remember. Funny . . . a woman wanting to see it.

JOE. Maybe she was assigned to cover it.

WARDEN. Yeah . . . maybe.

JOE. Warden!

WARDEN. Yes, Joe?

JOE. Do you think it's too late to hear anything?

WARDEN. You mean from the Governor?

JOE. That's right. I kinda hoped there might be something from him . . . for this one.

WARDEN. So did I, Joe . . . for this one.

JOE. And you don't think . . . ?

WARDEN. Possibly, but it's not likely . . . now. It's less than an hour till the time.

JOE *(Glances at his wrist watch.)* That's right.

WARDEN *(Rises and goes up to the percolator.)* And what's more, we have no reason to expect the Governor to take any action. *(Draws a drink in the paper cup.)*

JOE. How's that, sir?

WARDEN. Carson never even asked him to interfere, refused to appeal his case to a higher court. Just admitted he killed the man—and that was that. *(Drinks.)*

JOE. He's kind of religious. Do you suppose he feels he's paying his debt for what he did?

WARDEN *(Bitterly.)* Could be—and I'm helping him pay . . . a little . . . sweating it out this way. *(Lightning and thunder, followed by the ringing of the phone bell.)* Oh-oh!

JOE *(Pleased and a bit excited.)* The Governor, maybe?

WARDEN *(Hurries down to the desk and takes up the phone.)* Maybe . . . Hello . . . Yes, this is he . . . No! . . . With Miss Dayton? . . . We-l-l-l-ll, send them up. *(Replaces the phone on the holder.)* It wasn't the Governor. Your missing girl reporter has showed up with the wife of the man Carson shot.

JOE *(Amazed.)* Really?

WARDEN. That's right. Incidentally, the wife is Carson's sister—in case you've forgotten.

JOE. Why bring his sister here now?

WARDEN *(Explosively.)* You tell me!

JOE. Do you 'spose she's trying a last minute attempt—?

WARDEN. It's the reporter that's asking to see me, not the sister. *(A tap on the door upstage.)* Here they are! Open the door, Joe.

JOE *(Going up to the door.)* Yes, sir. *(The Warden stands behind his desk, facing up to the door as Joe opens it.)* How do you do, Miss? Come in, please.

DIANA *(As she enters, leading in Ellen.)* Thank you. *(Diana holds Ellen's arm and seems to be partially supporting her. Diana is a pretty brunette of about twenty-six—a little brisk in her manner, but not too over-confident. She gives the impression of easy efficiency. She wears a tailored suit with a plastic raincoat with a hood over it. Ellen looks younger, being actually eighteen. She is wide-eyed and ready to dissolve in tears—pretty, but wan-looking. She wears a colorless, cheap-looking coat and a draggled hat.)*

WARDEN *(Moving up to meet them.)* Good evening, Miss Dayton—or rather, good morning.

DIANA *(Coming down to him ahead of Ellen.)* Good morning, Mr. Burke. *(Offers him her hand.)*

WARDEN *(To Joe.)* I'll call you, Joe.

JOE. Yes, sir. *(Exits.)*

DIANA *(Drawing Ellen forward.)* Warden Burke, this is Mrs. Ellen Brady. *(The Warden and Ellen exchange greetings.)* I guess you know that Ellen is Jim Carson's sister.

WARDEN. Yes. Yes, I know.

DIANA. May we talk to you, Warden, for a few minutes
. . . about Ellen's brother?

WARDEN. Of course. Won't you take off your raincoat,
Miss Dayton? *(As Diana is shaking water from it, he moves
down a bit and they follow, Diana removing her coat.)*

DIANA. Thanks. I will.

WARDEN. And you, Mrs. Brady—your coat?

ELLEN *(Faintly.)* No, thank you. *(The Warden takes Diana's coat from her and crosses to the table at Right. Spreads
her coat over one of the chairs, picks another chair and carries it left to set it in front of the desk.)*

WARDEN. Please sit down—both of you.

DIANA. Thank you. *(She leads Ellen to the chair the Warden has set in front of the desk, and sits herself in the chair
at the right end of the desk. The Warden returns to his chair
behind the desk.)* Gracious! I wouldn't want to take *that*
drive again on such a night!

WARDEN. Pretty bad, was it?

DIANA. Terrible—and all the way from the capitol.

WARDEN. Really?

DIANA. I was talking to the Governor at midnight.

WARDEN. Well, well! Two hundred miles . . . but of course
you were to be here, anyway . . . later.

DIANA *(Soberly.)* That's right. I only hope the other trip
was justified. *(Opens her handbag and rummages in it.)* I
have a letter here . . . somewhere . . . from the Governor.

WARDEN *(Pleased.)* From the Governor?

DIANA *(Takes out a long envelope.)* That's right. Here it is.
(Takes a letter from the envelope.) Will you please read it?
(Hands it to him.)

WARDEN. Of course. *(As he takes the letter, there is a
brilliant flash of lightning followed by a long roll of thunder.
The letter is evidently brief, for he reads it quickly and lays
it on the desk.)* Well, Miss Dayton, the Governor suggests
that I help you follow up an idea. He seems to have a pretty
high opinion of you.

DIANA. He was very kind.

WARDEN. He seems to have some faith in what he calls
your hunch.

DIANA *(Eagerly.)* It may be nothing more than that, Warden, but isn't any idea—any hunch, if you please—worth following up if it may save a man's life?

WARDEN. It certainly is—in this case, Jim Carson's life?

DIANA. That's right.

WARDEN *(Glances at his wrist watch.)* What is this—this idea of yours, Miss Dayton?

DIANA. I'll be as brief as possible—and will you forgive me if I don't tell you *everything* right away?

WARDEN *(A bit doubtfully.)* We-l-l-l-ll . . . we haven't too much time, you know, but if you say . . . *(Ellen is sitting listlessly, her hands folded in her lap.)*

DIANA *(Nervous.)* May we—I'm almost afraid to ask this, but . . . but . . . ?

WARDEN *(Sharply.)* But what? Go ahead, please.

DIANA *(Still nervous.)* May I talk to the—may I talk to Jim Carson?

WARDEN *(Disturbed by her request.)* Really, Miss Dayton!

DIANA *(Begging earnestly.)* Please! I want, I *must* hear his story from his own lips.

WARDEN. At this time? Within less than an hour of his . . . of his . . . I've never had—I've never known of such a request!

DIANA *(Firmly.)* It may save his life. The Governor said . . .

WARDEN. Please, please! Don't misunderstand me. I'll do anything, *anything*, if there's the slightest chance . . . especially with Carson.

DIANA *(Leaning forward tensely.)* There *is* such a chance! A good chance! Believe me, there is. Yesterday I spent hours going over the transcript of the trial evidence. I found something. The Governor is willing . . . please!

WARDEN *(Still a bit dubious.)* Well, then . . . *(Still hesitates.)*

DIANA *(Eagerly.)* Yes, Warden?

WARDEN. It's such a terrible thing to do—to perhaps raise the man's hopes at the last minute and then . . .

DIANA. I understand that.

WARDEN. If this hunch of yours—if there's nothing to

your idea—I'll have to go ahead at the specified time and—
(Glances at his watch.)—and there isn't much time . . .

DIANA *(Leaning tensely forward as she begs.)* I know, I
know, but please, *please* . . .

WARDEN *(Rises as he makes his decision.)* Very well. I'll
have him brought here. *(The Warden runs his finger under
the desk's edge searching for the button. Finds it and presses
it. Offstage, faintly, a buzzer sounds.)*

DIANA *(Relieved.)* Oh, thank you, thank you!

WARDEN. I suppose Mrs. Brady knows about your hunch?

DIANA. Oh, yes!

WARDEN. And she also wants—?

ELLEN. Yes, yes—please!

WARDEN. I see. Believe me, Miss Dayton, no one would be
more delighted than I if Jim Carson could be saved.

DIANA. I had reason to think you felt that way, Mr. Burke.

WARDEN. Thanks. *(Joe enters, stopping just inside the
doorway.)*

JOE. You rang, Warden?

WARDEN *(Turning to him.)* Joe, I want you to bring Jim
Carson in here.

JOE *(Amazed.)* Carson here? Now?

WARDEN *(Sharply.)* That's right! And as quickly as possible!

JOE. Very well, sir, if you say. *(Exits briskly.)*

WARDEN *(Sits.)* It will take a little time.

DIANA. While we're waiting, there's something . . . Two
years ago a lifer—a Dave Mague—escaped from the prison
here.

WARDEN. That was before my time.

DIANA. I know—but you *do* know of the escape?

WARDEN. That's right. I read about it in the papers, and
I've gone over the records here. Why? What about it?

DIANA *(Ignoring his question.)* As I remember it, he was
serving a life sentence for murder—and knifed a guard here
when he escaped.

WARDEN. That's right. The guard died later.

DIANA. And they never caught Mague?

WARDEN. He's still on the loose somewhere right now.

DIANA. You never saw the man?

WARDEN. As I said before—

DIANA. Of course . . . Excuse me, please. *(She gropes in her hand bag and draws out another folded paper. Rises.)* This is part of my hunch, Warden—carrying it out. Do you have some Scotch tape?

WARDEN. I think I do. *(Opens the desk drawer and rummages for it, ad libbing.)* I'm sure I have somewhere in here, ets. *(As he is looking, Diana unfolds the paper and carefully tears off the lower portion of it, returning that portion to her hand bag. The Warden finds the tape and hands it to her.)* Here it is.

DIANA. Thank you. *(She goes upstage to the door.)* Please forgive me for being so secretive. Perhaps, it's my sense of the dramatic, but it's important to me.

WARDEN. Whatever you want.

DIANA *(At the door.)* I want to fasten this paper on the door here.

WARDEN. Go right ahead. *(She fastens the paper on the center of the door about eye level. On the paper is printed the large picture of a man's face and profile.)*

DIANA *(As she finishes.)* There! How could we get along these days without this tape?

WARDEN *(Rises so he can see what is on the paper as Diana stands aside to look at her handiwork.)* That man's picture, Miss Dayton! Who—?

DIANA. Please forgive me, if I don't tell you about it . . . yet . . . or why I put it there. *(Comes down to her chair.)*

WARDEN *(A trifle miffed at her reticence.)* Okay, if you like.

DIANA. I know I'm presuming.

WARDEN *(Still a little miffed.)* Not at all, not at all.

DIANA. As I suggested, I have a strong sense of the dramatic. In this case, it may contribute to the end we seek.

WARDEN *(Recovering his good humor.)* Then fine! Anything that will help. As I told you—or implied, at least—I have hoped that something might turn up to save Carson. I like him. I've never hated my job so much. *(A tap sounds on the door.)* That will be Joe—with Carson. *(Greatly agitated,*

Ellen rises and moves out Center as the Warden goes up to the door. Diana rises.)

JOE *(Outside the door.)* Here he is, Warden. *(As the door swings out, Joe moves in and stands with his back covering the paper fastened to the door so that Jim Carson, entering, does not see the paper. Warden backs away as Jim enters, passing Joe. He is a young man, slight of build, with a fine-featured, refined and sober face. He moves as one in a dream, listlessly. He wears khaki trousers and a white shirt, open at the throat. As Ellen sights him she runs upstage and throws herself into his arms.)*

ELLEN *(With excessive emotion.)* Oh, Jim, Jim!

JIM *(Holding her close.)* Ellen! Ellen honey!

WARDEN. Thank you, Joe. I'll call you.

JOE. Yes, sir. *(Joe exits, closing the door behind him.)*

WARDEN *(Moving back down to the desk.)* I'm sorry, Carson, to bring you here at this time, but there seems to be a good reason. *(Jim quietly disengages Ellen's grasp.)*

JIM *(Listlessly.)* It's all right, sir.

WARDEN. Please, Mrs. Brady, won't you go back to your chair and sit down?

JIM *(Giving her a little shove.)* Go ahead, honey.

ELLEN *(To the Warden.)* Yes, sir. *(She wanders listlessly back to the chair in front of the desk and drops into it, her head sinking forward into her hands.)*

WARDEN *(Indicating Diana.)* Carson, this is Miss Dayton. She's a newspaper woman.

DIANA *(Moving up to Jim and giving him her hand.)* How do you do, Mr. Carson?

JIM *(Dully.)* Hello, Miss Dayton.

WARDEN *(Moving over to them.)* Miss Dayton has come here to try and help you.

JIM. I haven't asked for help.

DIANA. For Ellen's sake, Mr. Carson.

JIM. All right, then—for her sake.

WARDEN. Won't you sit down, Miss Dayton?

DIANA. Thank you. *(Comes down to her chair and sits.)*

WARDEN *(Taking Jim's arm and leading him down Center.)* Miss Dayton is asking to hear your story, Carson.

JIM *(Tensely, staring at the Warden.)* Again? Now?

WARDEN. She thinks she's found something that may help.

JIM. I haven't asked . . .

WARDEN. I know, but please . . .

JIM. All right—if you wish. *(The Warden and Jim are now down Center. Warden moves to the table and starts to bring over a chair for Jim.)*

WARDEN. I'll get you a chair.

JIM. Please! Let me stand. I'd rather stand.

WARDEN *(Shoves the chair back.)* As you like. *(Returns to his desk and sits.)*

JIM. Thank you, Warden. *(He is down Center. As he talks he faces the audience much of the time, occasionally turning to face Diana or the Warden. Diana turns her chair to face him. Ellen has recovered from her emotional upset and now sits listlessly watching and listening.)*

WARDEN. Go ahead, Miss Dayton.

DIANA. Believe me, Mr. Carson, I wouldn't intrude on you —on your privacy at this time if I didn't think, if I didn't hope . . .

JIM. It's all right, Miss. It doesn't matter.

ELLEN. Jim! Please! You've got to help her if you can!

JIM. Of course, honey . . . anything . . . but you mustn't get your hopes up for nothing. *(Ellen drops her head back in her hand.)*

DIANA. Mr. Carson!

JIM. Call me Jim.

DIANA. Very well . . . Jim. Will you—do you mind telling me your story about what happened and why it happened— about this man you—you . . . ?

JIM *(Passionately and fiercely.)* Go ahead and say it! I killed him, all right, and I'd do it again!

WARDEN *(Sternly.)* Carson!

JIM *(Reverting to his lethargy.)* I'm sorry, Warden.

WARDEN. It's all right. I just want you to help Miss Dayton all you can.

JIM. I'll try.

DIANA. Now, Jim . . . Will you please tell me how everything came about—how it began?

JIM. All right. I guess you know I'm a miner. Coal. Ever since I was fourteen.

DIANA. Yes, I do know that.

JIM. I'm twenty-two now. I don't know the sun as well as you do, Miss Dayton.

DIANA. I'm sorry.

JIM. I'll get on. My father died eight years ago on Black Friday in the big cave-in. He's still down there—a mile down. My mother followed him soon after. She couldn't take what happened to him. Up to then, I was in school. After she died, I went into the mine. There was just Ellen and me. She was younger—she's only eighteen now. I tried to look out for her. We were happy together, weren't we, honey?

ELLEN *(With great feeling.)* Oh yes, Jim!

JIM. The life in the mine was hard, but like I said, we were happy enough, looking ahead to something better . . . And then *he* came!

DIANA. *He?*

JIM. Steve Brady—the man I killed. *(Suddenly fierce again.)* I never denied killing him! I never asked for mercy!

WARDEN *(Sternly.)* We know all that, Carson. Miss Dayton knows it.

JIM *(Again reverting to his dull recital.)* I'm sorry . . . Well, like I said, he came to our little town in the hills. No one knew or cared where he came from. The few who asked questions learned nothing. He talked a lot, but never about himself.

DIANA. Was he a miner before he came?

JIM. Not him! It was plain he had never worked in a mine. But he was big—strong as an ox. They needed men. They gave him a job right off, soon made him a foreman—just before he saw Ellen for the first time. *(Hesitates.)*

DIANA. Please go on. *(Ellen still sits with her head sunk in her hands.)*

JIM. He saw her one day in the store and set out to get her for his wife. She seemed to forget everything—everybody —even me.

ELLEN *(Raises her head quickly to protest.)* Jim! I didn't! I never did!

JIM. It seemed that way, honey . . . but maybe not. I'm sorry I said that.

DIANA. Please!

JIM. It was hard to take—him marrying Ellen—little Ellen. Maybe he bullied her into it. *(The last as though talking to himself.)*

ELLEN. He did! I—I—I—I didn't think I could help myself!

JIM *(Thoughtfully.)* Maybe it was my fault. Maybe I shouldn't have let her . . . I wasn't afraid of him, although he could have broken me in two. He was always picking fights with the boys. Even so . . . I thought if Ellen liked him, it was up to her.

ELLEN *(Hysterically.)* I—I—I—I—All the time I was afraid of him!

JIM *(A bit fiercely.)* Then why did you marry him?

ELLEN *(Brokenly.)* Oh, I don't know, I don't know! *(Drops her head back into her hands, sobbing.)*

WARDEN. The time is short, Miss Dayton.

DIANA. Please, Jim! Won't you . . . ?

JIM. Yeah . . . Well, there isn't too much more. She married him and I lived alone and worked in the mine and didn't care much whether I lived or died. Then I learned how he was treating her.

DIANA. How did you find that out?

JIM. No one had to tell me. I could see for myself. I met her in the company store one night. Her face was covered with bruises. I asked her who did it. I made her tell me. That was the first time.

DIANA. There were other times?

JIM. Many other times—and then the last time. *(Ellen is sobbing quietly.)* A neighbor woman told me Ellen was in bed from a beating he gave her. I had a gun. It belonged to my father. I cleaned it and got some new cartridges. I went to their house. He came to the door. He was drunk. And then Ellen came to the door.

ELLEN *(Raising her head.)* I was afraid for you.

JIM. When I saw her face, I lost my head. He cursed me.

ELLEN. He would have killed you!

JIM *(In the following, Jim works himself up to a frenzied climax.)* Maybe. He never got the chance. I emptied the gun into him before he got the chance to come at me, if he was going to. That's why they never let me plead self defense, even if I wanted to, which I never did. And I never asked for anything!

WARDEN *(A bit impatiently.)* I tell you Miss Dayton knows that.

JIM *(Again reverting to his former lethargy.)* I'm sorry, Warden.

DIANA. Warden, there's something I'm wondering. Wasn't there, at least, the implication of self defense?

WARDEN. The judge didn't seem to think so. If I'd been the judge—but that's no good.

DIANA *(Indignantly.)* The sentence was outrageous!

WARDEN. Maybe so.

DIANA. Tell me this, Warden Burke, if you know the answer. Suppose—just suppose that this Steve Brady turned out to be an escaped convict with a reward offered for his capture—dead or alive.

WARDEN *(Rises, startled, as he senses what Diana is getting at.)* Miss Dayton! Are you telling me—?

DIANA *(Quickly, also rising.)* Please, Warden! I'm telling you nothing!

JIM *(Dully, to the Warden.)* What does she mean by all this?

DIANA *(Quickly, before the Warden can answer.)* Just a minute, Jim! *(To the Warden.)* You didn't answer my question, Mr. Burke.

WARDEN *(Turning to the upstage door.)* That picture—

DIANA *(Cutting him off sharply.)* Please! Please! My question! *(The Warden turns to face her again, dropping back in his chair. Diana also sits.)*

WARDEN. Well, Miss Dayton, I'm not quite sure, but I would guess that if the man Carson shot turned out to be what you say, an escaped convict . . . *(Hesitates in some uncertainty.)*

DIANA *(Eagerly.)* Yes?

WARDEN. I would think Carson's act would be interpreted, e-r-r-r, more liberally.

DIANA. Wouldn't it be an act to be rewarded rather than punished? *(Jim is watching and listening to all this completely puzzled.)*

WARDEN. I don't know what the law would say. *(Glances at his watch.)* The time is—

DIANA *(Racing ahead.)* Surely it would change the punishment to a lighter sentence!

WARDEN *(A little irked.)* I told you I thought so, but I could be wrong, and—

DIANA *(Excitedly.)* You're not wrong, Warden! The Governor told me—*(Suddenly checks herself.)*

WARDEN *(Greatly interested.)* Told you what? What did the Governor tell you?

DIANA. Later, please.

WARDEN *(Irritated.)* Miss Dayton, I've gone a long way with you! It seems to me—

DIANA *(Unmoved and firmly.)* I'm sorry. Jim, have you told me all your story?

JIM. That was it, Miss Dayton—all there is to tell.

DIANA. One thing more, please. When did this man—this Steve Brady come to your little mining town? How long ago?

JIM *(Thinking.)* It was . . . about two years ago . . . I think.

DIANA. Are you sure of that?

ELLEN. That was when it was, Miss Dayton, in January, two years ago. I remember the time.

DIANA. Thank you, Ellen. *(To Warden.)* Well, Mr. Burke, I guess that's all.

WARDEN *(Amazed and greatly irritated.)* Wha-a-a-at? You mean to tell me—you mean you haven't learned what you thought—what you hoped to learn?

DIANA *(Firmly.)* Mr. Carson has told me his story and I have no more questions to ask him. *(Rises.)*

WARDEN *(More irritated.)* You mean to tell me that all this has been for nothing—that in twenty minutes . . . that we're just where we were before you came?

DIANA *(Firmly.)* I mean, Warden Burke, that my interview with Mr. Carson is ended.

WARDEN *(Protesting.)* You don't! And you want me to send him back to —to his cell?

DIANA *(Ignoring the Warden's question and turning to Jim.)* Please forgive me, Jim!

JIM. It's all right, Miss.

WARDEN *(Disgusted.)* It's no such thing! *(Presses the button under the desk's edge. Offstage faint buzzer.)* I don't mind admitting, Miss Dayton, that I'm mighty disappointed in you—after all your promises—

DIANA *(Snapping him off quickly.)* Warden Burke! I made no promises whatever!

WARDEN. Well . . . you're right about that. You didn't, I guess. It was rather what you led me to think, to hope.

JIM. It doesn't matter, sir.

WARDEN. It matters a lot, but apparently there's nothing I can do about it. *(There's a tap on the door and Joe enters. He hesitates just inside the door as the Warden turns to him. Ellen rises and rushes across to Jim. They embrace.)* Well, Joe, you can take Carson back . . . now.

JOE. Yes, sir. *(He comes down to Jim. Ellen is clinging to Jim. He gently disengages her arms and pushes her away.)*

JIM. Goodbye, honey.

ELLEN *(Distraught.)* Oh, Jim! Jim!

JIM. Now, now, honey. *(Ellen wanders back to the chair below the desk and stands there watching as Joe takes Jim's arm and starts to lead him upstage.)*

JOE. I'm sorry, Carson.

JIM. It's okay. *(As they move up to the door, Diana moves out Center, tensely watching them.)*

WARDEN *(Moving over with Diana.)* Miss Dayton, I must say—

DIANA *(In a tense whisper.)* Please! Wait! Watch! *(She and the Warden watch the two as they near the upstage door. Ellen also watches, standing in front of her chair. Jim walks beside Joe with a downcast face, but as he nears the door, he lifts his head and thus comes face to face with the picture fastened on the door. He stops, stares fixedly at the picture a moment. Then suddenly he hurls Joe's hand from his arm, snatches at the paper on the door, and rips it off. Crumpling the paper in his hand, he whirls and comes down to the Warden at Center with Diana. 'He shakes the crumpled paper in the Warden's face as he raves . . .)*

JIM *(Fiercely, biting off each word.)* Why . . . have . . . you . . . done . . . this . . . thing . . . to me?

WARDEN *(Taken aback, and retreating a few steps.)* For God's sake, Carson! What's come over you?

JIM *(Following him and shaking the paper.)* Why have you—? *(Joe has followed him and now seizes his arm.)*

WARDEN. Wait, Joe! *(Turns to Diana.)* Miss Dayton, that picture! What—?

JIM *(Still raging at the Warden.)* Why did you put it there?

DIANA. Please, Jim!

JIM *(Not to be distracted from the Warden.)*—where I would see it?

WARDEN *(Pointing at Diana.)* Ask *her*, Carson.

DIANA. Jim! I put that picture there! *(He turns to her.)*

JIM. Why? Why should you torture me now—at the last?

DIANA. Please, Jim! Who is it? Who is the man in the picture?

WARDEN *(Excited.)* Jim! Is it Brady—that picture—the man you . . . ?

JIM *(Fiercely.)* You know it is—and you—*(Ellen has run across to Jim and now chokes off his words as she throws her arms around him.)*

WARDEN. Miss Dayton! You're sure . . . ?

DIANA *(Taking the portion of paper she tore from the picture out of her hand bag.)* You say, Warden! *(Hands him the paper. He stares at the paper wonderingly, greatly pleased.)*

WARDEN *(Mutters.)* What a hunch, what a hunch—what a gal!

JIM *(Quietly now, his arm around Ellen.)* I don't understand all this. Please . . .

DIANA. I fastened that picture on the door, Jim. I was

312

trying to save your life—to prove something that *would* save it.

WARDEN. Please, Miss Dayton! What was it the Governor said—if your hunch was correct?

DIANA. It *is* correct, isn't it?

WARDEN. Not a doubt in the world. Of course, we'll have an absolute check. But what about the Governor?

DIANA. He mentioned a full pardon. He said there were details—*(Jim and Ellen are in each other's arms. The morning sun is streaming in the left window on them.)*

WARDEN. Details, huh! That dramatic instinct of yours, Miss Dayton—

DIANA. Paid off, didn't it? I just had to do it my way.

JIM. Warden, please! Does all this mean that . . . ?

WARDEN. That the bad times are over, Carson—for you and Ellen.

ELLEN *(Pointing to the window and the morning sun that is streaming in.)* Look, Jim! The sun!

DIANA. With a new day for you, Jim, and for Ellen.

CURTAIN

PUTTING FIRST THINGS FIRST

A PLAY IN ONE ACT

By

ETHEL D. POSEGATE

PRODUCTION RIGHTS

Copies of this play are available in single pamphlet form. The right to produce this play by one group of amateur players is authorized only by the purchase of four copies (one copy for each speaking part) at the current price of 50c each.

It is dishonest and illegal to copy parts.

CAST OF CHARACTERS
(For three women, one child)

Mrs. Dole—Hostess, the mother of two teen-age daughters

Mrs. Brown—Neighbor, the mother of . . .

Sue Brown—Baby in arms (or a life-like doll)

Betty Brown—Five or six-year-old child (as young as can handle the part)

Mrs. Shaw—Elderly grandmother and neighbor.

PUTTING FIRST THINGS FIRST

AT THE RISE OF THE CURTAIN: *Mrs. Dole and her neighbor Grandma Shaw are on stage. Mrs. Dole is talking on the phone.*

MRS. DOLE *(At the phone.)* Yes, this is Mrs. Dole. *(Pause.)* Oh yes, Gladys. How is my little neighbor this morning? *(Pause.)* So you think *you* have troubles? Well, you should hear *mine* and you will feel absolutely care-free. *(Pause.)* Sure! Come on over if you think I can be of any help—which I doubt. Mrs. Shaw, our neighbor on the north, is here. *(Pause.)* No-no! That is all right. You come right on over. I called her to come over and help me with my troubles—so perhaps she can help you too. *(Pause.)* Oh, that's all right. Bring them right along. At their ages they are no worry. Wait until they are in high school. *(Pause.)* Humph! That's what *you* think. Well, you come right on over. Be seein' you. Bye. *(Replaces the phone. To Grandma Shaw.)* Gladys Brown wants to come over. She thinks *she* has problems. *(Throws up her hands.)* Now I really do have them, do I not, Grandma Shaw?

GRANDMA *(Should be a slow speaking, motherly-type person.)* Well, my dear, if her troubles aren't any greater than yours, she hasn't much to worry about.

MRS. DOLE. Not any greater than mine! Why, Grandma Shaw! You know I have enough to drive me crazy!

GRANDMA. Just because your daughter Doris failed in two school subjects and Nancy wants to get married at seventeen? Is that enough to make you want to give up?

MRS. DOLE. Well, what could be worse? I never failed in a subject in school in my life and neither did her father and all this worry comes at a time when I need to have my mind free from worry. I simply do not have time for it. I have to entertain my club in a few weeks and this whole house has to be done over before then—and I am on five committees—chairman of two—*(A knock is heard. On the way to the door she says.)* and goodness knows what all else. *(Opens the door. Enter Gladys Brown with Sue and Betty.)* Oh, hello,

Gladys! *(To the children.)* and how is my little Sue and Brown Betsy?

GLADYS. Hello, Mrs. Dole. Good morning, Mrs. Shaw. Betty, speak to the ladies.

BETTY. Hello!

GLADYS. I hate to barge in on you like this and unload all my troubles, but I simply get swamped.

MRS. DOLE. You get swamped? You ought to be so thankful you don't have *my* problems that you would be shouting for joy—regardless of anything. What is bothering you, for pity's sake?

GLADYS. Oh, my baby-sitter moved away yesterday—very unexpectedly—and Jim, my husband, just raises cain if I so much as mention leaving them with a young girl and I was just elected president of our social club and that is such an honor, but it does take a lot of time, and I want to do even more than Mrs. Bell, last year's president, did, and to top it all Jim's mother wrote she wants to come for a visit right away, on her way to the coast. Jim is thrilled to death, but I've never even seen her; she lives so far away. *(Betty is seated on a low stool just a little back of her mother. She listens very attentively to the conversations and is quiet and good as can be. Gladys, a very nervous type person, looks all around the room and says.)* Betty! Where in the world are you? Is she into anything?

MRS. DOLE. She is not doing one thing, Gladys. Well, things have piled up on you a little, but just be glad that one of your daughters hasn't flunked in school and the other one doesn't want to get married.

GLADYS. Oh dear! Will I always have something to worry about with these children? I thought all my worries would be over when they grew up—if they ever do. *(To Grandma Shaw.)* Did you ever have any children, Mrs. Shaw?

GRANDMA. Yes—I had children. I had ten. *(Mrs. Dole and Mrs. Brown both show great emotion and horror.)*

MRS. DOLE. Ten!!! My soul and body, Grandma Shaw! How did you ever manage?

GLADYS. Ten children! Oh, you poor, poor woman.

GRANDMA. Now after all, girls, I said I had ten children.

You act as horrified as if I had said I had ten puppies. Gladys, you said "You poor, poor woman." I believe you really meant that and feel sorry for me. Girls, I feel I am the richest person in the world. My husband, my home, and those ten children were my life's work and it was a wonderful career. Two of my five sons are ministers, one is a doctor, one a farmer and one is a merchant. All of my daughters either taught or were nurses and they all have good homes and children of their own now.

GLADYS. Truly, Mrs. Shaw, I did not mean it exactly the way it sounded. But how did you find time for anything else? *(Looks around nervously.)* Betty, where are you? I simply can't keep track of her.

BETTY *(Calmly sitting as she was.)* Here I am, Mother. I'm not doing anything.

MRS. DOLE. She is quiet as a mouse and sitting right there behind you, Gladys. Stop worrying. Grandma Shaw, I know your children are grand to you and the ones I have met are wonderful people. How did you ever manage? Were you wealthy?

GRANDMA. About all we ever had plenty of was love. I always think of that when I hear that song young people sing sometimes nowadays—"I Can't Give You Anything But *Love*, Baby." Well, it takes more of that than any other one thing to build a home and if you do not have that—even though you have the finest furnishings in the world, your home will fall apart. When we started out and all through our early married years, that is about all we had.

GLADYS. What did you ever do for fun? Who took care of your children?

MRS. DOLE. Did any of your children ever fail in school subjects or want to get married at seventeen?

GRANDMA. You young mothers are as full of questions as a boy at a circus, but you asked for this so I am going to tell you. I'll take your questions in turn. Gladys wants to know what we did for fun? I guess we were so dumb we never knew we were having anything *but* fun. Our work together was fun. Our babies were fun. We drove six miles to church and we went every Sunday and to Prayer meeting every **Wednesday** night. Our church and school were close together and those were our community activities.

BETTY *(Who has been listening most attentively.)* Who kept your children, Grandma Shaw?

GLADYS. Hush, Betty! Let Mrs. Shaw talk.

GRANDMA. Remember, that was one of your questions too, Gladys. *(To Betty.)* Well, honey, believe it or not, we took them with us wherever we went.

BETTY. *Oh boy!* I wish I had been *your* little girl. *(All laugh.)*

GLADYS. *Betty!* I'm going to have to punish you if you don't stop interrupting.

MRS. DOLE. She was just trying to see if they had any baby-sitters *then*—I think.

GRANDMA. There were no baby-sitters. Everything planned at home or in the community included something for all ages. Oh, it wasn't easy, but our lives then were not cluttered up with a lot of outside interests that we had to dash hither and yon to do, whether the family was fed or not. We were just dumb enough to think those things came first in the sight of God—and I am awfully afraid I still think so, girls.

GLADYS. How would you avoid it if every one else did those things and you would be left out if you didn't do them too?

MRS. DOLE. You will have to admit, Grandma, that times have changed and that you could not do that today.

GRANDMA. If times have changed and are different today, it's because you have made them that way or allowed them to become involved. I know that if I had it all to do over, I would try to profit by my mistakes. But I would very definitely still follow my same rule that has guided me all through my life—"Put *First* Things *First*." That was drilled into me as a child by my parents. If you are at times hesitant as to which things come first, take it to God in prayer and don't try to help Him decide, just because you have something you would like to put first. Ask Him and then listen. If you are sincere and want to decide right, He will tell you in a way you will understand.

GLADYS. Well, maybe everyone did that then and it was easier. Now you just *have* to keep up with your crowd.

MRS. DOLE. There are so many more activities now, Grandma, that we just have to go to. Why, John and I seldom have an evening at home.

GRANDMA. Well, my dears, it all depends upon whom you would rather impress—the ladies in your club or organizations, or your families. "Put *first* things *first*." Of course, if you know which you want and are going to put that first anyway, praying for help won't do any good. That way you have already made your decision. Did you ever stop to think that maybe all the rest of the ladies in your crowd are sort of fed up and would welcome a slowing up in speed? It always takes one to start a change. You have to have the courage of your convictions. If you cannot take the presidency of this club of yours, Gladys, without making a nervous wreck of yourself and causing you to slight some other things of more importance—think it over. God only expects just so much of you and gives you no more than you can bear. Ask yourself—"How many of these activities are essential? How many of them benefit me, really, or my family? Or am I just trying to keep up with the Joneses and get ahead of last year's president in order to receive a few insincere compliments on my wonderful ability, and to the detriment of my health and family?"

GLADYS *(Going over and kissing Grandma Shaw.)* Grandma, may I call you that too? *(Grandma nods.)* You have just made me realize something. I don't have to do all this unnecessary worrying I have been doing. As you said, perhaps all the other ladies are tired of it too. I haven't felt so relaxed in years as since listening to you. I used to pray when I was younger, but I haven't had time—or taken the time—for years. I am not going to take that presidency. My time should be spent with my family. Now I can give Betty her birthday *(Spells it out.)* p-a-r-t-y.

BETTY *(Promptly.)* Oh, goody! I get to have my birthday party after all. *(Runs to her mother and hugs and kisses her.)* Thank you, Mother. *(All laugh.)*

MRS. DOLE. You will have to think up bigger words to

spell, Gladys. Grandma, I think your coming here this morning was an act of providence. You have given Gladys a new lease on life and I begin to see it was all my fault that Doris failed in her school subjects.

GRANDMA. Remember, I didn't say that, my dear.

MRS. DOLE. No, I know you didn't, Grandma, but I told you awhile ago that John and I scarcely ever have an evening at home and that is true. I just got to thinking that none of these things we have been going to pertain to school or the family's good, except P.T.A. once a month. Come to think of it, most of the time we give that up for something we would rather do. I should have been seeing to it that Doris did some homework. Then she wouldn't have failed.

GRANDMA. School isn't over. She could probably work and catch up yet if she had encouragement and help. She is a very bright child, I think.

GLADYS. Do you begin to feel better too, Mrs. Dole?

MRS. DOLE. Strange to say, I do. That motto of yours "Put First Things First" certainly hit me hard. I very definitely have been putting first things last and doing it because every one else did. You are right, Grandma, all the women I know are eternally complaining they are rushed to death. Maybe they would *all* slow up if someone had the nerve to start it.

GLADYS. Well, I am going to start it in my crowd whether they follow me or not. I am going to wire Jim's mother we will be happy to have her come. Jim will be so glad to have me slow down. What a fool I have been! It has really become quite a serious argument between us and I can see how right he is. Grandma, you are wonderful! I will have plenty of time to do other social things after my family is raised. How can I ever thank you?

GRANDMA. Tut tut! I'm just an old woman who was blessed with a wonderful mother in my youth, blessed with a wonderful husband and ten fine children and that is all there is to it.

MRS. DOLE. No, that isn't all. There is a reason why all those children are fine.

BETTY *(Coming in promptly.)* And I know what that rea-

322

son is. Grandma Shaw said she always did *First* things *First*, and that means I am going to get to have a birthday party, doesn't it, Mother? *(All laugh.)*

GLADYS. You surely are, dear. I hope I may be forgiven for even thinking that something else was more important.

GRANDMA. What would help this old world today more than anything, is for parents to realize that their children are entitled to a secure, Christian home life and the firm foundation that such training alone can give them for their future life. There needs to be more time for *thoughtful meditation* in the home. Children should see from *observation*, the *effect* of fervent prayer for divine *guidance*. I think one poem had more influence on my life than all others. I always kept a copy of it in my kitchen and one in our bedroom. Each of my children learned it and love it as I do.

BETTY. What is it, Grandma Shaw? Do you know it by heart?

MRS. DOLE. I am sure she does. Please read it for us, Grandma.

GRANDMA. Yes, I know it without reading it. It goes like this:

FIRST THINGS FIRST

My child, seek ye God's kingdom first, then all things in
their turn.

Put *first* things *first* throughout your life, soon they are
what you yearn.

Think not too *much* of *temporal* things. Jesus gave counsel
wise

By putting *first* things *first*, in life. Eternal life's the prize.

The things we *see* are temporal, the *common* things of *earth*,

The *unseen* are *eternal* things, of undetermined worth.

Instill within the smallest *child* life's most essential needs,

In his days of *maturity*, they'll govern *well* his deeds.

In daily life put *first* things *first* lest they be crowded out.

Let it be things of *lesser* worth which we must do *without*.

The *secret* of successful lives lies in the morning *prayer*.

God's counsel in those tranquil hours, for each trial will
  prepare.
Seek God and all His righteousness and if His will ye do,
All temporal necessities are added unto you.

BETTY. That is pretty, Grandma Shaw. May I have a
copy of it?

GRANDMA. Indeed you may, my dear. If you will always
keep that and learn it, it will prove a great help to you.

GLADYS. I am glad you asked for it, Betty, for I was going
to myself.

MRS. DOLE. Better make that two copies, Grandma. That
is going to go right up over my sink. I will need that in case
I might weaken.

GRANDMA. Another thing that will help you not to weaken
is to attend Sunday School and church services regularly.
I know you usually send your children, but taking them is
far better. Example is the thing that counts.

MRS. DOLE. You are right as usual. *(The telephone is
heard. Answers.)* Hello—yes, Nancy, this is Mother. *(Listens for some time.)* That is wonderful, dear. I am sure you
will never regret your decision. I am so glad you called.
Where are you? *(Listens.)* Well, you have a mighty sensible
father and I am so glad you both went to the office to talk
with him. *(Pause.)* Sure, that will be fine. Good-bye—and
God bless you both, my dear. *(Replaces the phone. To the
ladies.)* The world is a wonderful place after all. That was
Nancy. She said she and Bob, her boy friend, went down to
the office and talked to her father about wanting to get married. She said they had both decided that the smart thing
would be to wait until Bob had a better job and they were a
little older. Isn't that grand news?

GRANDMA. Indeed it is. I felt pretty sure everything would
straighten itself out. Usually most of the things about which
we worry most never materialize.

GLADYS. What a relieved feeling we both have, Mrs. Dole!
I must be getting home. I want to get a few things off my
mind, and *we* have a birthday party to plan, don't we,
honey?

GRANDMA. The greatest career any woman can have is that of homemaker, wife and mother and as Solomon said— "Her price is above rubies, the heart of her husband doth safely trust."

CURTAIN

THE HAPPY LIFE

A DRAMA OF FAITH IN THREE SCENES

By

ROBERT ST. CLAIR

PRODUCTION RIGHTS

Copies of this play are available in single pamphlet form. The right to produce this play by one group of amateur players is authorized only by the purchase of seven copies (one copy for each speaking part) at the current price of 50c each.

It is dishonest and illegal to copy parts.

CAST OF CHARACTERS

(For Four Men, Two Women, and Extras)

HARLOW JOHNSON..........a small-town business man

JULIA........................his wife; a housekeeper

BUNNY......................their teen-age daughter

REV. JAMES THORNE....................their pastor

HENRY BAKER......................a bank president

JOHN VARDON..................................

...chairman of the Every Member Canvass Committee

Several extra men and women for committee members

SYNOPSIS OF SCENES

SCENE ONE: Living room in the Johnson home. Early evening.

SCENE TWO: The same. Two days later.

SCENE THREE: The Board room at the church. The following Sunday.

LOCALITY: A small, Mid-western community.

TIME: Autumn of the present year.

PRODUCTION NOTE: It is not necessary to have a regulation "flat" stage setting for this play. All that is required for a successful production are a set of draperies, or a back "drop" curtain and the necessary side "tabs" or "wings" to form the entrances. Even the furniture and properties have been kept down to a minimum so that the play may be produced on almost any sized stage or platform, or even in the "central staging" manner if desired.

———

All characters and situations depicted in this play are entirely imaginary.

THE HAPPY LIFE

SCENE ONE

LOCALITY: *A small, Mid-western community.*

TIME: *An evening in early fall of the present year.*

SCENE: *A living room which may merely be indicated by a sofa and coffee table, standing halfway down Left Center, an armchair at Right Center and a small table and chair directly up Center at the back. On the table is a telephone, a desk-type calendar and a table lamp with a modern shade. There are two attractive floor lamps: one at the right of the table, the other at the right side of the armchair. On the coffee table is a nice arrangement of chrysanthemums or similar autumn flowers, and a number of unopened letters; two, of business size.*

LIGHTING: *The table and floor lamps are lighted as the play begins. The borders and footlights are not much more than halfway up. They may. be fairly bright at the beginning of the scene, but should dim down considerably. as the action progresses. The purpose of this is to suggest the fading daylight outside.*

AT THE RISE OF THE CURTAIN: *Bunny, the teen-age Johnson girl, sits beside the table up Center in typical teen-age relaxation, talking with animation into the telephone. On the table beside her elbow is a list of names and telephone numbers, also the stub of a pencil. Bunny's outfit consists of levis, sweater, bobby sox and loafers, or whatever casual outfit teen-agers happen to be affecting at the moment. A clock strikes six offstage as the curtains open.*

BUNNY *(Into the phone; speaking while the curtains are opening.)* Yes, that's right — the Pilgrim Fellowship — all next week — at the same time as the Every Member Canvass. We're going to wash cars, mow lawns. collect and sell newspapers and do every *other* kind of a job we can to get money to give to the church during the big fund-raising drive. Can you come to the meeting at the Youth Center tomorrow night at seven-thirty, Janice? We want to get everything organized and make out a list of the people in the congregation so we kids can call on them and ask them to give us jobs. It ought to be heaps of fun. Shall I put a check after your name, Janice? *(Slight pause.)* Thanks. That's fine. *(Grabbing up the pencil to check a name on the list.)* We can make a hundred dollars or more if we all really get behind the project and — push. See you tomorrow night then. *(Starts to hang up, but has another thought.)* Oh, wait. Do you have a date for the square dance coming up the first of next month? *(Slight pause, then gaspingly.)* Janice! You don't mean it? When did all this happen? Oh, golly! Tell me all the exciting details.

JULIA *(Entering down Left, wiping her hands on a dish towel. She is a gentle, sweet-faced woman of forty-five, wearing a neat house dress and a dainty kitchen apron.)* Oh, Bunny —

BUNNY *(Into the phone; speaking excitedly; failing to hear her mother.)* He did? Oh, he didn't?

JULIA *(Pausing near the sofa down Left Center; in a slightly louder tone of voice.)* Bunny. Whom are you talking to?

BUNNY *(Quickly turning her head; putting her free hand over the transmitter.)* Janice Dickerson. She's going steady with Sandy Jenkins. He asked her to last night. *(Into the phone again.)* I think that's wonderful, Janice.

JULIA *(Moving behind the sofa.)* So do I. Sandy's a very fine boy and Janice is one of your very best friends.

BUNNY *(Into the phone.)* Did you hear that, Janice? Mother thinks it's fine, too. I can hardly wait to tell the crowd. What's that? *(Slight pause.)* All right. I'll wait for *you* to tell 'em — tomorrow night. See you *then*. *(Quickly cradles the phone and runs her finger down the list of names on the paper beside the telephone.)*

JULIA. Is "going steady" the same thing as being engaged, Bunny?

330

BUNNY (*Without turning.*) Well, not exactly. It just means that the girl's not supposed to go out with another boy and vice versa.

JULIA (*Moving up Left Center.*) Then they're not really in love with each other?

BUNNY. Enough to want to go steady until their parents think they're *old* enough to get engaged. (*Lifting the receiver; dialing another number.*)

JULIA (*Chuckling.*) I — see. Whom are you calling now?

BUNNY. Dick Sayles. He's the last on my list. All the others, except one, said they'd come.

JULIA. My goodness. It looks as if your group's going to be very busy next week, doesn't it, dear? I only hope your school work doesn't suffer.

BUNNY. It won't. (*Talking rapidly, with the enthusiasm of youth.*) You see, what we plan on doing is spending a couple of hours after school every day the *first* part of the week lining up our jobs. Then we'll do the actual work on Friday afternoon and all day Saturday. There'll be over sixty of us, and if we go out in teams of four or more — (*As somebody supposedly speaks at the other end of the line.*) Hello? This is Bunny Johnson. Is Dick there, please? Yes, thanks — I would. (*To Julia again, as she starts toward the exit down Left.*) Just wait until *he* hears about Sandy and Janice. Poor fellow. He'll be fit to be tied.

JULIA (*Pausing down Left.*) Why? Does he like Janice, too?

BUNNY. Not as much as Sandy does. But he's taken her to a couple of movies lately and has started to call Janice his "girl," so — (*Quickly breaking off and speaking into the phone.*) Oh, hello, Dick. This is Bunny Johnson, calling about the new PF project to make money for the church.

JULIA (*In a loud, half-whisper.*) Don't *you* tell him, Bunny. Let him hear about it from some other source.

BUNNY (*Quickly putting her hand over the transmitter, speaking in a loud, half-whisper.*) That's just what I intend to do. What do you think I am, Mother — a gossip or something? *(Julia smiles, shakes her head and exits down Left, while Bunny goes on talking into the telephone.)* I'm sorry, Dick. I was talking to Mother. Now, about the Pilgrim Fellowship plans; I'm on the calling committee — I've been at it for two hours now — yours is the last name on my list. Want to do something to help, Dick? *You* could fix people's radios or TV sets and turn the money over to us — you're awfully good at that. What do you say? Can I check you off the list? *(Slight pause.)* Golly, that's fine. Thanks, Dick. Come over to the meeting at the Youth Center tomorrow night. Yeah — seven-thirty. We're going to have doughnuts and coffee afterwards. Okay? *(Slight pause.)* Okay. *(Cradles the phone and puts a check after the last name on her list. During this, her father enters from the right.)*

HARLOW *(Speaking as he enters; taking off his hat. He is a good-natured, friendly-looking and deeply religious man of forty-seven or thereabouts, dressed in a neat business suit. He carries a newspaper that he has supposedly just picked up off the front lawn.)* Hello, Bunny.

BUNNY. Oh, hi, Daddy. Be with you in a minute.

HARLOW *(Moving up Right Center.)* What are you doing?

BUNNY. Making my calls for the Pilgrim Fellowship. I just finished — How'd everything go at the store today?

HARLOW. Oh — pretty good. *(Crossing halfway down Left Center, calling toward the entrance down Left.)* Oh, Julia — I'm home.

JULIA *(Off Left.)* Good. I'll have dinner ready in thirty minutes.

HARLOW. No hurry — *(Goes to the sofa; puts his hat and the newspaper on the coffee table while nodding toward the letters on the coffee table and asking.)* Is this all the mail?

BUNNY. That's right. How come you're so late tonight, Daddy? *(Finished adding up the names on the list, she rises and moves down Center.)*

HARLOW (*Picking up the letters and looking them over.*) Some more of the Christmas stock came in just as it was time to leave. I stayed to help Jimmy itemize it. (*Referring to the letters.*) Nothing from your sister?

BUNNY. Not today — (*Goes to sit on the left arm of the armchair at Right Center.*)

HARLOW (*Disappointedly.*) She's getting careless. Only two letters from her in the past two weeks. (*Sits on the sofa, examining the letters. Julia enters down Left in time to hear the latter part of his line.*)

JULIA (*Smilingly; pausing near the sofa.*) Listen to the doting father complain, will you? Gladys isn't careless, Harlow — just too busy to write, that's all.

BUNNY. Sure, Daddy. College is all new to her —

JULIA (*Sitting beside Harlow on the sofa.*) And it's the first time she's ever been away from home. Remember how it was when you were a freshman? The excitement of getting your courses all lined up, meeting so many new people, the rushing and so forth? I'm glad she accepted the Delta Gamma bid.

HARLOW (*Grinning; putting his hand over hers.*) That isn't surprising, you Delta Gamma mother, you!

BUNNY. I suppose they felt they just *had* to give her one — being a legacy and all.

JULIA (*Quickly and defensively.*) Being a legacy sometimes prejudices a sorority against a girl, Bunny. (*To Harlow, who had replaced all the letters except one on the coffee table.*) To tell you the truth, *I* was afraid she'd go Theta as so many of her friends did.

HARLOW (*Opening the letter.*) Not our Gladys, dear. She'd never think of letting her mother down like that. (*Indicating the letter.*) This is from my insurance agent, Mr. Carpenter.

JULIA (*Rising.*) Well, I'd better go back to the kitchen. We're having a roast — (*Starting down Left.*)

HARLOW. Sounds wonderful. (*Reading the notification from the insurance man.*)

BUNNY (*Rising and walking rapidly up Center toward the telephone.*) And *I've* got to call in my report —

HARLOW *(Exclaiming; surprised at the notification.)* Well, what do you know about *that?*

JULIA *(Pausing down Left. Bunny pauses up Center.)* What is it, Harlow?

HARLOW. My insurance policy covering the store and merchandise. I've allowed it to lapse!

JULIA *(Concerned; taking a quick step to the left end of the sofa.)* How did that happen?

HARLOW *(Indicating the bill.)* According to this notification it *should* have been renewed the day-before-yesterday. And here *I* thought I had until the middle of next week! *(Bunny sits beside the table up Center, lifts the receiver and quickly dials a number.)*

JULIA. Doesn't Mr. Carpenter *automatically* renew?

HARLOW *(Interrupting.)* Ordinarily, yes. But I instructed him to wait this time — until I had a chance to decide how much more I wanted to add to it — to cover the new toy department, you see. *(Bunny talks into the telephone in pantomime, giving her report about how many people on her list have indicated that they would cooperate in the fund-raising drive.)*

JULIA. Perhaps you'd better call him and —

HARLOW *(Interrupting.)* I will — just as soon as Bunny gets through with the phone. What's the date? *(Replacing the paper in the envelope.)*

JULIA. September 30th. *(Rising.)* Tomorrow's our anniversary, in case you'd forgotten. *(Starting down Left again.)*

HARLOW. Of course I haven't forgotten. *(Rising.)* I'm going to take you and Bunny out to dinner and a show.

BUNNY *(Quickly.)* Really, Daddy?

JULIA *(Pausing down Left.)* Oh, how nice!

HARLOW *(To Bunny; moving up Left Center.)* To celebrate your mother's and my twenty-fifth wedding anniversary.

JULIA *(Smiling at him, with deep affection.)* And twenty-five wonderful, happy years they've been, too.

HARLOW *(Making light of it, but feeling greatly com-*

plimented just the same.) Why, thank you, Mrs. Johnson. I didn't know you cared. *(They laugh.)*

BUNNY *(Into the phone.)* I'm sorry, George. Tomorrow's Mother's and Daddy's wedding anniversary. We're all going out to dinner and a show. *(To Harlow, cradling the phone.)* He wanted to take me out.

JULIA *(Surprised.)* He did?

HARLOW *(To Bunny.)* Why did you turn him down?

BUNNY *(Rising and going closer to him; taking his coat lapels in her hands, playfully.)* Because I'll have more fun with you two. It'll be fun listening to you talk about all the things that've happened to you during all those years. And it wouldn't seem right not to have at least *one* of your kids along to remind you of all the trouble and expense we've been —

HARLOW. Say! Where do you get that stuff? Why, you and your sister are two of the biggest reasons *why* the years have been so happy and wonderful to us. *(Gives her a light kiss on the cheek.)*

JULIA *(Laughingly.)* My goodness! He's full of compliments this evening, isn't he? We'd better feed him as quickly as possible so he'll stay in the same mood. Will you set the table, darling?

BUNNY. Okay. *(Hurrying down Left, via the back of the sofa.)* Tell him about the beautiful sweater I got from Gladys today. *(Exits down Left.)*

HARLOW *(To Julia; crossing down Left Center.)* Another present?

JULIA *(Nodding a smiling affirmative.)* A cardigan — with a note saying how much she misses her "little sis."

HARLOW *(Picking up the newspaper off the coffee table.)* I don't see how she can spare the money. Her budget isn't big enough to allow for presents every few — *(Crosses toward the armchair while taking off the elastic band that holds the paper folded together.)*

JULIA *(Interrupting; moving in front of the sofa.)* It would be just like her to go without lunches for a while to make it up. Oh, Harlow, isn't it wonderful that they're so close? *(Looking off Left where Bunny has gone.)*

HARLOW. That's due to the way you've raised them, my dear. I'd better send her an extra check the first of the week. *(Sits in the armchair, looking at the headlines.)*

JULIA *(Moving Center.)* I wish we could have Gladys with us tomorrow.

HARLOW. I wonder if she'll remember?

JULIA. Why, of course. She always does. She gave me an orchid last year — and knitted you a pair of argyle socks.

HARLOW *(Grinning and looking at her over the top of the paper.)* Which were almost two sizes too large for me.

JULIA. But we couldn't persuade you to give them to someone else.

HARLOW *(Chuckling; turning the page of the paper.)* No. There're still upstairs in my dresser drawer.

JULIA. She'll probably send us a telegram. *(Going closer to him; soberly.)* We ought to be very grateful, Harlow.

HARLOW. For the girls?

JULIA *(Simply.)* For — everything. We've been greatly blessed.

HARLOW *(Lowering the paper; nodding a slow, thoughtful affirmative.)* Yes. God's been very good to us.

JULIA. And even though business hasn't been as good as it used to be.

HARLOW *(Interrupting; optimistically.)* Business has been bad all over, Julia.

JULIA. And we've managed to keep our heads above water — *(Crosses toward the sofa.)* — so I guess we shouldn't complain.

HARLOW. That's right. We're getting along okay. Of course, we can't *save* very much now that Gladys is in college and Bunny's at an age where she needs so many things. However, the Christmas trade ought to put us on top again for a while. *(Leaning forward.)* Look, Julia —you're not worried, are you?

JULIA *(Quickly.)* No — I'm not worried. God's always taken care of us and I know He always will. *(Sitting on the left end of the sofa.)* I don't usually think much about money, you know — I leave all that up to you. However, it'll soon be time to renew our pledge at the church — next Sunday they start the Every Member Canvass, and — well — since it took nearly all our savings to pay for the alterations and redecorating at the store — *(Shrugs; hesitating.)*

HARLOW. Are you suggesting that perhaps we ought to reduce our pledge this year?

JULIA. Well, I certainly wouldn't feel *right* in doing so —

HARLOW *(Stuffing the newspaper down into the chair and rising.)* Neither would I. We've had little business depressions before — two of which I remember were quite serious. *(Crossing toward the sofa.)* And yet we've always managed to go on giving our ten per cent to the church. It's little enough for all God's done for us, Julia. If we have to cut down, we'll do it somewhere else. *(Smiling again; abruptly changing the subject.)* Now I'd better call Mr. Carpenter and instruct him to take care of that renewal. He ought to be home from the office by now. *(Going up Center to the telephone.)*

JULIA *(Rising and crossing down Left.)* Are you going to be on the committee this year?

HARLOW. What did you say? *(Picking up the telephone and dialing a number.)*

JULIA *(Pausing down Left.)* The Every Member Canvass Committee?

HARLOW. I don't know. I haven't been asked. *(Sits beside the table, waiting for his connection to be made. At the same time, a doorbell rings off Right.)*

BUNNY *(Calling, from off Left.)* Want me to get it, Mother?

JULIA *(Calling off.)* No, dear. I'll go. *(Walking rapidly to the right.)* Have you heard what the Pilgrim Fellowship plans to do?

HARLOW. Yes. *(Then to himself as Julia exits at Right.)* Nobody answers. I guess they aren't home. *(Cradles the phone.)*

JULIA *(Off Right; in pleased surprise.)* Why, Reverend Thorne!

REV. THORNE *(Off Right; jovially.)* Hello, Julia? I hope you're not having dinner? *(Harlow rises, looking in the direction of the voices.)*

JULIA *(Off.)* Oh, no. It isn't quite ready yet. Won't you come in?

THORNE *(Off.)* Well, just for a few minutes. Is Harlow here?

JULIA *(Off.)* Yes —

THORNE *(Off.)* Good. I want to talk to him. *(Harlow moves halfway down Center.)*

JULIA *(Off.)* I think I already know what it's about —

THORNE *(As he enters from the right, with Julia following. He is a distinguished-looking man of forty, dressed in a dark business suit. He is holding his hat as he comes in, nodding a friendly greeting to Harlow while saying:)* Good evening, Harlow.

HARLOW. Oh, hello, Reverend Thorne. *(Meets Thorne halfway down Center and shakes hands with him.)*

JULIA. Let me take your hat. *(Pauses beside Thorne.)*

THORNE. Don't bother. I don't want to hold up your meal —

HARLOW. Why couldn't you stay and join us? I understand Mrs. Thorne's out of town.

THORNE *(Nodding affirmatively.)* Visiting her mother over in Centerville for a few days.

JULIA. Then you simply must stay. *(Takes his hat and crosses down Left Center to put it on the coffee table.)*

THORNE. I'd surely like to, but, you see, I've already accepted an invitation from John Vardon. I'm on my way to his house right now. He's going to be chairman of the Every Member Canvass Committee this year.

HARLOW. That's fine. John will do a very good job.

JULIA *(To Thorne; indicating the armchair.)* Well, at least you can sit down for a few minutes?

THORNE. Thank you. *(Going to sit in the armchair.)* I've been *trying* to get you on the telephone for the past two hours, but the line's been busy —

JULIA *(With a light laugh; sitting on the sofa.)* Yes. Bunny's been calling for the Pilgrim Fellowship.

THORNE *(Chuckling.)* The Youth Group are certainly enthusiastic once they get going on a project, aren't they? And, the best part of it is, they always carry things through.

HARLOW *(Sitting on the sofa beside Julia.)* Which is principally due to your inspired leadership, I'd say.

THORNE. Now don't say that. All I do is supervise. I like to keep in close touch with their activities. The kids are so vital and come up with so many interesting ideas. However, the real credit goes to Johnny Warren, our Youth Director. Now there's a hard worker if I ever saw one. Your Gladys was a hard worker, too. We certainly miss her in Sunday school. How's she getting along in college, by the way?

JULIA. Just fine. She pledged Delta Gamma, you know.

THORNE. Yes. So I heard.

JULIA *(Calling off Left.)* Oh, Bunny, look at the roast, will you, dear? I don't want it to burn.

BUNNY *(Off Left.)* I just did. It's okay.

THORNE *(Nodding toward the entrance down Left.)* She's doing all right, too. The children love her. *(Changing the subject.)* And now I'll get my business over with. *(To Harlow.)* Can you come over to the Verdon's for an hour or so this evening, Harlow? The men want you to serve on the committee again this year, if you will.

HARLOW. Why, sure. I'd be glad to.

THORNE *(Grinning.)* They haven't forgotten how you came in with more pledges than any of the rest *last* year about this time.

HARLOW *(Modestly.)* Oh, that was just because I had a good list.

THORNE *(Crisply.)* We'll use the same procedure; divide the men up into teams with each team covering a specified part of town. It's much less embarrassing when two men call on a family together. That way, each man can give the other his moral support as it were. *(Chuckles.)*

339

JULIA. Harlow's never embarrassed, are you, Harlow?

HARLOW. Why should I be? It's for the good of the church.

THORNE. And *you* firmly believe in what you are *"selling,"* Harlow. *(To Julia, indicating Harlow.) He* knows how to talk to people who claim they can't *afford* to give a little to the furtherance of God's work, and yet spend all kinds of money on clothes and entertainment and so forth. *(Leaning back in the chair.)* Faith is contagious. In the vernacular of the times, it "rubs off" on people; people who may be wavering and need someone like *you* folks, who have found the peace and joy of Christian living, to show them where they're wrong.

HARLOW *(Self-consciously.)* It — it's nice of you to say that, Reverend Thorne.

THORNE. Well, it's true, Harlow. I wonder if you people know what an inspiration the family life of the Harlow Johnsons has been to others around town? *(Rising; jokingly.)* Now don't let that go to your heads!

HARLOW *(Laughingly; he and Julia rise.)* It won't —

JULIA *(Shrugging.)* We've just tried our best to live according to the teachings of Jesus. Almost everybody we know is doing the same thing. *(Linking her hand in Harlow's arm.)* Harlow and I think it's the only *happy* way of life.

THORNE *(Musingly.)* "The — happy way of life." *(Smiling again.)* That's a lovely way of putting it, Julia. I'll use it for the title of a sermon one of these days if you've no objections?

JULIA. Oh, my goodness. I'd love to have you, Reverend —

THORNE *(Interrupting.)* I wish you'd call me "Jim." Lots of the other people in the congregation do, you know. *(Looking at his watch.)* I'll have to go now. Tell Bunny I said "hello." *(Crossing toward the right entrance.)*

HARLOW *(Following him.)* Be glad to —

JULIA *(Quickly getting his hat off the coffee table.)* Oh! — your hat!

THORNE *(Pausing at Right.)* That's right. I would have forgotten it. *(To Harlow, as Julia hurries toward him with the hat.)* I was raised in Southern California — men hardly ever wear hats out there except when the weather's bad. Consequently, I'm always leaving it some place and then forgetting where. Half the congregation have had to bring it back to me at one time or another! *(Taking the hat; Harlow and Julia chuckle.)* Thank you, Julia.

HARLOW. You say the meeting's at seven-thirty?

THORNE *(As he exits at Right.)* That's right.

HARLOW *(He and Julia exit at Right.)* I'll be there.

JULIA *(Raising her voice a bit.)* We've enjoyed your little visit, Reverend —

THORNE *(Off Right. All talk loud enough to be heard by the audience.)* Jim —

JULIA *(Off.)* Well — if you insist — *(Bunny — now with a dainty kitchen apron tied around her waist — enters quickly down Left and hurries up Center to get her list of names off the table.)*

THORNE *(Off.)* Good-bye now.

HARLOW *(Off.)* Come again.

THORNE *(Off.)* Thanks, I will — many times, I hope.

JULIA *(Off.)* Good-bye. *(We hear the front door closing. During this, Bunny takes her list down Left Center, checking over the names with her stub of a pencil.)*

HARLOW *(Off.)* Fine fellow, isn't he?

JULIA *(Starts this line off Right and enters during it, with Harlow behind her.)* Yes. *His* faith is certainly contagious —

HARLOW. I'll say —

JULIA *(Crossing toward Bunny, who is now sitting on the arm of the sofa.)* Did you know Reverend Thorne was here, Bunny?

BUNNY. Yes —

HARLOW *(Going to the armchair to pick up the newspaper again.)* Then why didn't you come in?

BUNNY. I thought you'd call me if you wanted me.

(Dropping the list and pencil onto the coffee table.)
Everything's ready to be taken up, Mother.

JULIA. Then suppose we do it. *(Crossing down Left.)*
Your poor father must be just about starved. *(Pauses as the telephone rings.)* Now who do you suppose that is?

BUNNY. I don't know, but I'll soon find out. *(Hurries up Center to answer the phone, which rings again before she can get there.)*

HARLOW *(To Julia.)* Might be Gladys. *(Crosses toward the sofa.)*

JULIA. Oh, no. She won't call until Sunday evening — when she'll be sure we'll be at home.

BUNNY *(Into the phone.)* Hello?

JULIA *(To Harlow.)* By the way, did you get Mr. Carpenter?

HARLOW *(Sitting on the sofa with his newspaper.)* No. They didn't answer. Maybe they're eating out tonight.

BUNNY *(Into the phone.)* Talk louder, will you? I didn't understand what you said.

JULIA *(To Harlow.)* Well, you can try again after dinner. I honestly don't think you ought to let it go until — *(Breaks off, glancing quickly toward Bunny, who becomes increasing excited as a result of what she hears over the telephone.)*

BUNNY *(Into the phone; speaking on the cue, "ought to let it go until —")* Yes, he's here. What's the matter? You're all excited. Is anything wrong?

JULIA. It's for you, Harlow. *(He drops the paper, rises quickly and hurries up Center.)*

BUNNY *(In the phone.)* What's all that noise? It sounds like fire engines!

JULIA. Fire engines?

HARLOW. Who is it, Bunny?

BUNNY *(Gaspingly; into the phone.)* Oh, *no!*

JULIA *(Taking a few, quick steps up Left Center.)*
Bunny —

BUNNY *(To Harlow; talking rapidly and breathlessly.)*
It's one of the men at the gas station across the street

from the store, Daddy. He says there's a *fire in the store!*

JULIA (*Gaspingly.*) The *store!*

HARLOW (*Explosively; together with Julia.*) What?

BUNNY (*With a rush of words.*) It must've started at the back — nobody noticed it until they saw the reflection of the flames through the windows. Then the man called the fire department and —

HARLOW (*Interrupting; violently agitated; rushing toward the entrance over Right.*) Tell him I'll be right there! (*Exits.*)

BUNNY. Oh, isn't it terrible, Mother? How on earth do you suppose —

JULIA (*Interrupting and running to Right.*) Take the things off the stove. I'm going with your father. I'll call you back as soon as I can! (*Calling loudly as she exits at Right.*) Wait, Harlow. I want to go, too! (*The front door slams shut off Right.*)

BUNNY (*Into the phone.*) My father's on his way. (*Cradles the phone, looking dazed and horrified.*)

CURTAIN

NOTE: *The curtain only remains down long enough for the people backstage to remove the newspaper, Harlow's hat, Bunny's list and pencil, and the flowers. Then, the curtains part or rise again for —*

SCENE TWO

TIME: *Two days later. Late afternoon.*

LIGHTING: *The stage lights are brighter than they were at the finish of Scene One. The table and floor lamps are turned off.*

AT THE RISE OF THE CURTAIN: *A worried-looking Julia sits at the table up Center, talking into the telephone. If she can arrange her costumes so that she can change quickly enough between scenes, then she will now be wearing another fall house dress. She is talking at the rise of the curtain.*

JULIA *(In the phone.)* Yes, it happened two nights ago, Gladys. We haven't let you know before because — well, because we didn't think it was wise. What did you say, dear? *(Slight pause; she sighs.)* Yes, it's pretty bad — the store was gutted — most of the stock's a total loss. Isn't that terrible? And the worst part of it is, we can't collect any insurance. No, none at all. The policy lapsed a few days ago — your father was going to renew it last Thursday, but didn't have a chance to before the fire. Mr. Carpenter's been very nice, but there's nothing *he* can do about it, of course.

BUNNY *(Entering from the right, wearing a sweater and skirt.)* I'm home.

JULIA. Good. Gladys is on the phone. She just got our letter. Would you like to say a few words to her, dear?

BUNNY. Oh, sure. *(Hurries up Center to take the phone.)*

JULIA *(In a loud, half-whisper, as she rises; handing Bunny the phone.)* Don't talk too long. I don't want it to go over three minutes if we can help it. *(Moves slowly halfway down Left Center, suppressing a little sniff; absently brushing a tear away from her eyes.)*

BUNNY *(Into the phone.)* Hi, sis. I knew you'd call. Isn't it awful about the fire? You ought to see the store. It's a perfect mess. Daddy says he doesn't think we can salvage enough stuff to even have a fire sale. Huh? What's that?

JULIA *(Standing behind the sofa.)* I want to speak to her again as soon as you're through, Bunny.

BUNNY *(Into the phone.)* Oh, sure — there's still quite a bit of merchandise in the warehouse — Christmas stuff, you know. Mr. Vickers — you know him, Gladys — you had his little girl in your Sunday School class —

JULIA *(Interrupting; crossing up Center beside her.)* Make it brief, darling. *(Glances at her watch.)*

BUNNY *(Into the phone.)* Well, *he* says we're welcome

to use that empty store building of *his* on Main Street —
rent free — temporarily. And since it's already equipped
with counters and *shelves* —

JULIA *(Cutting in.)* Hurry, Bunny. Hurry.

BUNNY *(Into the phone; after a quick look at Julia.)*
Mother wants to talk to you again. Too bad Daddy isn't
here. *He's out trying to get a loan* —

JULIA *(Quickly.)* Bunny! I didn't want *her* to know!

Bunny. Oh, golly. I'm sorry. *(Into the phone.)* Here's
Mother again. 'Bye, sis. You can help when you come
home for your Christmas vacation — save the wages of
a clerk, like Mother and I are going to do. *(Hands the
receiver to Julia and steps aside to the left.)*

JULIA *(Into the phone.)* Hello, darling. We'll have to
stop talking now. Thank you for calling; it's been wonderful hearing your voice; makes me feel better somehow.
(Very slight pause.) Oh, no. We'll manage — we always
have. There's a good reason for everything that happens
to us in life, so all we've got to do is put ourselves in
God's hands and — wait. Good-bye, sweetheart. Remember we love you. And say a little prayer for us, won't you,
dear? *(Slowly cradles the phone while saying to Bunny:)*
She wants to come home.

BUNNY. Give up college, you mean?

JULIA *(Nodding a slow, sober affirmative.)* That's
right.

BUNNY. Well, it will be kind of hard to keep her there
without any money coming in.

JULIA *(Rising.)* We'll have money. We're going to
mortgage the house. Now I'd better start thinking about
what we're going to have for dinner tonight. *(Crossing
down Left.)*

BUNNY *(Moving down Center, on a line with Julia.)*
But what about the store? So much of the stock's on con-
signment. *That'll* all have to be paid for.

JULIA *(Pausing down Left.)* Of course.

BUNNY *(With an expressive gesture.)* And it'll cost
several thousand to have the place cleaned out and fixed
up before it's fit to do business in again.

JULIA. That's perfectly true.

BUNNY *(Crossing in front of the sofa.)* Do you think we can do all that, pay our bills here and keep on sending Sis money every month from what we can get on the *house?*

JULIA *(Quietly.)* No, dear. The house is old — we probably won't be able to raise more than a couple of thousand on it.

BUNNY *(Beginning to look frantic.)* Then what're we going to do, Mother? Daddy's only got a couple of hundred left in the bank; he told me so. *(Sitting on the edge of the sofa.)*

JULIA *(Taking a step or two closer to the left end of the sofa.)* You might as well know that it'll take us several years to get on our feet again, Bunny. However, you mustn't worry or be down-hearted. You heard what I just said to your sister over the telephone? Well, I believe that and so must you. People will help — I know they will. Look what Mr. Vickers has done. Already we have a place where we can sell the Christmas stock that was in the warehouse. That'll help. We'll at least be staying in business on a modest scale.

BUNNY *(Disgustedly.)* Yeah, a very modest scale!

JULIA *(Sitting beside her; putting her hand on the girl's shoulder.)* Maybe we'll even be able to *keep* Mr. Vickers' place until the store is renovated, restocked and we're ready to open it up again. You see, dear, all we really need is a substantial *loan* — on top of the mortgage, of course. Your father is sure he can get it from Mr. Baker at the bank. He's on the Board of Administration at the church, you know — a very kind and understanding man. He's loaned us money in the past and it's always been paid back promptly.

BUNNY *(Dejectedly.)* But it's never been as much as we'll need *now.*

JULIA *(Sighing a little.)* No. And *this* time it will have to cover a period of several years — *(As Harlow enters at Right.)* Harlow! *(Rises quickly.)*

HARLOW *(Looking dejected and weary unto death.)*

Hello, folks. (*Takes off his hat and goes to sit in the arm-chair. Now wearing another business suit.*)

BUNNY (*Rising.*) Daddy! You look terrible.

HARLOW (*Forcing a small grin; Julia moves around behind the sofa to Center.*) Do I, honey? Well, it's no wonder — I'm terribly tired. I've been a lot of places today. (*Sighs again and leans his head against the back of the chair, closing his eyes for a minute.*)

BUNNY (*Going to take his hat and put it on the coffee table.*) You'll feel better after a good, hot dinner.

JULIA. Goodness! I haven't even decided what we'll have.

HARLOW (*Without opening his eyes.*) Doesn't matter. I'm not hungry anyway.

JULIA (*Moving closer to him; hesitantly.*) Did you — did you talk to Henry Baker at the bank?

HARLOW. Yes. We had a nice, long talk.

JULIA. And — and what did he say?

BUNNY (*Quickly; sitting on the right arm of the sofa.*) Did he give you the loan, Daddy?

HARLOW (*Lowly; raising his head; staring at Julia.*) No.

JULIA (*With a slight gasp.*) Harlow!

BUNNY. Why not?

HARLOW (*Still, to Julia.*) He said he'd be happy to take a mortgage on the house for twenty-five hundred, but said that that was all he could do.

JULIA (*Looking slightly dazed.*) I — I can't believe it!

BUNNY. How much do you actually need, Daddy?

HARLOW. In even numbers, about ten thousand —

BUNNY (*Looking frantic again.*) Oh, golly!

HARLOW (*Rising; too restless and nervous to be able to sit still for very long.*) Oh, I can't blame him. That's a lot of money to put out without good collateral, and all I have *now* to give him is my — word. (*Crosses up Right.*)

BUNNY. Isn't that enough?

JULIA (*To Harlow.*) It should be — when he knows that the money will put us in business again.

BUNNY (*Rising and moving to Center beside her mother. Harlow crosses back down Right.*) And we'll do a rushing business as soon as we can open up again. Everybody in the church'll buy from you, Daddy — and they'll even bring all their relatives and friends.

HARLOW (*Pausing down Right.*) So they all tell *me*. And that's what I told Henry Baker. But he just doesn't think he can afford to take the risk. (*Crossing to Julia at Right Center.*) Frankly, I don't know where to go next.

JULIA. Aren't there any *individuals* in town wealthy enough to — ?

HARLOW (*Interrupting.*) Give me a private loan? No, dear. All the people I know with money are cold, practical business men, who feel the same way about that as Henry Baker does. (*The telephone rings.*)

BUNNY. I'll get it. (*Hurries up Center to answer the phone.*)

JULIA (*Placing a comforting hand on his arm.*) Oh, well, *some* door will be opened to us. We must pray without ceasing and not allow ourselves to be depressed. Remember what you said the very day of the fire, Harlow — when we were talking about the way business had dropped off lately?

HARLOW. No. I've forgotten. (*Moves in front of her, going toward the sofa.*)

JULIA (*Quietly.*) You said, "We've had business depressions before" — and we've always managed to come out on top. So I see no reason why we can't surmount *this* difficulty — once we've been shown the way.

BUNNY (*Who has been conversing on the telephone in pantomime. Now turning to Harlow.*) It's for you, Daddy.

HARLOW. Okay. (*Crossing up Center.*)

BUNNY (*Into the phone.*) He's coming. (*To Harlow, handing him the telephone.*) Gladys called a few minutes before you came in.

HARLOW. Poor child. I wish we could have spared her the shock — (*Into the phone. Bunny moves down Left*

Center behind the sofa.) Hello? Oh, hello, Reverend —
I mean, Jim.

JULIA *(Crossing down Left.)* Like to help me figure
out what we're going to eat, Bunny?

BUNNY. Oh, sure — *(Follows Julia down Left.)*

HARLOW *(Into the phone.)* The committee? *(Hesitantly.)* Well — er — I don't know. You must realize
that I certainly don't *feel* much like it just now.

BUNNY *(Standing beside her mother down Left. In a
loud, half-whisper.)* What does he want you to do,
Daddy?

HARLOW *(Into the phone.)* Just a minute, please. *(To
Bunny and Julia; in a lowered tone of voice; placing his
hand over the transmitter.)* It's about the Every Member
Canvass —

JULIA *(Taking a quick step closer to the sofa.)* Oh,
that's right. They're going out next Sunday, aren't they?

HARLOW *(Nodding "yes.")* Directly after church.
(Into the phone again.) Couldn't you get somebody to
take my place.

JULIA *(Quickly moving halfway up Left Center.)* No,
Harlow! It's too late for you to back out now.

HARLOW *(Into the phone.)* I'm sorry — Julia's saying
something. *(To Julia; in the same, loud, half-whisper;
again covering the receiver.)* But, darling, I should be
trying to figure out ways and means of trying to raise —

JULIA *(Interrupting; going closer to him; speaking
rapidly and confidentially.)* Not on Sunday, Harlow.
Don't you see — they're depending on you — it's your
job — you gave them your *word.*

BUNNY. And it'll do you good, Daddy. Take your
mind off your troubles for a while.

HARLOW *(Lowly; thoughtfully.)* Yes, I — I guess
you're right. *(Bunny exits down Left as Harlow speaks
into the phone again.)* Well, okay. I'll be there. We'll
all be in church as usual. Thanks for reminding me — er
— Jim. *(To Julia, as he cradles the phone.)* My heart
won't be in it this time, I'm afraid.

JULIA *(Smiling.)* Oh, yes, it will — once you get

started. You'll forget yourself, like you always do, and just think about how many new pledges you can get for the church. *(Starts down Left again.)*

HARLOW *(Moving halfway down Center.)* But what are *we* going to do? The committee members always hand in their *own* pledges before they start calling, you know

JULIA *(Pausing down Left; thoughtfully.)* Oh, yes. I hadn't thought of that.

HARLOW. And I just *can't* do any tithing *this* year.

JULIA. But we ought to be able to give *something* — even a *little* —

HARLOW *(Going closer to the right end of the sofa.)* How? Why, *we'll* be fortunate if we're able to keep body and soul together — for the next six months at least. And I don't like to make any promises that I may not be able to keep.

JULIA. And yet we should make *some* sort of pledge.

HARLOW. When we haven't the faintest idea where it would be coming from? No, Julia. That just wouldn't be good sense. *(Goes toward the armchair.)*

JULIA *(Looking at him in some surprise.)* It seems rather strange to hear you talk like that.

HARLOW. We've got to think of ourselves, Julia. I've always laughed at the saying before, but it's true — charity *does* begin at home. None of our friends will *expect* us to do anything considering the terrible loss we've just suffered. I'm sure God wouldn't either. *(Taking a notebook and pencil out of his pocket.)* And now I'm going to do some figuring while you get us something to eat. *(Sitting in the armchair.)* Thanks to Mr. Vickers we can get rid of some of the Christmas stock at least. That'll keep us busy for a while. *(He starts to do some figuring in the notebook, holding it on his knee. Soft, incidental music fades in as an atmospheric background while Julia looks at him for a slow count of five, then sighs, shakes her head and exits down Left.)*

CURTAIN

NOTE: *In order to preserve the continuity of the story, the offstage music should continue through the short intermission. This is only long enough for the furniture and properties to be removed and a long wooden table, with ten chairs surrounding it, substituted. On the table are several little piles of pamphlets, held together by elastic bands, a number of pencils, and a map of the "city." As soon as all is in readiness, the music fades away and the curtains open or rise, for —*

SCENE THREE

TIME: *The following Sunday. About 1:30 P.M.*

SCENE: *A Board Room at the church, which is merely indicated by the long table and the ten chairs. There is a chair at either end and four on each side. Reverend Thorne sits at the head of the table or at the right end of it. Henry Baker, the bank president, sits at the opposite end. Henry is a rather pompous-looking individual with a florid countenance, white hair and moustache. He wears a neat, conservative business suit and rimless glasses. John Vardon, the chairman, sits behind the right end of the table, close to Thorne's left elbow. He is a pleasant-faced man of forty. Harlow faces the audience at the left end of the table close to Henry Baker's right elbow. The other chairs are occupied by men and women on the committee.*

LIGHTING: *The stage lights are up to their full strength. No electrical fixtures are in evidence.*

AT THE RISE OF THE CURTAIN: *Reverend Thorne is reading aloud from a mimeographed letter. During this, Harlow rises and quietly moves around the table, distributing little packets of pledge cards held together by elastic bands. He gives a small packet to each member of the committee, then sits down again.*

THORNE (*Starts speaking this line just before the curtains open.*) During the past week, every church family has received a copy of this letter. However, there are a couple of paragraphs which I consider pertinent and which

— with your indulgence — I should like to read to you
again before you all start out on your sacred mission.
Afterwards, I'll turn the meeting over to Mr. Vardon,
(Nodding toward him.) your chairman, again. *(Clears
his throat, preparing to read.)*

BAKER *(To Harlow confidentially, as Harlow is about
to sit down.)* I'm sorry I had to turn you down on that
matter the other day, Harlow.

HARLOW *(Nervously, resuming his seat.)* Oh, th-that's
all right, Henry.

BAKER. I couldn't sleep all that night for thinking
about it.

HARLOW. Don't worry about it, Henry.

BAKER *(While the others are looking at their pledge
cards, etc.)* But I do worry. If only you had some good
collateral.

THORNE *(Without knowing he is interrupting Baker.)*
I call your attention to the final paragraph — *(Reading.)*
"Because the work of our church represents the individual work of *all* its members, it is believed that all of
you will wish to take an active *part* in our Loyalty Sunday ceremony and the Every Member Canvass — "

VARDON: Excuse me for interrupting, Reverend, but in
view of that letter, it was interesting to see how many
people filled out their cards at *church* today.

THORNE. Yes. I was extremely gratified by the response. *(Reading again.)* "With sufficient canvassers and
a large attendance for Loyalty Sunday, the number of
calls which must be made to cover the entire congregation
should be rather small. *(Looking around the table.)* That
means that you ought to be all finished well before six
o'clock.

1ST LADY *(To the person sitting next to her.)* I do
hope we find everybody at home.

BAKER. It's such a nice day. *I'd* probably be taking my
family out for a drive if I hadn't volunteered to do this.
*(Looks at Harlow, who isn't looking at him. Then
glances quickly away again as Harlow raises his eyes.)*

THORNE *(Indicating the letter.)* In this letter, we endeavored to impress everyone with the need for extra sacrifice this year. We mentioned the $25,000.00 budget recommended by the finance committee; the necessity of an expanded Youth and Sunday School program; and, of course, the building fund we are trying to accumulate for the chapel we hope to erect some day. In short, every member has been made to realize just where all the money goes, and why. I sincerely trust that the people will respond with courage and generosity. And now I'll turn the meeting back to your chairman. *(Smiles at Vardon and leans back, replacing the letter in his pocket.)*

VARDON *(Looking around the table.)* I guess there isn't much more to say. You've had your instructions; you know what areas you are to cover; you've been given the packets of pledge cards, and your teammates are all waiting upstairs in the Social Hall for you to join them. The ladies are serving coffee and sandwiches. There'll be plenty left for us when we're all through here. However, I hope you won't *dawdle* over your lunch — *(Waits for the others to laugh a little, then goes on.)* — because we want to start on our rounds as soon as possible. We'll meet here in the Board Room again this evening, at six o'clock. If you haven't completed your calls by that time — or fail to find some people at home and wish to contact them later — you may do so at your convenience during the week. However, I'd like to impress on you all that the signed cards must be returned to the church office not later than Friday. Is that understood?

ALL *(Except Harlow and Rev. Thorne.)* "Yes," "Of course," "Sure. I understand." *(Et cetera.)*

VARDON *(Rising.)* According to tradition, we, the members of the committee, are required to have our *own* pledges made out before the canvass begins. How many here have done so? Will you please raise your right hands? *(All except Harlow do this. He merely sits quietly, arms resting on the table, staring down toward the little pack of cards before him. The others notice this, but quickly look away, pretending not to. Vardon continues.)* Good. Will you kindly pass them along to *me?* *(They all do so, except Harlow, from one to the other until the single cards reach Vardon's hands. During this, he is saying:)* Thank you. Thank you. That's fine. *(After he has all the cards, he snaps an elastic band around them and turns to Thorne, saying:)* And now, Reverend Thorne, if you'd like to offer up a little prayer for the success of our enterprise — ?

THORNE. Be glad to, John. *(Rising; the others follow suit, and stand behind their chairs with bowed heads during the prayer.)* Dear God, we ask thee to bless these consecrated men and women who are about to go forth in thy service. Make their efforts fruitful. Accept their sacrifice of time and money as a token of their love and gratitude for the joys of home, family, friends and church which Thou hast so bountifully bestowed upon them. It has been truly said, that to live by the teachings of Jesus is — *(Looking directly at Harlow; with significant emphasis)* — "the *happy* way of life." *(Harlow looks up quickly; remembering that it was his wife who said this to the pastor a few days previous. Thorne bows his head again and Harlow does likewise, now with a thoughtful expression on his face, as Thorne continues.)* Let us remember this and always be happy in the knowledge of thy great love. May we remain steadfast in Thy service; may our faith grow like the mustard seed, which, when it is grown," is the greatest among herbs, and becometh a tree, so that the birds of the air can lodge in the branches thereof." These things we ask in the name of Our Lord, Jesus Christ, who gave himself on the Cross for our sins. Amen. *(Looks up, smiling brightly. At once the people collect their packets of pledge cards, pencils, etc. Baker takes a notebook out of his pocket and makes a notation therein with his pen.)*

VARDON *(Glancing around the table.)* And now let's go upstairs and eat our lunch. Try to leave the grounds within a half hour if possible. Are there any questions?

ALL *(Except Thorne, Harlow and Baker.)* "No," "I understand everything all right," "You've made everything very clear," "All *I* want to do is get started." *(Et cetera.)*

VARDON. Very well then — the meeting is adjourned. *(He and Thorne walk up Right, conversing together in pantomime. The others ad lib appropriate comments to each other as they exit to the right. Baker puts his pen down on the table, thrusts the notebook into his pocket, looks at Harlow and follows the others out. Harlow slowly picks up his packet of cards, frowning thoughtfully. Finally, Vardon takes his leave of Thorne and exits after Baker. Harlow waits until Thorne starts walking toward the entrance down Right, then takes a few, quick steps to the center, behind the table.)*

HARLOW *(Hesitantly.)* Rev. Thorne — *(Pauses, self-consciously.)*

THORNE *(Pausing down Right.)* It's "Jim" on Sunday, too, Harlow.

HARLOW. Could I — speak to you a minute?

THORNE. Why, of course — *(Walks closer to Harlow up Center.)* What's on your mind?

HARLOW *(Finding it difficult to say.)* Well, you see, it's about the pledging. Julia and I have been tithing for years.

THORNE. Yes, I know.

HARLOW. And, on top of our ten per cent, we've always tried to give extra amounts at Thanksgiving, Easter and Christmas. *(Hesitates again, looking extremely embarrassed.)*

THORNE *(Quietly.)* You've been very generous, Harlow.

HARLOW. *(After clearing his throat a little.)* Julia and I were talking things over the other day and I told her that — in view of our present circumstances — it just wouldn't be good sense for us to pledge anything *this* year, when we haven't the faintest idea where the money would be coming from.

THORNE *(Smiling again; placing a reassuring hand on his shoulder.)* Nobody *expects* you to, Harlow.

HARLOW *(During this, Baker enters down Right and comes to a sudden stop as he hears what Harlow is say-*

ing. Neither Harlow nor Thorne realize he is in the room.) However, I've been doing a lot of thinking since then, and — well, it seems to me that *my* faith would be even *smaller* than a mustard seed if I didn't at least make an effort to go on contributing what I can to the Lord's work. So I thought I'd like you to know that I'm going to fill out my card the way I always have, and trust God to make it possible for us to come through.

THORNE. You'll "come through" all right, Harlow. This is a mighty fine demonstration of faith. *(Harlow tenses as he looks past Thorne and sees Baker standing down Right. Thorne turns to see what causes this reaction.)*

BAKER. Er — I'm sorry. I left my pen behind. *(Crosses to the left end of the table, via the front of it, to get his pen.)*

THORNE *(To Harlow.)* Now don't you feel like bolting down a couple of sandwiches and some coffee before starting out? *(Crossing down Right.)* I do. I'm as hungry as a bear after that long-winded sermon of mine this morning. *(Exits down Right as Harlow starts to follow him.)*

BAKER. Oh, Harlow — *(Hesitates.)*

HARLOW *(Pausing down Right; looking as if a burden had suddenly been removed from his shoulders.)* Yes, Henry?

BAKER. I — I couldn't help overhearing what you just said to Rev. Thorne.

HARLOW *(Grinning.)* And I suppose you think I'm all kinds of a fool for taking on another big obligation when — ?

BAKER *(Interrupting, moving to Center, in front of the table.)* No. On the contrary, I think you've taught *me* a little lesson — a lesson in faith. Here you've just suffered a great loss. You and your family will really have to deprive yourselves in order to meet that pledge. But I've never had to deprive myself of anything. I haven't even missed the money *I've* given for the past ten years. Consequently, it's been easy for me to keep faith.

HARLOW (*Moving a few steps closer to him.*) But you have kept it, Henry, and that's all that matters, isn't it?

BAKER. No. One has to live their faith. And apparently I've forgotten the "do unto others" admonition, and that's — bad. Look, Harlow, about the loan you asked me for the other day —

HARLOW (*Interrupting.*) Oh, yes — the loan. I don't think I'm going to need it now, Henry.

BAKER (*Greatly surprised.*) Why? What's happened?

HARLOW (*Simply.*) I'm going to sell the building — as is — for as much as I can get. That will pay off my creditors, I hope. The loan you're going to give me on the house will take care of our living expenses for a while. Meanwhile, we'll be starting all over again — in a smaller way — in the building that Mr. Vickers has so kindly offered for our use. He'll let us have it rent free until after the holidays, and then I'll take a lease. (*Putting his hand on Baker's shoulder.*) So you see we're going to get along all right. It'll be tough sailing for a while, but with the help of God — and all our friends — I know the Johnsons will come out on top. (*He takes Baker's arm and they start walking toward the exit down Right. During this, soft, background music fades in.*) Now let's forget about *my* problems and concentrate on the canvass. *I* want to top the record I made last year, if I possibly can. (*He chuckles. Baker does likewise and, as they start to exit down Right* —)

CURTAIN

RADIO JERUSALEM, THE STORY OF JESUS

AS TOLD IN RADIO STYLE

By

CATHERINE MAGEE

PRODUCTION RIGHTS

Copies of this play are available in single pamphlet form. The right to produce this play by one group of amateur players is authorized only by the purchase of five copies (one copy for each speaking part) at the current price of 50c each.

It is dishonest and illegal to copy parts.

RADIO JERUSALEM,
THE STORY OF JESUS

A script for high school groups in the church school.

CAST OF CHARACTERS

MASTER OF CEREMONIES

SPEAKER 1

SPEAKER 2

SPEAKER 3

VERSE CHOIR of from 6 to 20 voices

CHARACTERS can be either boys or girls. Master of Ceremonies and Speakers 1, 2, and 3 should be chosen for contrasting voices, to avoid confusion.

No scenery is needed. Appropriate music such as The Old Rugged Cross; Stand Up, Stand Up for Jesus; Holy, Holy, Holy, can be furnished by a record player or live.

The New Testament references are inserted to insure accuracy and are not to be read.

MUSIC, *fading.*

RADIO ANNOUNCER *(If given at a radio station. If not, let one of the group read this and the concluding part.)* Today the members of the .... class of the church school of .... Church are appearing in a radio drama called *Radio Jerusalem.* Master of Ceremonies for the program is ....

MUSIC, *15 seconds, fading.*

M. C. This is ...., a member of the .... class of the church school of .... Church. We have been studying the life of Jesus, and have tried to imagine ourselves living in Palestine during the time when he was growing into manhood and beginning his ministry. To make the New Testament scenes more vivid, we have invented an imaginary radio station which we shall call *Radio Jerusalem.* Our verse choir will give us a background of familiar quotations from the Revised Standard Version of the New Testament. Return with us now to the year 12 A. D. and listen to *Radio Jerusalem*.

SPEAKER 1. This is *Radio Jerusalem*, in the third month of the 75th year of the Roman occupation of Palestine. The headline story of the day is still the Feast of the Passover, which ended yesterday. The largest crowds in history have attended the celebrations, and are now dispersing to their homes in the various towns of this country.

SPEAKER 2. Attention all Jews! Attention all Jews! King Archelaus, reigning in the name of the Roman Emperor, reminds you of the law in regard to carrying packs for the Roman soldiers. Any Roman soldier can require any Jewish citizen to carry his pack for one mile. Local festivals such as the Feast of the Passover are no excuse for refusing this service to soldiers of Rome.

SPEAKER 3. Here is a special bulletin! A twelve-year-old boy, Jesus by name, is reported missing from the caravan returning to the province of Galilee. The anxious parents, Joseph and Mary of Nazareth, who had supposed him to be with friends in the caravan, are going back to Jerusalem to look for him.

VERSE CHOIR. "After three days they found him in the temple, sitting among the teachers, listening to them and asking them questions. And all who heard him were astonished at his understanding and his answers . . . *(Pause.)* And Jesus increased in wisdom and stature, and in favor with God and man." (Luke 2:46-47, 52)

M. C. Time passed. The boy Jesus became a man, the oldest son in a large family. We assume that Joseph had died by the time Jesus was grown, and that Jesus was in charge of the family carpenter shop. But he was thinking of more than carpentry. Eighteen years after his first Passover Feast in Jerusalem, Palestine was still occupied by the Romans. The promised "Kingdom of God" seemed to be very slow in coming. Let's listen again to our imaginary *Radio Jerusalem*, eighteen years later.

SPEAKER 1. This is *Radio Jerusalem*, in the ninety-third year of the Roman occupation. We have been receiving questions from every part of Palestine about the strange events now taking place on the banks of the River Jordan. Two of our best reporters have reached the scene and will give you an on-the-spot account of what is happening. We take you to the banks of the River Jordan for an eye-witness account.

SPEAKER 2. I am speaking to you from the banks of the River Jordan, a few miles from where it empties into the Dead Sea. There are hundreds of people in this out-of-the-way spot. Some are curiosity seekers, no doubt, but most have been attracted here by the rumor that the man who is preaching is the forerunner of a new era. His name is John, and though he is poorly dressed, he speaks with authority of things to come.

VERSE CHOIR. "The voice of one crying in the wilderness: Prepare the way of the Lord, make his paths straight."
(Luke 3:4)

SPEAKER 3. We find that John has been instructing the people, and baptizing many in the river. He must be very tired. A man from Jericho tells me that he lives on wild honey and locusts. The crowds are falling back now. I can see John and a newcomer speaking together. John appears to be protesting, the stranger insisting. A man beside me has just told me that the newcomer is a carpenter by the name of Jesus, from the province of Galilee. Now John is baptizing Jesus. The crowd is quiet, watching and listening . . . Watching . . . And listening . . .

VERSE CHOIR. . . . "And a voice came from heaven, 'Thou art my beloved Son; with thee I am well pleased'."
(Luke 3:22)

M. C. In the days of his ministry Jesus was misunderstood by those who thought that the strict laws and customs of the Jews were more important than the spirit of love. He taught that the kingdom of God was at hand if only men would open their hearts to it. Some few became his disciples. News flashes from our imaginary *Radio Jerusalem* will give an insight into what was going on.

SPEAKER 1. This is *Radio Jerusalem bringing* you daily news notes from the provinces. First, from Galilee. Four young men have joined forces with one Jesus of Nazareth. They are the brothers Simon and Andrew; and the sons of Zebedee, James and John. Zebedee tells our reporter that James and John left so suddenly that he found himself alone in his fishing boat with only the hired servants to mend his nets.

SPEAKER 2. Here is a news report from the village of Nazareth. Jesus, a resident of Nazareth until a few months ago, returned today with four friends. Asked to assist in the synagogue by reading the day's lesson, he gave the congregation to understand that the Scripture had been fulfilled and that the kingdom of God was at hand. Murmurings against him were heard, and he and his companions left quickly. His four brothers, James, Joseph, Judas, and Simon, could not be reached for comment before we went on the air.

VERSE CHOIR. "And they rose up and put him out of the city, and led him to the brow of the hill on which their city was built, that they might throw him down headlong. But passing through the midst of them he went away."

(Luke 4:29-30)

SPEAKER 3. Here is a last minute bulletin from Galilee: A civil service examination will be held in the near future to fill the vacancy caused by the sudden departure of Levi, son of Alphaeus, who yesterday left the tax office abruptly to become one of the company of that Jesus of Nazareth whose name you have heard on this program in recent weeks. Surprise is expressed by citizens of Galilee with whom your reporter has talked that this man Jesus should associate with a tax collector.

VERSE CHOIR. "And the scribes of the Pharisees, when they saw that he was eating with sinners and tax collectors, said to his disciples, 'Why does he eat and drink with tax collectors and sinners?' And when Jesus heard it, he said to them, 'Those who are well have no need of a physician, but those who are sick; I came not to call the righteous, but sinners'." (Mark 2:16-17)

M. C. Yes, Jesus ignored social barriers, to go where he was most needed. People who were "born on the wrong side of the tracks," as we say today, found that he was their friend, though he also gave attention to the problems of more fortunate men. Many students wiser than we have studied the life and teachings of Jesus, and today we are still looking for the answer to the question, "When will this kingdom of God come?"

SPEAKER 1. To the Jews, under the yoke of Roman occupation, political freedom seemed to be a necessary part of the "kingdom."

SPEAKER 2. But Jesus told the Pharisees that "The kingdom of God is not coming with signs to be observed."
(Luke 17:20)

SPEAKER 3. In this twentieth century, we often identify the "kingdom of God" with world peace between the nations, but Jesus said,

VERSE CHOIR. " . . . behold, the kingdom of God is in the midst of you." (Luke 17:21)

M. C. When we study the parables that Jesus told, we notice that several of them are stories of growth. Our imaginary *Radio Jerusalem* would not have dared to carry these parables, but perhaps a radio station of the Jewish underground might have used them, hopefully:

SPEAKER 1 *(In hushed voice.)* "Hear then the parable of the sower." " . . . A sower went out to sow . . ."
(Matthew 13:18 and 3)

SPEAKER 2 *(In hushed voice.)* "The kingdom of heaven is like a grain of mustard seed which a man took and sowed in his field; it is the smallest of all seeds, but when it has grown it is the greatest of shrubs and becomes a tree . . ."
(Matthew 13:31-32)

SPEAKER 3 *(In hushed voice.)* "The kingdom of heaven is like leaven which a woman took and hid in three measures of meal, till it was all leavened." (Luke 13:21)

VERSE CHOIR. "The kingdom of God is as if a man should scatter seed upon the ground . . . and the seed should sprout and grow, he knows not how." (Mark 4:26-27)

M. C. After Jesus became known for his teaching and healing, it was hard for him to get away from the crowds even long enough to eat and sleep. If our *Radio Jerusalem* had actually been in operation in those times, there would have been many startling broadcasts, like these:

SPEAKER 1. Flash! Thousands of people have followed Jesus of Nazareth to a lonely place near the sea of Galilee. A usually reliable informant tells this reporter that many sick people have been healed and that Jesus talked to the crowds for a long time, and then gave them all barley bread and fish for supper, as much as they could eat.

VERSE CHOIR. "And they all ate and were satisfied." — "And those who ate were about five thousand men, besides women and children." (Matthew 14:20, 21)

SPEAKER 2. Here is a late news bulletin on the story we gave you about Jesus of Nazareth. It seems that the people who were fed so bountifully were greatly impressed by what they called a miracle, and wanted to make Jesus their king. They were even attempting to persuade him by force that he must become ruler of all Israel, but he avoided them and went off into the hills, alone.

SPEAKER 3. This is *Radio Jerusalem,* with a last-minute bulletin from the capital. Special messengers have complained to the chief priests here that unlawful acts are being committed on the Sabbath by Jesus of Nazareth and his followers. Local Pharisees assert that some of these men have picked wheat and eaten it on a Sabbath afternoon; that Jesus himself has recently broken the law by healing a man with a withered hand on the Sabbath. The chief priests are taking these complaints under consideration.

VERSE CHOIR. Jesus said, "It is lawful to do good on the Sabbath . . . And many followed him, and he healed them all." (Matthew 12:12 and 15)

M. C. Yes, Jesus did his work well here on earth. He planted the seed that is still growing in the hearts of men. A long view of history shows us that much has been accomplished:

SPEAKER 1. The brutal sports of two thousand years ago have disappeared.

SPEAKER 2. Slavery was commonplace in the time of Jesus, but now it has almost disappeared from the earth.

SPEAKER 3. The dignity of the individual is acknowledged in our own and many other countries.

VERSE CHOIR. "For whoever would save his life will lose it, and whoever loses his life for my sake will find it."

(Matthew 16:25)

M. C. Yes, the seed of Christianity is growing. We, too, can live in the kingdom if we only believe it is possible. The requirements are simple, and yet very difficult. Jesus speaks to us today as he spoke to his disciples:

VERSE CHOIR. "A new commandment I give to you, that you love one another; even as I have loved you, that you also love one another. By this all men will know that you are my disciples, if you have love for one another."

(John 13:34-35)

MUSIC *15 seconds, fading.*

RADIO ANNOUNCER. You have been listening to a program given by the .... Class of the .... Church, with an original script by Catherine Magee. Those taking part were: ...., ...
MUSIC

(CURTAIN)

THE LOVE OF RUTH

A COMEDY DRAMA IN ONE ACT

By

BEATRICE M. CASEY

PRODUCTION RIGHTS

Copies of this play are available in single pamphlet form. The right to produce this play by one group of amateur players is authorized only by the purchase of eight copies (one copy for each speaking part) at the current price of 50c each.

It is dishonest and illegal to copy parts.

CAST OF CHARACTERS
(For Four Men and Four Women)

LONNY BLAKE .... Marsh Oldfield's secretary

TRACY OLDFIELD .... Marsh's daughter

RUTH OLDFIELD .... Marsh's daughter-in-law

SHEILA OLDFIELD .... Marsh's wife

MARSH OLDFIELD .... a businessman

DENISE VALLEE .... Ruth's friend

PETER STERLING .... Tracy's admirer

BRECK HATHAWAY .... Ruth's suitor

TIME: *A summer afternoon.*

PLACE: *The Oldfields' living-room.*

TIME OF PLAYING: *About twenty-five minutes.*

COSTUMES AND CHARACTERISTICS

Lonny, about 25, is tall and fair; he moves and speaks with a deceptive lightness, always smiling and debonair, but he is earnest when the occasion demands gravity. Tracy is 20, petite and vivacious, with a sleek and sophisticated coiffure which belies her "little girl" face; she affects a blase attitude until she becomes frightened; then, she is just a frightened, clinging vine. Ruth, 25, is a delicate, graceful young woman, with serene strength in her lovely face, with fair hair, and blue eyes that smile. Her voice is low and moving. Sheila is an attractive woman of 46, somewhat pale and wan, obviously unhappy, but warm and friendly. Marsh, 47 or 48, is an impressive, tall man with hair graying at the temples; his manner and speech are brusque until, at the last, he becomes repentant and kindly. Denise, 24, is a tall, dark-haired and dark-eyed girl, poised and straight-forward, somewhat crisp of speech, but showing flashes of humor. Peter, 25, is a big, good-humored young man, with an ingratiating manner; he speaks drawlingly, grins often, and reveals a courteous and protective attitude toward the women in his company. Breck is 27, handsome and distinguished. All the members of the cast are well dressed in summer attire.

PROPERTIES

Lonny brings in a briefcase at first; later, he has a newspaper. Ruth has a large manila envelope with papers in it. Denise has a briefcase. Peter has a notebook.

THE LOVE OF RUTH

SCENE: *The Oldfields' attractive living-room. There is a door in the back wall at Right, and a window in the back wall at Left. Between them is a long, narrow table holding a lamp, flowers, books, and a telephone. There is a door at the right, well down stage; above it against the right wall is a long sofa flanked by end tables bearing lamps, etc. In the left wall, at Center, there are colorful draperies which appear to cover a wide window. Two easy chairs with a table between them are placed at Left. Other furnishings may be added as desired, to create an atmosphere of good taste and cheer.*

AT THE RISE OF THE CURTAIN: *Tracy is discovered at the back table, arranging the flowers, her back to the audience. Lonny enters with his briefcase at Right. He sees Tracy.*

LONNY *(Coming to Right Center, saluting Tracy airily.)* Ha! The beauteous Miss Tracy Oldfield, in person. How're you, Tracy?

TRACY *(Over her shoulder, casually.)* Oh, hello, Lonny. What are you doing here? Why aren't you over at Dad's office, secretary-ing?

LONNY *(Dropping upon the sofa.)* I am an indispensable man. Your father had to go to Hampden this afternoon, but he wanted to see these papers the moment he returned home. So, *(He stretches his legs out lazily.)* here they are.

TRACY *(Coming to Center, grinning.)* Well, he's back. He's storming at Mother about that meeting that Ruth wants Mother to attend at church this afternoon.

LONNY. Where is Ruth?

TRACY *(Tartly, returning to the table at back.)* I really don't know. *My* world doesn't revolve around my precious sister-in-law, as Mother's does.

LONNY *(Leaning forward, quizzical.)* No? Now, who is the great sun in your solar system at this moment?

TRACY *(Sparkling, hands to her breast, dramatically.)* Oh, you don't know him, but he's big—and exciting, and masterful. *(She sighs, swaying as if dancing.)*

LONNY *(Jumping up with his briefcase.)* That reminds me. I'd better look up *my* master, eh?

TRACY *(Going to Right, perching on the lower arm of the sofa.)* Better put on your catcher's mask; he's in a bad mood.

LONNY *(Turning at back, near the door.)* Isn't that the same mood that he's been in ever since your brother, Roger, was drowned? *(He continues earnestly.)* I tell you, Tracy, if I ever had a fine son like Roger, a fellow who died to save one of his Sunday School boys, I would try to be worthy of him. I wouldn't change into an ogre, and scoff at all that is sacred, and make everyone about me unhappy.

TRACY *(Coming to face Lonny, as both come down Center.)* Dad is a man. He can't weep on Ruth's shoulder, as Mother does. He never whimpers.

LONNY *(Raising his eyebrows.)* Scarcely. There are moments when his tone does not remotely resemble a whimper. *(He chuckles, then grows grave.)* Tracy, other men have lost their only son, but they have kept their faith.

TRACY *(Cynically, shrugging.)* Dad had faith; what did it get him?

LONNY. Our faith does not depend upon what we get, young lady. *(He goes to the back door, pausing there.)* Your father has a lovely wife, a daughter—*(He surveys Tracy critically.)* just *fairly* attractive, *(Tracy grimaces at Lonny.)* and his son's young widow—all looking to him for strength, and he screams and kicks and bites, like a four-year-old having a tantrum.

TRACY *(Wagging a finger, dropping into a chair at Left.)* Look out, Mr. Secretary! If I tell your boss, you'll get the two weeks' notice.

LONNY *(Grinning.)* Then you don't know that I have wanted to leave him for a year? Your mother and Ruth thought that I might help by staying.

TRACY *(Mischievously.)* Of course, you don't stay so that you can see Denise Vallee more often; she is Ruth's shadow.

LONNY *(Striding with arms out to Tracy, in mock delight.)* Why, Tracy Oldfield, I do believe that you're jealous. I believe that you love me madly.

TRACY *(Pushing Lonny away, half laughing.)* Lonny Blake, you're a nut. I like my men dark and handsome and mysterious, like . . .

LONNY *(Grinning.)* Like Pete Sterling?

TRACY *(Scoffing.)* Humph! Pete! *(She sits up, eager.)* I mean Bart Hegelmann. I met him two weeks ago at the Schillers'.

LONNY *(Frowning, concerned.)* Tracy, you're a nice little girl, even if you're a trifle obnoxious. Keep away from those Schillers. They're poison.

TRACY *(Flippantly, grinning.)* There's nothing I like better than a little cyanide, Lonny darling. *(She springs up suddenly and shakes a vehement fist close to Lonny's face.)* And don't you preach to me, either! *(Ruth enters at the back with her envelope of papers.)*

RUTH. Hello, Lonny.

LONNY *(Turning and coming up to Ruth's left.)* Ruth! Protect me from her.

RUTH *(Smiling, coming down Right, speaking to Tracy.)* Was he telling you that you should help me with our Young Folks' program, Tracy?

TRACY *(Indifferently.)* Can't do it. I have a very special date for that evening. Mother will help you, *(She shrugs and turns up Left.)* if Dad hasn't put his foot down.

RUTH *(Laying her envelope on the end table at Right, near the door.)* Did he say anything?

TRACY *(Grinning.)* At the top of his lungs, he did. He said, quote: "Most of this religious feeling that you women experience is escapism." Unquote. He thinks that Mother should give more time to her other responsibilities, and less to these church activities. *(She looks defiantly at Ruth.)* I do, too.

RUTH *(Gently.)* Tracy, please listen . . .

TRACY *(At Center, frowning.)* Now, don't you start preaching to me, too. I shall manage my own life. *(She goes to the door at back and turns to add sharply, speaking to Lonny.)* I may even experiment with a little—poison. *(Tracy flings herself off at the back. Lonny whistles, gazing after Tracy.)*

LONNY *(Calling loudly after Tracy.)* Happy antidote to you, little one.

RUTH *(Shaking her head ruefully.)* What has happened to her, Lonny?

LONNY. It's her father's influence, Ruth. *(He comes down to face Ruth.)* It's not my affair, but she is being seen with some rather Bohemian characters. Her father sets the example. He calls these lunatics intellectuals—moderns. *(He growls.)* Modern crackpots!

RUTH. Marsh Oldfield is a man groping in the dark. He can't see people and things as they really are. *(She touches Lonny's arm and speaks brightly.)* But he will be brought into the light again: I know that he will. *(She nods confidently.)* Something will happen to bring him back. Sheila's prayers for him—and mine—will be answered. *(She turns and goes to the Right again.)*

LONNY *(Following Ruth, admiringly.)* You and your mother-in-law are like Ruth and Naomi in the Bible story, aren't you?

RUTH *(Smiling.)* I think so. You see, Sheila has been my mother—my whole family, indeed—ever since I was six, when my parents died. I suppose that I really married Roger to please his mother. But those two years with him were happy years. *(She sighs.)*

LONNY. Roger was a great fellow.

RUTH. But Marsh was like him. You remember, Lonny? Losing Roger was his first experience with sorrow. His rebellious and angry self fights his real self. He is like two persons.

LONNY *(Grinning.)* And I'd enjoy knocking his two heads together. *(Steps are heard from outside at the back.)*

RUTH *(Warningly, to Lonny, as she crosses to Left.)* Sh! It may be Sheila.

SHEILA *(From near the back door, calling.)* Ruth?

RUTH *(Coming up Left.)* In here, Sheila. *(Sheila enters at back.)*

SHEILA. Good afternoon, Lonny. Marsh is waiting for you in his study. I asked Annie to bring some coffee to you men in there.

LONNY *(Facing Sheila near the back door.)* Thank you, Mrs. Oldfield. *(He leans confidentially closer to Sheila.)* If Denise comes, will you send up some flares at once? I'll come running.

RUTH *(Firmly, shaking her head, coming to take Sheila's left arm.)* She will be here in a moment, but we won't even let you know, because we both have to go to our committee meeting.

LONNY *(Tragically.)* I'm going to swallow my typewriter. *(Lonny goes off with his briefcase at the back.)*

RUTH *(Leading Sheila to the upper chair at Left.)* You aren't coming with me? Tracy told me that Marsh . . .

SHEILA *(Sitting in upper chair at Left.)* He made a dinner engagement for us with those Islingtons. *(She sighs.)*

RUTH *(At Center, shocked.)* Islington? The author of those atheistic articles? How can Marsh endure their company?

SHEILA. He pretends to believe that the man is a genius, an intellectual phenomenon.

RUTH. A phenomenon is something rare. I suppose that that type of blasphemous creature is rare!

SHEILA *(Both hands out, leaning forward.)* Ruth, what shall I do? Not even my boy's death tore my heart in two like this terrible wall that Marsh is building between us.

RUTH *(Going to Sheila's right, speaking gently.)* But, Sheila dear, that wall will crumble. You will have Marsh back, his old self again. Have faith.

SHEILA. But you—you can't be happy in this household. He is unkind to you. Tracy is growing away from us, too. You must make a new life for yourself. Roger would want that.

RUTH *(Kneeling on one knee near Sheila's chair.)* I won't leave you while you need me.

SHEILA *(Caressing Ruth's hair.)* But you must, dear; you're young.

RUTH *(Smiling, leaning back.)* Remember my namesake in the Bible? "Entreat me not to leave thee. Whither thou goest, I will go. Thy people shall be my people" . . . Remember?

SHEILA (*Drawing Ruth near to her.*) Oh, I am selfish. I do want you to stay. But you know that Breck Hathaway loves you, and he is so . . .

RUTH (*Shaking her head, smiling.*) I'm thinking of you—only you—and I know that God will show Marsh the way back to Him soon. (*She takes Sheila's hands.*) We'll pray—together. (*Marsh enters abruptly at the back, frowning.*)

MARSH. Sheila, you have scarcely time to dress for our dinner engagement. (*He comes down a few steps.*) Ruth, don't detain her. (*Ruth rises.*) I thought that you had gone to your world-shaking meeting. (*He smiles sarcastically.*)

RUTH (*Gently, facing Marsh.*) I am going in a few moments. It is a meeting to plan our Young Folks' program. We miss you on the committee, Marsh.

MARSH (*Turning toward the back door.*) I have more important things to do. Come, Sheila. (*Marsh goes off at the back.*)

SHEILA (*Rising and going slowly to the back.*) Thank you, Ruth. I'll remember. (*Sheila smiles at Ruth, then goes off at the back. Ruth comes thoughtfully down to Left. Denise enters at Right, with her briefcase.*)

DENISE. Am I late, Ruth?

RUTH (*Going to meet Denise.*) Oh, Denise, come in.

DENISE (*Looking about, speaking in a lowered tone.*) I am glad that you're alone. I don't know whether it would do any good to speak to Tracy, but . . .

RUTH (*Disturbed.*) Tracy? What is wrong, Denise?

DENISE. For about two weeks, she has been seen with Adam Schiller and his wife and their hanger-on, Bert Hegelmann. They are not good associates for her. I believe that they are under surveillance as subversives.

RUTH (*Alarmed.*) Oh! We must keep Tracy from being identified with them.

DENISE (*Drily, setting her case on the sofa.*) You will have to use tact. She doesn't take kindly to advice, I have noted.

RUTH. I don't want Sheila to know; she has enough to bear. (*Lonny hurries on at the back, carrying a newspaper.*)

LONNY (*His face lighting as he goes to Denise.*) Denise!

(He beckons to Ruth, who comes to Lonny's left.) Girls, look at this. *(He points to a newspaper line.)* "Adam Schiller and his wife and Bart Hegelmann questioned." Aren't those Tracy's new friends?

RUTH *(Taking the paper and reading with an anxious expression.)* Yes. We must do something, Lonny. Tracy hasn't seen this paper?

LONNY. No. It just came. *(He frowns.)* If those crackpots name her as a character reference, knowing that the Oldfield name is sacrosanct around here . . .

DENISE. That is what I fear.

RUTH *(Giving the paper back to Lonny, and starting for the back determinedly.)* I shall talk to them.

LONNY *(Catching Ruth's arm.)* To those Schillers? No!

RUTH. Yes; I shall appeal to them to keep Tracy's name out of this. They must have some decency. She's only a young, impressionable girl.

LONNY. Ruth Oldfield, you aren't going to be seen going to their apartment. It is closely guarded, and you . . .

DENISE *(Coming to Lonny's right.)* That is right, Ruth.

RUTH *(Between Denise and Lonny at the back.)* They can't harm me. Think of Sheila. This would be the last straw. I'll go to them now. *(She is firmly waving Lonny and Denise away. Peter and Breck, after knocking lightly, enter at Right. Peter has his notebook.)*

PETER. Is anyone at home? *(He grins at Ruth.)* Hello, everybody.

RUTH *(Coming down Center, smiling.)* Peter, and Breck, this is nice.

BRECK *(Crossing hurriedly to come to Ruth's left.)* Ruth, you look disturbed. What is wrong?

LONNY *(Tapping his newspaper, coming down a few steps.)* It's our Tracy.

PETER *(Quickly, interestedly, coming up Right.)* Tracy? What happened to her?

LONNY *(Drily, handing the paper to Peter.)* That's it, it didn't happen. She didn't get spanked at the proper time.

DENISE *(To Peter.)* She has been seeing those imported pests. *(She points to the names in the newspaper.)*

PETER *(Troubled.)* No! It's her father's fault, with his crazy notions about these intellectuals.

DENISE. Ruth is determined to appeal to them to keep Tracy out of this.

BRECK *(Laying his hand on Ruth's arm.)* Ruth! Not you. I'll telephone Jeff Dawson and ask him to do what he can. Everything that they say will be laid before him. I'll tell him that Tracy is just a silly little girl.

PETER *(Protesting, to Breck, coming across to Left.)* Now, Breck . . . *(He lays the newspaper on the end table above the sofa.)*

LONNY *(Grinning.)* Pete, you should have been masterful with her. She likes her men mysterious and masterful. She just told me so.

DENISE. Ruth, Breck's idea is worth trying.

RUTH. Then, go across the street to telephone, please. At all costs, Sheila must not know. *(Ruth comes with Breck to the door in the right wall.)*

BRECK *(Tenderly, to Ruth, taking her hand.)* Don't look so troubled, dear. I'll come back in two minutes. *(He looks at Ruth for a moment, then goes off. Lonny and Denise move to the Left, smiling back at Breck and Ruth. Peter goes up Left, looking at his notebook. Marsh and Sheila enter at the back.)*

SHEILA *(Smiling, coming down Right.)* Good afternoon, Denise, and Peter.

MARSH *(At Center back.)* Has the church committee meeting moved over here, Ruth?

PETER. Not exactly, Mr. Oldfield. *(He smiles and steps nearer to Marsh.)* I am accepting contributions in our annual church drive. May I put you down for your usual amount?

SHEILA *(Pleasantly, sitting at Right, on the upstage end of the sofa.)* Of course, Peter.

MARSH *(Harshly, looking coldly at Peter.)* No. I am not interested.

SHEILA *(Gently.)* Marsh, dear! *(Ruth moves quietly to stand at Sheila's right.)*

MARSH *(As his bitter glance embraces all.)* My wife and daughter-in-law would like me to conform to their pattern, but I find meekness and resignation not to my taste. I am a man. *(Tracy enters at the back in time to hear this line.)*

TRACY *(Patting her father's arm.)* Good for you, Dad. Hi, Pete. *(She waves a careless hand at Peter, who crosses to Right to join Tracy.)*

PETER. Then, I'm to understand that you don't wish to make a contribution to the drive this year?

MARSH *(Coldly.)* That is correct. *(He goes a few steps toward the back door, then turns to smile sardonically at Ruth.)* No doubt, my wife and daughter-in-law will immediately begin to pray for me.

RUTH *(Pleasantly.)* I do pray for you. It is the only way in which I can help you.

TRACY *(Belligerently, to Ruth.)* Dad doesn't need help; he can take care of himself. *(Sheila covers her face with her hands, head bowed.)*

LONNY *(Coming to look at Marsh, speaking courteously, but firmly.)* No one is self-sufficient. Mr. Oldfield, you are closing a door, and leaving all your real friends on the outside, if you will permit me to say so.

MARSH *(Furious.)* I will not! You are impertinent to lecture me, young man. *(Louder.)* You are discharged.

SHEILA *(Looking up, startled.)* Marsh! No!

LONNY *(Smiling, crossing to Right.)* Thank you, sir. I have hoped to hear that for a year.

SHEILA *(Rising, unhappy, going to Marsh.)* I'm sure that Marsh does not really mean that.

RUTH *(Quietly.)* It is nearly time for the meeting, Denise. Lonny will drive you over, and I'll come later.

LONNY *(Smiling, going to shake hands with Sheila.)* I'll see you often, Mrs. Oldfield. Come on, Denise. *(Lonny and Denise go to the door at Right, smile at all, and go off together.)*

MARSH. We'll be late for the dinner with the Islingtons, Sheila. Do come along. *(He turns and says airily to Peter.)* Good luck with your begging, Peter. *(Marsh goes off at the back.)*

SHEILA *(As Ruth joins her at Right.)* I won't go. I don't feel equal to it, anyway.

TRACY (*Crossing to the end table above the sofa.*) I'd like to meet them. They are modern—sharp. (*Tracy idly picks up the newspaper, and suddenly cries out.*) Oh! (*Tracy stares stricken at the paper. Ruth hurries to Tracy.*)

SHEILA. What is it, Tracy dear?

TRACY (*In a choked voice, trying to appear calm.*) Nothing, Mother, nothing.

RUTH (*Brightly.*) Don't worry about anything, Sheila. You'd better go if Marsh wants you to. Maybe, you can tell Mr. Islington a few truths which he needs to hear.

SHEILA (*With unaccustomed spirit, at the back door.*) I shall tell him what I think of his shocking philosophies, and Marsh can explode, if he will. (*Sheila goes off, head high, at the back. As soon as Sheila is off, Ruth hurries to Tracy, who is bending over the newspaper, frightened, with Peter at her right, bending to reassure her.*)

TRACY (*Wailing.*) Ruth! Pete! I'm scared. What will I do? Will they arrest me?

RUTH (*At Tracy's left, speaking gently, patting Tracy's arm.*) No, no. Breck is telephoning to Jeff Dawson, dear. Don't be so worried.

PETER. Why *did* you, Tracy?

TRACY (*Tearful.*) Oh, I thought that they were exciting. They were older and terribly sophisticated.

PETER (*Frowning with mock ferocity.*) Well, I am five years older than you, and you have no idea how sophisticated I can be. (*He crosses to Left, poses with an aloof expression and haughtily folded arms.*)

RUTH (*Gently easing Tracy down into the easy chair down Left.*) Now, try to be calm, Tracy. Your mother doesn't know that you ever saw these persons, does she?

TRACY. Horrors, no! She would be shocked. (*She sits up, wailing again.*) Oh, Ruth, she'll know when they arrest me!

RUTH. Hush! Not so loud. Please do not let her see that you're frightened. She has looked pale and wan lately. We must spare her this. Trust us, dear. (*Ruth pats Tracy's hand reassuringly.*)

TRACY (*Clinging to Ruth's hand.*) How can you be so nice to me, Ruth? I've been—obnoxious, as Lonny said. I'm

—I'm sorry. *(Breck hurries on at Right, looking troubled.)*

RUTH *(Crossing hurriedly to Right.)* Yes? What did Mr. Dawson say, Breck?

BRECK. He already knew about—about Tracy, because a gold evening bag was found in the apartment, and . . .

TRACY *(Rising and clinging to Peters arm.)* My evening bag! I put it into Bart's pocket while we were dancing, and it had my name and address in it.

PETER. But you told Jeff that Tracy is only an acquaintance of theirs, that she couldn't be involved in their schemes?

BRECK. I told him. He promised not to question them about Tracy, but, if they bring her name in, he can't do anything about it.

TRACY *(Excitedly, loudly.)* Oh, they will! They will! What shall I do, Pete?

RUTH *(Coming to Center, troubled.)* Peter, Tracy will never be able to keep her worry from her mother. I wish that she could go somewhere for the week-end.

PETER. My sister, Nan, invited us both to her place in the mountains for the week-end, but Tracy declined.

TRACY *(Pleadingly.)* I'll go, Pete, I'll go. Please take me.

PETER. Let's go and telephone Nan to see whether it's still all right.

TRACY *(Gratefully.)* Thanks. You and Ruth are my best friends. I've been so silly. I need a guardian.

PETER *(Pretending to drag Tracy to the back door by the hair.)* You need a strong, handsome, mysterious, and masterful—husband, Woman! *(Peter and Tracy go off at the back.)*

BRECK *(Coming with Ruth to Center back.)* They may have the decency to leave her name out of their answers. She may grow up a little after this.

RUTH *(Kindly.)* Poor Tracy! *(Denise, after knocking lightly outside at Right, enters.)*

DENISE. I forgot my briefcase. *(She takes it from the sofa.)*

RUTH *(Crossing to Denise.)* Denise, Tracy's evening bag was found there, and her name and address were inside.

DENISE. No! Does her mother know?

RUTH. Heaven forbid! Pete will take her to his sister's for the week-end.

DENISE. This may blow over by Monday. *(Lonny pokes his head in at Right, grinning.)*

LONNY. Is this a woman's two minutes, Denise? *(The telephone bell sounds.)*

RUTH. Wait, both of you. *(Ruth answers the telephone.)* Yes, this is the Oldfield residence . . . Who? . . . No, Miss Tracy Oldfield is not here at the moment . . . Will you try again later? . . . Oh? . . . You may not be able to? . . . May I tell her who called? . . . *(Then, in a choked voice, looking about at the others.)* Oh! Bart Hegelmann! . . . Goodbye. *(Ruth replaces the receiver, disturbed.)*

LONNY *(Angrily, starting to Right.)* He wants to enlist her sympathy, of course, the wretch! Let me at him. I am going straight to his apartment.

BRECK *(To Ruth.)* We might talk to him.

RUTH *(Going to restrain Lonny.)* No, no. It's too late. That call was overheard, no doubt. We must think of some other way. We have to spare Sheila. *(Sheila appears quietly in the doorway at back, unnoticed. Ruth continues firmly.)* and we must save Tracy's good name.

SHEILA *(Starting forward.)* Ruth! *(Ruth, Lonny, Denise, and Breck turn, aghast, to face Sheila.)* You must save Tracy from what? What has happened? Tell me.

DENISE *(With forced cheerfulness, going to Sheila's left.)* Oh, you know these young girls and their pranks, Mrs. Oldfield.

SHEILA. Ruth does not get disturbed over pranks. Ruth, what is it? *(Sheila comes in front of the sofa and Ruth comes to her right. Tracy and Peter enter at the back.)* Tracy, what have you done? Tell Mother, dear. *(Sheila puts her right hand out to Tracy.)*

TRACY *(Head down, coming to her mother's left.)* I didn't want you to know, Mother, but I . . .

PETER *(With attempted lightness.)* She went dancing with this Bart Hegelmann and went to the Schillers' parties, and it appears that they are . . .

SHEILA *(Tensely.)* Go on, Peter.

RUTH *(Quickly.)* No. *(Ruth shakes her head at Peter.)*

TRACY. It's no use, Ruth. *(Tracy clings to her mother, tearful.)* They are being arrested, and I may go—to jail! *(The last is a wail.)*

SHEILA *(Both hands out, eyes closed, sits down suddenly on the sofa.)* Tracy! *(The word is spoken in a faint, trembling tone.)*

RUTH *(Leaning to Sheila, anxious.)* Sheila, are you ill?

SHEILA *(In a low voice, opening her eyes.)* No, no; it's nothing.

BRECK *(Coming to Center, reassuring.)* We have Jeff Dawson's assurance that Tracy won't be mentioned in the case, if he can possibly avoid it.

SHEILA *(One hand to her heart, the other reaching for Tracy's hand.)* And if he can't?

PETER *(Bursting out, indignantly, going to put an arm about Tracy.)* If anything unpleasant happens to Tracy, it will be her father's fault. She only wanted to imitate him.

RUTH *(Gently.)* Peter! Don't be hard upon him. He is lost in a dark and tangled wood, but he will find his way home, poor Marsh. *(Marsh enters at the back, frowning blackly.)*

MARSH. I heard. It's flattering to be the subject of this conference, I am sure, but, Sheila, *(He looks puzzled as he glances at the bowed head of Sheila.)* are you deliberately delaying our dinner? . . . *(He looks at Tracy.)* And what is wrong with you, Tracy? You have been weeping. *(Marsh comes nearer to Tracy.)*

TRACY *(Dabbing at her eyes.)* I—I am scared!

SHEILA *(Looking up, more calm, but still speaking in a low tone.)* Tracy has become involved with some questionable persons, the Schillers, and . . .

MARSH. Adam Schiller and his wife? They are friends of the Islingtons.

PETER *(Grimly.)* Yes, birds of a feather: all crows! *(He grates the last word out.)*

RUTH. The Schillers and their protege, Bart Hegelmann, are being questioned as suspected subversives.

MARSH *(Shaken.)* And Tracy . . . *(He raises his voice angrily, whirling upon Tracy.)* Why were you so stupid, Tracy? But I know. *(He glares at Ruth.)* It's because you try to fashion her life to your dull and strait-laced pattern. She had to find gaiety and diversion elsewhere, and . . .

BRECK *(Stepping to face Marsh, controlled, but speaking in an icy tone.)* Permit me to interrupt you, Mr. Oldfield. Your thinking is completely distorted. *You* have chosen for your friends shallow thinkers, pseudo-intellectuals, or worse, and, as Tracy admires you, she believed that it was smart and modern to follow your example.

MARSH *(Haughtily.)* Breck Hathaway, you dare . . .

BRECK *(Coolly.)* It doesn't require great daring to point out that you are a great disappointment in your church, that you are antagonizing your business associates, and . . .

RUTH *(Touching Breck's arm lightly, trying to check him.)* Breck!

BRECK *(Covering Ruth's hand with his.)* Let me finish, Ruth. I was about to add, Mr. Oldfield, that we, who are your friends, are grieved to see your family so unhappy because of . . .

MARSH *(Enraged, shouting, starting toward Breck, a hand up.)* Why, you young upstart, I'll . . .

TRACY *(Frightened, trying to draw Marsh backward.)* Dad! Don't!

MARSH *(Shaking Tracy off.)* Out of the way, Tracy! I'll throw him out! *(Breck remains unruffled, Ruth puts a pleading hand out to Marsh.)*

SHEILA *(Trying to rise, crying out in a choked voice, distraught.)* Marsh! *(Sheila then falls back, head back upon the back of the sofa, both hands to her throat, panting.)* Ohhh! *(All look at Sheila in alarm.)*

MARSH *(Subdued, sitting at Sheila's left.)* Are you ill? Sheila!

RUTH *(Hurrying to kneel at Sheila's right.)* I was afraid of that. Call Dr. Pierce at once, Tracy. *(Ruth rubs Sheila's hands.)*

TRACY *(Hysterically, crying out.)* Oh, Mother! Mother!

RUTH *(Quietly.)* Quiet, Tracy. Peter, please take her out, and call Dr. Pierce. *(Peter takes Tracy off at Right.)*

MARSH *(Pleadingly.)* Sheila, dearest, tell me what . . .

RUTH. I'll help you get her on the bed, Marsh.

BRECK *(Coming to Right.)* Let me, Ruth. *(Breck and Marsh draw Sheila to her feet, Ruth helping.)*

MARSH *(Miserably, near the back door.)* Ruth, what have I done? What can I do?

RUTH *(Soothingly, standing behind Breck, Sheila, and Marsh in the doorway.)* Pray, Marsh, pray. *(Marsh, Breck take Sheila off at the back, followed by Ruth, who turns first to send a pleading glance at the others, her hands clasped.)*

DENISE *(After a troubled pause, turns to Lonny.)* I believe that this will bring him to his senses. No matter how defiant and self-sufficient a man may be, when he is frightened, he turns to God.

LONNY *(Sitting in the easy chair near the front at Left.)* He has been like a man bedeviled, running away from something.

DENISE *(Going to look out at the back door.)* His conscience, no doubt. . . . I do hope that Mrs. Oldfield's attack will not prove serious. Ruth loves her so much.

LONNY. Her husband loves her, too.

DENISE *(Turning to look at Lonny.)* Does he? *(She looks skeptical.)*

LONNY. Yes. I am sorry for him.

DENISE *(Coming down Right, smiling.)* You're generous. He just discharged you.

LONNY *(Rising, grinning, hands in his pockets.)* That's right. I forgot. I am unemployed. *(He crosses to Denise.)* You would be kind to a man on the relief roll, wouldn't you?

DENISE *(Drily.)* I would probably relieve him of his roll. *(She goes to look out at the window at Left.)*

LONNY *(Following Denise, hopeful.)* You mean . . . ? Darling! *(As Denise still has her back turned to Lonny, he pretends to stumble against the chair.)* Don't torture me. I'm in a coma. *(He slumps into the chair.)*

DENISE *(Going to the back door again.)* I wondered what

was wrong with you. *(Ruth appears in the back doorway, her face anxious.)*

RUTH. Did Tracy get Dr. Pierce?

DENISE. I thought that was his car driving up. *(Denise points to the window.)* How is she, Ruth?

RUTH. The pain is severe. I'll let the doctor in. Please stay, both of you.

LONNY *(Sitting up in the chair, serious.)* I'm worried. *(He drops his head in his hands, leaning forward. Denise goes to stand at Lonny's right, touching his hair lightly. Tracy and Peter enter at Right, looking anxious.)*

TRACY *(Running to Ruth.)* Oh, Ruth, is she . . . ?

RUTH. Dr. Pierce is here. I'll go up with him and try to get your father to come down. Ask Anna to make some coffee, Tracy, please. *(Ruth hurries off.)*

TRACY. I'm going up to see for myself. Pete, you tell Anna. *(Tracy hurries off at the back. Peter goes off at Right.)*

DENISE *(Gravely.)* Lonny, let us ask God to spare Mrs. Oldfield.

LONNY *(Rising, more cheerful.)* He will. Ruth's devotion and love and faith make me ashamed of my worry. *(Lonny takes Denise's two hands, speaking earnestly.)* Love and faith can work miracles. Let us hold on to ours, my dearest.

DENISE *(Low, smiling.)* I have a good hold on it, Lonny. *(Breck comes on at the back.)*

BRECK. The doctor is with her. Tracy was crying, so he turned her out. *(He comes to sit on the sofa.)* That husband of hers is a frightened man, but Ruth . . . *(He smiles at Denise and Lonny.)* what a girl!

DENISE *(Crossing to Breck.)* Take her away from here, Breck. Be masterful. *(She smiles.)*

BRECK *(Rising, troubled.)* Denise, I am not worthy of her but I would spend my life trying to make her happy. Only . . . she is so loyal to this family that . . .

LONNY. Do as I do. Make her believe that you are a storm-tossed soul in a leaking boat. She'll drag you out of the waves, as Denise did for me.

DENISE. I'll toss you right back in soon, I expect. *(All*

laugh. Peter comes at Right and Tracy enters at the back, at the same moment.)

PETER. Anna says that there will be coffee for everyone in a few minutes. I could use some. *(He goes to take Tracy's hand and leads her to up Left.)*

TRACY *(Nervously.)* I wish that Ruth would come down and tell us . . .

PETER *(Soothingly.)* Chin up, my girl. Sophisticated Pete is standing by.

TRACY. But I wish that Ruth would come. If Mother is going to be all right, I'll tell Ruth that I'll help her with her Young Folks' program. *(Tracy sits disconsolately in the easy chair up Left.)* Oh, Pete, I feel as if I had been lost, and had just got back home. Oh, Mother! *(Tracy covers her eyes. Marsh enters slowly, at the back, looking anxious, subdued. Tracy springs up and goes to Marsh.)* Dad, is she . . . ?

MARSH *(Gently.)* Dr. Pierce is with her. He will let us know soon. *(Marsh goes to droop at the upstage end of the sofa.)*

DENISE *(Crossing to Right.)* Be of good courage, Mr. Old-field.

MARSH *(Looking up.)* Thank you, Denise. *(He looks at Lonny.)* Oh, Lonny, you're here. *(Marsh rises and goes slowly to Lonny.)* Will you believe that I am sorry for my outburst, and stay on? I want you very much.

LONNY *(Pleasantly, offering his hand which Marsh takes.)* Gladly, if you wish, sir.

MARSH. I thank you. *(He turns to Peter and Breck.)* Peter, Breck, I wish to apologize for my inexcusable conduct. You were both right. I have been an insufferable boor ever since my son was taken from me. I deserve to be punished, but . . . *(Marsh steps back, his two fists up suddenly, shaken.)* but not Sheila, please, God, not Sheila! *(Marsh turns his back and takes a few uncertain steps up back.)*

TRACY *(Following Marsh to console him.)* Dad, don't! *(Ruth comes quickly on at the back, smiling.)*

RUTH *(Gaily.)* Smile everyone, smile! *(All turn to Ruth, eager.)* Dr. Pierce says that this is only a nervous crisis, and that Sheila will be as good as new. He orders a complete

rest; he says that she has been under a severe strain. So . . .
no excitement.

MARSH. Thank God! *(The telephone rings.)*

TRACY *(Answering the telephone.)* Hello . . . Who? . . .
Yes, he is. It's for you, Breck.

BRECK *(In the telephone.)* Yes? . . . Jeff? . . . *(All show
interest.)* Yes . . . Oh, that is great! . . . Yes. . . . Jeff, thank
you; you have been very kind. . . . Very well; thanks. *(Breck
turns from the telephone, delighted.)* Jeff says that no one
even mentioned Tracy's name. He will drop her bag off here
on his way home. *(All show relief and joy.)*

TRACY *(Throwing her arms about Peter.)* Oh, Pete, Pete!
(Tracy runs to hug Ruth.) Ruth, isn't Breck wonderful?
(As Ruth looks confused and embarrassed, all laugh.)

PETER *(Crossing to draw Tracy back to Left, looking
firm.)* There. That's over. Now, *(He grins at Marsh.)* with
your permission, sir, I am going to marry this daughter of
yours, to keep her out of mischief.

TRACY *(Sparkling, looking mischievously up at Peter.)*
That's such a good idea.

MARSH. I am glad for you young folks. *(He goes to shake
Peter's hand.)* Now, I shall go up to Sheila. I am going to
plan a long cruise together. That will be good for her. Lonny,
you can carry on while I am away. And, Peter, of course,
you may put my name down for the usual contribution.
(Marsh goes to Ruth.) Ruth, what can I say to you, my dear,
for your patience and your loyalty? God bless you, Ruth,
God bless you. *(Marsh holds Ruth's two hands for a moment,
then goes off.)*

RUTH *(Very still at Center back, radiant, head bowed.)*
Thank you, Father! He has found the way back!

DENISE *(Glancing at Breck who stands dejectedly down
Right.)* Everyone looks happy except you, Breck. Why the
long face?

BRECK *(With a wry smile.)* Envy. I can't endure the sight
of you two happy couples. *(He starts for the Right door.)*
I am going to—to Tibet.

RUTH *(Hestitantly, her right hand out to Breck.)* Wait,

Breck. I—I have always been curious—about Tibet. *(Ruth smiles.)*

BRECK *(Incredulous, staring at Ruth.)* Ruth! You . . . you mean . . . ? But you said that Mrs. Oldfield . . .

RUTH *(Coming down Center slowly.)* Sheila will be happy now, with Marsh his old self, and so . . .

BRECK *(Striding to meet Ruth at Center and seizes her hands.)* Ruth! You will?

RUTH *(Softly, gravely, looking at Breck.)* "Whither thou goest, I will go" . . . *(She laughs suddenly, releasing her hands, and tucking her left hand into Breck's right arm.)* even to—Tibet.

BRECK *(Seizing Ruth's free hand and drawing her to him, cries out with unaccustomed abandon.)* Ruth! You do mean it! *(Breck is about to kiss Ruth, but he glares around at the other two couples.)* Go away, you ordinary folks, go away!

LONNY *(Going to drag at Breck's arm while Tracy gaily tugs at Ruth's left.)* No such luck for you! Come on, getting engaged always makes me hungry, so we're all going to celebrate with some of that coffee. Come along. *(Laughing, Peter and Denise go first, off at back, with Lonny pushing Breck ahead of him, and Tracy following, with her arm about Ruth.)*

CURTAIN

BY CHRIST ALONE

AN EASTER PLAY IN THREE SCENES

By

WILLARD S. SMITH

PRODUCTION RIGHTS

CAST OF CHARACTERS

(For Twelve Males and Three Females*)

A Blind Beggar
A Shepherd
Ada
Sarah
Mary of Bethany
Judas
Nathan
Barabbas
Abimilech }
Benjamin } High Priests of the temple
Samuel
Thomas
Peter
Matthew
James

Time: The afternoon of the Crucifixion

Scene I: A hillside outside Jerusalem not far from Calvary

Scene II: The Court of the High Priests in the temple at Jerusalem

Scene III: Same as Scene I

*The Beggar, the Shepherd, and Nathan can easily double as three of the disciples in Scene III.

SUGGESTIONS FOR STAGING

With the exception of Judas none of the characters appears in more than one scene. Each scene can be rehearsed separately until the last one or two rehearsals.

Scenes One and Three are the same . . . a hillside outside Jerusalem and within sight of Calvary. If the depth of the stage makes it at all possible, extend the "hill" out on to the stage. Use sturdy tables, boxes, etc., to give realistic contours. Cover all with grey and brown cloth. It will add much to the effectiveness of Judas' exit in Scene Three if he goes part way up the hill, then exits behind an evergreen which would serve as an effective screen.

A few bare shrubs, an evergreen or two, a few real rocks scattered about will lend realism to the scene. The overall effect should be that of a rather desolate spot. The background beyond and above the hill should be of dark material to simulate sky.

In Scene Two a curtain of rich-appearing material extends across the back. If possible, this should be divided in the center so that one of the high priests may look out occasionally. This curtain conceals Scene One, the lower part of which may have to be pushed back if the stage is narrow.

A large pillar is on each side down front, and two more are part way back, set in a trifle. These can easily be made of light weight wallboard, the cheaper kind that is much like heavy cardboard. Cut pieces to the right length and width, then bend lengthways to form a semi-circle. Fasten with wire or string and cover with marble-like wall paper.

Two or three large and appropriate pieces of furniture should be somewhere in the scene; they are not used so arrange them to best fit the stage. Be sure they "fit" the scene. The judicious use of appropriate drapery material will help. Pulpit chairs might well be used.

An effective way to produce the noise of the crowd is by the use of a sound-effect record such as used in radio studios. Be sure the machine you plan to use will take the large studio transcription record, and that it can be run at the proper speed. Occasionally designated individuals offstage should add, "Crucify him!" "Away with him!" "Behold the King of the Jews!" (mockingly) and similar remarks, keeping them in the distance, as is the general noise of the mob.

As the play progresses the noise of the crowd fades down but never entirely out. At times it is heard clearly. In Scene Three it is used but little; the crowd has thinned out. It should also be remembered that in Scene Two the noise should be from the *left* since the temple is in Jerusalem.

Music, preferably organ music, will be very effective if used where indicated. Selections from Wagner would be appropriate—a sombre, heavy type of music. The organist should rehearse with Judas, or wherever music is indicated, as much as do the characters with speaking parts.

Recorded music might be used. If so, one person should have charge of it and should rehearse for timing, volume, etc.

The glow at the end of Scene Three adds much to the effectiveness of the scene. If possible have the light for this hooked up to a rheostat so that it can be brought up gradually. It should not be too bright, even at its peak.

It will help the characters sense the atmosphere of the play if they bear in mind that the action takes place at the time of the crucifixion; the first words of Jesus from the cross are spoken soon after the play opens.

BY CHRIST ALONE

SCENE ONE

SCENE: *A hillside not far from Calvary.*

TIME: *The afternoon of the crucifixion.*

The music starts as the house lights go off. Though not loud it should be rather heavy and is played for fifteen or twenty seconds to create the desired atmosphere. Gradually it fades down and out as the curtain opens.

The light is that of a dark, brooding afternoon—Good Friday. The wind blows fitfully and there is occasional thunder and lightning.

The noise of the mob is heard in the distance off Right. It continues throughout the scene, as background only except where indicated.

After a few moments a blind beggar enters at Right, bewildered, feeling his way along with his staff.

BEGGAR. Help! Help! Will no one help a poor blind beggar? Help! I am lost! Help me! Help me! *(A shepherd enters at Right at the end of the Beggar's speech. His cloak is wrapped tightly about him as protection from the wind.)*

SHEPHERD. What is it, man? Why dost thou bleat here like a lost sheep?

BEGGAR. Because I *am* lost! And I feel the chill of a cruel wind such as I have never known before.

SHEPHERD *(Not realizing the Beggar is blind.)* Come then, and follow me down the slope. *(He starts out at Left.)* The path is just below.

BEGGAR. But I am blind! Help me!

SHEPHERD. Blind! I would to the God of my fathers that my eyes had been blind to what I have seen this day.

BEGGAR. I heard the cries of many people—I still hear them. They sound like mad men. But no one has told me the meaning of it all.

SHEPHERD. They *are* mad men! They go to Calvary to crucify One who claims to be the Son of God.

BEGGAR. The Son of—Thou speakest blasphemy! *(He draws back.)*

SHEPHERD. I speak the truth.

BEGGAR. But how would they dare to . . . ?

SHEPHERD. I know not how nor why, but so it is. I am going. Is thy piety greater than thy need of a guide?

BEGGAR. Nay! Nay! I will go with thee! *(He reaches out and the Shepherd helps him.)* The Son of—God, crucified! *(Both exit at Left. There is a brief pause with a roll of thunder. Then, in a moment of calm, from distant Calvary come the words, "Father forgive them, they know not what they do." Then again, thunder and the cries of the mob. Sarah, followed by Ada, enters at Right. Ada, near exhaustion, is plainly close to despair. Sarah, also tired and discouraged, is more vehement in her attitude. Both hold their cloaks tightly about them.)*

ADA *(Stopping and sinking down at the foot of the hill.)* Sarah! Wait a moment, I pray thee! We have hurried all the way from Calvary, and I must rest.

SARAH *(Turning back.)* Forgive me, Ada. I had hoped to reach the home of Mary and Martha in Bethany before— before it is too late.

ADA. But it is already too late. And what could they hope to do, two women against that crowd that cries out for the death of Jesus? I can still hear them! *(She covers her ears.)*

SARAH. I only know that in this dark hour when all who claimed to love Him have deserted Him, Mary and Martha and Lazarus will be true to Him.

ADA. But perchance they came to Jerusalem. All morning the city has been like a hornet's nest with people running this way and that. *(Mary enters at Right, sobbing as she hurries along.)*

SARAH *(Not recognizing Mary in the dim light.)* Who art thou, weeping in the loneliness of this place?

MARY. What matters it where I weep? Are tears less bitter in one place than another?

SARAH. Mary! Ada and I were on our way to Bethany to seek thee.

MARY *(Trying to control her weeping.)* Evil tidings travel

fast. It was hardly daybreak when Ezra the tanner brought word that the Roman soldiers had seized Jesus. Lazarus and I left at once for the city, leaving Martha to care for the flocks. Surely, we thought, they will not dare to hold Him, a Jew, and we thought to bring Him to Bethany where He would be safe, for a time at least.

ADA. But they *did* hold Him! They tried Him; the Sanhedrin tried Him and passed sentence!

MARY. What right had they to try Him before dawn? And without the witnesses as required by our laws?

SARAH. They had no right. And witnesses? They were there. Paid, it is whispered, to testify against Him.

ADA. Paid? By whom?

SARAH. What matter? We know Him to be innocent, as do others. He had committed no offense for which the Romans could put Him to death.

MARY. Yet there He hangs, crucified on Calvary!

ADA. Where is Lazarus now?

MARY. Somewhere in the city, helpless to help Him who gave him back his life.

SARAH. Didst thou hear the people shouting that Barabbas be freed and Jesus crucified?

MARY. We heard the tumult while still outside the city wall. But only when we reached the Gate of the Camel did we know that Pilate had given the crowd its way.

ADA. How could the people demand His death when all He sought to do was to help them?

SARAH. Blame the high priests! They knew that if the way of Jesus prevailed they would lose power and wealth.

ADA. Not so loud, Sarah!

SARAH. Who is there to hear in this desolate place? And what matter? It is the truth.

MARY. Pilate asked, "What is truth?"

SARAH. But he did not have courage to find the truth. He might have saved Jesus, but he did not dare.

ADA. How could anyone have saved Him?

MARY. He saved others . . .

SARAH. And His own denied Him!

MARY. Sarah, what meanest thou?

SARAH. I mean that even Peter denied that he ever knew Jesus.

MARY. Peter? No, Sarah! No!

SARAH. My brother's wife's sister is a maid-servant in the household of Pilate. She heard those about the fire name Peter as one of Jesus' disciples, and Peter denied it, not once but thrice, and the last time with an oath.

MARY. Peter!

SARAH. Yea, and worse than that, when the Roman soldiers went to the garden to find Jesus, it was one of His own that betrayed Him.

MARY. Sarah! Who could be so base?

SARAH. Judas Iscariot!

MARY. Judas of Kerioth?

SARAH. Yea. He betrayed the Son of God with a kiss.

ADA. Denied! Betrayed! Forsaken! . . . Crucified! What hope is there left for Israel?

MARY. What hope for the world while men deny Him, betray Him, forsake Him?

ADA. Will they always?

MARY. Some will. But some will never leave Him, whether in life or in death. They have crucified Him this day. Over there on the crest of Calvary Jesus is dying . . . But . . . But Lazarus died . . . and Lazarus lives . . . *(There is wonderment in her voice, but not certainty. Perhaps only a wistful, a new hope.)*

SARAH. Mary! Thinkest thou that . . . that . . .

MARY. I know not what may happen to Jesus. I wonder more what will happen to the world that has crucified Him.

ADA. Surely reason will return . . .

MARY. It is not reason that is needed, it is faith. Faith in Him who said just last eventide at the Passover, "I am the resurrection and the life."—James met Lazarus before daybreak and told him all that happened in the upper room where they were met.

SARAH. The resurrection and the life!

MARY. Come with me to Bethany, both of you. There we will wait for Lazarus to return. Perchance he will have heard what next they plan. *(She looks toward Calvary, then with a sob turns and goes out at Left.)*

ADA *(Glancing toward Calvary.)* What greater evil can they plan? *(Exits at Left.)*

SARAH *(She, too, looks toward Calvary as she says, half to herself.)* The resurrection—and the life! *(Exits at Left. There is a brief pause, the noise of the crowd still heard in the distance. There is a roll of thunder. Then the words of Jesus drifting across from Calvary: "This day shalt thou be with Me in paradise." There is a rumble of thunder, lightning, the shouting of the mob—and Judas enters at Right. He is distraught, his conscience gnawing.)*

JUDAS. So it is done . . . They have crucified Him . . . And I . . . I have betrayed Him . . . I led them to Him . . . But they would have found Him. For days they have watched and waited . . . since last Sabbath when He rode into the city . . . If only He had not looked at me as He did when I kissed Him! . . . His eyes . . . they looked into my soul! . . . And— there was love in them! . . . O God! I did not know! I thought Him greater than His enemies! . . . And there on Calvary they have crucified Him! . . . *(On this last sentence Judas, almost against his will, turns and looks toward Calvary.)* . . . I betrayed Him into their hands! I betrayed Him . . . my Master! *(He stumbles toward Center and sinks to the ground, sobbing. There is a roll of thunder for a moment or two before Nathan enters hurriedly from Right, glancing back over his shoulder. He does not see Judas and nearly stumbles over him.)*

NATHAN. Who sleeps here at such an hour as this? Or art thou sick?

JUDAS. I shall never sleep again, and my soul is sick unto death.

NATHAN *(Not particularly impressed.)* Thus have many said this day. *(Lighter.)* But the morrow will bring sunlight and a change of heart.

JUDAS. For me it can but bring fresh agony.

NATHAN. Wert thou one of His disciples, perhaps, that His death moves thee to despair? After all, He is not the first, nor will He be the last, to be crucified. **Curse** these Roman dogs!

JUDAS. But . . . but He was Jesus!

NATHAN *(Not impressed.)* Yea, He was named Jesus, and one of the others is Dysmas, and the third—I have forgotten his name. And what matter now?

JUDAS. But Jesus . . . He was my Lord!

NATHAN. So thou wert one of His band. Little help you can be to Him here, or elsewhere now. Already they had crucified the other two and were raising His cross when I left.

JUDAS. Raising Him on a cross! What was it He said? . . . "I, if I be lifted up, will draw all men unto Me."

NATHAN *(Scornfully.)* Draw men to the cross? Is that all your Jesus can offer? Come, man, if thou art wise thou wilt leave this place before nightfall. Jackals run over the face of it, some with four legs and some with two! *(He laughs as he draws his cloak about him and goes off Left.)*

JUDAS *(He sinks against the rocks.)* Crucified! . . . Dying! He saved others, why will He not save Himself? . . . Come down, come down, Jesus! Come down from thy cross! *(He has risen and faced toward Calvary.)* . . . No. He will not. *(Dully.)* His kingdom . . . where is it? It needs Him as king . . . "Follow Me" he said . . . and I followed Him . . . Spring and summer and winter I followed Him, and never once did He claim the crown of His kingdom . . . Last Sabbath He had but to speak and every Jew in the city would have hailed Him as the Messiah . . . But no! . . . He railed against the high priests. He scorned the rulers and ridiculed those who held the power of life or death over Him . . . I had nothing to do with that! They plotted to do away with Him . . . they sent their soldiers to seize Him in the garden . . . and there . . . there I . . . I betrayed Him! *(He sinks to the ground, sobbing. There is a rumble of thunder; then from the distant hilltop come the words of Jesus: "Woman, behold thy son! Behold thy mother!" Again there is thunder, and the noise of the mob swells, then dies down as Judas cries out . . .)*

JUDAS. O God of mercy! Have pity, O my God!

BARABBAS *(He has entered, Right, on Judas' words.)* Who cries out for pity and mercy in such a place as this?

JUDAS. I, who pray for both and merit neither!

BARABBAS. It is He on yonder cross who deserves pity, since none have shown Him mercy.

JUDAS. Who knows better than I?

BARABBAS. I do! Were it not for Him I would be hanging there on His cross. What manner of man is this that so stirs the people that they free Barabbas in order that Jesus might die?

JUDAS *(Rising.)* Thou . . . thou art Barabbas?

BARABBAS. Yea, I am Barabbas. Free—and yet not free. For all my days I shall be in debt to this Nazarene who dies in my place.

JUDAS. But—He was the Son of God! He did not need to die!

BARABBAS. Son of God or son of man, I know not. But this I know, never was there man like Him. I mingled with the crowds after I was loosed from prison, lost in the throngs that mocked Him on His way to Calvary. And He answered them not a word. Almost I would have carried His cross.

JUDAS. And none defended Him?

BARABBAS. Bah! Cringing cowards! Of all who claimed to be His disciples, not one dared speak for Him before Pilate.

JUDAS. But what could they do?

BARABBAS *(Fiercely.)* They could die with Him! Instead, one, I hear, led the Roman soldiers to where He prayed in Gethsemane.

JUDAS. Yea, I . . . I know.

BARABBAS. Led them there and then with a kiss marked Him for the Roman dogs!

JUDAS. Thou . . . dost thou know . . . which follower it was?

BARABBAS. I know his name, that is all. Judas! It is on the lips of many, to be spat out. And as long as men live the name of Judas will be despised. I am a robber—or have been. Now—I know not what I will do with the new life this Jesus hath given me. But I tell thee, had one of my band betrayed me, or any of his fellows, I would have hunted him down like a jackal, had his tongue cut out and his body thrown to the dogs that slink in the rubbish of Gehenna! *(Judas cringes at Barabbas' vehemence.)* Judas and his thirty pieces of silver—even the price of his betrayal is known—cursed be his name forever! Would that I knew where he crouched in hiding while the One he claimed to love, the One he betrayed . . . the One who died for me, hangs on yonder hill! *(Exits at Right.)*

JUDAS. Thirty pieces of silver! *(Bring in music softly.)* Even Barabbas knows the price they paid me! *(He takes out the bag containing the money, holding it from him.)* Thirty pieces! Damned! Bloody! . . . I'll . . . I'll take them back! I'll redeem my soul that much! Let them take back their silver and free me from its curse! . . . Yea, that is what I will do! . . . I will not be cursed by future generations . . . The name of Judas may be forgotten, but not spat upon, despised, hated! . . . O God, had I but known! . . . But now . . . to the temple! To the temple to give them back their thirty pieces of silver! *(Goes off at Right as the music swells for the curtain.)*

CURTAIN

SCENE TWO

SCENE: *The Court of the High Priests in the temple at Jerusalem.*

TIME: *Shortly after Scene One.*

As in the previous scene there is the semidarkness of the storm with wind, occasional thunder, and lightning. Care must be taken that the noise of these does not interfere with the speeches. Since this scene is inside the temple the noise of the storm will be somewhat less distinct than in Scene One. Also, the cries of the mob are barely heard since the temple is some distance from Calvary and the shouting has died down now that Jesus has been crucified. When the shouting is heard it comes from Left instead of Right.

Abimilech, Benjamin, and Samuel, high priests, are at the rear Left looking toward Calvary at Left. Abimilech and Benjamin are little moved, but throughout the scene it is apparent that Samuel is stirred and troubled, though still conscious of his position as a high priest.

ABIMILECH. That should bring an end to this talk of Him being some sort of a messiah.

BENJAMIN. A strange sort of a messiah indeed, hanging on a cross. *(He chuckles at the idea.)*

SAMUEL *(As he turns and comes down Right.)* Nailed there by the cursed Romans.

ABIMILECH *(Coming down.)* What else could they do? Didst thou not hear the shouts of the mob: "Crucify Him! Release unto us Barabbas!"

SAMUEL. Yea, I heard.

BENJAMIN. Had He been content to teach, even to heal the sick, it would have been well with Him. Oh, some grumbling and fault-finding, but to set Himself up as one with authority to—well, to drive the traders from the temple—that is something else.

SAMUEL. Yea, that brings Him close to us.

ABIMILECH *(Missing Samuel's subtle meaning.)* Too close. If there are no sheep and doves to buy, how can the people make their offerings and sacrifices unto the Lord God?

SAMUEL. And so add to the temple treasury.

BENJAMIN. It is legal, well within the law.

SAMUEL. Even the usury of the money changers?

ABIMILECH. Yea, there is usury. But that is not of our doing.

SAMUEL. Nay, but we get a greater share, whether of the silver shekels of the rich or the copper denarii of the poor.

ABIMILECH *(With a slight smirk.)* It that not well?

SAMUEL. For our purses, perhaps. For our souls . . . well, what thinkest thou?

BENJAMIN. Tell me, Samuel, have the teachings of this Jesus found lodgement in thy head?

SAMUEL. In my heart perhaps.

BENJAMIN. It were well for thee to forget Him. *(He goes back to look off Left.)*

SAMUEL. Forget Him. Yea, perhaps. But how can I forget the joyous laughter of my sister's child when he leaped with joy after this Jesus had restored his crippled leg?

ABIMILECH. And doth one miracle make a wandering healer king of Israel, the messiah of his people?

BENJAMIN *(Looking out.)* Well, He is dead, or will be soon. And soon His followers will see their folly and return to the God of their fathers.

ABIMILECH. Even those who were closest to Him are nowhere to be found. And one was glad to lead the soldiers to Him for thirty pieces of silver.

SAMUEL. *Our* thirty pieces. I know not whether to pity that one or to despise him.

ABIMILECH. Pity a traitor? Curse such as he, I say.

SAMUEL. We need not curse him. God will judge him.

BENJAMIN. But he did make it easier for us. Caiaphas seemed pleased.

ABIMILECH. Satisfied, yea. But Caiaphas would scorn this Judas if they met. To kill a valiant foe in battle is good; to poison his drink is the way of a coward.

SAMUEL. And what of those who pay the coward to poison —or betray?

BENJAMIN. By the beard of the prophet, Samuel, I believe this Galilean *hath* converted thee!

SAMUEL. I but marvel that we who paid this Judas his thirty pieces of silver can so easily despise him, and yet think ourselves innocent of all wrongdoing.

ABIMILECH. It was a bargain struck! We paid the price agreed; he led the soldiers to the garden.

SAMUEL. And betrayed his Master with a kiss.

ABIMILECH. Yea, and I despise him. But Jesus is crucified as it had to be. Now let this Judas be forgotten!

SAMUEL *(Partly aside.)* He never will be forgotten. *(There is commotion outside at Left and voices saying, "Nay! It is forbidden to enter." "This is the Court of the High Priests!" "None may enter!" Etc. Judas bursts in.)*

BENJAMIN. Judas!

ABIMILECH. Why dost thou desecrate the sanctity of this place? This is the Court of the High Priests!

JUDAS (*Registering the intense emotion he feels.*) Yea, but thou art here. (*His "thou" includes all three.*) Thou didst pay me . . . this! (*He holds out the bag containing the thirty pieces of silver.*)

ABIMILECH. And well we paid thee. Thirty pieces of silver, such was the price agreed on . . .

JUDAS. Yea, I know. But I want . . .

BENJAMIN. Not another denarius! The Nazarene was seized, the bargain is ended.

JUDAS. Nay, it is not ended for me! It will never be ended!

ABIMILECH (*Striding to the rear Left and looking off.*) I tell thee yea. (*Gestures toward Calvary.*) Go to Golgotha and see Him whom thou hast betrayed.

JUDAS. I have been! O God, I have seen!

ABIMILECH. Then begone, traitor! We have nothing more for thee!

JUDAS. I seek nothing. I . . . I have come to return the thirty pieces of silver! (*The three priests are taken aback.*)

SAMUEL. Return them, Judas?

JUDAS. Yea! Take them back! (*He holds out the money bag. The priests draw away.*) They are like fire that burns into my heart! They are heavy, weighing my soul down . . . down . . .

BENJAMIN. What is that to us? Thou art the traitor.

SAMUEL. Do we not share his guilt?

ABIMILECH. We? It was agreed that this Jesus should be done away with. Annas, Caiaphas, Benjamin, thou—all of us knew that. Had He been allowed to continue his blasphemous teaching not one of us would dare face the people.

SAMUEL. Now dare we face God?

ABIMILECH. The deal is done! (*To Judas.*) We bargained for thirty pieces of silver. It was paid. Thy kiss marked this Jesus as agreed so the soldiers could know it was He and seize Him.

JUDAS. But I beg thee, take back the money! Free my soul from the weight of this! (*Holds out the bag. The priests draw away as Judas takes a step toward them.*)

SAMUEL. It is forbidden that we take it back, Judas.

JUDAS. But I must be rid of it! Free me from my sin for I have betrayed innocent blood!

BENJAMIN. What is that to us?

SAMUEL. Because it is the price of blood, it is not lawful to put it in the treasury of the temple. *(Judas has reached into the bag. He brings out a handful of coins that trickle out of his hand.)*

JUDAS. Take them back! Take them back! *(He steps toward the high priests who back away in horror, for this is a terrible violation of the sanctity of the Court of the High Priests. Samuel is less concerned than the others; he does little more than step out of Judas' way.)*

ABIMILECH. It is blasphemy!

JUDAS. Thirty pieces of silver! Thirty pieces of silver for my soul! *(The last of the coins fall from his hand. He throws down the bag with a few coins remaining in it.)* O God, let me die! Let me die as He is dying! *(He rushes off at Left.)*

SAMUEL. Nay, Judas, no man will ever die as He dies.

BENJAMIN. Fool!

ABIMILECH. Traitor!

BENJAMIN. What of the money?

ABIMILECH. It is the price of blood and forever defiled. *(Pushes the coins nearest him with his foot.)* Let the servants gather it up and with it buy the potter's field. *(Thunder, lightning. Shouts outside.)*

VOICE OUTSIDE. The veil of the temple is rent!

ABIMILECH. Someone has blasphemed against the most high God!

BENJAMIN. Can it be that the blasphemy of Judas hath done this? *(He and Abimilech hurry off Right.)*

SAMUEL. Nay, not the blasphemy of Judas, but the sin of all who have betrayed and crucified this Man. *(Samuel has stepped to the curtain, Left rear, and looks off toward Calvary, Right, as he speaks. Then he seems to be listening as though faintly hearing the voice of Jesus that again drifts across the city from Calvary: "My God, my God! Why hast thou forsaken Me?" Fade in music softly as Abimilech and Benjamin go off. Keep it low until after the words of Jesus, then swell for the curtain.)*

CURTAIN

SCENE THREE

SCENE: *Same as Scene One.*

TIME: *Shortly after Scene Two.*

Again, the music should be heavy, gradually fading out as the curtain opens. The wind blows, but not so strongly as in Scene One. The noise of the crowd is heard only occasionally, and then "thinner" than before.

Thomas, Peter, Matthew and James enter at Right. They are deeply moved by what has transpired—bewildered, heavy-hearted. Every word they speak shows this.

THOMAS. The wind is dying down.

PETER. Yea, but it is still dark.

MATTHEW. Will there ever again be light? *(He drops to a nearby rock.)*

PETER. *He* said, "I am the light of the world."

JAMES. He said many things that seemed of God when He spoke them.

THOMAS. And we believed when he said there would be peace, and the kingdom. Peace! There is more turmoil in my soul than I have ever known before. *(He sits on a rock at Left.)*

MATTHEW. When He bade me leave the seat of custom and follow Him, I rejoiced. I believed that I had found greater wealth than the gold and silver that came to me as my share of the tax money.

PETER *(He paces restlessly to and fro.)* "It is easier for a camel to go through the eye of a needle . . ."

MATTHEW. ". . . than for a rich man to enter the kingdom of heaven." I know. I remember. I have never regretted my decision to leave all and follow Him . . . but to what end . . . now? *(He sinks to a rock at Left Center.)*

JAMES. At least John and I can return to the nets of our father Zebedee.

THOMAS. And I to my old life, forever to wonder, wanting to believe, yet torn by doubts and questionings.

MATTHEW. These we all have . . . this day. Yet . . . I think He would understand.

PETER. Perhaps. But He never could understand how I . . . I, Peter, who loved Him . . . denied Him, not once, but thrice . . . O Jesus, Son of the Living God! . . . I cannot understand myself!

JAMES. Have we not all denied Him in leaving Him? He hangs yonder on Calvary; we crouch here in the shadows, afraid.

THOMAS. But what could we have done? The crowd would have turned on us, yea, crucified us with Him.

MATTHEW. To die with Jesus might have been better than to live without Him, knowing we have forsaken Him.

PETER. Denied Him!

MATTHEW. At least we did not betray Him, as did Judas.

PETER. And which is the greater sin, betrayal or denial?

THOMAS. What madness possessed Judas? True, for many days, yea for weeks, he hath acted strangely at times. But who could believe that he would betray the Master?

JAMES. Jesus knew. Dost thou not recall last evening as we sat together at the Passover He warned that one should betray Him?

MATTHEW. And Judas left at once! How blind we were!

PETER. Yea, blind and stupid! If only I had known then, I . . . (He hesitates.)

JAMES. What wouldst thou have done, Peter?

PETER. I know not. God forgive me! For when I might have done something, even speak a word for Him, I . . . I denied Him!

THOMAS. Together we must share the blame, the guilt. Our silence, thy denial, Judas' betrayal—only God can say whether one sin is greater than the other.

MATTHEW. Only God can bring back our lost faith, our lost hope, our lost Christ. For now the hopes of Israel are laid in the dust.

PETER. Could it be that the hope, the faith of the world will be built on . . . on what has happened this day?

THOMAS. Faith? Hope? On what? A shattered kingdom? A vain and vanished dream? On a crucified Christ? *(There is wind and distant thunder. Then, from Calvary— "It is finished." The disciples are unaware of the voice.)*

PETER. How many times have the hopes and dreams of men been born again from ruins and ashes?

JAMES. How often hath the Son of God come into the world to show men the way to build God's kingdom on earth? *(His tone says, "Never.")*

PETER. I wonder—how many times? *(Judas has entered at Right, unseen by the others.)*

JUDAS *(Distraught and broken.)* I thought I might find thee here—some at least . . . in darkness . . . in fear . . . in doubt.

JAMES *(Rising.)* We want nothing to do with thee, Judas. Begone!

JUDAS. Here beneath the brow of this hill I can look across to Calvary and see Him.

THOMAS. And gloat over his agony, perhaps?

MATTHEW *(Rising.)* How tastes the kiss upon His cheek, traitor?

PETER. Had I my sword I would gladly use it to pierce thy traitorous heart!

JUDAS. Pity, I beg! Pity! Yea, I . . . I betrayed Him, I cannot deny my guilt. But I did not believe He would allow the Roman dogs to crucify Him! I thought . . .

PETER. Thy thoughts were of thyself! Scheming, plotting, even as He sat with us in the upper room.

JUDAS. Nay, I tell thee! I never denied Him!

PETER *(Though Judas' remark was not deliberate, it strikes home.)* O God, I denied Him!

JUDAS. It was not for the thirty pieces of silver that I led them . . .

MATTHEW. Then they did pay thee a price! The price of a slave's ransom! Thirty pieces of silver for that kiss in the garden!

JUDAS. O Jesus, Master, forgive!

THOMAS. Let us leave the traitor to beg forgiveness. Perhaps God can listen to the babbling prayers of a Judas, but not I. *(Exits at Left.)*

MATTHEW. Nor I. Thirty pieces of silver! *(Exits at Left.)*

JAMES. Pray for thy soul, Judas, for it is doomed to everlasting hell. Men will forever despise thee, and God will cast thee out. *(Exits at left, carefully avoiding, as have the others, contact with Judas who crouches on the rocks.)*

PETER *(Half to himself.)* Denial ... betrayal; betrayal ... denial! God forgive *me!* Master, forgive! *(Exits at Left. He does not deliberately avoid Judas. Fade in music softly for background.)*

JUDAS. Forgiveness! What hope of forgiveness can there be for me, Judas, betrayer of the Son of God? *(He stumbles to his feet and looks across to Calvary.)* There He hangs on a cross on Calvary for all to see against the darkened sky. Why does He not show His power? ... Jesus! Master! Lazarus came forth from the grave at Thy bidding ... Save Thyself! ... Come down! Come down from the cross! Come down! ... *(Sobbing, he sinks to the ground. There is a faint rumble of thunder and as it passes the last words of Jesus come across the hills: "Father, into Thy hands I commend my spirit.")*

JUDAS *(Calmer.)* Nay, there is no hope ... He will not come down from the cross ... He dies ... I, Judas Iscariot, betrayed Him into the hands of His enemies ... and they crucified Him ... As long as men remember Jesus of Nazareth, my name will be despised ... For me there is no forgiveness, no redemption ... only death. *(He has risen, and taking the cord from around his waist he loops it over his hand significantly, but not too pointedly, e.g. no noose, as he continues.)* He dies to live forever in the hearts of men. I die that men, even as they curse my name, may know the fate of him who betrayed his Christ. *(Slowly he turns and goes up the hill at Left, and off as the music swells.)*

* *(The wind increases, the darkness deepens, there is thunder and lightning. Do not overdo this, but strive to convey the impression of Judas' hanging. Through all the noise of the elements the music is heard, gradually building up to a*

final crashing crescendo—then three or four seconds of absolute silence. Then the music again, very soft.

From offstage, Right, high up as though shining from Calvary—or heaven—shines a soft radiance. Then from offstage, Left, and from high up as though coming from the hilltop, is heard the voice of Judas . . .)

JUDAS *(As though in greeting.)* Jesus! Master! *(Then with the deepest of humility and the greatest of hope.)* Thou once said, "Ask what ye will and it shall be done unto you." . . . O my Master! . . . Forgive! Forgive!

THE VOICE OF JESUS *(From where the radiance shines at Right.)* He that cometh to Me shall in no wise be cast out. Judas, Judas, I forgive. Come unto Me, and ye shall find rest unto your soul. *(The radiance, Right, increases as the music swells slightly for a slow curtain.)*

Continue the music softly for a few seconds before the house lights go on, and perhaps after.

It is suggested that nothing follow the final curtain unless it be a simple benediction.

* If there is objection to the voice of Jesus answering Judas, the following alternative is suggested:

After Judas has made his exit, Peter re-enters at Left. Keep the music soft until after he finishes speaking.

PETER *(Speaking as he comes on.)* I cannot go with them yet. Perhaps even now I can do something to earn the forgiveness of my Lord. *(He looks toward Calvary.)* Darkness settles over Calvary, over the world, over my soul. *(The music swells, the thunder rumbles, the lightning plays as Peter draws his cloak about him, half in wonder, half in fear. Then comes the voice of Judas. For a moment Peter is startled, then he understands.)*

JUDAS *(As though in greeting.)* Jesus! Master! *(Then with the deepest humility and the greatest of hope.)* Thou once said, Ask and it shall be done unto you . . . O, my Master, I ask . . . I ask Thee to forgive! Jesus forgive me!

PETER *(With feeling.)* Judas! Judas! Hast thou forgotten —"He forgiveth all our iniquities"? And his words: "Come unto Me and ye shall find rest, peace, unto your soul."? *(The radiance at Right increases as the music swells slightly for a slow curtain.)*

CURTAIN

I SAW THE CROSS

DRAMA OF THE FIRST EASTER

By

JEAN M. MATTSON

PRODUCTION RIGHTS

Copies of this play are available in single pamphlet form. The right to produce this play by one group of amateur players is authorized only by the purchase of ten copies (one copy for each speaking part) at the current price of 50c each.

It is dishonest and illegal to copy parts.

CAST OF CHARACTERS

(For 5 women, 17 men, extras)

NARRATOR (May be a woman)
JUDAS
CAIAPHAS
PRIEST I
PRIEST II
SERVANT OF CAIAPHAS
PETER
GUARD I
GUARD II
GUARD III
GUARD IV
MAID I
MAID II
PILATE
PRIEST I (First 2 may be re-used)
PRIEST II
SERVANT OF PILATE
MOB (Voices offstage)
SIMON OF CYRENE
JESUS
LONGINUS
SOLDIER I (Guards may be re-used)
SOLDIER II
SOLDIER III
(The SERVANT OF CARAPHAS and the SERVANT OF PILATE could be played by women.)

PLAYING TIME: About thirty minutes.

SYNOPSIS OF SCENES

SCENE ONE: Palace of the High Priest, Caiaphas.
SCENE TWO: The courtyard outside the palace.
SCENE THREE: Pilate's office.
SCENE FOUR: The road to Calvary.
SCENE FIVE: The barracks.

I SAW THE CROSS

(The Narrator should read his continuity at one side of the stage or platform while the principal character who introduces each scene should appear on the opposite side. Of course, it will be more effective if the Narrator and the principal character were spotlighted in turn.)

NARRATOR *(Speaks.)* Now that centuries have passed since the time of Christ, can we imagine the three ugly, blood-stained crosses which once stood on Golgotha? The followers of Christ who were in Jerusalem at the time of the Crucifixion found it easy to understand the horror of those crosses. They may have only caught a glimpse of Him as they were jostled by the screaming mobs. Or perhaps they crouched at the foot of the cross and endured the insults of the soldiers in order to be near their Christ. But they surely knew what the Crucifixion meant.

And they had only to take a little walk down to "Joseph's lovely garden" and view the empty, rock-hewn tomb to be assured, to know that Easter means "He is risen."

It is hard for us, perhaps, to think of these things as really happening when we were not there. But we should try. Easter is the most important day of our church year, and we should try to make these events real and close to us. The glory of the Resurrection should not be blurred by the years between.

The best way to see the whole drama is to use the eyes of those who *were* there and who *did* take part in Christ's destiny. Seeing through their eyes and understanding more clearly what took place may teach us new lessons and help us to live our lives more fully and more completely Christian in this century.

JUDAS *(Entering from the opposite side and speaking in an informal, conversational way.)* I am Judas. Oh, I know what you think of me. I'm the man who betrayed the Saviour of the world. How can I forget it? How can I forget the wonderful days I spent with Him, listening and learning.

(Pauses a moment.) How can I forget the look on His face after I kissed Him in the garden and He said, "Friend, why are you here?"

I wonder the same thing myself. "Why was I there? *(Desperately.)* Why was I there?" It looks as if it were the thirty pieces of silver which led me to betray my Master. But what a paltry payment for such a dastardly deed!

(More softly.) I try to figure it out sometimes. I guess I didn't really think that Jesus would let Himself be crucified. After all, He was the Son of God. He could have saved Himself, couldn't He?

I remember hearing the crowd yelling that. "Son of God, save yourself now!" They taunted Him with it at the trial, on the way to Calvary, and on the cross. But He didn't save Himself. He died there on the cross.

I thought that He had died forever, and I didn't want to go on living myself. Perhaps if I had been there on Easter morning, my sin would have seemed less wicked, and I would have been comforted.

I know that Jesus died *because of* me, and my only hope is that He also died *for* me.

SCENE ONE

(Curtain Opens)

SCENE: *Palace of the high priest, Caiaphas. Caiaphas and the priests are seated around a table.*

CAIAPHAS. We must do something about that Jesus of Nazareth. *(Strikes the table with his fist and springs to his feet.)* He's upsetting the whole country with His wild talk. There's no telling what will happen if He is allowed to continue His ridiculous preaching.

PRIEST I. And they flock to hear Him. There was a regular migration over to Gennesaret the other day when word got around that He would be there.

CAIAPHAS. They're all taken in with this talk of love and so on. They're actually beginning to follow this religious fanatic instead of the true Jewish religion.

PRIEST II. I'd hate to try to do anything to Him in front

of all those people who are always swarming around. Why, we'd have a riot on our hands.

CAIAPHAS. Exactly. We must do it in secret, before they realize what has happened.

PRIEST I. But how? We don't know where He'll be when we act.

CAIAPHAS. That's the problem. And we have to figure it out. *(Servant enters.)* Well, what do you want? *(Annoyed.)*

SERVANT. A man by the name of Judas Iscariot is outside to see you.

CAIAPHAS. Judas Iscariot? I don't know any Judas. Tell him to go away.

PRIEST I. Wait a minute. Isn't that one of the men who keeps going around with Jesus? Sure it is. There are twelve of them. And he's one, I know it.

CAIAPHAS. Is that right? *(Craftily.)* I wonder what his errand can be. Send him in. *(Servant exits.)* Perhaps this is just what we've been waiting for. *(Servant admits Judas.)* Judas Iscariot, eh? One of the twelve?

JUDAS. I am one of them, yes. *(Uneasily.)*

CAIAPHAS. And what brings you to the palace of the high priest? Surely it's not a friendly call. *(Sarcastically.)*

JUDAS. I understand you are after Jesus of Nazareth.

CAIAPHAS. That's putting it mildly, yes.

JUDAS. Perhaps I am in a position to help you.

CAIAPHAS. And no doubt, we are in a position to help you. Will thirty pieces of silver do it?

JUDAS. Yes, yes.

PRIEST II. What we should do is to take him quietly with no fighting or noise.

CAIAPHAS. Do you have any suggestions?

JUDAS. Jesus and His disciples are planning to go to the Garden of Gethsemane tonight.

PRIEST I. Alone? Just He and the twelve.

JUDAS. Yes, just He and the *eleven*. He intends to commune with God. If you wish, I will lead you to the place.

CAIAPHAS. Oh, this will work out remarkably. *(Chuckles.)*

PRIEST I. But how will we know which one He is?

JUDAS. I will show you. I will kiss the Master.

CAIAPHAS. Oh, that's even better. Betrayed with a kiss. What perfect irony! We will take you up on your plan. *(To the priests.)* Round up a band of soldiers to meet at the gate at sundown.

PRIEST II. We won't need many. I hear this fellow is set against violence.

JUDAS *(Quickly.)* Yes, but it would be better to be prepared. There are a couple of disciples who may not share His ideas. And *(Pause.)* I want to be sure of protection.

CAIAPHAS. Very well. See that there is a company of soldiers—*(Smiles at Judas.)*—well-armed. See that there are torches and lanterns ready. *(They leave to do his bidding.)* Oh, this is working out perfectly. *(All exit, leaving Caiaphas rubbing his hands together gleefully.)*

(CURTAIN)

NARRATOR *(The spotlight is centered on him.)* To betray means to violate a trust. We may not be responsible for nailing Christ to a cross. But are we guiltless? We play the role of betrayer in a thousand treacheries. We are entrusted with our lives and the lives of others. We are entrusted with God's world and the plants and creatures in it. Listen now. *(Pause.)* Don't you hear the faint hollow clinking of thirty pieces of silver?

PETER *(Enters from the opposite side of the stage, as the spotlight is thrown on him.)* I am Peter. I was a fisherman on the Sea of Galilee until Jesus came along. "Follow me," He said, "and I will make you fishers of men." And I followed Him, and it changed my whole life. I lived near the Master as He taught, preached and healed. *(Pause.)* I was with Him when the temple police came to the Garden of Gethsemane to take Him away.

I couldn't bear to see them take Jesus, so I grabbed my sword and cut off the ear of one of the high priest's servants. And how well I remember how Jesus healed the ear saying to me, "Put your sword back in its place. For all who take the sword will perish by the sword." So I put my sword away and watched them take Jesus—to His crucifixion and death.

I have never been so happy as I was on that Easter morning when I ran to the tomb to find the stone rolled away and knew that Jesus had risen from the dead.

Yet, whenever I think of Holy Week, I am ashamed, because I was not true to my Lord. At supper the night He was taken, He told me I would deny Him. He warned me that before the cock crew I would deny Him three times. I told Him I never would. I really believed that I could never deny someone I loved so much. But I did.

I wish I couldn't remember it. I followed the temple police that night when they took Jesus to the palace of Caiaphas. In the courtyard of the palace there were a lot of guards and soldiers, sitting around the fire eating and talking. A maid from the palace was bringing them food. I wanted to find out what was happening to Jesus if I could, so I went on in and warmed myself by the fire.

SCENE TWO

SCENE: *The courtyard outside the palace of Caiaphas.*

GUARD I. And He came willingly enough. There wasn't any fighting or clashing of swords.

GUARD II. Except that one of His friends cut off the ear of one of the men working here at the palace.

GUARD I. Yes, but Jesus healed it right back in place and made it plain He didn't want that to happen again.

GUARD III. I can't figure the man out. He surely knows that Caiaphas means business.

MAID I. That bunch is unpredictable. *(Looks at Peter.)* Say, aren't you one of the men who was with Jesus, the Galilean?

PETER *(Disturbed.)* I don't know what you mean? *(Maid shrugs her shoulders.)*

MAID *(To the soldiers.)* Have some more bread. There's plenty in the kitchen. Help yourselves. *(Offers Peter some and looks at him curiously. He accepts.)*

PETER. Where is this Jesus now?

GUARD II. He's inside, *(Gestures.)* with the scribes and elders. They are trying to get the goods on Him. And with that whole council in there and all the witnesses they've rounded up, it shouldn't take long.

PETER. What can they accuse Him of?

GUARD II. I don't know, but they'll find something. *(Peter moves to the door.)*

MAID II *(Just entering, looks at Peter, then speaks to the soldiers.)* This man was with Jesus of Nazareth, if I'm not mistaken.

PETER. I don't even know this man. Mind your own business. *(Angrily.)*

MAID II. Well, pardon me. *(Swings off. Guard IV enters.)*

GUARD IV. They've got Him now.

GUARD II. What do you mean? What's going on in there?

GUARD IV. They just made Him admit He's the Son of God, the worst kind of blasphemy He could make. He'll deserve death for that.

GUARD I. Yes, imagine anyone having the nerve to say a thing like that.

PETER. He had nerve perhaps, but it takes more than that for a man to say such a thing.

GUARD IV. Why you're a Galilean, aren't you? I can tell by your accent. You must be one of the disciples.

PETER. I don't know what you're talking about. *(Cock crows.)*

GUARD III. The cocks are crowing. It's almost dawn.

GUARD I. What a long night this turned out to be. *(Guards begin to gather their things together.)*

PETER. Yes, the cocks are crowing. *(Stands abashed as realization comes. Then covers his face with his arm and rushes out.)*

CURTAIN

NARRATOR. Yes, Peter denied his Lord. But is Peter any worse than we? We have to face neither armed soldiers or malicious high priests. Yet we deny Him every day. We deny Him when we refuse to do the things we know are Christian, when we don't go to church, when we are angry, when we lie and are selfish. We hurt only ourselves and will suffer as Peter suffered.

Our lives should be lived so that when people observe our actions and hear us talk, they can say, "You were with Him too. I can tell by your accent." For that is the greatest compliment of all.

PILATE *(On the opposite side of the stage or platform.)* I am Pilate, Governor of Judea during the time of Christ's trial. It was the high priest Caiaphas who was determined to kill Jesus. I didn't really want to do it. I didn't know what to do. I was between two fires.

If I didn't have Jesus killed there would be riots and trouble. If Rome heard that I was allowing riots and unrest —and Caiaphas and the rest of the Jews would make sure that Rome did hear—I might lose my position. I had only been governor three years and hated to leave in disgrace.

Then on the other hand, I'd heard of all the things this man could do. And although I believed in the Roman gods, I couldn't help but believe that this Jesus was rather remarkable, that there must be some kind of power behind Him. I was almost afraid to do anything against Him. I finally sent Him to Herod, but he only sent Him back to me.

Then my wife showed how she felt about the matter, and I was even more confused. My wife is a very intelligent woman and not given to small talk. I couldn't help but listen to her.

What should I do?

SCENE THREE

SCENE: *Pilate's office. He sits pondering. Servant enters with a tablet.*

PILATE. Eh, what's this?

SERVANT. A message from your wife, Governor Pilate. *(Servant exits.)*

PILATE *(Reading.)* Have nothing to do with that righteous man. I have suffered much over Him today in a dream. *(Pilate shakes his head and sighs. Priests I and II enter.)*

PRIEST I. Come, what is your decision, Pilate?

PILATE *(Makes a futile gesture.)* I can find nothing wrong with Him.

PRIEST I. But we have found Him perverting our nation, forbidding us to pay tribute to Caesar, and saying that He Himself is King.

PILATE. I cannot find Him guilty as you charge. And neither can Herod. He sent Him back to me right away.

PRIEST II. He calls Himself the Son of God. For that alone He deserves death.

PRIEST I. If this man hadn't done anything wrong, we wouldn't have given Him to you. He's disrupting the whole country.

PRIEST II. He calls Himself the King of the Jews. And anyone who says he's king is no friend of Caesar's. Caesar would not like that.

PILATE. But He says that His kingdom is not of this world. If it were, He would be fighting for it now. I just can't see that He deserves death. I am going to chastise Him and release Him. *(With sudden determination.)*

PRIEST I. Release Him? Do you know what kind of a riot that will cause? They are milling outside now.

PILATE *(Confused.)* I shall ask them. We shall see. *(Goes to the window.)* My people, I have found no crime in this man, Jesus. There is a custom on the Passover that a prisoner be released. Shall I then release to you the King of the Jews or Barabbas?

MOB. Release Barabbas!

PILATE *(Surprised.)* But Barabbas is a rebel who has committed murder.

MOB. We want Barabbas!

PILATE. What evil has this Jesus done? I should release Him . . .

MOB. Release Barabbas!

PILATE. What, then, should I do with this man you call King of the Jews?

MOB. Crucify Him!

PILATE. Even if He is innocent? Shall I crucify your king?

MOB. Crucify Him! We have no king but Caesar.

PILATE *(Closing the window and turning.)* Very well. Take Him yourselves and crucify Him. But I want to wash my hands of the whole affair. I am innocent of the blood of this righteous man. *(Washes his hands.)* Deliver this man Jesus to be scourged. *(When they do not move he waves them away.)* See to it yourselves. *(Priests exit happily, leaving Pilate with his head in his hands.)*

CURTAIN

NARRATOR. How many times do we do the very same thing? "How does that concern us," we say. "What could we do anyway?" "It's not my affair." As Christians some of these affairs should bother us, should prick our consciences, should stir us to action. To be Christian is not a passive thing. We should commemorate Christ and His cross by reaching out whenever the opportunity is ours to show that to be a Christian is a matter not only of being but also of doing.

SIMON OF CYRENE *(On the opposite side of the stage or platform.)* I am Simon of Cyrene. I just happened to be walking through the streets of Jerusalem when the procession to Calvary was passing. I was coming in from the country and heard the noise. I saw the excited mob, the flashing armor of the guards, the tears of sorrow and the looks of hatred. From the conversations and shouts, I gathered what had taken place. A blasphemer was to be put to death.

I tried to get a bit closer and before I knew it, the soldiers were yelling at me to carry the cross. And there, before me, was the drooping figure of the man who claimed to be God.

He had fallen on the street, too beaten and weak to continue the long steep climb to Golgotha. The soldiers *forced* me to carry the cross that day, but as I watched this poor man stumbling ahead of me, I was glad they had. There was something glorious about Him, even in His degradation. He turned and comforted the wailing women. His words were gentle and His eyes were kind. The few phrases of thanks He haltingly spoke to me, I shall remember always.

Before we reached the place of the crucifixion, I felt inside of me, I knew, that I had actually carried the cross for the Son of God. I shall treasure my experience forever, knowing that perhaps I did something for my Lord.

SCENE FOUR

SCENE: *The road to Calvary. Christ, drooping but brilliantly lighted, with Simon the Cyrene in the shadows carrying the cross. The tableau held briefly while soft music is played in the background.*

CURTAIN

NARRATOR. Simon of Cyrene carried the cross when Jesus' broken body could no longer support the heavy beams of wood. He did what Jesus was not then able to do. And today, Christ is not here in the flesh to do things for Himself. We who have strong bodies must fill in for Him, must manage the jobs which He cannot do. We must learn to notice the situations which Christ would change were He walking with us, and try to do as He would do.

Do we really believe Paul when he says, "We are the body of Christ"? Are we ready to bear our crosses willingly for Him?

LONGINUS *(On the opposite side of the stage or platform.)* I am Longinus, the Roman centurian who stood guard under the cross on which Jesus was crucified. Until I got that assignment, I really didn't know what all this talk about the King of the Jews was all about. I was in the occupational army there, had only been in a few years, and didn't pay too much attention to the people of Palestine and their religions. I'm a Roman and had my own gods.

From what I could gather though, this man, Jesus, certainly was no criminal and didn't deserve that horrible death. Nevertheless, I helped nail Him to the cross, helped drive those big spikes into His hands and feet. You know, He didn't yell and scream and curse like most of them do. He didn't resist at all. I'd crucified a lot of people, but for the first time in my career, I was a little ashamed of my job. *(Pause.)*

I was on duty when He died, only nine hours after He was crucified. When I heard Him say His last words, "Father, into thy hands I commend my spirit," I somehow knew that there, hanging on the cross, was the Son of God

422

Himself. And when the sky became dark and the earth rumbled I felt that it was God's answer to the cruel treatment of His Son.

I wanted to know more about this man. And in the barracks several days later I found out the rest of what happened to Jesus of Nazareth.

SCENE FIVE

SCENE: *The barracks. The soldiers are polishing their armor. Soldier I enters.*

SOLDIER I. I just left the council of high priests and elders. We've got our orders.

SOLDIERS. What did they say? *(Ad lib, etc.)*

SOLDIER I. We're supposed to go around and spread the word that those disciples of His came to the tomb at night and stole the body when we were asleep.

SOLDIER II. Hey, listen. I don't like that story. I never sleep on duty. I don't want that going around.

SOLDIER I. You'd rather have them hear that, than the story that a certain Roman soldier—namely you—*(Points to him.)* was sent back to Rome in irons, wouldn't you?

SOLDIER II. Well, yes. But now wait a minute. What's Pilate going to think about our going to sleep? He could put us in irons too, you know.

SOLDIER I. They said they'd fix it up with Pilate, if we got into any trouble about the tomb being open. And they sent along this bag of gold for our trouble.

SOLDIER II. Well, that's different. Why didn't you say so?

SOLDIER III. What difference does it make anyway?

SOLDIER I. The high priests don't want the people getting the idea that Jesus rose from the dead like He said He would.

LONGINUS. Well, did He?

SOLDIER I. I don't know. *(Evasively.)*

LONGINUS. What did happen at the tomb?

SOLDIER I. I don't know. *(Emphatically and then a pause.)* But it was something peculiar.

LONGINUS. Tell us about it.

SOLDIER I. Well, we were stationed in front of the tomb

right by the stone. It was almost light when we heard some women coming down the road.

SOLDIER II. We didn't pay much attention to them because we knew they couldn't roll the stone away by themselves and take the body.

SOLDIER I. Then all at once there was a blinding flash of light, and the stone rolled back, and we seemed to make out a figure standing there.

SOLDIER III. What did you do then?

SOLDIER I. Nothing. We were scared to death. At least I was. *(Looks at Soldier II.)*

SOLDIER II. And so were the women. But whatever, or whoever it was, said to them—let's see, what was it now? *(Thinks.)* "Do not be afraid, for I know that you seek Jesus who was crucified. He is not here for He is risen. Come and see where He lay." *(Speaks as if remembering.)*

SOLDIER I. And I could see that the tomb was empty and the grave clothes were lying inside.

SOLDIER II. And we didn't wait to hear any more. We left in a hurry.

LONGINUS. Do you really think He came back to life?

SOLDIER I. I don't know what to think. *(Begins to polish furiously.)*

SOLDIER III. Are you sure He was in there to begin with?

SOLDIER II. I was right with this Joseph of Arimathea when he took the body to the tomb. And I watched the women annoint it and dress it.

SOLDIER I. And we both helped seal it. Oh, He was in there all right. Of course, *(Pause.)* He may not have been dead. I suppose that could . . .

LONGINUS. Yes, He was dead. I watched Him die. I was there when they took Him off the cross. You know, I hated to see Him die. I think I'd be glad to know He did rise again.

SOLDIER I. Why this sudden change of attitude? You were getting just as big a laugh as the rest of us when we dressed Him up and crowned Him King of the Jews.

LONGINUS. I know. But after I watched Him on the cross, it all seemed different. I read the sign Pilate had nailed above Him and wondered. "This is the King of the Jews."

SOLDIER III. Well, for being a king He sure wasn't dressed for it. Those clothes of His that I won in the dice game aren't worth a talent. The first time I've won in months too.

LONGINUS. I don't understand the whole thing either. But there must be more to it than we think. One thing I know is, that Jesus of Nazareth was no fool. The priests have been after Him for a long while. And He's outwitted them time after time. I've heard Him myself.

SOLDIER III. Well, they finally got Him for blaspheming.

SOLDIER I. Yes, no man can say He's the Son of God and get away with it.

LONGINUS. No. Unless it's true! *(All look startled.)*

CURTAIN

NARRATOR. Longinus recognized the spirit of God shining through the cross. He saw something divine in the person of Jesus. Can we traverse the years and stand beside that Roman soldier to recognize in Jesus the Son of God, the Saviour of the World?

These people of the passion story were ordinary men and women like you and me. They responded to the Christ who walked among them. And today, are we any different? Likewise we also feel and experience the guilt of the betrayer, Judas; the sorrow and joy of Peter, His disciple; the heavy burden of the visitor from Cyrene; the indifference of Pilate; and the bewilderment and wonder of the Roman soldier. We feel these things because Jesus Christ is alive and with us now. We know. We are sure. That is what the Resurrection means. That is Easter!

NOTE: *This presentation will prove more effective if music is used before and after the various monologues and the speeches of the Narrator.*

PRODUCTION NOTES

SETTINGS:

The settings need not be extravagant. In Scenes I, III, and V, there need be only a few pieces of simple furniture —a table, a chair and a bench or two. In Scenes I and III, the homes of the high priests and Pilate, a few gold and silver vases, pitchers or other ornaments may be used to indicate luxury. And perhaps a rich tapestry or drapery could be thrown over a table or chair. In Scene V, the quarters of the soldiers, perhaps a shield and crossed lances or swords could be hung on the wall.

Pilate's home, of course, will need a window or a door supposedly leading to a balcony.

Scene IV needs no setting. A few people could be placed in the shadows indicating the crowd in the streets.

Scene II is in the courtyard. There should be an open fire in the center of the stage with logs or benches placed around it. On one side there may be a gate in the wall which surrounds the courtyard.

COSTUMES:

For the most part, a loose flowing type of costume may be used—a simple tunic as a foundation with a cape or shawl draped about the body and perhaps caught up on one shoulder. On the feet simple sandals should be worn.

Pilate and the high priests should wear richer-looking material, perhaps fringed with gold. Pilate, a Roman, might wear a band about his forehead. The high priests may wear a headdress which could be made out of cardboard, gilded and decorated.

The maids in Scene II may wear a belt or cord around their waists and perhaps some jewelry.

The soldiers and guards wear knee-length tunics with armor and a cape. The armor and helmet may be made by covering pieces of cardboard with aluminum foil.

MUSIC:

1. "The Message of the Cross" by F. Sheldon Scott and published by Willis Music Company has some very appropriate music in it. The introduction especially could be used as a theme throughout, ending either with the hymn or the aria from Handel's "Messiah," "I Know That My Redeemer Liveth."

2. Parts from Bach's "Passion According to St. Matthew"

could be used ending with Handel's "I Know That My Redeemer Liveth."

3. Then, the following group of hymns could be used. Aside from the beginning and the ending, the hymn for each part can be played softly after the lead character has given his monologue and after the scene. Then it can be played loudly or even sung after the narrator's comment on the scene.

Introduction—"There Is A Green Hill Far Away"

Judas—"Go to Dark Gethsemane"

Pilate—"More Love To Thee, Oh, Christ"

Simon—"I Gave My Life For Thee, What Hast Thou Done For Me?"

Longinus—"Beautiful Savior"

Closing—"I Know That My Redeemer Liveth"

THE LIGHT OF THE WORLD

(Lux et Tenebrae)

A DRAMA OF CHRIST'S PASSION
IN NINE SCENES

By

BROTHER FINIAN, F.M.S.

CAST OF CHARACTERS

(Seventeen Men and Extras)

RUBINUS......................the unrepentant thief

BARABBAS....................a political opportunist

DISMAS.........................the repentant thief

PILATE......................the Roman Procurator

ANNAS....the former High Priest, Caiphas' father-in-law

CAIPHAS............................the High Priest

JESUS................................. the Christ

JOSEPH....................a rich man of Aramathea

JUDAS..................................the traitor

ABEL

NATHANIEL }..............servants at the court of Pilate

JAMES

BENJAMIN......................a servant of Caiphas

THREE PRIESTS OF THE TEMPLE

THE CAPTAIN OF THE GUARD

SOLDIERS AND SERVANTS

VOICES OF THE CROWD

In this play, "THE LIGHT OF THE WORLD" (*Lux et Tenebrae*), there is the portrayal of light and darkness in the souls of men. It is the stroke of the Great Artist's brush depicting the brilliancy of grace and the shadows of guilt, the gleaming of hope and the gloom of despair. It is like the somber interior of a tree-packed forest where slivers of sunlight cut through the towering pines and lie in bright patches on the needled floor. And then, all the "Tenebrae" is dissolved and only the "Lux" remains, in the splendid glory of the Risen Savior. . .

THE LIGHT OF THE WORLD

SCENE ONE

SCENE: *The scene is a dank, dark prison cell in the Fortress Antonia where three bodies are chained to posts: Rubinus, Barabbas, Dismas. All appear to be slumbering uneasily. Open with a portion of the Gregorian Lamentations or Were You There When They Crucified Our Lord? With the voice of Rubinus the music subsides, recurring at the scene's end.*

RUBINUS. The end of an empire! Hear me, Barabbas, it is the end of your empire and the king, the christ, Barabbas, is rotting in a cell for want of subjects. Most kings rot in spite of their subjects; Barabbas rots for the want of subjects.

BARABBAS. Be still, you son of the devil, you loose-tongued, traitor-hearted, self-righteous scum of the unholy earth. Be still and listen or I shall yet see you sorry for your words. Pilate fails to release me, yes! But I shall live to see him sorry for his silence and you, my friend, sorry for your lack of it. I walked in Galilee and was a leader; indeed, a king. The Galileans cheered me — I was the king.

DISMAS. You *were* the king.

BARABBAS. I *am* the king. Shall they forget? Shall my people forget their leader? I alone hold the power to give them freedom from Rome. I alone have the force necessary to drive the foreigner from the city gates; yes, to see all Jerusalem free. The people know me; they want me to lead them. I am Barabbas, Barabbas the Christ!

RUBINUS. Then hail, O King, who sets his people free. See the freedom you have given me. *(He holds up his chains.)*

DISMAS. It is indeed a strange freedom we have gained. I am afraid, O King, that you are at best an actor. If you are a successful actor it is because you allow no critic but yourself. You are a strange king — what should we have sought but a strange freedom. We, your subjects . . .

BARABBAS. You, my subjects. What subjects! When I led the mob in the market place, you were with me; when I spoke in the streets with words of iron-clad force, you were my subjects. Yes, ave Christ, ave Barabbas. But let a defeat come, let the jealous Sadducees plot my ruin and then see them turn on their King of a moment ago. If I am not to deliver the people through my strength, who shall? Rubinus, who shall?

RUBINUS. Perhaps Jesus, the Nazarene. He is free. *(Rubinus and Barabbas laugh and mock.)*

DISMAS. We laugh and mock, yet . . .

RUBINUS. And yet, what?

DISMAS. And yet, I once heard Him speak. He called Himself, not a ruler but a Shepherd, and said something about a lost sheep that I never can forget, no matter what.

BARABBAS. Listen, Rubinus, is it any wonder the Sad-. ducees trapped me, when following close behind me all the time was a lost sheep? You fool, Dismas, you stumbling, weak-minded, jelly-hearted fool! Would you have that man, that self-styled prophet as a leader? I, too, have heard Him rave in public. Such words from the heart of a leader! He speaks of flowers of the fields, birds of the air, and service to God! Are these the words of a libera-tor? Are they fashioned to drive out Pilate? Do the words of dreamers out-weigh the argument of a fist?

DISMAS. Perhaps they do, Barabbas, when dreams come true.

RUBINUS. I agree with you on the issue of the Naz-arene, Barabbas, but in so doing I must call you a weak failure. The soft-spoken champion of love for hate walks freely while we rot in prison. He gains power while you lose all strength, even that of your own body. He has out-done you.

BARABBAS. Idiot! Do you not know that even now the Pharisees are plotting His arrest? There was one time He made a mistake! He attacked the Pharisees, and not as you say, with soft words. They will make Him pay. We shall see then if His people scream: "Hail, Christ."

Christ! If He is Christ, then let me be called the anti-Christ.

DISMAS. Be still! It sounds *(Sound of the mob without.)* like a mob without, at the court of Pilate.

RUBINUS. They *do* sound as if they approach the court of Pilate. What could it be?

BARABBAS. Think, you fools, think! There is to be released today one prisoner. Who shall they demand? Now, you idiots, my day begins. This is the birth of my true glory. They want me.

RUBINUS. No, it is not so. But, if it is — if it is so, Barabbas, will you liberate us?

BARABBAS. You, you traitors? May you decay and putrefy on this spot when I become King of the Jews. And may Jesus the Christ be made your servant in this prison on the day I start my rule. *Rule. Rule. Rule.* Soon shall I rule. Hear me, you Jews, hear your Ruler, King Barabbas, Anti-Christ the First!

CURTAIN

SCENE TWO

SCENE: *The scene is the courtyard of Pilate's palace. Pilate, Caiphas, Annas. Voices and shouts.*

PILATE. Citizens of the Empire, this morning you came to me as true subjects of Caesar to ask for a judgment, a judgment on one who is, like yourselves, a Jew. The charges are that He calls Himself a God and seeks to override the lawful authority of Rome. For the first charge, I have no concern. If a man calls himself your God, who but your God can call Him a liar? For the second charge, I have only contempt; having spoken to the Man, I find He claims no right which is Rome's. He says He is the King of that Kingdom which is in another world. He claims as His weapon, truth. Now, of what import is such a Kingdom; and, indeed, what is truth? But I am a man of experience and, as such, I am not over-confident of my own judgment. For, if experience teaches us nothing else, it teaches us that we make mistakes and that we often lose true judgment, since we do not even know what truth is. Therefore, I have learned to make appeal to others before placing a seal on my written word. Nor do I appeal to my friends alone, because good friends may be lost in disagreement, and bad friends are too cautious to disagree. So it was that I sent Jesus to the court of the visiting Herod, under the pretext that He was of Herod's jurisdiction. Yet, Herod, like myself, must have found no cause for punishment in this Man, for he sent Him back, as you have seen. Jesus the Christ is within my walls. This is the day of release. We find no guilt. Why do you ask for one who is marked with murder and revolt against authority? Why do you ask for Barabbas? I thought that if you could see this filthy criminal you would change your minds, and so I have sent for him. Guards, bring out Barabbas for all the citizens to see. Then they shall ask for Christ Jesus and we shall have peace.

ANNAS. Pilate, before the final decision is made, I feel that Caiphas, our High Priest, should have an opportunity to speak to the people.

PILATE. I will let him speak before Barabbas is brought forth. But I advise that his words be in keeping with the prudence of his past deeds.

ANNAS. He will speak from his heart.

PILATE. And that might prove a mistake. We should speak from intelligent conviction and not from the prejudice of sentiment.

ANNAS. You are a wise man, Pilate. May Caiphas speak now? (*Pilate nods consent and turns away. While Caiphas ascends, a messenger boy brings a letter to Pilate.*)

CAIPHAS. My chosen brothers, Pilate in his kindness, consents today to release one prisoner of the state. Two of those in prison stand out in your mind in such a way that the choice seems to be between them. One stands out because the people overwhelmingly desire his release. This alone would seem to indicate who shall be chosen. But let us weigh the case without reference to the dealings which led us into the necessity of such a choice. Let us look at Barabbas first. Here is a man who has always been desirous of a prosperous Jewish people under the leadership of Rome. As any leader might have done, he made a mistake. In a meeting of his loyal followers, he was carried away by the emotion of his just cause, and became the murderer of a hard, misunderstanding foe. Is he to be punished for misguided zeal, for one mistake?

CROWD. No! Release Barabbas!

CAIPHAS. Let us look at Jesus the Christ now. Here is a Man who calls Himself God, and — God forbid — may even believe it. His sins, His crimes, His trespasses against God and state are many. Are we to endure such insults, such mistakes, from One Who sets Himself up as a King and Leader of the Jewish nation?

CROWD. No! Crucify Him! (*Pilate looks angrily at Caiphas. Annas perceives the wrath of Pilate.*)

ANNAS. Well said, friends, crucify Him that all may see what becomes of these enemies of Pilate, Rome, and God.

PILATE (*To the two.*) You have said enough.

ANNAS. Indeed, Pilate, and enough has been said.

PILATE. Guards, bring forth Barabbas. (*Enter Barabbas and guards. Pilate goes inside his house.*)

BARABBAS. I knew you would want me back. I knew I would speak again to you all. What would I do without my people and what would my people do without me? I have always fought for you. I am going to continue. You know we have a just cause. You know what that cause is. Here I am, a savior of my people. Take your leader, and when he is free we shall go forward together into a grand tomorrow.

ANNAS. Let me hear you cheer and ask for your leader. (*Crowd cheers and shouts "Barabbas!" Re-enter Pilate.*)

PILATE. Guards, stay close to that rabble-rouser. Citizens, while the hero, the hero *in chains*, was yet speaking, I had Jesus brought to the pillar and scourged. (*Cheers.*) I saw him crowned with thorns and draped in purple robes, spit upon, and beaten. All this I enforced to satisfy His enemies' lust for revenge. It is my hope that when they gaze upon this pitifully beaten figure their burning envy will be quenched and the Man allowed His rightful freedom. Guards, bring into our view Jesus the Christ. *(Christ is led out onto the balcony and placed beside Barabbas.)* Behold the Man. *(When Christ appears He stands for a full two minutes, while "Vexilla Regis" or "Nearer, My God, to Thee" is heard sung offstage.)* Citizens, it is fitting that one should be released to you this day. Whom do you choose?

ANNAS. Barabbas!

CROWD. Barabbas! Give us Barabbas!

PILATE. And what shall I do with the King of the Jews?

ANNAS. Crucify Him!

CROWD. Crucify Him!

PILATE. My judgment is favorable towards Him. My wife writes, warning of His innocence. He has committed no crime. There is no cause for punishment. *(Pauses. Loudly, to the crowd.) Shall I crucify your King?*

CAIPHAS. We have no king but Caesar. Let this Man be crucified.

CROWD. Crucify Him! *(Pilate whispers to his messenger boy, who runs off.)*

PILATE. And what law shall I write down as having been broken?

CAIPHAS. We have a law that condemns to die those who call themselves "Son of God."

PILATE *(Turning towards the messenger who re-enters with a water bowl.)* Then, look to it yourselves. I wash my hands of the blood of this just Man.

VOICE. His blood be upon us . . .

ANOTHER. . . . and upon our children.

CAIPHAS. Guards, lead our would-be God down to the people. *(Guards lead off Jesus. Annas and Caiphas follow close behind. Pilate retires slowly, his boy following. The sound of the voices reaches its peak after a moment and then dies away. Barabbas is alone and all is quiet.)*

BARABBAS. Come back, someone, come back and free my hands. I shall lead you, my people. Come and hear your king speak. *(Softly.)* How soon to forget a leader. But they shall learn, and I shall be their teacher.

CURTAIN

SCENE THREE

SCENE: *The court of the High Priest. A long table surrounded by priests. At the head of the table is Caiphas; next to him is Annas. Joseph of Aramathea is present.*

CAIPHAS. That, then, is the full report. We have acted wisely and we are rid of Jesus, the self-styled King of our race. Are there any questions?

ANNAS. Caiphas, I would only suggest that we avoid over-confidence in the matter. We have only this hour left the mob with the three offenders of the law. The Nazarene is not yet dead and His past deeds would seem to indicate that . . .

JOSEPH. . . . that He is not subject to the laws of nature, nor of men. Is that it, Annas?

CAIPHAS. Joseph, your opposition to the action of this court was tolerable in its place. But, the deed having been done, all bitterness must be avoided.

JOSEPH. It is good to defend justice, even in the past tense.

CAIPHAS. Annas meant to imply that the cunning of our foe might well enable Him to escape the just punishment of the enforced law. His point is well made. Crucifixion marches travel slowly. I shall go myself with Annas to ensure the desired results of our day's labor. *(Enter Benjamin, a servant boy.)*

BENJAMIN. Excuse me, Caiphas. Barabbas awaits admission at the gate.

CAIPHAS. Barabbas! We have a guest at our meeting. *(To Annas.)* This shall be worth the delay. Admit the scoundrel and let us hear what he has to say.

ANNAS. Barabbas is the leader of all those who are too stupid to follow. *(Enter Barabbas.)*

BARABBAS. Excellent friends, you have saved me this day. I thank you. But simple words cannot repay such omens of trust. I have come to offer you, not words, but action.

CAIPHAS. And what shall it be, Barabbas, a dance?

ANNAS. Or a street-corner murder?

BARABBAS. A dance for our nation and a murder of our conquerors! I am a leader. You all know that I seek freedom for the Jews and their land. Give me the means of supplying my followers and we will make this court the high court, the final judge of all.

ANNAS. The means? Give you the means?

CAIPHAS. He wants money, Annas; our money.

BARABBAS. Time after time I have shown you my power with the people. Use me as an arm and you shall strike with strength. Or, better yet, be my arm and I will win the victory myself.

ANNAS. Be your arm, Barabbas?

CAIPHAS. He means he wants to lean on our resources, Annas.

BARABBAS. Think, please think, and then let me know the wise decision of the court, so long subjected to the foreigners' judgment.

CAIPHAS. Barabbas, we need no thought nor time to see a dying calf play the part of a bull. Our finger is on the pulse of the people. We know that your power died the day you killed a fellow citizen. Your popularity disappeared the hour you were dragged into prison crying for the mercy of Rome. The mob that followed you, Barabbas, has been disillusioned by your own display of weakness. Now you have had your day, rest quietly in some obscure corner and let the world pass you, unmolested by your ambitious hands.

BARABBAS. How . . . how can you speak so foolishly? Only a few short hours before, the throngs were shouting my name, demanding my release. How can you attribute obscurity to Barabbas the Christ?

CAIPHAS. My poor friend, the mob moved as I instructed. They did not demand your release. Those crude shouts you heard were but the echo of my whisper, Barabbas, nothing more. When I am forced to whisper, "Crucify him," the shouting mob shall echo, "Crucify Barabbas." See to it I am not forced. Now leave, please.

BARABBAS. False and deceitful lovers of fame and power! No son from Adam come can speak so to me and leave the price of insolence unpaid. I shall yet hear the echo revolt against its master's voice.

ANNAS. Were you to hear the entire world shout defiance to this court, it would cost me no ease. Sounds in reality and sounds in a mad-man's ear are not to be honored by like sentiments.

CAIPHAS. Enough said! Let us go, Annas, to remain silent only when the Nazarene is silenced; to stand our ground until the come-lately king be raised from that ground. *(Exit Caiphas and Annas.)*

JOSEPH. Barabbas, you seem to place great value on temporal power. Have you ever thought of eternal power?

BARABBAS. Temporal power shall make eternity mine.

JOSEPH. No, friend, only truth can make eternity yours.

BARABBAS. And is not all power truth?

JOSEPH. By no means, my blind orphan, by no means! All truth is power, but all power is not truth. *(Enter Judas with clamorous haste.)*

VOICES. Judas! The informer! His friend!

JUDAS. Judas, yes. The informer, yes. His friend, no. The measure of friendship is loyalty; the essence of friendship is sacrifice; the manifestation of friendship is understanding; the result of friendship, sweetness. Have I been loyal? Let the unbearable jangling of this miser's purse answer for me. Have I sacrificed? If sacrifice is oblation, is giving, then I have often been the object of sacrifice, but never the subject. Have I understood? Not while understanding might have been of use, had I done so. Only now do I understand; now, when prophesies have come to pass. And sweetness? Once I thought gold sweeter than honey, yet now I find it turns sour before it has left my tongue. What can wash away the sour foulness, save blood? His friend? Not I, not Judas, the informer.

BARABBAS. Do you know me, Judas?

JUDAS. Had I never seen you, I would know you, for in your eyes as in mine life's deeds are written in crimson symbols.

BARABBAS. Take heart, take life, comrade, and join hands with me. The union of two such hands may give birth to power.

JUDAS. I have already taken heart — my Savior's heart, and I have ground it in my traitor's fist. I have already taken life — my God's life, and cast it as a victim for the devil's hate. Were my hand to join with yours, it would drag you with me to my doom. My own weight alone carries me downward too swiftly. Here, honorable court, relieve me of some weight. Take your cherished silver before it burns a hole into my own heart. I cannot stand its sting. I cannot stand to live.

JOSEPH. Learn to live anew in the death of your Master. He will take you back and teach you love.

JUDAS. Fool! My Master, I have killed. How am I to ask life where I have taken it, or love where I have denied it. Be silent! I do not want life; it costs more than my poor soul can pay. There is one path left for me; do not hold me from it. Pity the tree that shall bear my weight, the weight of all my sin. (Exit Judas.)

BARABBAS. The weak man. What is more repulsive than the weak man? I am strong and stronger yet shall be. Remember me, good priests and friends. You shall hear my name again. For the present, good day. (Exit Barabbas.)

JOSEPH. Judas is blind to the light about him and Barabbas is blind to the darkness he enters. Two blind men, and both too proud to know it.

A PRIEST. Joseph, what are we to think in the midst of all this confusion? How has Christ Jesus, your friend, caused all this misery we witness?

JOSEPH. Christ Jesus brought love to the world. To receive the Spirit of Love, however, we have first to surrender the things nearest our heart. We have to give up lust of possessions in His Name before we can possess Him. The failure to do so has caused the misery; Christ is not guilty of it. Judas deemed silver of more worth than God and so he is without both God and silver. Barabbas sought power before the one great Truth. Now he is blind to truth, and powerless. So shall it be with this court that holds self-esteem so close to the eye that it fails to recognize injustice behind it. We must all remember that the surest way to lose all temporal things is to love them too intensely.

PRIEST. You are a strange man, Joseph.

ANOTHER. With a philosophy stranger yet.

A THIRD. Let us go; our duty is done. *(The priests file out in groups, leaving Joseph alone.)*

JOSEPH. Perhaps they would all be happier if they could learn to love their lives a little less. *(He moves to the center stage and picks up the purse of Judas. Regarding it, he continues.)*

> Decay will sooner find the rose loved best
>   If clasped too warmly in an anxious hand.
>   A child at play within his world of sand
> Will lose his castle with a fond caress.
>
> We single out the one we love from rest
>   And send thereto the best our souls command.
>   And yet, it's true, that love by which we stand
> Will kill, if we allow that it obsess.
>
> In loving much we carry death abreast,
>   Destroying swiftly what we would hold near,
>   And soon life goes away and leaves a tear
> That makes a mocking world our constant guest..
>
> It's wise to see that, when our love is great,
> We bar the object at Expression Gate.

(As a background to this sonnet, Newman's "Lead, Kindly Light" may be given. Upon completion of the lines, it grows in volume. Joseph remaining still until the end of the hymn.)

CURTAIN

SCENE FOUR

AT THE RISE OF THE CURTAIN: *The Court of Pilate. His room. Pilate sits musing as his servant boy, Abel, arranges a tray of fruit on a table.*

PILATE. Abel, come here, please.

ABEL. Yes, sir.

PILATE. Abel, tell me; you speak often with the other servant boys down in the court yard, and you are familiar too with the servants and guards. What do they say of the events of this day?

ABEL. What events in particular, sir?

PILATE. Be spontaneous, Abel; it becomes youth.

ABEL. It becomes youth, sir, but rarely insures old age.

PILATE. If that is your only worry, boy, speak frankly. I have asked concerning the Christ because I seek truth, not because I desire flattery.

ABEL. What is truth, sir?

PILATE. Child, I am losing patience with you. Tell me, now, what do your friends say of the Nazarene?

ABEL. I have heard expressed as many shades of thought as I have heard speakers today. I will try to give you the general trends of opinion, sir — frankly.

PILATE. Do so, my boy — frankly, remembering, however, that frankness and gruffness are much at odds with each other.

ABEL. There are those, especially among the guards and the older servants, who say that Christ, so-called by His friends, is an evil man who receives powers from Satan to blind men and lead the weak to damnation. They are pleased with the successful flight of the High Priest and his court. They are pleased with the condemnation.

PILATE. They are pleased, then, but why have they looked so upon the Christ, so-called? And why do they rejoice at His death?

ABEL. Sincerely, I cannot say, sir. What I know of their opinion, I have learned by listening as they shouted and ranted earlier today. At this moment few of them are here for me to hear, since they have followed after the crucifixion march, throwing stones through the air from their places behind the guards.

PILATE. And the others. You said there were others.

ABEL. The others of my acquaintance are comprised chiefly of the younger servants and boys of the court. They say that the Christ may be properly so called, or that He is at least the Greatest of the prophets. They are greatly saddened by the events of the day and lament that you failed in what they expected of you.

PILATE. Failed! How have I failed? It is my duty to dispense justice as the people see it. How have I failed? — I am sorry, boy. Continue as you have been speaking.

ABEL. They think that, rather than to dispense justice as the people see it, it is your duty, sir, to dispense justice as it exists.

PILATE. A point well made. But, more important, do these few have expressed reasons for their positions?

ABEL. They do not speak too freely, nor do they speak openly. I know, though, that they base their stand on the wonders worked by the Christ — so-called; and they feed their belief on the sermons they have heard the Man speak or about which they have been told. Of all those things you have heard, I know, and I shall not waste your time in repetition now. Of only one thing would I like to speak. You may not know of it.

PILATE. Do so, Abel.

ABEL (*During this speech, a background chorus may sing "Pange Lingua" or "I Walk in the Garden Alone," fading out during the indicated silence following Abel's story.*) It is a story told to the believers by an inn-keeper of the town. He watched the Nazarene eat last evening with the twelve. His story is a strange one and none of those who hears pretends to understand. After the repast, as the keeper stood nearby, ready to see to the needs of his guests, the Christ took bread and gave a portion of each to His followers, telling them it was His own body. They say He then took wine and, dividing it among them, told all that it was His blood. Finally, He asked those present to do this same act when He would be gone from them. And, as those last words were spoken, the inn-keeper claims he himself felt a great interior joy and the tears welled in his eyes and his feet begged to move him closer to this Master, and his whole body trembled, half in fear, half in joy. Indeed, he told his friends, it was only the feeling that something sacred was happening that kept him from moving into the scene before him and becoming a part of it.

PILATE (*After a moment's reflection.*) You tell the story well, Abel, but no narration can infuse reason into the heart of such a tale. But, tell me one more thing, boy. If these things are spoken of quietly by those timid followers of the so-called Christ, how do you know of them so well?

ABEL. You are a good man, Pilate, and so I can tell you frankly. Of all who believe, none does so more firmly than I.

PILATE. Then why are you here when your King is dying?

ABEL. I like to think it is because it is my duty to be here. But perhaps it is because the sight of that pain-filled face swells my heart so that each beat becomes a torture.

PILATE. That is all. Thank you, Abel. (*Exit Abel.*) Now, what am I to make of all these things? To a segment, I am the oracle of justice; to another segment, the instigator of deicide. But why should I worry about these things? Why should a busy man waste the sprite-like hours in weighing the affairs of a moment? I shall dwell in the company of more worthy thoughts. (*He reclines in a chair and voices are brought back by his memory's ear.*)

VOICES:

CROWD. Crucify Him! Give us Barabbas!

PILATE. . . . if experience teaches us nothing else, it teaches us that we make mistakes . . .

CAIPHAS. Are we to endure such insults?

CROWD. Release Barabbas!

ANNAS. Let us see what becomes of these enemies of Pilate, Rome, and God.

BARABBAS. What would my people do without me?

CROWD. Crucify Him!

CAIPHAS. We have a law!

ANNAS. Crucify Him!

CROWD. Crucify Him!

BOY. A letter from your wife . . .

CAIPHAS. Ask for your leader.

CROWD. Barabbas!

ABEL. What is truth, sir?

ANNAS. Crucify Him!

CAIPHAS. Such insults!

CROWD. Release Barabbas!

ABEL. . . . dispense justice as it exists . . .

CROWD. Crucify Him! Crucify Him! (*Pilate silences voices by smashing an urn to the floor from a nearby table.*)

PILATE. Se still! Insidious Jewish rabble, I am a Roman. Be still! Where is your Christ now? And where, Barabbas? Where is my wife's letter? Where is the crowd? I have none of these present. Then, why be concerned? Only things present and their presence are real. All else is the product of an over-fed body or an over-worked mind. I have both, no doubt. A rest! Yes, a rest and the morrow will bring a sun which refuses to cast shadows. Be still, you demirep, Imagination, so that I may rest!

CURTAIN

SCENE FIVE

SCENE: *A small chamber in Pilate's Palace. A group of servant boys are gathered together sharing the experiences of the day. Before the curtain rises, a few bars of "I Know that My Redeemer Liveth" from Handel's "Messiah" may be given. Follow the scene with the entire piece.*

BENJAMIN. And one of the old men told me that Christ would vanish from sight if they approach him with a nail.

NATHANIEL. That is only conjecture, Benjamin. What I heard came directly from a guard who was there when it happened. As they went to arrest Him, the Man but raised His hand and all were paralyzed until He allowed them to move.

BENJAMIN. And the ear He cut from a servant's head — what of that?

NATHANIEL. He did not cut it, but healed it after an angry-looking stranger had severed it with a sword.

ABEL. And, Nathaniel, Haman told me of the one who had kissed him there in the garden. He has already taken his own life.

BENJAMIN. That he has killed himself may or may not be true, Abel, but I do know that he told Caiphas before the whole court that he would do so shortly. *(Enter a fourth boy.)*

JAMES. Here is news for you all! It comes from a traveler who passed by way of Calvary's Hill.

ABEL. Speak, James! Speak quickly!

JAMES. He is crucified!

ABEL. God have mercy upon us.

NATHANIEL. And forgive us all.

JAMES. The traveler remained there but a few moments, however, and he left the three still living on their crosses. The Nazarene is in the center with a thief on each side. One mocks the Christ, calling down curses on the heads of all there present.

BENJAMIN. That would be Rubinus.

JAMES. The other prays and is even comforted by the Christ.

ABEL. And that would be Dismas. Continue.

JAMES. But the saddest report of all is the last which he gave to me. At the foot of the cross there stand some women and two men, and in front of them all is His Mother.

ABEL. Help her and love her, dear God.

JAMES. She stands erect at the base of the cross and as the traveler watched he saw only one tear draw a thin, wet line down the side of her sorrow-filled face. One tear which was matched, he said, by a line of blood traced down the side of the cross by which she stands.

ABEL. It is proper that the blood drop and the tear drop should match in form. Both stem from the same source, the mother's heart.

BENJAMIN. Let us meet here again to speak of these events.

NATHANIEL. Yes, and also of the events to happen.

JAMES. Do you think that more shall yet occur?

ABEL. I hope so. At this moment, my Christ would seem to have been defeated. I hope that some events will yet make Him the victor — the Victor to be hailed for all time.

CURTAIN

SCENE SIX

SCENE: *Twilight. The Court of Pilate. His room. Enter a man servant as Pilate sits musing.*

SERVANT. Sir, excuse me.

PILATE. What is it now?

SERVANT. At the entrance, sir. He's insisting on admission; claims you would desire to have him admitted. The guards are angry and may strike him down if he tries to pass.

PILATE. Who, blast you, who?

SERVANT. Oh, pardon me, sir; Barabbas, sir. He is insane.

PILATE. Barabbas! How long must I bear with these puppets and demigods? Have him dragged to the city gates.

SERVANT. Yes, sir. Gladly, sir.

PILATE. No, wait. Admit him.

SERVANT. Admit him, sir?

PILATE. Yes, and as soon as you have done so, send a boy in search of the Captain of the Guard. I want to speak to him.

SERVANT. It shall be done. *(Exit, servant.)*

PILATE. These sly, proud Jews with their mincing steps. How I long to be free of them and to speak my mind without reservation, without consideration! But, then, popularity is a pearl of power, and he who wants to own it must pay the price of independence. *(Re-enter servant with Barabbas.)*

SERVANT. Here is Barabbas.

PILATE. Greetings, my friend. What troubles bring you here? Or is this a social visit, one leader to another?

BARABBAS. Yes, yes, a social visit; a powerful subject to a wise ruler! I am powerful. You are ruling. Wed power and authority and you have greatness! Am I correct? Am I correct?

PILATE. Of course, Barabbas. Your words would seem to prove themselves as they are pronounced, as they have the very tone of veracity about them.

BARABBAS. Then hear my plan, Pontius Pilate. Join forces with me and we shall rule together the whole expanse of this land. And more, perhaps. Hear my plan now.

PILATE. You interest me, Barabbas, and I shall hear your plan. But, if you please, not now because I am fatigued by the day's events and my weary mind could not do justice to your clever thoughts. Return. Tomorrow perhaps I shall be well rested.

BARABBAS. Your words are poetry; strong and potentially militant poetry. With the new sun I must return to gladden you for having so spoken to me. For today, I shall content myself to speak in the market place to my people. Good day, sir.

PILATE. Good day, Barabbas, and good morrow. *(Exit, Barabbas.)* Go, Barabbas, and expostulate against all who oppose you. Speak today in the market place, and tomorrow I shall be well rested. *(Enter Captain of the Guard.)*

CAPTAIN. You desire to see me, sir?

PILATE. Enter, Captain, enter! My business is brief. You know Barabbas?

CAPTAIN. All the soldiers and guards both know and detest him. I have just passed him at the entrance.

PILATE. He is going to the market place to speak to the people.

CAPTAIN. There are few people there at this moment.

PILATE. Excellent! When Barabbas speaks, he often says foolish things. But I much love that man, as do you all, and would greatly regret seeing him exposed to danger through foolish words. It would please me if a group of soldiers were to watch carefully and save my dear friend all such embarrassment. Do you understand?

CAPTAIN. I understand clearly, sir.

PILATE. Then attend to your duty well. That is all. (*Exit captain.*) There! At last, peace. Come, Pilate, rest this tired frame and forget. Forget the Jews and their Caiphas, their Christ, their Barabbas, and their ill-timed expressions of pretended loyalty. For me, they are only steps to things higher. I refuse to stub my toe on so narrow a stone as they.

CURTAIN

SCENE SEVEN

SCENE: *A small room in Pilate's Palace where Abel lies sleeping. It is evening of the same day. Enter Joseph. Open with "Inviolata" or Handel's "Faithful Shepherd" Suite.*

JOSEPH. Abel, Abel, wake up. It is Joseph.

ABEL. Joseph, what has happened? I long for news of the Master but I found myself too exhausted to continue. What has happened?

JOSEPH. It is all finished, boy. The Master died on the cross.

ABEL. Dear God . . .

JOSEPH. His sufferings are finished now, Abel. It is for those remaining we must mourn.

ABEL. His Mother?

JOSEPH. She remains at the foot of the cross to receive the body. That is what brought me here. I received Pilate's permission to take the body away, but I feared it would be touched by unfriendly hands before I could return there. I have just sent ahead one of your friends to inform the guards and His Mother of Pilate's permission to me. As soon as I am rested, I shall follow after and lead them to a tomb which I own. It is hewn in stone and truly worthy of the Master.

ABEL. That so much misery could come into being on the same day!

JOSEPH. All the sorrow of so many hearts springs from the same source. Those who believe feel a sorrow that shall be turned to joy when the Master shall conquer and reign as King in His own Kingdom. Those who do not believe feel a sorrow that shall haunt them forever. Judas believed once but he drowned his faith in a whirlpool of avarice. His sorrow endures. Barabbas might have learned and believed but he holds the love of power so dear that it shrouds his heart and excludes all other considerations. His sorrow endures. Pilate does believe, but he starves his convictions until they are imperceptible to himself. He starves his convictions to feed his pride. And his sorrow endures. *(Enter Benjamin.)*

BENJAMIN. News of Barabbas, Abel.

ABEL. What news can encourage me when I am crushed by the loss of my Master?

BENJAMIN. It is not to encourage you that I come. The news will amaze you, perhaps. Within this very hour Barabbas stood in the market place and spoke of his ascent to the throne of a new Jerusalem. There were only a handful of people there, but even they ignored him. Two boys mocked him as he spoke. Then, gradually his voice grew louder until he was shouting incomprehensible phrases. No one listened to him seriously. His face grew flushed and he cried as he shouted, when out of nowhere there came a group of soldiers and they moved towards him from all sides. Barabbas grew hysterical and took flight down the blind alley that separates the two houses on the north side of the square. One Roman soldier with a spear walked into the alley after him and following a minute of complete silence we heard a scream of pain. The soldier came out and all his companions laughed at what he said. And not one person in the market place paid attention. Does it not amaze you?

ABEL. No, I am not surprised at the news.

JOSEPH. Nor I. But I must return now that I have had enough rest to enable me to make the trip. I have tarried too long already.

ABEL. Before you leave us, Joseph, tell us briefly what is the meaning of those words the Master spoke over the bread and wine last evening?

JOSEPH. I am not certain, boy. But if my supposition is correct, then our Master died beautifully.

ABEL. Is death ever beautiful?

JOSEPH. No, death never is, but dying life may be beautiful when it departs in generosity.

BENJAMIN. I do not understand.

ABEL. Nor do I.

JOSEPH. It is merely that when a living creature surrenders life with an act of benevolence, it gives rise to a beauty surpassing all that it had in life possessed. Dying life may be beautiful and our Master has died in the greatest act of beauty ever to take place on our earth.

> The leaves of northern trees in death are bright
>   And flowers breathe a scent no death corrodes,
>   Our heroes die upholding life-long codes —
> Give death a day, yet beauty wins the fight.
>
> Give death a day to show its armored might
>   And see all cowards fall along the way,
>   As Christians dare to fight on as they pray,
> And never fear death's universal sight.
>
> The keenest death is blinded by life's light:
>   Men often face the blade to save ideals,
>   And nature fades in sweetness which it yields.
> Thus, death was killed on Holy Thursday night.
>
> The cross was not enough for Christ: He gave
> Himself to all mankind, a helpless slave.

(Close with the singing of "The Lord's Prayer.)

CURTAIN

SCENE EIGHT

SCENE: *Pilate's room. Holy Saturday morning. Pilate sits and Joseph stands nearby.*

PILATE. I have sent for you because I am filled with a sorrow which confuses me. I cannot trace its source.

JOSEPH. I shall do all I can to help you.

PILATE. Thank you, Joseph. The events of yesterday were of small import in my eyes as they occurred, but since then, I have relived every movement and every syllable ten times over. Why should it be so?

JOSEPH. Because Jesus the Christ is no ordinary man. My people know that man once sinned against God. An offense is as great as the one offended and an offense against God must require infinite retribution. Yesterday that retribution was given by One Who of necessity had to be both God and Man: God, to afford the cost; and Man to pay the price. Is it any wonder that such an event should haunt you through the night?

PILATE. You speak of things I can at least understand, I am pleased to say. I cannot, however, believe them, even after having understood.

JOSEPH. Oh, it may be that you fight against belief because of other considerations.

PILATE. Attribute it to what you like. You do believe. I cannot believe.

JOSEPH. Indeed, I thank God that I do believe, that He has given me the eyes of faith. Also, I pray that the sign shall soon be given that will feed the belief of all like myself, so that the message of our Christ may be carried down through the ages to all people, everywhere.

PILATE. Then, you believe also that a sign shall be forthcoming.

JOSEPH. I do.

PILATE. Believing would cost me too much. *(Pilate shakes his head and leaves the room.)*

JOSEPH. Please, God, let the sign come soon.

CURTAIN

SCENE NINE

SCENE: *Outside the tomb. Two guards sit drowsing. Before the curtain rises, use "The Holy City."*

OFFSTAGE:

CROWD. Crucify him! Give us Barabbas!

PILATE. . . . if experience teaches us nothing else, it teaches us that we make mistakes . . .

CAIPHAS. Are we to endure such insults?

CROWD. Release Barabbas!

ANNAS. Let us see what becomes of these enemies of Pilate, Rome, and God.

BARABBAS. What would my people do without me?

CROWD. Crucify Him!

CAIPHAS. We have a law.

ANNAS. Crucify Him!

CROWD. Crucify Him!

BOY. A letter from your wife . . .

CAIPHAS. Ask for your leader.

CROWD. Barabbas!

ABEL. What is truth, sir?

ANNAS. Crucify Him!

CAIPHAS. Such insults!

CROWD. Release Barabbas!

ABEL. . . . dispense justice as it exists . . .

CROWD. Crucify Him! Crucify Him!

JAMES. One mocks the Christ, the other prays.

ABEL. God have mercy on us.

JAMES. She stands erect at the base of the cross.

ABEL. Help her and love her, dear God.

BARABBAS. I am powerful; you are ruling!

PILATE. Those sly, proud Jews with their mincing steps.

BARABBAS. Hear my plan, Pontius. Pilate.

PILATE. I refuse to stub my toe on so narrow a stone . . .

JOSEPH. The Master died on the cross.

ABEL. His Mother? His Mother?

JOSEPH. It is hewn in stone . . .

BENJAMIN. . . . we heard a scream of pain.

ABEL. I do not understand.

JOSEPH. The cross was not enough for Christ: He gave Himself to all mankind, a helpless slave.

PILATE. You do believe. I cannot believe.

JOSEPH. Please, God, let the sign come soon. *Please, God, let the sign come soon. (Chorus sings "The Holy City." Then, with a rumble, the stone of the tomb rolls back. The guards prostrate themselves and the figure of Christ appears with great light. The figure of Christ remains fixed in view as His voice is heard offstage.)*

CHRIST. I am the Resurrection and the Life: he that believeth in Me, although he be dead, shall live: and every one that liveth, and believeth in Me, shall not die forever. . . . All power is given to Me in heaven and in earth. Going therefore teach ye all nations: Baptizing them in the name of the Father, and of the Son, and of the Holy Ghost. Teaching them to observe all things whatsoever I have commanded you: and behold I am with you all days, even to the consummation of the world. *(Close with "The Alleluia Chorus" from "The Messiah.")*

CURTAIN

THE END

A SUGGESTED TABLEAU

If a Tableau is desired, it might be executed in the following manner:

The curtain opens again with Christ in His same position (as the last scene). The entire stage is very brightly illuminated. Immediately to the right of Christ and slightly in front of Him, kneel Benjamin and James. Behind them stands Joseph of Aramethea, his gaze fixed on Christ. Immediately to the left and in the same position as Benjamin and James, are Nathaniel and Abel. Behind them stands Dismas. About midway between the wings and the central figure, to the right, are Annas and Caiphas. They face the audience, heads bowed. In a fixed pose of bewilderment behind them and to their right are the other priests of the High Court. Midway to the left is Pilate, body front, head turned from the Resurrection scene. At the extreme left and front, the Captain of the Guard stands facing off-stage, spear in hand. Before him kneels Barabbas, hands joined in begging mercy. Like the Captain, Rubinus is at the extreme right, facing offstage. In front of him and facing the audience, Judas kneels, eyes fixed down upon the purse held in his hands. The soldiers have kept the prostrate positions of the last scene. Slowly, as the music rises and swells, all light fades from the extremes and fixes upon the person of Christ. The figures nearest Him are viewed in reflected rays, while the others are swallowed in varying degrees of darkness.

CURTAIN

SUGGESTIONS FOR STAGING AND MUSIC

Where a live chorus and music is not possible, recorded music may be used.

For those scenes where voices occur, the lines can be read offstage under organized direction. However, it would be far better to have the voices on tape recording, ready for playing at the exact moment. The action on stage can be rehearsed this way with no fear of a change in timing. Renting a tape recorder for a week would allow sufficient practice for this one routine, if such an instrument is not owned.

N.B.: In the music selection, care was taken to have the words of the hymns coincide with the lines of the scenes. Where the same selections are given for Catholic and Protestant groups, the pieces are known to both groups. Protestant hymns are given in italics.

SCENE ONE
A prison cell in the Fortress Antonia.

Open with a portion of the "Gregorian Lamentations."
Open with *"Were You There When They Crucified Our Lord."*

With the voice of Rubinus, the music subsides, recurring at the scene's end.

SCENE TWO
The courtyard of Pilate's palace.

When Christ appears, He stands for a full two minutes, while Vexilla Regis is heard sung offstage.

At the same time, "Nearer, My God, to Thee" offstage.

SCENE THREE
The court of the High Priest

As a background to the sonnet that closes the scene, Newman's *"Lead, Kindly Light."* Upon completion of the lines, it grows in volume, Joseph remaining still until the end of the hymn.

The same.

SCENE FOUR
Pilate's chamber.

At Abel's line "It is a story told to the believers by an inn-keeper . . .," background chorus of Pange Lingua, fading out during the indicated silence following Abel's story.

As above, with "I Walk in the Garden Alone" as the selection.

SCENE FIVE
Another chamber in Pilate's palace.

Before the curtain, a few bars of "I Know that My Redeemer Liveth" from Handel's "Messiah." Follow the scene with the entire piece.

The same.

SCENE SEVEN
A small chamber in Pilate's palace.

Open with Inviolata. Background as before (Scene Three) for the closing sonnet, "Mother of Christ."

Open with playing of Handel's "Faithful Shepherd" Suite. Close (during sonnet) with singing of "The Lord's Prayer."

SCENE NINE
The tomb of Christ.

Before the curtain, "The Holy City."

Closing with the "The Alleluia Chorus" from the "Messiah."

The same.

Where available material makes the Resurrection scene a problem, suspended rock-paper or gray curtains may serve well in place of the rolling rock.

Costumes: Simple togas of the period can be fashioned from dyed sheets.

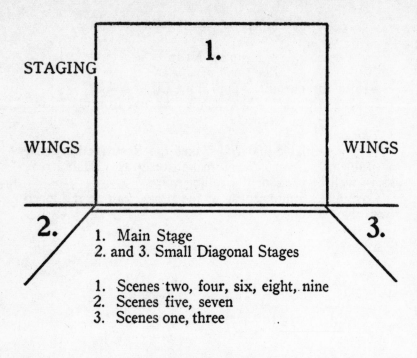

STAGING

WINGS   **1.**   WINGS

2.   **3.**

1. Main Stage
2. and 3. Small Diagonal Stages

1. Scenes two, four, six, eight, nine
2. Scenes five, seven
3. Scenes one, three

ALTERNATE PLAN

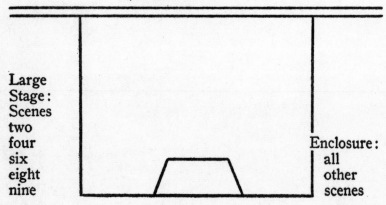

Large
Stage:
Scenes
two
four
six
eight
nine

Enclosure:
all
other
scenes

Walls are set up to create a small enclosure front and center. The curtain is drawn back for scenes involved just to the side walls. For the large scenes, this enclosure is removed.

PROMISE OF THE ANGELS

A Drama About Easter in Four Acts

By

Elaine Walker Getzinger

PROMISE OF THE ANGELS

FOR THREE WOMEN AND TWO MEN

———

CAST OF CHARACTERS

REUBEN, *a poor man of the people, a native of Jerusalem.*

HANNAH, *his wife.*

MIRIAM, *their cousin from Galilee.*

JOHN, *her son, a farmer of Galilee.*

RUTH, *his wife.*

———

SETTING: Jerusalem during Holy Week. One simple interior for three scenes, garden for last scene.

PROMISE OF THE ANGELS

SCENE ONE

Jerusalem during Holy Week. Interior of simple peasant home. Afternoon. Business of exchanging greetings as guests arrive.

HANNAH. Come in, come in! How good to see you! You must be tired after your long journey.

MIRIAM. Yes, it was a long way, and I am growing old. Riding so far on that donkey's back has left me weary indeed.

JOHN. Why not lie down for a while, Mother? Now that we're here there's nothing for you to do but rest up for the feast. Ruth will help Cousin Hannah if there's anything she wants done. I'll take care of our animals and help Reuben with the chores.

REUBEN. Time enough for that later, John. Sit for a moment first. You've come a long way.

HANNAH. Yes, do rest a while, all of you. We don't want you to be too tired to enjoy the Passover Feast after coming so far to share it with us. Our preparations are almost complete so there is little to do just now.

RUTH. We certainly appreciate your kindness in opening your home to us, Cousin Hannah. We've all been looking forward to this day for a long time.

MIRIAM. Indeed we have, and I too thank you for your hospitality. How are the children? Are they around somewhere? We didn't see them outside.

HANNAH. Oh, you'll see them soon enough, no doubt. They're both well, but very excited about all the goings on this week. I've hardly been able to keep them around the house long enough to help their father with the chores.

MIRIAM. Excitement? About what? The Passover has not yet begun.

HANNAH. Oh, there has been a teacher—some call him a prophet—who has been going around the city stirring up the people and making speeches. He even went into the Temple and turned over the tables of the moneychangers!

RUTH. Serves them right! They make too much money at the expense of poor people like us. But why did this teacher drive them out? By what authority?

HANNAH. He said something about the Temple being a place of prayer, and not a den of thieves. And he criticized the scribes and the Pharisees who pretend to be so holy, and yet allow the Temple to be used that way.

MIRIAM. He sounds like a wise and good man, Hannah. What is his name?

REUBEN. He is truly a wise man, Miriam. I have heard him speak and he made my very heart thrill within me at his words. It is not his words only, though, but his voice and his eyes that somehow impel you to listen and believe his teachings.

MIRIAM. What does he teach? What are his words that move you so?

REUBEN. Oh, if you could only hear him! He speaks of Jehovah as a loving heavenly father who cares for each one of us, no matter how lowly . . . even those who have sinned and turned away from the faith of their fathers. If they repent, they are welcomed back into the fold as I would welcome back a sheep that I had lost and once more found.

JOHN. Aye, then the sinner would be welcome indeed, for no shepherd can afford to lose sheep in these hard times.

REUBEN. That is what he meant, John. That each of us is as precious to God as our sheep are to us. And that He is not willing for one of His sheep to perish, Jesus said.

MIRIAM (*Excitedly.*) Did you call this teacher Jesus? Where is he from? Where was he born?

REUBEN. That I know not, Miriam. But he is from Nazareth, they say. His father was a carpenter there— Joseph, I think his name was. The man who told me, once knew the family and was surprised that the son of a carpenter could speak so well and with such authority.

MIRIAM (*Half to herself.*) That's right. They were from Nazareth, I remember now. That night in Bethlehem, Mary—yes, that was her name—Mary—spoke to me of people in Nazareth we both knew.

RUTH. What did you say, Mother? Oh, you came from Nazareth, too, didn't you? Did you know this Jesus?

MIRIAM. No, I didn't know him. I left Nazareth when I was a young girl. But I did see Jesus once—the night when he was born—in Bethlehem, in the stable of the inn where I worked as a serving girl.

REUBEN. Are you sure, Miriam? A man like Jesus, a teacher and leader of the people, born in a stable?

MIRIAM. Yes. I am sure. Perhaps he will yet be king.

HANNAH (*Looking about fearfully.*) Be careful what words you use in this city, my cousin, I beg of you! Even the walls have ears! King Herod would have his soldiers on us if he heard of any such talk. And Pilate, too, would seize any who favor the rule of a new king. (*Softly.*) But why do you say, "He may yet be king?"

JOHN. Mother, are you referring to that old story about the Messiah being born in Bethlehem? Surely you know by now that it was only a dream father had that night when he thought he saw angels in the sky.

REUBEN. Angels in the sky? What does he mean, Miriam?

HANNAH. Yes, tell us about it!

RUTH. It is only a folk tale of our village. I have heard it since I was a child, but there are few who believe it any more.

MIRIAM. I believe it! And it is not a folk tale, but an actual happening that I myself saw and heard. A child was born one winter night in a stable in Bethlehem, and I saw him and talked to his parents. They had come to be enrolled for the tax and since there was no room for them in the inn, they spent the night in the stable. I myself waited on them and I saw their tiny newborn son lying in the manger there.

JOHN. I know, Mother, a baby was born in the stable that night, but he wasn't anybody special. Just the son of a carpenter. He couldn't have been the Messiah, the king of the Jews! Not born in a stable!

MIRIAM. But he was the Messiah! The angels said so. Your own father, Jethro, and the other shepherds heard them. They were tending their sheep on the hillside when they suddenly saw a great host of angels above the hills, glorifying God and singing of the birth of the Promised One. An angel even spoke to them telling them to follow a certain radiant star that had appeared in the sky. He told them the star would lead them to the newborn king.

REUBEN. But even if this is true, what makes you think this teacher is the Messiah? How do you know he is the same person?

MIRIAM. Oh, I know! I know he is the Messiah! The child born in Bethlehem was called Jesus, and his father too, was a carpenter from Nazareth. But that is not how I know. I know because my heart tells me that I have found him again—the promised saviour of our people! All my life I have sought him, but none knew where he had gone. (*Musingly*.) He was such a beautiful baby. Sturdy and bright-eyed. It was easy to see why the shepherds and the wise men knelt down before him and called him the Son of God, the Messiah we had long been waiting for.

JOHN. But if he were truly the Messiah, where has he been all these years? Why hasn't he led our people against the Romans and established his kingdom here in Israel? Why is he only a wandering teacher, without power or station?

MIRIAM. I don't know, John. It may be that he has been preparing for this very time. Perhaps that is why he has come into Jerusalem now at the Passover season when so many of our people are gathered here. Perhaps he plans to lead them on to victory now, against our enemies.

HANNAH. Why, yes, Reuben, do you not remember? You told me Jesus came into Jerusalem at the head of a long procession of his followers. You said they threw their garments and branches of palms and flowers in his path. And they shouted praises to him as he rode by.

REUBEN. That's right, they did. And he certainly acted like a man of authority and importance when he threw the money changers out of the Temple. No mere teacher would have dared do that.

MIRIAM. Then the long looked-for day of our liberation is almost at hand! Jesus must be busy even now martialling his forces for the assault on Herod's army! How blessed am I to have been present at both his birth and at his ascension to the throne of Israel! May God be praised for sparing me to see this day!

CURTAIN

SCENE TWO

Early the next morning.   Setting the same.

REUBEN (*Enters at Right, excitedly.*) Hannah! Hannah! Where are you?

HANNAH (*Entering from Left.*) Here I am, Reuben. What is wrong? Has something happened?

REUBEN. Oh, Hannah, they've taken him prisoner! They've taken him before Pilate!

HANNAH. Who, Reuben? What has happened?

REUBEN. Jesus! They've accused him of starting an insurrection among the Jews! Herod and his men are demanding his death! (MIRIAM *and* JOHN *enter from Left, closely followed by* RUTH, *fastening the sash.*)

MIRIAM. Reuben, tell me my ears played me false! That what I thought I heard you say is not true! They have not arrested him?

JOHN. Surely it can not be so, Reuben. Why would Pilate concern himself with a simple teacher?

MIRIAM. He is the Messiah, and Herod and Pilate both fear him. Jesus and his followers will sweep them both from their thrones!

RUTH. Like he swept the money changers from the Temple? I wondered that they let him go unpunished for that. Now I see that they were only biding their time. They will put a hasty end to your messiah now—your king-from-a-stable!

REUBEN. Truly I fear you are right, Ruth. King, messiah, prophet—I know not what he was. Yet do I know that he was good and wise and he held out such hope for our people as we have not known since the reign of David. I wish there was some way we might help him, but we are powerless. Many of his disciples have fled from the city, and others have gone into hiding. They all fear Herod.

JOHN. But how did it come about, Reuben? Was it not sudden?

REUBEN. It all happened last night when Jesus went up to the Mount of Olives to pray after celebrating the Passover with his disciples. Some of Herod's men seized him even as he prayed, and took him before Caiaphas. They accused him of blasphemy and insisted that he be put to death.

JOHN. Then how does Pilate figure in this? Surely a Roman governor would not take sides in a purely religious quarrel?

REUBEN. That is where Herod is clever. He wanted Pilate to be the one to pass sentence on Jesus because he feared the vengeance of the people. So he charged Jesus with rebellion against Rome to force Pilate to act. If Pilate believes Herod, Jesus is doomed.

MIRIAM. Pilate must not condemn an innocent man. Someone should tell him of Herod's true purpose in turning Jesus over to him. Someone should tell Pilate that Jesus is kind and good. That he heals the sick and maimed, and teaches love and brotherhood.

RUTH. It matters little now, what this teacher did. He will soon be dead, and that will be the end of it.

MIRIAM. No, no! It must not be! Jesus is the promised Messiah who is to bring salvation and hope to our people. We can not let him be killed before his work is finished. Not after all these years of waiting. Reuben, isn't there something that can be done to save him? Surely someone will appear in his behalf?

HANNAH. They dare not, Miriam, or they and their families would also be put to death. If Herod is determined to end the power of this new teacher, he would not hesitate to kill all his disciples.

JOHN. You are right, Cousin Hannah, and yet it is not just that this good man should die only because he opposes Herod.

RUTH (*Bitterly.*) And what things are just or right in these days? There is wickedness and oppression on every hand, yet we keep quiet if we wish to live. If we are God's chosen people why must we suffer so? Why must we live in such fear and degradation in the eyes of our enemies?

REUBEN. It is indeed hard to understand, and I had thought this new teacher might be the one to lead us out of our troubles. But it is too late, and once more our hopes are to go unfulfilled.

MIRIAM. It is not too late! If Jesus is still alive there may yet be time to save him. I will go to Pilate myself and tell him of the happenings which occurred on the night when Jesus was born . . . how the angels announced his birth as the Son of God. And how the shepherds and the wise men followed the star and brought gifts to the infant king and knelt low before him. Then will he know that Jesus is the Messiah and he will not dare kill him. Not even a pagan from Rome would dare to kill the Son of God!

HANNAH. Miriam, my cousin, you know not what you say! Would you bring death to us all that live in this house?

RUTH. Mother, you are out of your mind! Hannah is

right. We would all be seized and put to death if you did so foolish a thing! And it would be all for naught anyway, since Pilate would not see such lowly people as we are. Herod has his ear now, and you would not be allowed near Pilate.

JOHN. I fear she is right, Mother, and though you mean well, you could not help him now. You would only bring punishment to us all. Besides, if Jesus is the Messiah, God Himself will save him.

RUTH. There! Now you can find out if your messiah is what he claims to be! God would not let harm befall his own Son. And if Pilate and Herod are able to put him to death, you will know for sure that this Jesus is just another prophet.

MIRIAM. Perhaps what you say is right, I do not know. I only know that I must do all I can to save him. If Jesus is only a prophet, and not the Messiah, still he is a good and holy man. One not deserving death at the hands of the evil Herod. And if he is indeed the Messiah, perhaps I am to be God's agency to save him. Am I not the only one in Jerusalem who was present at his birth and who saw the wonders of that night? And is this not the first year we have been able to come to Jerusalem for the Passover in many years? Yet it is the one time when what I alone know may be the means of saving the Son of God from death at the hands of his enemies.

REUBEN. God has ever chosen human agencies to work his wonders for him—Abraham and Moses and Elijah. You may well be the chosen one to bear this message to Pilate, Miriam.

RUTH. Oh, this is foolishness! Chance alone has brought these circumstances about. Last year Mother was not well enough to make the long journey, and the year before John was stricken with a strange fever that left him weak and helpless for many months. The year before that the drought destroyed our crops and we had no money to—

REUBEN. Yet this year you are here, Ruth. What Miriam knows may convince Pilate that Herod is only jealous for his own power and cares nothing for the fate of Rome. Wait! Suddenly a thought has occurred to me! It is always the custom at the Passover for the Roman governor to release a condemned man to the people. Perhaps he could be persuaded to release Jesus if the people demanded it.

JOHN. That's it! We will go talk to some of Jesus' followers and urge them to go to Pilate and demand his release. Then Mother won't have to risk going to Pilate herself. I fear what might happen to you and to all of us if you did go, Mother.

HANNAH. John is right, Miriam. You do not live in this evil city so you can not know how bad things are. Many of our people have disappeared in the night and none have dared ask where they have gone, but sorrowed in silence for lost loved ones. And surely you have seen with your own eyes as you came into the city, the bodies nailed to crosses and left by the roadside as a warning to others who dare rebel against injustice.

REUBEN. Our people desperately need a leader to save them from such cruelty and wickedness and that is why they turned to Jesus. He must not die! Pilate can not kill him!

MIRIAM. That is why I must go. I am old and my life is almost over. If I can save my king, I will gladly die. It is a small price to pay. No one knows me in this city, so they will not connect me with you. None of you will be harmed because of what I do. They will think me just another Passover visitor. But do not try to stop me, for I go to serve my king!

REUBEN. And I will go with you, for he is my king too. I would rather die serving him than live on without the hope his words have brought, to our people.

HANNAH. Oh, Reuben, my husband, you can not go! I will not let you! Think of our sons and of our home—

REUBEN. I have thought of them, and of you, my dear wife, and it is for them I must go. For if we succeed, they will have a better world in which to live than we have ever known. A world of righteousness and mercy, the brotherhood of man Jesus spoke about so often.

JOHN. But if you fail—

REUBEN. We can not fail. We must not. John, guard them for me—Hannah and my two fine sons. Let no harm befall them because of what I do. And if I do not come back—

JOHN. I understand. I will take care of them for you.

HANNAH (*Crying.*) Reuben! Reuben!

REUBEN (*Embracing her.*) God keep you, dear wife. Pray that we reach Pilate in time. Come, Miriam, I will show you the way to the palace of the governor.

CURTAIN

SCENE THREE

Late afternoon of the same day. Same setting.

(*Enter* MIRIAM *and* REUBEN *at Right, weary and heartsick. Others rush forward to greet them warmly.*)

HANNAH (*Embracing* REUBEN.) Oh, my husband, I did think you were never coming back! I feared you were dead or in prison, you have been gone so long!

JOHN. Mother! Are you all right? Did they harm you in any way?

MIRIAM (*Dully.*) They did not harm me. They would not even listen to me. I did not get to see Pilate at all. I begged and pleaded with his guards but they would not let me enter.

HANNAH. Then we are safe? We will not be punished for befriending this teacher?

REUBEN (*Bitterly.*) Do not fear, wife. We are safe enough. The time for fear is past. He is dead, and nothing worse can befall us, now that our one hope is gone.

RUTH. So he was not the messiah after all! He could not deliver himself out of the hands of his enemies. He died like a common criminal, and with him, his kingdom!

MIRIAM. No, Ruth, he did not die like a common criminal. If ever in all his short life he was a king, it was there, nailed upon a crown, that he revealed himself. His crown was but a crown of thorns and his poor body, beaten and bruised, bore no king's robes. Yet his indomitable spirit and great compassion even toward those who crucified him, made clear his kingly estate.

REUBEN. Aye, you should have seen him! He gave no thought to himself—to his pain and agony—but thought only of others. There were two other men crucified with him—robbers, they were—and when one of them repented of his sins and begged forgiveness, Jesus said to him, "This day thou shalt be with me in paradise."

RUTH. But that was blasphemy! Only God can forgive sins!

REUBEN. Ah, but he was the Son of God! Never was I more sure of it than when he asked his heavenly father, as he calls God, to forgive the very men who were crucifying him! He said, "They know not what they do."

JOHN. You are right, Reuben. Surely no *man* could have that much forgiveness in his heart. Think of it! To bear the humiliation and suffering of the cross, and yet intercede for those who inflicted it upon him. Did this not have a favorable effect on those who heard him?

REUBEN. On some perhaps, but they are hardened men, used to these crucifixions. They happen so often. They mocked him for the sign Pilate had caused to be placed above his head, "This is the king of the Jews," and called to him to save himself if he were really a king.

MIRIAM. If tore my heart to see him suffer so and yet be powerless to help him, but there was one there who suffered more than all the rest—Mary, his mother. I know not how she bore it. I thought of how she had looked that night when Jesus was born—sweet and young and so proud of her newborn son. Now she is old and heart-broken. I wondered if she were thinking of the promises the angels made that night long ago and how they had failed to come true.

REUBEN. Jesus was thinking of her too. Even in his pain, he thought of her welfare and asked his favorite disciple to provide for her after he was gone.

HANNAH. I begin to see what you mean, Reuben, and why you were willing to die for him. Yes, he was truly a king. I wish I might have heard him speak just once before he died. I have heard of those whom he has healed and once I saw a man who had been lame since birth, now standing straight and tall, walking down the road as well as any man. It was no trick, for often I had seen him dragging his poor crooked limb behind him as he passed by. Healing such as that can come only from God—or the Son of God.

RUTH. You knew this man—this cripple who was healed?

HANNAH. Aye, I knew him well. Eli, son of Isaac, whom a careless serving girl let fall to the stone floor when he was but a babe, they say. And there were others, too—Anna who had been blind since birth, and Jacob whose hand was withered. These I heard of, but did not myself see. But Eli I knew and saw walking down this very lane.

REUBEN. But it was not these miracles of healing only that drew the people to him. It was his message of hope and salvation for our people that made them eager to hear more of his words. And he spoke as one with authority to make the promises he did, and not just as another teacher telling the people to fear God and keep His commandments. He even gave us two new commandments.

JOHN. Two new commandments? We have enough laws now.

REUBEN. But these were different from the rest and in a way, they summed up all his teachings. He said, "Thou shalt love the Lord thy God with all thy heart, with all thy soul, and with all thy mind, and thou shalt love thy neighbor as thyself."

RUTH. "And thy neighbor as thyself." It would indeed be a better world if people obeyed that law. It is the law of a dreamer, and yet it is the only basis on which a better world might some day be built. Yes, I too, would like to have heard this teacher. Messiah he may not be, but he was very wise.

JOHN. Obedience to God and love of one's fellow man. Yes, that is all the law one needs. It covers everything.

MIRIAM. I never heard him speak save for those few words from the cross and in all my life I have seen him but two times. Yet I know he is what my heart has been seeking since that night in Bethlehem. Often I have asked travelers to our little village if they had heard or seen Jesus, but no one knew where he had gone. Now that I have found him again only to see him die, my heart is heavy within me and I too would die, save for a tiny spark of unreasoning hope that will not be extinguished by all the horror of this day. I do not understand it, yet still it is there.

REUBEN. I know. I feel it too. I can not believe it is all over. And yet we saw Joseph of Arimathea claim his body and lay it in a new tomb.

MIRIAM. Mary, his mother, and some of the other women are going over to anoint his body with spices after the Sabbath is over. I have only a few coins left, but I will spend them to buy spices too. It will be the last thing I can do for him. Once I spread hay in a manger to make a soft bed for him and this—this is his last bed.

HANNAH. May I go too, Miriam? I have some herbs I have saved—

RUTH (*Hesitantly.*) And I would go too, for something draws me beyond my power to resist.

CURTAIN

SCENE FOUR

Easter morning. The garden where Jesus was buried.

MIRIAM (*Entering at Left, followed by* RUTH *and* HANNAH.) Over this way now, just a little farther. There! There it is. Is it not beautiful?

HANNAH. Aye, it is a fitting place even for the Messiah. What a peaceful, quiet spot it is, with the trees and flowers all around!

RUTH. But the stone! Where is the stone that sealed the tomb?

MIRIAM. The stone? Why, it is gone! Well, doubtless the others were here before us and rolled the stone away.

RUTH. But you said it was a great stone. That Mary of Magdala was wondering how they could move it to get into the tomb today.

MIRIAM. Perhaps Peter and some of the other disciples came with them to help them.

HANNAH. Well, someone moved it away, luckily for us. But why did they put a stone before the tomb, Miriam? Surely they knew the women would be coming to anoint his body as soon as the Sabbath was over.

MIRIAM. The Roman soldiers put the stone there and sealed it to keep all intruders away. I heard their leader say something about rumors of Jesus rising from the dead.

RUTH. But that is fantastic! Surely no one believes such things?

HANNAH. It is hard to know what to believe. Jesus brought others back to life—Lazarus and the daughter of the centurion. I've heard stories about it, but I didn't know whether to believe them or not. If he did do that, why could he not raise himself?

RUTH. This I refuse to believe! He may have healed the sick or roused someone from a coma resembling death, but restoring the dead to life? Oh no, it can not be!

MIRIAM. Look! Here come John and Reuben! They seem excited about something.

HANNAH. I wonder what has happened?

RUTH (*Sarcastically.*) Perhaps they have seen your messiah alive again!

JOHN (*Entering with* REUBEN *at Left.*) I have not seen him, Ruth, but others have! He *is* alive again! He lives!

REUBEN. Aye, it is true! Mary of Magdala has seen him! Here in this very garden! He spoke to her, and she knew his voice!

JOHN. And the other women, too! They touched his robes, and he spoke kindly to them, telling them to tell others what they had seen.

MIRIAM. Could it be? Can he be alive again? But no! I saw him die in horrible agony upon the cross. I felt the earth tremble beneath my feet and saw the sky grow dark as the very universe was torn by his anguish. How can he be alive again?

REUBEN. I, too, saw him die, and yet do I know he lives, even if the women had not told us so. That same spark of hope that was with me throughout the terrible day of the crucifixion still persists in saying, "It is not the end. This can not be the end of our dreams, the promises of a better world. The Messiah has come, he will not fail us!"

MIRIAM. I feel it too, yet how can he be alive? I must go into the tomb and see for myself. If it is empty— (*She enters the tomb at Right.*)

RUTH. When she sees the broken body of her messiah lying cold and still in his grave clothes, then will she know that hopes and dreams are not for such as we are. Our God has forsaken us, and our people are crushed beneath the power of Rome forever.

HANNAH. And yet, Ruth, if what John and Reuben say is true—if Jesus is alive again, it means he is truly the Son of God. That he is more powerful than all the legions of Rome and as our leader, he can free us from our cruel bondage.

RUTH. Aye, if what they say is true—

MIRIAM (*Steps forth from the tomb, her face alight with great joy and happiness.*) Jesus *is* alive! He is gone from the tomb! And in his place I saw—an angel! He was dressed all in white, and from his being there glowed a great and shining light like the star that shone over Bethlehem so long ago. He looked at me and spoke gently as if he sensed my fear and distress. "Fear not," he said, "for I know ye seek Jesus which was crucified. He is not here, for he is risen." "Fear not," he said, just as the angel said to Jethro that night in Bethlehem when he and the other shepherds were frightened by his sudden appearance. "Fear not, for he is risen!" Jesus is alive again! The Messiah has come to deliver his people! And I will follow him and do his bidding. All my life I have waited for this day and now at last it has come! I have found him who was born king of the Jews!

CURTAIN